THE GENDERING
OF MELANCHOLIA

JULIANA SCHIESARI

THE GENDERING
OF MELANCHOLIA

Feminism, Psychoanalysis, and
the Symbolics of Loss
in Renaissance Literature

CORNELL UNIVERSITY PRESS

ITHACA AND LONDON

This book is dedicated

to my mother, Nives, to my father, Louis,
and to my aunt Velis

and written for Christina

Contents

Preface   ix

Introduction   1

1. The Gendering of Freud's "Mourning and Melancholia"   33
   Freud's Essay and the Narcissism of Excessive Grief 36
   The Question of Female Melancholia (Irigaray, Silverman,
     Kristeva) 63

2. Black Humor? Gender and Genius in the
   Melancholic Tradition   96
   Aristotle and the Humor of Outstanding Men 101
   Ficino's Philosophical Celebration of Loss 112
   Diabolical Melancholia in Hildegard of Bingen 141

3. Appropriating the Work of Women's Mourning:
   From Petrarch to Gaspara Stampa, and from
   Isabella di Morra to Tasso   160

4. *Soverchia maninconia*: Tasso's Hydra   191

5. Mourning the Phallus? (Hamlet, Burton, Lacan,
   and "Others")   233

Index   269

Preface

This book is about the cultural status of an affect. The affect in question is variably called depression, melancholia, or even mourning. How such different namings come about is an issue of cultural politics, and the role of gender in these designations is not innocent. What I try to show, in the following pages, is the insistence of what could be called a politics of lack in a certain cultural representation of loss known as melancholia. By a politics of lack, I mean the attribution of value to some subjects who lack but not to others who appear equally "lacking." To anyone with a feminist perspective, it is no surprise that this politics of lack operates along gender lines: as I show in my readings of various texts, women's lack (ironically) never turns out to be quite lacking enough, while the sense of lack foregrounded in such great men as Petrarch, Ficino, and Tasso or the character of Hamlet paradoxically works to their credit as the sign of inspired genius. This gender dissymmetry is not simply an effect of my interpretation; it is the historical legacy of these canonical figures.

Unlike many contemporary feminist critics, I do not restrict myself to texts written by women; nor is my aim the deconstructive one of discovering the repressed femininity supposedly to be found in the most misogynist of male texts. Rather, I seek to situate the texts of male melancholia along with their received cultural values in relation to other texts, notably lesser-known ones by women, that question the ways lack is symbolized in the melancholic tradition. It is precisely this gendered politics of melancholia and lack that organizes and motivates my work. My aim is not to reattribute value to canonical male texts, since this kind of recuperation could only reproduce the same politics of lack that I am calling into question (which is not to say that these texts are not worth reading and rereading). Rather than pursue revisionist readings of particular texts, I aim to encourage a revisionist understanding of the canon itself. If one were to describe my project in psychoanalytic terms, my approach could be called a "transferential" one that studies the relation between texts rather than explicating what is within them.

For example, my opening chapter rereads Freud's essay "Mourning and Melancholia" in the direction of the feminist critics Luce Irigaray, Kaja Silverman, and Julia Kristeva. A subsequent chapter studies the humoral tradition of melancholia from Aristotle to Ficino against the proto-feminist analysis of Hildegard of Bingen. Later chapters study the relation of Italian women poets of the Renaissance (Gaspara Stampa, Isabella di Morra) to melancholic poets such as Petrarch and Torquato Tasso. Finally, a concluding chapter reads *Hamlet* and the very male tradition of *Hamlet* criticism from the point of view of Ophelia and Gertrude. In foregrounding these moments of feminine resistance or revision, I hope to have done more than simply recount a tale of misogynist male privilege and also to have avoided the trap of a postfeminist utopian denial of the very real effects of a phallocratic symbolic order. While my work highlights the ways myths of the "sensitive" male have co-opted or reappropriated a certain femininity for the benefit of men and to the detriment of women, my selection of female responses to the masculine myth of melancholic genius also argues for the possibility of an alternative symbolics of loss and lack.

As I explain more fully in the Introduction, my use of psychoanalysis as a methodological approach to the reading of Renaissance texts is a critical one. I am well aware of Freud's own entrenchment in the humanist legacy of Renaissance manhood and its myths of inspiration through impairment. One need look no further, in fact, than "Mourning and Melancholia" and its allusions to *Hamlet*. As a category that is both clinical and cultural, melancholia has a particular fascination for psychoanalysis that may blind psychoanalysis to how much it remains within the tradition of melancholia passed on from Aristotle to Ficino to Tasso to Burton. Melancholia has appeared to these male thinkers as the disease of great men, if not the secret of their inspiration, but it strikes me that the less glorious double of melancholia, mourning, is a traditional women's ritual. As a feminist critic, I aim to displace the androcentric privilege of the psychoanalytic *and* Renaissance view of melancholia as creative lack by reading the disparaged practice of women's mourning as an alternative—and less narcissistic—expression of grief and loss. My interpretive strategy is thus an avowedly transformative one that critically revises psychoanalysis through a feminist reading of Renaissance texts and offers new insight into the Renaissance through the feminist critique of psychoanalysis. It is my hope that this work will thus alter not only the way melancholia has been understood but also the relation between psychoanalysis, feminist theory, and Renaissance studies.

I am grateful to Miami University in Ohio for a semester leave that gave me time to begin work on this book. *The Gendering of Melancholia* was completed at Cornell University thanks to a grant from the Andrew W. Mellon Foundation. A portion of Chapter 4 appeared in *Quaderni d'Italianistica* 11 (Spring 1990) under the title "Mo(u)rning and Melancholia: Tasso and the Dawn of Psychoanalysis"; parts of the Introduction and Chapter 3 were published in *Refiguring Woman: Perspectives on Gender and the Italian Renaissance*, ed. Marilyn Migiel and Juliana Schiesari (Ithaca: Cornell University Press, 1991) as "The Gendering of Melancholia: Torquato Tasso and Isabella di Morra." Portions of Chapter 1 and another part of Chapter 3 were published as "Appropriating the Work of Women's Mourning: The Legacy of Renaissance Melancholia," at the Center for Twentieth-Century Studies, Working Paper No. 2 (Fall–Winter 1990-91).

Many people deserve thanks for the emotional and intellectual support they have given me during the writing of this book. Among these I would like especially to name Carla Freccero, Geraldine Friedman, Marjanne Goozé, Keala Jane Jewell, Katie King, and Nancy Schiesari. Verena Andermat Conley, Teodolinda Barolini, Mitchell Greenberg, and Tania Modleski gave particularly informed and encouraging feedback. I am also grateful to Kathy Woodward, who invited me to present some portions of this work as a talk at the conference "Discourses of the Emotions," held at the Center for Twentieth-Century Studies at the University of Wisconsin, Milwaukee, in April 1990. Jann Matlock and Kris Straub gave detailed readings of an early draft of the third chapter. I also owe many thanks to Barbara Spackman for intellectual encouragement and warm friendship throughout. Timothy Murray's analytical wit and scholarly prowess were a continual source of renewed thinking. I am especially indebted to Marilyn Migiel for her longstanding support as well as for her invaluable readings and comments. I also thank Bernhard Kendler of Cornell University Press for believing in the project and for generously seeing this book into print. Madelon Sprengnether and an anonymous reader commissioned by the Press gave particularly helpful and insightful comments, and I appreciate their close consideration of the manuscript. Many thanks go to Elizabeth Holmes for her terrific copyediting, and to Laura Moss Gottlieb for help with indexing.

Finally, it is to two people whom I love deeply that I owe my deepest gratitude. My daughter, Christina, on whose nineteenth birthday I am writing this Preface, has given me, as well as her endless wit and charm, a sustained and inspired feeling of joy and beauty, one that certainly points beyond mourning and melancholia! I thank my husband, Georges Van Den Abbeele, for untiringly listening to, reading, and commenting on various aspects of this manuscript; also and most important, I give him thanks beyond thanks for encouraging a division of labor in our household that gave me the freedom to pursue this project *sine curae*.

JULIANA SCHIESARI

Davis, California

THE GENDERING
OF MELANCHOLIA

Introduction

After two decades of proclaiming new beginnings and new sciences of all sorts, contemporary theoretical discourse seems given over to a rhetoric of loss and to a general sense that things are at an "end." No longer the uncritical advocate of textual free play or of a limitless plurality of meaning, current poststructuralist thinking has issued in such odd assertions as "every work is a work of mourning"[1] and "there is meaning only in despair."[2] Those who utopically saw desire as revolutionary now ask if "a vigorously melancholic humanity [would not be] the proof that [humanity] is 'progressing toward the better'?"[3] Where the "ends" of man, modernity, or Western metaphysics were once greeted with morbid glee and anarchistic celebration, now the apocalyptic tone of such pronouncements seems somewhat hollow, and even tinged with a sense of defeat and anguish. Writes another poststructuralist philosopher: "I am on the side of *melancholia*, . . . I am nostalgic, sad, elegiac."[4]

---

[1]Jacques Derrida, in an as yet unpublished lecture, given at Cornell University in October 1988, titled "The Politics of Friendship."

[2]Julia Kristeva, *Soleil noir: Dépression et mélancolie* (Paris: Gallimard, 1987), p. 15; *Black Sun: Depression and Melancholia*, trans. Leon Roudiez (New York: Columbia University Press, 1989), pp. 5–6.

[3]Jean-François Lyotard, *The Differend: Phrases in Dispute*, trans. G. Van Den Abbeele (Minneapolis: University of Minnesota Press, 1988), p. 179.

[4]Philippe Lacoue-Labarthe, "A Jean-François Lyotard: Où en étions-nous?" in *Comment Juger*, ed. M. Enaudeau and J.-L. Thibaud (Paris: Minuit, 1985).

What does all this mean at the end of a twentieth century whose intellectual energies have been long directed toward debunking every conceivable mythology? What has been lost that now requires such a wide-ranging work of mourning? Has not the debunking of myths left behind a sense of the loss of something that may have once (even delusionally) given meaning and plenitude to life? <u>Are we mourning</u>, then, <u>what we have strived so hard to rid ourselves of</u>? If so, what does this mean? And should we be so eager to join the bandwagon? If the deconstruction of the Western metaphysical tradition leaves contemporary *post*structuralist, *post*modern, *post*-Marxist, *post*-Freudian, even "*post*feminist" critics positioning themselves as various kinds of melancholics, we need to consider what is at stake in such a prevalent mode of intellectual self-definition, especially at a time when thinkers such as Allan Bloom and William Bennett are mobilizing the same *fin-de-siècle* sense of loss to urge an uncritical return to "traditional values." I do not wish to suggest a complicity between the latter's agenda and the critical labors of those whose work in the last two decades comes under the rubric of "theory." Rather, I wish to question what might be at stake in the rhetoric of loss and melancholia, and whether the adoption of it is either as innocent, as defeatist, or as recent as it might appear to be.

Of course, this is not the first time that melancholia has surfaced as a dramatic cultural phenomenon among a Western intellectual elite, even to the point of signifying what it means to be a thinker, scholar, or poet. I am thinking of that other great era of melancholia that coincides with what the nineteenth century first called the Renaissance: from the fifteenth-century philosophy of Marsilio Ficino, through the etchings of Dürer and the poetry of Tasso, culminating in the seventeenth century with the tragic character of Hamlet and the publication in 1621 of Robert Burton's monumental and encyclopedic *Anatomy of Melancholy*.

One could probably attempt to multiply the analogies between Renaissance and postmodern melancholias, but my suspicion is that we are dealing not with two different periods of dramatized loss but rather with the historical boundaries of a great age of melancholia (in Foucauldian terms: an epistemic formation), whose edges are coterminous with the historic rise and demise of "the subject" as the organizing principle of knowledge and power. The prominence of the discourse of melancholia at the edges of that historical block does not point so much to a disjunction or repetition as it does to the continuity of a tradition inaugurated by the Renaissance, refined by the Enlightenment, flaunted by Romanticism, fetishized by the Decadents and theorized by Freud, before its current resurgence. During this time, melancholia has been the subject of innumerable clinical, philosophical, and theoretical studies; and in literature its preponderance is such as to suggest a veritable genre, including such writers as Tasso, Rousseau, Hölderlin, Chateaubriand, and Nerval, and such literary characters as Hamlet and Vigny's Chatterton.

The question remains, though, as to why such a vast body of texts exists on this subject, and what its particular fascination for Western thought might be. Perhaps the melancholic sense of ineffable loss in conceptual, affective, and historical terms is only the flip side of the modernist espousal of progress, its objective or even chronological correlative: the self-critical tedium that comes *after* the euphoria of modernism, namely postmodernism.[5] Such a conclusion may seem inordinate to scholars of melancholia, who remain divided into two camps that are less mutually opposing than mutually neglectful: in one are contemporary theorists of melancholia largely informed by psychoanalysis; in the other, Renaissance scholars interested in the iconographical and historical issues relevant to a condition once characterized by humoral medicine as an "excess of black bile." Despite the obvious confluence of interests, research by these two groups almost never meets.[6] One of the aims of the following chapters is to broach an articulation of the two fields.

That is not, however, the only aim. Looking over the list of those one could consider "great melancholics" (Petrarch, Ficino, Tasso, Rousseau, Chateaubriand, Hölderlin, De Quincey, Nerval, Dostoevsky, Walter Benjamin), one is struck by the notable absence of women, an absence that surely points less to some lack of unhappy women than to the lack of significance traditionally given women's grief in patriarchal culture. In contrast to the distinguished epithet by which men are called "melancholic," women who fall into the depths of sorrow are all too easily

---

[5]As Lyotard has argued, the postmodern should be understood not as a temporal period but as the transhistorically "critical" moment *within* modernism (*Postmodern Condition*, trans. Geoff Bennington and Brian Massumi [Minneapolis: University of Minnesota Press, 1984], p. 79).
[6]Notable exceptions are Giorgio Agamben, *Stanze: La parola e il fantasma nella cultura occidentale* (Turin: Einaudi, 1977); and Michel de Certeau, *La fable mystique, XVIe–XVIIe siècles* (Paris: Gallimard, 1982).

dismissed with the banal and unprestigious term "depression."[7] The other aim of this book is thus to examine the possible systematic exclusion of women from the canon of melancholia. Hence the title *The Gendering of Melancholia*. There have, of course, been many women at different historical moments who have lamented, complained, spoken ironically, sorrowed, and despaired about losses suffered or grievances felt under oppressive and exclusionary conditions. In fact, there is a rather significant body of women's literature on these issues, and much of it has begun to appear thanks to the efforts of recent feminist editors.[8] It seems, however, that when it comes to the rubric of melancholia as an expression of a cultural malaise embodied within a particular individual or system of thought, women do not count as so-called great melancholics. In some respects, this book could be said to aim at a feminist reconceptualization of Klibansky, Panofsky, and Saxl's classic *Saturn and Melancholy*, the thesis of which, about sadness and artistic triumph in the Renaissance, only tangentially speaks to women.[9]

Because of its pivotal role looking back to the great figures of Renaissance melancholia while serving as the quintessential reference for

[7]On this gendered distinction between melancholia and depression, which is reconfirmed throughout this work, see as an initial point of reference Jennifer Radden's "Melancholy and Melancholia," in *Pathologies of the Modern Self: Postmodern Studies on Narcissism, Schizophrenia, and Depression*, ed. David Michael Levin (New York: New York University Press, 1987), p. 243.

[8]Among the most prominent such anthologies of premodern women writers are the four-volume series on Italy (ed. Beverly Allen, Muriel Kittel, and Keala Jane Jewell), Spain (ed. Angel Flores and Kate Flores), France (ed. Domna Stanton), and Germany (ed. Susan L. Cocalis) titled *The Defiant Muse*, series editor Angel Flores (New York: Feminist Press, 1986); *Medieval Women Writers*, ed. Katharina M. Wilson (Athens: University of Georgia Press, 1984); *Women Writers of the Renaissance and Reformation*, ed. Katharina M. Wilson (Athens: University of Georgia Press, 1987); *Women Writers of the Seventeenth Century*, ed. Katherine M. Wilson and Frank J. Warnke (Athens: University of Georgia Press, 1989). See also Elaine V. Beilin, *Redeeming Eve: Women Writers of the English Renaissance* (Princeton: Princeton University Press, 1987); Peter Dronke, *Women Writers of the Middle Ages* (Cambridge: Cambridge University Press, 1984); Constance Jordan, *Renaissance Feminism: Literary Texts and Political Models* (Ithaca: Cornell University Press, 1990); and my "In Praise of Virtuous Women? For a Genealogy of Gender Morals," *Annali d'Italianistica* 7 (1989), 66–87; as well as the entirety of that special issue of *Annali*, edited by Rebecca West and Dino S. Cervigni, "Women's Voices in Italian Literature."

[9]Raymond Klibansky, Erwin Panofsky, and Fritz Saxl, *Saturn and Melancholy* (New York: Basic Books, 1964), p. 248. Other general works on the history of melancholia are subject to the same charge: Rudolf Wittkower and Margot Wittkower, *Born under Saturn: The Character and Conduct of Artists: A Documented History from Antiquity to the French Revolution* (New York: Random House, 1963); Lawrence Babb, *The Elizabethan Malady: A Study of Melancholia in English Literature from 1580 to 1642* (East Lansing: Michigan State College Press, 1951); Agamben, *Stanze*; (Torino: Einaudi, 1977): Attilio Brilli, ed., *La malinconia nel Medio Evo e nel Rinascimento* (Urbino: Quattro Venti, 1982); Stanley W. Jackson, *Melancholia and Depression from Hippocratic Times to Modern Times* (New Haven: Yale University Press, 1986).

contemporary discussions of this celebrated pathology, Sigmund Freud's influential essay of 1917, "Mourning and Melancholia" (the title already evokes the familiar topos celebrated in the famous etchings of Dürer, the character of Hamlet, the poetry of Tasso, and the *Anatomy* of Burton), serves as the initial point of departure for my discussion.[10] Freud's essay can be shown to possess more than a casual complicity with the Renaissance discourse on melancholia. Freud differentiates between mourning as the more or less conscious working through of a concrete loss and melancholia as a pathological fixation on an imaginary sense of loss, a neurosis whose symptom indicates the persistence of something repressed deep in the subject's unconscious. In distinguishing the two states, Freud is clearly much more taken with the category of melancholia than with the apparently more pedestrian practice of mourning, which the former nevertheless imitates. Later, Freud goes on to argue that in the melancholic subject what is displayed is a heightened sense of morality, even if this morality acts mercilessly on the person who is suffering from melancholia: "In the clinical picture of melancholia, dissatisfaction with the ego on moral grounds is the most outstanding feature" (pp. 247–48). Such remarks alert us to an understanding of melancholia that exceeds a clinical appraisal of this illness. A tacit but demonstrable admiration sets in for this neurosis, seen to be inflected by "heightened self-criticism," moral "dissatisfaction," and what generally seem to be the effects less of a turbulent unconscious than of an overdeveloped superego.

As we know, in Freud, the superego is that psychic entity equivalent to the introjected figure of the father, such that the "heightened self-criticism" of the melancholic subject is related to "the agency commonly called conscience" (pp. 246–47). Given the tragic grandeur of this neurosis, it should perhaps come as no surprise that in "Mourning and Melancholia," Hamlet turns out to be the figure who most strikingly emblematizes the confused man at a loss, plagued by moral scruples and self-doubt (p. 246). But in its crystallization around the figure of Hamlet, Freud's melancholic subject also falls within a venerable cultural tradition that has, in fact, historically legitimated loss in terms of melancholia for men. By privileging a nostalgic ideal that is also kept absent and deferred, the self not only reconverts the loss into self-display but also legitimates

---

[10]Sigmund Freud, "Mourning and Melancholia," in *The Standard Edition of the Complete Psychological Works*, trans. J. Strachey, 24 vols. (London: Hogarth, 1953–74), 14: 243–58. Further references are given in the text.

that display as part of a cultural myth— that of the melancholic intellectual and artist—whose roots reach at least as far back as the Renaissance.

Melancholia has, of course, a very long tradition that is virtually coextensive with the history of Western culture. The word "melancholia" is a Latin transliteration of the Greek μελαγχολια meaning black bile or *atra bilis* (whence modern English "atrabilious"), the body fluid whose excess was deemed responsible for the melancholic temperament understood by Aristotle as an unfortunate malady that invariably affected "all" great men: "Why is it that all men who have become outstanding in philosophy, statesmanship, poetry or the arts are melancholic, and some to such an extent that they are infected by the disease arising from black bile, as the story of Heracles among the heroes tells?" Among the other great *men* said by Aristotle to have been afflicted by melancholy were Ajax, Bellerophon, Empedocles, Plato, and Socrates.[11] Given this status of "eminence," melancholy could thus become a praiseworthy attribute in its own right. This conclusion, however, was not drawn by ancient or medieval writers on melancholia, who characteristically viewed the condition as an unwelcome disease. Nonetheless, by the end of the Middle Ages a change in attitude began to occur. In his *Life of Dante*, for example, Boccaccio would write that Dante was "malinconico e pensoso,"[12] words that themselves recall the lines of Petrarch's celebrated sonnet, "Alone and filled with care, I go measuring the most deserted / fields with steps delaying and slow" [Solo e pensoso i più deserti campi / vo mesurando a passi tardi e lenti].[13] As Klibansky, Panofsky, and Saxl note in their famous study, Petrarch was "perhaps the first of a type of men who are conscious of being men of genius" and "had himself experienced the contrast between exultation and despair very poignantly indeed."[14] But, as these scholars also and accurately note, Petrarch was still "far from describing" the contradictory ecstasy of sadness as melancholy, referring to his condition instead as "acedia," a medieval term

---

[11]"For Aristotle's discussion of melancholia as a not altogether desirable disease that typically afflicts "great men," see his *Problems* xxx, trans. W. S. Hett (Cambridge: Harvard University Press/London: Heinemann, 1953–57), 2: 154–69.

[12]"Giovanni Boccaccio, *Trattatello in laude di Dante*, ed. Pier Giorgio Ricci (Milan: Mondadori, 1974), chap. viii.

[13]"Francesco Petrarca, *Petrarch's Lyric Poems: The Rime Sparse and Other Lyrics*, ed. and trans. Robert M. Durling (Cambridge: Harvard University Press, 1976), xxxv, 1–3, p. 95.

[14]"Klibansky et al., *Saturn and Melancholy*, p. 248.

that, "as [Petrarch] uses it, seems to hover half-way between sin and disease."[15]

It was the fifteenth-century Florentine philosopher, Marsilio Ficino, a self-described melancholic, who revised such negative or at least ambiguous assessments of the melancholic temperament by insisting that those who fell under the unlucky planet of Saturn, as he himself had, were especially gifted. As the deity or planet traditionally associated with melancholia, and thus previously viewed only negatively, Saturn took on a positive aspect with Ficino, becoming a *iuvans pater* for men of intellect. Equating the Aristotelian clinical category of melancholy with the Platonic poetics of "divine frenzy,"[16] Ficino thus turned melancholia into a positive virtue for men of letters and "popularized" it to the rest of Europe.[17]

In other words, depression became translated into a virtue for the atrabilious man of letters. And it is significant that melancholia—at least this form of it—became an elite "illness" that afflicted *men* precisely as the *sign* of their exceptionality, as the inscription of genius within them. The fluctuations between "exultation and despair" became a hallmark whereby the *homo melancholicus* defined his difference from the common crowd or *vulgus*, and the exaggeration of emotional states could be seen as that perilous course that the creative *man* set upon in order to create a trajectory that was extraordinary. Depression for "qualified" men thus became a sign of spiritual greatness that, in turn, empowered such men to capitalize on their difference by making it a difference that counts. The *homo melancholicus* might be seen as mad; but a blessed lack or holy curse signifying proximity to Truth granted him cultural and literary

[15]Ibid.

[16]Ibid., p. 254. Marsilio Ficino's discussion of this "divine frenzy" can be found in his *Commentarium in Phaedrum*, in *Marsilio Ficino and the Phaedran Charioteer*, ed. Michael J. B. Allen (Berkeley and Los Angeles: University of California Press, 1981), pp. 65–129. The most pertinent passages are found in chapter 4, "De furore poetico ceterisque furoribus et eorum ordine, conjunctione, utilitate" (pp. 83–87). The Wittkowers also provide an invaluable service in tracing the historical influences of classical texts on Renaissance notions of madness and melancholy and their particular promulgation through Ficino's rereadings of Plato and Aristotle (*Born under Saturn*).

[17]In a letter addressed to Giovanni Cavalcanti, Marsilio Ficino states his desire to find a way to rethink Saturn's negative influence over melancholic temperaments and to "seek a shift" such that if melancholia does come from Saturn, "I shall, in agreement with Aristotle, say that this is a unique and divine gift." See *The Letters of Marsilio Ficino*, vol. 2 (Liber III), trans. Language Department of the School of Economic Science, London (London: Shepard-Walwyn, 1978; rpt. New York: Gingko Press, 1985), pp. 33–34. Cf. Klibansky et al., p. 250; on popularizing, see pp. 254–74.

legitimacy. The "victim" of such a malady was thus able to identify his illness as a gift of inspiration. Even in its distress, the masculine ego is thereby preserved and even affirmed through literary and cultural production.

Thus as early as Ficino and as late as Freud melancholia appears as a specific representational form for male creativity, one whose practice converted the feeling of disempowerment into a privileged artifact. The melancholic not only became perceived as an exclusive someone but also perceived himself as exclusive. Like Molière's misanthrope, a character who in the play's subtitle is specifically diagnosed as "atrabilious," the melancholic's identity visibly displayed the supposed traits of his differ-ence from all else. At the same time, the hyper-exclusivity of his world required the negation of everything different from himself. The very nature of the melancholic was to be that of a self split against itself, fleeing the social into a perpetual dialogue with its own Imaginary, to use Lacan's term. Such a morbid turning-in on itself, however, frustrates the implicit desire for a fusion of selfhood because a distinction is thereby established between the self and its *objectification* of itself. The "sufferer" thus bemoans this inability to suture the self or to overcome the necessity of lack. As elaborated since the Renaissance, the discourse of melancholia glorifies this frustration as heroic suffering and consecrates the situation of lack as blessed. In some cases, as with Michelangelo, melancholia was even seen to be "the artist's joy": [La mia allegrezza è la maninconia].[18] In other words, the more the artist suffered, especially through self-denial, the more he became emblematic of superior aesthetic virtues. More than just the undesirable *disease* that humoral medicine had tra-ditionally diagnosed as caused by an excess of black bile, melancholia by the time of the Renaissance had *also* come to be perceived as an eloquent form of mental disturbance—a special, albeit difficult, gift— as hierarchically superior to mere depression as were the individuals afflicted by it.[19]

Freud's long-range indebtedness in "Mourning and Melancholia" to the tradition inaugurated by Ficino is evidenced by his attributing to the melancholic a moral—hence superior—quality, but that indebted-ness is even more manifestly mediated by that other avatar of Renaissance melancholia, the character of Hamlet. In fact, the figure of Hamlet falls

---

[18]Michelangelo Buonarroti, "I'sto rinchiuso come la midolla," in *Poesia Italiana del Cin-quecento*, ed. G. Ferroni (Milano: Garzanti, 1978), p. 150.

[19]Cf. Jackson, *Melancholia and Depression*, esp. pp. 99–103.

squarely within this Ficinian tradition with its ethos of suffering, an ethos that points to the (male) subject's difficult—and extraordinary—encounter with the "martyrdom" associated with "true greatness." Freud writes: "[the melancholic] has a *keener eye for the truth* than others who are not melancholic . . . [and] it may be, so far as we know, that he has come pretty near to understanding himself; we can only wonder why a man has to be ill before he can be accessible to a truth of this kind. For there can be no doubt that if anyone holds and expresses to others an opinion of himself such as this (an opinion which Hamlet held both of himself and of everyone else), he is ill, whether he is speaking the truth or whether he is being more or less unfair to himself" (emphasis mine).[20] Freud's analysis is pleased to uncover something virtuous and exceptional in Hamlet, whose illness makes of him a possible speaker of truths and a visionary. In other words, Hamlet's melancholic humor elevates him above ordinary men—as in Ficino's model. It is what we could call an *accredited pathology*, justified by the heightened sense of conscience that the melancholic is said to display ostentatiously: "Dissatisfaction with the ego on moral grounds is the most outstanding feature" (p. 248).

Freud further posits *within* the individual psyche of the melancholic a structure of dominance and disempowerment: "We see how in him one part of the ego sets itself over against the other, *judges it critically*, and as it were, *takes it as its object*. . . . What we are here becoming acquainted with is the agency commonly called 'conscience'" (p. 247; emphasis mine). Here the critical agency of the moralizing conscience functions in terms of an objectification, which positions a superior moral side of the psyche over and against a lesser "immoral" one. As Freud says later in his essay, "The ego may enjoy in this the satisfaction of knowing itself as the better of the two, as superior to the object."[21]

My feminist suspicion is that this object, at once vilified, desired, and judged by a "superior, moral" instance, is situated *in the same way* as woman in classic phallocentrism (that is, as a devalued object, as

<hr />

[20]Freud, "Mourning and Melancholia," p. 246. As Jacqueline Rose points out, "The relationship of psychoanalysis to Hamlet has in fact always been a strange and repetitive one in which Hamlet the character is constantly given the status of a truth, and becomes a pivot for psychoanalysis and its project" (*Sexuality in the Field of Vision* [London: Verso, 1986], p. 133).

[21]Freud, "Mourning and Melancholia," p. 257. While Freud is arguing at this point in terms of a cure for the melancholic that would entail a mental separation from the incorporated object of loss, nevertheless, the subject at that moment still remains locked in a polarized conflict between the ego and an object that it seeks to dominate.

abject and at fault). This suspicion can be corroborated if we look again at the Renaissance text of *Hamlet*, and especially at the role given the female figures in it. While the gloomy prince continually desires the attentive gaze of others, the women in the play (Gertrude and Ophelia) are the persistent objects of his aggressivity and derision. In fact, Hamlet's brooding mourning has been situated by psychoanalytic readers within an oedipal structure whereby the feminine is both desired and devalued. Thus Hamlet's melancholia points to an overinvested tie to his mother, Gertrude, although that fixation is certainly not her fault, as some critics would have it, nor that of any other woman.[22] Spurned and ridiculed, Gertrude and Ophelia lose all, even their lives. Yet it is the question of Hamlet's sense of lack that makes Shakespeare's tragedy so compelling for male subjectivity: Hamlet underscores the possiblity for men to display loss, thus encoding a gendered bias within the melancholic syndrome. Concomitantly, the women's losses are delegitimated or made to seem insignificant by men's melancholic display of loss.[23] The superiority of the *homo melancholicus* thus lies in his privileged understanding and in the exceptional marginalization or alienation that grants him cultural legitimacy.

It is indeed striking that in Freud's "Mourning and Melancholia" the only named subject of melancholia is Hamlet. The other examples Freud provides are mere *types* of women such as the deserted bride or

[22]As Jacqueline Rose astutely remarks: "The fact that Hamlet constantly unleashes an anxiety which returns to the question of femininity tells us above all something about the relationship of aesthetic form and sexual difference, about the fantasies they share—fantasies of coherence and identity in which the woman appears repeatedly as both wager and threat. ...The problem of the regulation of subjectivity, of Oedipal drama and the ordering of language and literary form—is *not*, to put it at its most simple, *the woman's fault*" (*Sexuality in the Field of Vision*, p. 139; emphasis mine).

[23]See Elaine Showalter, "Representing Ophelia: Women, Madness, and the Responsibilities of Feminist Criticism," in *Shakespeare and the Question of Theory*, ed. Patricia Parker and Geoffrey Hartman (New York: Methuen, 1985), pp. 77–105. In addressing the question of how Ophelia has been historically represented, Showalter remarks that the Elizabethans would have diagnosed Ophelia's behavior as a "female love-melancholy, or erotomania," which needs to be contrasted with that other type of melancholy for which "Hamlet himself is a prototype" and "hero," although one could easily say that Hamlet too suffers from some type of lovesickness as many psychoanalytic critics have argued. I think what needs to be underscored here is that, as Showalter has suggested, "the epidemic of melancholy associated with intellectual and imaginative genius curiously bypassed women" and "women's melancholy was seen instead as biological and emotional in origins" (p. 81). Also see Jacques Lacan, "Desire and the Interpretation of Desire in *Hamlet*," trans. James Hubbert, *Literature and Psychoanalysis: The Question of Reading: Otherwise*, ed. Shoshana Felman (Baltimore: Johns Hopkins University Press, 1982), pp. 11–52. Lacan rereads Freud's "Mourning and Melancholia" in terms of Hamlet's lack of proper mourning, but he too (like Freud) situates the feminine as the object of a judgmental male gaze in his discussion of the relation between Hamlet and Ophelia.

the self-deprecating wife, suggesting that, for Freud, Hamlet's pathology exceeds mere depression (pp. 245, 248); Hamlet, has claim to a status beyond the commonplace. This notion of a privileged lack functions to produce a specifically male-oriented subjectivity that invests its eros by appropriating the putative lack of some other, in particular, by appropriating the feminine. (By "feminine" here, I do not mean an unchanging essence of woman; but the social constitution of her by and within patriarchal culture as the projected object of male desire, a point to which I return later in this Introduction.) In other words, the polarization mirrored in the Freudian model places the melancholic subject— say Hamlet—in a privileged position vis-à-vis the feminine. The critical function of the moralizing conscience, split as it is, is symbolically defined in terms of its power to reduce an other to control its difference, but then the moralizing conscience becomes dependent on that now delegitimated "inferior" other in order to eroticize its own subject position by bemoaning its fate. That unnamed, "feminized," objectified, inferior other is the condition for the morally superior, male subject of melancholia, the grandeur of whose name is a function of his expressive self-criticism, that is, repressed criticism of that devalued other.

Yet the heightened consciousness that both Ficino and Freud attribute to the *homo melancholicus* is dialectically aggravated through the ego's warring over the object of loss, such that the loss itself becomes the dominant feature and not the lost object. Thus in Freud we can see two sides of this illness. On the one hand, Freud gives us a "clinical" picture of the pathology of melancholia; but on the other hand, by referring to Hamlet and the melancholic's visionary talents (i.e., his "keener eye for the truth"), he points to a cultural apotheosis of its victims, whose sense of loss and "melancholy" is thus the sign of their special nature. This set of convergences suggests the degree to which the psychoanalysis of melancholia remains within the Ficinian tradition. The question I must ask myself, however, is just where, if, and how women fit into this "creative" form of mental disturbance.

In pursuit of such an inquiry, this book explores how male fantasy is implicated within the rise of melancholia as a specific cultural as well as pathological phenomenon. As I argue, the "grievous" suffering of the melancholic artist is a gendered one, an eroticized nostalgia that recuperates loss in the name of an imaginary unity and that also gives to the melancholic *man* (the *homo melancholicus*) a privileged position within literary, philosophical, and artistic canons. This implicitly empowered

The Gendering of Melancholia

display of loss and disempowerment converts the personal sorrow of some men into the cultural prestige of inspired artistry and genius. At the same time, such an impressive translation of lack seems persistently denied to women, whose association with loss or grief is expressed by less flattering allusions to widow's weeds, inarticulate weeping, or other signs of ritualistic (but intellectually and artistically unaccredited) mourning. This cultural devaluation of women's sense of loss does not exclude, however, the frequent representation of melancholia by the figure of woman (for example, in Dürer's famous etching); for in such cases, as I argue, she functions as a metaphor of male sorrow.[24] The vulnerability and sensitivity, or "feminization," typically claimed by the melancholic male thus seem concomitant with the traditional denial of importance to expressions of loss by women.

Melancholia thus appears as a gendered form of ethos based on or empowered by a sense of lack; at the same time, it finds its source of empowerment in the *devaluing* of the historical reality of women's disempowerment and of the ritual function that has traditionally been theirs in the West, that of mourning.[25] If such a gender dichotomy obtains between (female) mourning and (male) melancholia, then the mimetic relation Freud describes wherein melancholia imitates the trappings of mourning points to something considerably less innocent than what the father of psychoanalysis sees as "heightened self-criticism." Not only does the male display of loss convert it into gain, but the "loss" displayed

[24] As Klibansky et al. argue, the representation of the winged woman in Dürer's etching was to be understood as expressing the "melancholia naturalis" of the mentally creative man who has also "been overcome by a fit of depression" (*Saturn and Melancholy*, pp. 349, 350). For Sander L. Gilman, "melancholia is a feminine noun" and therefore representable as a woman, although Gilman also goes on to argue that such a representation of melancholia accordingly signifies that the female is "especially prone to the exaggeration of emotional states" (*Disease and Representation: Images of Illness from Madness to AIDS* [Ithaca: Cornell University Press, 1988], p. 19). But whether the "femininity" in question is grammatically justified or whether it is understood as emotional excess, its reference persistently remains but the "feminine" *within man*.

[25] Diane Owen Hughes ("Invisible Madonnas? The Italian Historiographical Tradition and the Women of Medieval Italy," in *Women in Medieval History and Historiography*, ed. Susan Mosher Stuard [Philadelphia: University of Pennsylvania Press, 1987], pp. 25–57) has shown how a feminine symbolic became obviated by a masculine one: "The ordering of the commune [was] an exclusively male corporation whose earliest laws not only excluded women from membership but also sought to limit their dominance in the private sphere, restricting those marriage festivities, mourning ceremonies and birth celebrations that had accorded women a central role" (p. 31). Also see Sharon Strocchia, "Funerals and the Politics of Gender in Early Renaissance Florence, "in *Refiguring Woman: Perspectives on Gender and the Italian Renaissance*, ed. Marilyn Migiel and Juliana Schiesari (Ithaca: Cornell University Press, 1991), pp. 155–68.

is one whose expression is derived from the devalued cultural form of women's mourning. That is, the ideology of melancholia appropriates from women's subjectivities their "real" sense of loss and, in Lacanian terms, recuperates that loss (whose sense both philosophers such as Ficino and psychoanalysts such as Freud attribute to moral superiority) as a privileged form of male expression, if not as an expression of male privilege. In turn, that recuperation legitimates the male in his "excessive" suffering, even in his "femininity," but leaves women as an oppressed and nameless (or generic) other.[26]

By such an "appropriation," I mean that the (cultural) expression of women's losses is not given the same, let us say, representational *value* as those of men within the Western canon of literature, philosophy, and psychoanalysis. Thus, oftentimes, a woman's lament, grievance, or suffering is seen as the "everyday" plight of the common (wo)man, a quotidian event whose collective force does not seem to bear the same weight of "seriousness" as a man's grief.[27] The value of "his" grief would lie, on the other hand, in its uncommon or unparalleled expression, which is to say that his "loss" is transcoded once again as a privileged suffering that all too often displays (and belies) the desire for a transcendent relation with the world, a transcendence of difference (whether social, sexual, ethnic, or linguistic). Such a desire for transcendence is especially evident in the trope of "sensitivity," whose aesthetics may even seem to undo or fragment the rigid binarism of what is traditionally called masculine or feminine. Hence, even if sexual difference is ques-

---

[26]Such a male appropriation of a *male* representation of women, which then doubly excludes women, can be seen in Ficino: "To achieve poetic madness (the madness that may instruct men in divine ways and sing the divine mysteries), the soul of the future poet must be so affected as to become almost *tender* and *soft* and *untouched* too. The poet's province is very wide, and his material is varied; so his soul (which can be formed very easily) must subject itself to God. This is what we mean by being 'soft' and 'tender.' If the soul has received alien forms or blemishes because of its ability to be formed so easily, then it cannot be formed in the meantime by the divine forms; and this is why Socrates added that the soul must be completely 'untouched,' that is, unblemished and clean" (in Allen, *Marsilio Ficino and the Phaedran Charioteer*, p. 82). A very interesting reversal of this notion, in which women are seen to "corrupt" but which nevertheless betrays a similarity to Ficino's appropriation of "femininity," is described by Freud in reference to critical appraisals of the *Mona Lisa*: "The most perfect representation of the contrasts which dominate the erotic life of women; the contrast between reserve and seduction, and between the most devoted tenderness and a sensuality that is ruthlessly demanding—consuming men as if they were alien beings" (Leonardo da Vinci and a Memory of His Childhood," *S.E.* 11: 108). On this passage, also see Rose, *Sexuality in the Field of Vision*, p. 127.

[27]While the figure of the *mater dolorosa* may iconographically seem to include grieving women, let us not forget that the grief expressed is over the loss of a divine *son*.

tioned within the melancholic subject, any ambiguity of gender turns out to be recuperated by male power as individual triumph in the guise of moral conscience, artistic creativity, or heightened sensitivity, and the melancholic thus stands both in reaction to and in complicity with patriarchy. On the other hand, and to the extent that women are persistently situated as the mere objects of patriarchal desire, their material existences become dehistoricized by their conversion into the representation of a "timeless" and anonymous femininity.[28]

Within the hierarchy of such a scheme, the historical and political reality of women remains obfuscated by their absorption into discourses that superimpose a transcendental lack over women's own losses, thus denying validity and significance to the expression of those losses. As if in confirmation of this gendered dissymmetry, a topos of the medical tradition from Avicenna to Burton states that melancholia is more frequent in men but more severe in women: as Avicenna says, "Of sexes both, but men more often; yet women misaffected are far more violent, and grievously troubled" [Et hic quidem egritudo plus accidit in viris, sed in mulieribus est deterior].[29] Yet precisely in these rare cases when women do suffer from melancholia, they appear more afflicted by its negative or pathological effects than creatively inspired by the potential for "eminence" it seems to encode in men. For the sixteenth-century physician John Weyer, melancholia's implicit masculinity makes it more harsh in women: "They are cruelly used and violently disturbed by it, for melancholia being more opposed to their temperament, it removes them further from their natural constitution."[30]

For Burton, these troubles are most extreme in women whose "fire" is not domesticated by a husband (i.e., "maids, nuns, and widows"):

---

[28]A similar dissymmetry between the named and historical particularity ascribed to men and the timeless anonymity of women is discussed by Elizabeth Cropper in terms of Renaissance portraiture: "Many portraits of unknown beautiful women are now characterized as representations of ideal beauty in which the question of identity is immaterial. No identified male portrait, on the other hand, is ever said to be a beautiful representation made for its own sake" (The Beauty of Women: Problems in the Rhetoric of Renaissance Portraiture," in *Rewriting the Renaissance: The Discourses of Sexual Difference in Early Modern Europe*, ed. M. Ferguson, M. Quilligan, and N. Vickers [Chicago: University of Chicago Press, 1986], p. 178).

[29]Avicenna, *Canon* bk. III, fen. 1, tr. 4, chap. 18; cited in Donald A. Beecher and Massimo Ciavolella, ed. and trans. of Jacques Ferrand, *A Treatise on Lovesickness* (Syracuse: Syracuse University Press, 1990), p. 527—also see Beecher and Ciavolella's extensive note on this topos on the same page; Robert Burton, *The Anatomy of Melancholy* (London: Dent, 1932), 1: 140.

[30]John Weyer, *De praestigiis daemonum*, 1563; cited in Radden, "Melancholy and Melancholia," p. 243, n. 50. Cf. Michel Foucault, *Madness and Civilization: A History of Insanity in the Age of Reason*, trans. Richard H. Howard (New York: Vintage Books, 1965), p. 120.

"Many of them cannot tell how to express themselves in words, or how it holds them, what ails them, you cannot understand them, or well tell what to make of their sayings; so far gone sometimes, so stupefied and distracted, they think themselves bewitched, they are in despair ... yet will not, cannot again tell how, where, or what offends them, though they be in great pain, agony, and frequently complain, grieving, sighing, weeping, and discontented still, *sine causa manifesta*."[31] Far from being inspired to express themselves in some heightened artistic way, women melancholics—especially those who by lack of a husband are most alienated from phallic authority—lapse into utter inarticulateness and can no longer find a place in the symbolic order's prime system, language. Although, of course, both women and men can be depressed, the *discourse* of melancholia has historically designated a topos of expressibility for men and has accordingly given them a means to express their sorrows in a less alienated way, while relegating women to an inexpressive babble whose only sense (at least for the doctors of melancholia) is their need for a good man. As we shall see on a number of occasions in this book, melancholia is at best made available to woman as a debilitating disease and certainly not as an enabling ethos.

My intention, then, is not to set up a simple polarity between male and female melancholia, nor to argue the existence of male melancholia as precluding the possibility of female melancholics. My intention, rather, is to show how the *discourse* of melancholia legitimates that neurosis as culturally acceptable for particular men, whose eros is then defined in terms of a literary production based on the appropriation of a sense of lack, while the viability of such appropriation seems systematically to elude women. Melancholia occurs, on the one hand, as a clinical/medical condition and, on the other hand, *as a discursive practice* through which an individual subject who is classified as melancholic or who classifies himself as melancholic is legitimated in the representation of *his* artistic trajectory. This book is therefore not a historical study of melancholia as a clinical phenomenon. Nor do I seek to unpack what melancholia, depression, and mourning "really" are in constitutive or ontological terms. Even a historian of medicine such as Stanley Jackson has considerable difficulty in distinguishing the different affects of bereavement in mourning, melancholia, and depression.[32] And in purely

---

[31]Burton, *Anatomy of Melancholy* 1: 416.
[32]In "Mourning and Its Relation to Manic-Depressive Stages," Melanie Klein sees a fundamental continuity and interrelated development between mourning and the later ap-

clinical terms, one can have just as many unhappy men as unhappy women.

Rather than attempting to define what melancholia "is" in clinical terms, I am interested in ascertaining how this clinical category serves to legitimate a certain ego-formation in men. One could argue, in fact, that while on the clinical level mourning and melancholia are distinguishable, depression and melancholia are clinically identical and indeed are distinguishable only on the cultural level. In other words, while we can at least provisionally distinguish mourning from melancholia in terms of the difference between a "literal" loss and a figural sense of loss, depression and melancholia can be read as differently valued terms for the same etiological complex: the great melancholic of yesteryear would have been a tortured but creative male genius, but the stereotypically depressed person of today is an unhappy and unproductive woman. Nothing more eloquently expresses what I call the gendering of melancholia than this split between a higher-valued form understood as male and a lower-valued one coded as female. Moreover, the "higher" form (melancholia) is made to represent a sensitive or exquisite illness characterized by representation itself, whereas the "lower" form (depression) remains characterized by an incapacity to translate symptoms into a language beyond its own self-referentiality as depression. And not only is the male form empowering and the female one disempowering, but melancholia is romantically garbed in the past while depression is given only the banality of the present.

Alternatively, one could represent the lexical shift from melancholia to depression as a historical one from valued to devalued, from masculine to feminine. Rather than attempting, however, to construct some all-encompassing "grand narrative" from this difference, this book seeks to explicate some *symptomatic* moments in the discursive construction of melancholia. A textual approach based on psychoanalysis, poststructuralism, and feminism is deployed to reveal the workings of the gendered valuation that subtends and motivates the production of melancholia as a privileged psycho-physiological category or neurosis. Obviously, the gendered workings of the discourse of melancholia are not the same in every one of the moments I have decided to study, and these differences

---

pearance of various kinds of grief or depression (in *Contributions to Psycho-Analysis: 1921–1945*, intro. Ernest Jones [London: Hogarth, 1948], pp. 311–38). On Klein's theory, see Jackson, *Melancholia and Depression*, pp. 322–23. And on the relation between mourning and depression, also see John Bowlby, *Attachment and Loss* (New York: Basic Books, 1969–80).

point to a historicization of the neurosis. At the same time, the persistence of a gender imbalance in the ways melancholia is discussed from Aristotle to Freud, from Ficino to Benjamin, or from Burton to Kristeva, testifies to a *transhistorical* oppression of women's loss in Western phallocentrism that exceeds any neo-historicist insistence on the particularity of a single historical moment.

The unraveling of the gendered bias that structures Freud's 1917 essay is pursued in Chapter 1 through a close reading of his text followed by an extended consideration of some recent feminist reappraisals of the twin categories of mourning and melancholia. In propping the etiology of melancholia on the practice of mourning, Freud is nonetheless shown to be at pains to explain exactly what is different about melancholia just as he is later at pains to distinguish melancholia from hysteria. A criterion of differentiation is found in the *narcissistic* identification said to be carried out by melancholia. This narcissistic basis for differentiation is consonant with an implicit masculinizing of the neurosis as well as with its disassociation from the stereotypically feminine conditions of mourning and hysteria. The question of narcissism is also at the heart of the debate between Luce Irigaray and Kaja Silverman over whether women are incapable of melancholia or are constitutively melancholic. Some resolution in the terms of this debate can be found, again, if we differentiate between the symbolically accredited category of melancholia and the devalued status of depression. While Irigaray is right to argue that women are denied "access to the signifying economy" that is the discursive apparatus of (male) melancholia, Silverman is also correct to demonstrate the necessarily depressed psychical makeup of women in a patriarchal society that requires them to renounce a mother with whom they must *also* identify. Female melancholia, or depression, can be shown to be a perpetual mourning for the barred status imposed on them. This mourning, however, not only points to a resistance to patriarchy that would serve as the radical basis for a collective refiguring of women's identities but also suggests the possibility of rethinking a symbolics of loss that would displace a patriarchal symbolic. Such a refiguring, which would take place as a revolution in the symbolic order, is the occasion for a critical reading of Julia Kristeva's *Black Sun: Depression and Melancholia*. Kristeva's "matricidal" therapy for depression is shown to be disturbingly complicitous with the same symbolic order that privileges the artistic expression of male melancholia and devalues the depression of women as personal failure.

This feminist reconceptualization of the Freudian categories then allows for their further displacement—a historicizing one—by a set of readings of texts from the tradition of humoral medicine that replicate in curious and complementary ways the same insights, and the same blindnesses, that Freud reveals. Chapter 2 explores the relation between melancholia and femininity in a number of premodern texts, focusing especially on Aristotle's influential *Problems* XXX and Marsilio Ficino's crucial writings *On Love* and *On Life*. The parameters of a tradition are staked out in terms of a gendered set of values: when melancholia is considered undesirable it is stereotypically metaphorized as feminine or viewed as an affliction women bring onto men; when melancholia is valued as a creative condition, however, its privilege is grounded on an implicit or explicit exclusion of women. A critical alternative to this misogynist tradition (women included but melancholia devalued, or melancholia valued but women excluded) is found in Hildegard of Bingen. Perhaps the most acerbic critic of melancholia, she sees its cause not in women but in the male misogynist disdain for women. Nor does melancholia offer men any philosophical privilege or artistic potential. Furthermore, Hildegard's radical departure from the melancholic tradition is demonstrated by her unparalleled delineation and sympathetic discussion of female melancholia as a distinct category.

Chapter 3 considers the revaluing of melancholia as an elite male affliction in its historic coincidence with the Renaissance assault on mourning, and most particularly on mourning insofar as it took place as a collective women's ritual. Interestingly, the same men who most disparaged the value of mourning, such as Ficino and Petrarch (the latter even going so far as to demand that wailing women be confined to the home), also figure as early incarnations of the melancholic genius and were the recipients of grandiose public funerals. The question of (male) melancholia as a possible displacement if not appropriation of (female) mourning is then examined through a set of contrastive readings of men and women poets of Renaissance Italy. To Gaspara Stampa's reaffirmation of the collective power of women's mourning in her revisions of the Petrarchan poetic tradition corresponds Torquato Tasso's self-aggrandizing appropriation in his "Canzone al Metauro" of the kind of disempowered situation represented by Isabella di Morra in one of her autobiographical laments.

Fueled by the drive for an intellectual distinction based on individualism, the prestigious pathos of melancholy emerged as a grief more akin to Freud's notion of melancholic mourning than to the affective reaction to a concrete loss. In this Renaissance pathos of grief, there existed a sense of the tragic, a feeling of finitude whose expression presupposed its reconnection to an exhilarating infinitude, coupled with a heightened awareness of the self as "different" from the common *vulgus* and by virtue of this difference, extraordinary. Within this Renaissance thematics of the artist as melancholic, the figure who emerged as the most explicit embodiment of the pathological status given those who grieve too long for an impossible union with the Ideal through their fixated desire to negate finitude was Torquato Tasso. Chapter 4 is thus dedicated to a reconsideration of his work. Tasso came to define the new subjectivity of the *homo melancholicus* at an extreme: one full of doubts and fears, one for whom the existence of any alterity in the world comes at the cost of his exclusivity— which is necessarily impugned by his inevitable participation in the society of women and men. With Tasso, therefore, we see the rise of a subjectivism that finds its source of identity within melancholy, an identity whose contours proceed from the ambiguous point of intersection between clinical limitation and philosophical (spiritual) transcendence. The figure of such a "divine" madness wherein the melancholic also suffers the exclusive fantasy of his elect status precisely because he suffers, Tasso also emblematized the risk of severe states of depression, persecutionary fantasies, and babbling madness.

My intent here, again, is not to criticize melancholy from the point of view of some hypothetically pure or normative state of "health," but rather to unravel the stakes in this historicized form of self-identity, a form for which Tasso became a European model, as evidenced by such illustrious imitators and admirers as Rousseau, Hölderlin, Goethe, Byron, and Nerval. In Tasso's own time Montaigne saw him as representing melancholic madness. Tasso embodied the dilemma of the *belle-âme* who, having directed his imaginative energy in accordance with an insuperable desire for an ontological and epistemological certitude that cannot be had, mourns this loss by incorporating the ideal back into himself as a condition for an idealization of the self. His "suffering" becomes the incremental sign of an unappreciated, or even persecuted, but nonetheless divinely accredited genius.[33] As we shall see, this absolute

[33]For the standard biographical information on Tasso's persecutionary fantasies, Angelo Solerti's *Vita di Torquato Tasso* (Turin: Ermanno Loescher, 1895) remains unsurpassed. One of the first men of letters to spread the news of Tasso's illness and imprisonment and whose

desire for an ideal incorporated as self-presence is at best the ego's self-display projected onto its ideal, and at worst an attempt to deny difference (in psychoanalytic terms, castration) empowered by the classic obsessions of Western culture and metaphysics: aestheticism, immanence, the communality of sameness, the logic of identity.

More than the classic case of madness as inspiration, an embodiment of the Ficinian ethos, or a textbook case for medical discourse, Tasso is exemplary for his discussions of his own psychic condition, evincing a self-analysis unparalleled by any contemporary—and matched in its representational power only by the character of Hamlet. In fact, a lost Elizabethan play titled *Tasso's Melancholy* may have served as a model for Shakespeare.[34] Tasso is also crucial to this book for his appropriation of a "feminine" position of melancholic lack, both through his foregrounding of powerful and/or mournful women in his epic *Gerusalemme liberata* and through his self-celebrating display of loss and victimization in his autobiographical lyric of reclusion. Both a theorist and a "practitioner" of melancholia, Tasso thus reifies and is a model for the discourses found in other writers of melancholy. Assuming his social and mental "alienation" almost with pride, thus presaging the Romantics, Tasso also models the poet's relation to modern society as an always contested phrasing of the boundaries between public and private. In turn, the troubled question of the Ferrarese court poet's infamous in-

---

description of Tasso was to have no small impact on future writers and scholars was Michel de Montaigne. There has been much controversy as to whether Montaigne visited Tasso in the prison hospital of Sant'Anna. Solerti believes that Montaigne did indeed encounter Tasso during his voyage to Italy but doubts that Montaigne actually went to Sant'Anna in the prison (*Vita* 1: 324–25). In his *Essais*, Montaigne recalls having met with Tasso in Sant'Anna, whereas his *Journal de Voyage en Italie* says little about his trip to Ferrara and nothing of his having met the Ferrarese poet. Some recent scholarship has renewed the question, notably that by Mario Roffi, "Montaigne, il Tasso, l'Ariosto, il Bucintoro, e i cittoli di Ferrara," *La Pianura* no. 2 (1981), 51, and by Edwina Vittorini, "Montaigne, Ferrara, and Tasso," in *The Renaissance in Ferrara and Its European Horizons*, ed. J. Salmons (Cardiff: University of Wales Press, 1984), pp. 145–69. My concern is not whether Montaigne actually visited the poet. What interests me is that Tasso's fame and "madness" were soon known outside Italy, becoming a cultural legacy. Montaigne's view of Tasso's illness, moreover, was less sympathetic than critical. For example, in the *Essays* Montaigne says: "I felt even more vexation than compassion to see him in Ferrara in so piteous a state, surviving himself, not recognizing himself or his works, which, without his knowledge and yet before his eyes, have been brought out uncorrected and shapeless" (trans. Donald M. Frame, *The Complete Essays of Montaigne* [Stanford: Stanford University Press, 1957], p. 363). Vittorini, in citing this passage, mentions that Montaigne's criticism of Tasso upset the Romantics, notably Vigny and Chateaubriand, who saw in it a certain callousness and lack of compassion (p. 156).

[34]C. P. Brand, *Torquato Tasso: A Study of the Poet and His Contribution to English Literature* (Cambridge: Cambridge University Press, 1965).

carceration for melancholic madness during the turbulent politics of Counter-Reformist Italy points to the cultural role of that clinical/poetic condition long before its current revival.

A final chapter explores the legacy of the Tassian/Ficinian paradigm as crystallized in melancholia's classic figure, Hamlet. The gloomy prince's simultaneous appropriation and exclusion of femininity is then analyzed along with Burton's encyclopedic *Anatomy of Melancholy*. Given the contemporary spread of witchcraft trials, the rise of such figures of sensitive manhood appears coincident with the brutal suppression of any or all forms of femininity understood as excessive or threatening. Unable to master and classify all the differences he considers under the rubric of melancholia, Burton compares his task to that of combating a "many-headed beast," a Hydra-like figure of feminine multiplicity that had already surfaced in the texts of Ficino and Tasso.[35] Finally, the repressive features of the melancholic syndrome condensed in the figure of Hamlet are examined in two modern readers of Hamlet and melancholia: Walter Benjamin and Jacques Lacan. While both insist with a certain awe on the historical importance of Hamlet's melancholia as the representation of an "epochal moment," they also testify to the significance of gender—and class—in the status of the melancholy hero, whose "heightened self-criticism" (to use Freud's characterization) demarcates the advent of "modern" subjectivity.

By historicizing the gendered appropriation of lack, sorrow, and loss in the poetic and philosophical traditions of Renaissance melancholia, this book mobilizes a psychoanalytic and feminist approach in order to reexamine and re-situate the conceptual limits of Freud's "Mourning and Melancholia" and to signal its historical indebtedness to the Renaissance discourse on that neurosis. Given such a realignment and revision of Freud in terms of the Renaissance ethos of melancholia, I would like to exploit the possibility provided by the simultaneous reading of psychoanalytic and Renaissance texts in order to pursue a feminist critique of the discourse of melancholia. Such a critique requires a critical displacement of both psychoanalytic methodology and the historical construct we call the Renaissance. To the extent, however, that these readings will remain recognizably psychoanalytic in approach to many

---

[35]Burton, *Anatomy of Melancholy* 1: 78–79; Ficino, "The Apology of Marsilio Ficino," in *The Book of Life*, ed. and trans. Charles Boer (Irving, Tex.: Spring Publications, 1980), pp. 188–89; Torquato Tasso, *Il messaggiero*, in *Prose*, ed. Ettore Mazzali (Milan: Riccardo Ricciardi, 1959), p. 19.

a reader, some clarification of my approach may be in order, especially in the light of recent attacks on theoretically informed readings of early modern texts in general and on psychoanalytically inspired readings in particular.

The dialogue between literature and psychoanalysis has provided some of the most virulent paradigms for critical practice in the twentieth century.[36] Until recently, though, comparatively little has been done to question the historical and cultural limits of Freud's theoretical constructs (in fact, quite a bit has been done, notably by the Jungian movement, precisely to dehistoricize Freud's categories into universal truths of the human condition). Such a questioning does not seek to dismiss those constructs out of antiquarian reaction or to insert them into a comfortable narrative of development, but it does seek to bring differences to bear on the Freudian models in order to rethink their applicability and pertinence. Within this project, the elaboration of a *history* of the neuroses also means the analysis of the ways their differing symptoms are embedded in literary and cultural representations. The collective weight of those representations thus does away with any notion that the psychoanalyst diagnoses or invents them objectively as if from a vacuum. Rather, such historicizing work should make clear how psychoanalytic theories about various pathological categories are informed by their role in preceding ideological paradigms. Much has, of course, been written in this vein on the subject of hysteria as a pathological construct implicated in all kinds of relations between power and knowledge.[37] An equivalent "situating" of melancholia has no doubt been hampered by its "glamour" as a pathology with whose symptoms the majority of commentators on melancholia (from Ficino to Burton to Freud to Kristeva) all too willingly identify.

[36]On the relationship between the two disciplines, see the introductions to the following special issues of journals: "Literature and Psychoanalysis: The Question of Reading: Otherwise," ed. Shoshana Felman, *Yale French Studies* 55/56 (1977), 1–10; "Psychopoetics-Theory," ed. Mieke Bal, *Poetics* 13 (October 1984), 279–98; "The Trial(s) of Psychoanalysis," ed. Françoise Meltzer, *Critical Inquiry* 13 (Winter 1987). Also see Michel de Certeau, "The Freudian Novel: History and Literature," *Humanities in Society* 4, nos. 2–3 (1981), 121–41.

[37]For some recent interpretations of hysteria that stress its articulation as a resistance to patriarchal culture, see the volume of essays edited by Charles Bernheimer and Claire Kahane, *In Dora's Case: Freud-Hysteria-Feminism* (New York: Columbia University Press, 1985); Georges Didi-Hubermann, *L'invention de l'hystérie* (Paris: Macula, 1982); and Sharon Willis, "A Symptomatic Narrative," *Diacritics* 13 (Spring 1983), 46–60. On the general history of hysteria, see Ilza Veith, *Hysteria: The History of a Disease* (Chicago: University of Chicago Press, 1965); and most recently, Philip R. Slavney, *Perspectives on "Hysteria"* (Baltimore: Johns Hopkins University Press, 1990).

In an already celebrated and somewhat infamous essay, Stephen Greenblatt seems to impugn the validity of applying psychoanalytic criticism to Renaissance texts. In his critique, psychoanalysis is understood as that which presupposes a "continuity of selfhood," which is, however, the mere "historical effect" of the early modern redefinition of the relation between "body, property and name." According to this logic, then, psychoanalysis cannot legitimately be used to explain the "causes" of a selfhood whose very definition not only precedes psychoanalysis but is also presupposed by it. Thus, for Greenblatt, psychoanalysis would not simply be "irrelevant," nor even an "anachronism," but "causally belated, even as it is causally linked: hence the curious effect of a discourse that functions *as if* the psychological categories it evokes were not only simultaneous with but even prior to and themselves causes of the very phenomenon of which in actual fact they were the result."[38]

A more attentive look at Greenblatt's argument reveals, however, that a certain kind of psychoanalysis is utterly pertinent to the study of early modern literature. While Greenblatt is right to reject the ahistoricism of those psychoanalytic approaches that posit a "universalizing mythology"[39] or the depth psychology that uncovers the same invariant motivation (i.e., repressed sexual desire) behind all human behavior and in all cultural and historical periods, his argument about the developing Renaissance paradigm of the self as derived from the institutional accrediting of one's external persona is strikingly congruent with the Lacanian revision of psychoanalysis. This Lacanian revision rejects the hypothesis of a self-contained and self-originating psychological subject and instead grounds subjectivity in the "discourse of the Other."[40]

[38]Stephen Greenblatt, "Psychoanalysis and Renaissance Culture," in *Literary Theory/Renaissance Texts*, ed. Patricia Parker and David Quint (Baltimore: Johns Hopkins University Press, 1986), p. 221. For a critique of Greenblatt's "historicist" approach as implicated in a "denial" of gender and racial difference among other differences, see Marguerite Waller, "Academic Tootsie: The Denial of Difference and the Difference It Makes," *Diacritics* 17 (Spring 1987), 2–20, and Elizabeth J. Bellamy, *Translations of Power: Narcissism and the Unconscious in Epic History* (Ithaca: Cornell University Press, 1992).

[39]The critique seems less apt in regard to Freud or to psychoanalysis in general, as Greenblatt would seem to have it, than to that renegade of psychoanalysis, Jung, whose monistic positing of a "universalizing mythology" in the form of his famous archetypes was directly responsible for his split with Freud. Also see Greenblatt, "Psychoanalysis and Renaissance Culture," pp. 217–18.

[40]See Jacques Lacan, "Subversion of the Subject and Dialectic of Desire," in *Ecrits: A Selection*, trans. Alan Sheridan (New York: Norton, 1977), pp. 292–328, esp. p. 312; Fredric Jameson ("Imaginary and Symbolic in Lacan: Marxism, Psychoanalytic Criticism, and the Problem of the Subject," in *Literature and Psychoanalysis*, ed. Felman, p. 365) defines the

Within the Western world, that *symbolic* Other is the social institution
of patriarchy, which organizes, through a determined set of injunctions
and prescriptions (the "symbolic order"), the very nomenclature of family relations, to which Lacan refers—in his characteristic shorthand—
as the *nom du père*: the father's name, which is also the powerfully
interdictive "no" of paternal authority.[41] Within this revised Freudian
schema, the phallus, as a *metaphor* for the *nom du père*, would be a
principle of sexual differentiation that is at least as social as it is biological.[42] No longer the deep, dark "subconscious" of traditional or
vulgar Freudianism, the Lacanian "structural unconscious" is what "exceeds" the subject, or "decenters" its supposed centrality, by ascribing
the very core of its individuality to a mirror reflection of something
external to it,[43] and hence, although Lacanians do not always draw this
conclusion, to the particularity of a social order or of a historical
moment.[44]

According to Greenblatt, psychoanalysis "can redeem its belatedness
only when it historicizes its own procedures," and indeed, the *uncritical*
application of any conceptual schema to any object of analysis is invariably suspect.[45] In its strongest forms, however, psychoanalysis is not
the application of a set of concepts (castration anxiety, penis envy, the
oedipal triangle, etc.) to a given subject matter. Rather, psychoanalysis
is itself a critical approach whose terms and procedures are always and

---

Lacanian "structural" unconscious in opposition to "the classical image of the Freudian unconscious as a seething cauldron of archaic instincts." This latter understanding of the Freudian
subject as one whose psyche is embedded in an ahistorical primal organization must be criticized
for its assumption that a given subject's entry into the world of exchange is wholly predetermined by its personal history. Thus Greenblatt would be correct to refuse *the* ahistoricism of
such "psychoanalytic" readings that view the subject's experiences as simply what pours out
of that "seething cauldron of archaic instincts."

[41]See Lacan, "Function and Field of Speech and Language," in *Ecrits*, esp. pp. 65–68.

[42]See Jacqueline Rose, "Introduction II," in Jacques Lacan, *Feminine Sexuality: Jacques
Lacan and the Ecole Freudienne*, trans. Jacqueline Rose, ed. Juliet Mitchell and Jacqueline Rose
(New York: Norton, 1982), pp. 38–40.

[43]Cf. Lacan, "The Mirror Stage," in *Ecrits*, pp. 1–7; also see John Brenkman, *Culture and
Domination* (Ithaca: Cornell University Press, 1987), esp. pp. 157–58, for an analysis of the
mirror stage as that moment which is fraught with conflict given that the Gestalt of the image
in the mirror is one of wholeness the fictionality of which is belied by the child's recognition
of its dependence on *others*. Thus such "autonomy" is questioned just as the child's acquisition
of and dependence on language are not acts of "self-sufficiency" but of "participation" and
"interaction" (p. 157).

[44]Cf. Brenkman who states: "The importance of Lacanian theory lies precisely in the fact
that it restates the psychoanalytic problem in *social and cultural terms*, while at the same time
maintaining the integrity of the psychoanalytic experience" (*Culture and Domination*, p. 151;
emphasis mine).

[45]Greenblatt, "Psychoanalysis and Renaissance Culture," p. 221.

already unendingly revised *in their very implementation*. It is the "inter-minability" of the analysis (and not some fixation on the phallus) that most forcefully marks the work of the later Freud as well as Lacan, and explains much of their so-called "obscurity."[46] If, as Greenblatt states, the Renaissance is that period that undertakes "the prepsychoanalytic fashioning of the proprietary rights of selfhood" that makes the later invention of psychoanalysis possible, then psychoanalysis is indeed capable of shedding *some* light on the literature of that period.[47] Moreover, the psychoanalytic reading of such texts—also and necessarily—transforms the very theory that carries out the interpretation through contact with those texts that seem to prefigure psychoanalytic categories. Psychoanalysis, if you will, is less a theory than a *practice* of interpretation that lends an ear to what is not said, to what is "repressed."

The difficulty (and urgency) of such a self-transformative critical practice when brought to bear on historical texts at the very inception of the modern notion of selfhood is compounded when the historical perspective is doubled by a feminist one.[48] For, just as the autonomy of the subject is historically compromised by the symbolic order within which it is located, so too the centrality of the phallus to that order is contested by a feminism that hears what remains unspoken within or is repressed by Western patriarchy: the voices of women. Again, if the very conditions of the patriarchal subject were first made possible in the Renaissance, then the combined feminist and psychoanalytic criticism of texts from that period is valuable, not only for a better understanding of the Renaissance but also for a rethinking of psychoanalysis itself. In sum, the psychoanalysis of Renaissance texts is warranted insofar as it allows or wills the transformation of its own conceptual apparatus through the twin displacement of feminist criticism and of the confrontation with older texts.

[46]On the notion of "interminability," see Sigmund Freud's late "Analysis Terminable and Interminable," *S.E.* 23: 209–53.

[47]Greenblatt, "Psychoanalysis and Renaissance Culture," p. 223.

[48]On the relation between psychoanalysis and feminism see, for example, Juliet Mitchell, "Introduction I," and Jacqueline Rose, "Introduction II," in Lacan, *Feminine Sexuality*; Jane Gallop, *The Daughter's Seduction: Feminism and Psychoanalysis* (Ithaca: Cornell University Press, 1982). For a recent volume of essays dealing with the uneasy dialogue between psychoanalysis and feminism and the call for a third term to disrupt any easy duality between the two, see Richard Feldstein and Judith Roof, eds., *Feminism and Psychoanalysis* (Ithaca: Cornell University Press, 1989). In that same volume, Mary Poovey's "The Anathematized Race: The Governess and Jane Eyre" argues for the insertion of history as the necessary third term that will give psychoanalytic and feminist analyses a social and political dimension to the ways the unconscious is structured (pp. 230–54).

Finally, any psychoanalytic approach to Renaissance material should also take note of Freud's indebtedness to the works of that period in the elaboration of his own most cherished principles. Whether we consider (critically or uncritically) Freud's studies of Leonardo and Michelangelo or the prominence of various Shakespearean figures throughout his opus, psychoanalysis has since its inception been involved in rereading the Renaissance. The key, formative role played by Renaissance texts (exceeded only by the role of Greek mythology) in the development of Freud's thought is less surprising than it may at first seem, given that Freud appears at the historical end of that great era of Cartesian selfhood (defined by the autonomy of a self who needs only to "think" to know he "is") whose first stirrings, following Greenblatt, would have been laid down during the Renaissance. Freud is also said to have undertaken a "Copernican revolution" (another Renaissance reference!) in our notions of selfhood. The psychoanalysis of Renaissance texts is thus implicated in the genealogy of psychoanalysis, a situation that is less a vicious circle than the necessity—and the possibility—for a critique of psychoanalysis from *within* psychoanalysis itself.

Much has been said, for instance, about the ways women constitute their subjectivities in or through the symbolic order, and how such a constitution differs from that of men. While both men and women are constructed as gendered subjects in and through social and discursive practices, the positioning of women and men within those practices and their varying responses to those positionings chart differences between genders (and *within* genders if we consider not only sexual but also class and racial differences). As such, differences arise out of the specific and multiple ways the subject encounters herself/himself within various social and psychological practices. The symbolic order, as governed by certain discursive practices, has indeed formed of the ways women interpret their social and psychological roles. Within psychoanalytic paradigms, for example, the symbolic has been dominated either by the Freudian superego or by the Lacanian Law of the Father. Within both categories, however, it has become more and more apparent (and has become a contested issue) that both the Freudian and Lacanian models are in fact dominated by a masculine economy that understands only the development of the male child, and that is constructed in terms of *his* ego self-preservation. The Freudian superego as the agency of the father also implicitly situates the relationship of identification between son and father (no matter how askew it can become, now matter how oedipally antagonistic it may be) within a realm of distinct privilege and presupposed empowerment.

The same can be said for the Lacanian model, in which the phallus as the mark of lack paradoxically comes to symbolize the Law of the Father to which both sexes are subjected. It is precisely the slippage between penis and phallus, however that cannot be denied. The lexical choice of phallus cannot help but remind us of penis as if penis were a metonym for phallus, and thus implicitly positions the male subject in terms of a subjectivity that is favored—from penis, to phallus, to Law of the Father.[49] Such psychoanalytic paradigms resemble what Kaja Silverman after Michel Foucault has called "fellowships of discourse," or the "strict" regulating of a discourse's production and circulation within a given community "without those in possession being dispossessed by this very distribution."[50] Thus, within psychoanalytic theory, the foregrounded recourse to a male term in order to designate the (putatively ungendered) subject's role within the community of symbolic exchange grants to the male subject a privileged status. The refashioning of the current symbolic order is a key project of contemporary feminism, and feminist theorists who work in psychoanalysis need to revise Freudian schemas and assumptions in accordance with that project.[51] In any case, this volume resulted from the necessity I faced in my own research and teaching to rethink the fundamental psychoanalytic notions of lack and loss in terms of gender.

Before this Introduction closes, some clarification of these terms is in order. In melancholy, depression, or mourning, the question of loss is inevitably inscribed, but it does not seem to me that that inscription is always the same. One loss is the literal (or figural) death of someone dear to us, but there is another loss that may intensify it and determine its connotations and associations. This other loss can be called by its more technical name, the primordial loss of the original (lost) object. For Lacan, "aphanisis of being" comes through the loss of and separation

[49]As Jane Gallop puts it, "The masculinity of the phallic signifier serves well as an emblem of the confusion between phallus and male which inheres in language, in our symbolic order" (*Reading Lacan* [Ithaca: Cornell University Press, 1985], p. 135).

[50]Michel Foucault, *The Archeology of Knowledge and the Discourse on Language*, trans. A. M. Sheridan-Smith (London: Tavistock, 1972), p. 255. Also see Kaja Silverman, "Disembodying the Female Voice," in *Re-Vision*, ed. Mary Ann Doane, Patricia Mellencamp, and Linda Williams (Los Angeles: American Film Institute, 1984), p. 131.

[51]On the possibilities for such a refashioning, see Teresa Brennan, ed., *Between Feminism and Psychoanalysis* (London: Routledge, 1989); and Juliet Flower MacCannell, *Figuring Lacan: Criticism and the Cultural Unconscious* (Lincoln: University of Nebraska Press, 1986).

from the mother, a loss whereby the subject assumes lack. For Lacan, all subjects undergo this lack, a differential lack that can never be filled, for it is the condition of the subject's sense of itself, of its being: "Being comes into existence as an exact function of this lack. Being attains a sense of self in relation to being as a function of this lack, in the experience of desire."⁵² In this way, the subject's being is that of a subject without a center, a non-subject or a non-being, which is only constituted through this *difference*. Lacan specifies: "It isn't the lack of this or that but lack of being whereby being exists."⁵³ And this lack of being, this primordial lack that is a decentered center propels the subject into desire, a desire motivated by the impossibility of ever achieving a fixed point, of ever recuperating the original lost object (the mother). Neurosis would thus occur as an obsessive and necessarily doomed desire to fix or find plenitude, to recover an absolute presence in this absence.

My concern, however, as I situate myself within and without a Lacanian model, is as follows: even if, rigorously speaking, the Lacanian lack is something that cannot be named—something that we all share (consciously or unconsciously)—given that we have all lost the original object (the mother), nonetheless this lack, which works as a transcendental sign to that lost object (referent), may on a general level appear, like original sin, to equalize and democratize men and women in that

⁵²Jacques Lacan, *Seminar II: The Ego in Freud's Theory and in the Technique of Psychoanalysis, 1954–1955*, ed. Jacques-Alain Miller, trans. Sylvana Tomaselli (New York: Norton, 1988), p. 223.
⁵³Ibid. Cf. the following lines from "The Field of the Other and Back to the Transference": "By separation, the subject finds, one might say, the weak point of the primal dyad of the signifying articulation, in so far as it is alienating in essence. It is in the interval between these two signifiers that resides the desire offered to the mapping of the subject in the experience of the discourse of the Other, of the first Other he has to deal with, let us say, by way of illustration, the mother. It is in so far as his desire is beyond or falls short of what she says, of what she hints at, of what she brings out as meaning, it is in so far as his desire is unknown, it is in this point of lack, that the desire of the subject is constituted" (Lacan, *The Four Fundamental Concepts of Psycho-Analysis*, ed. Jacques-Alain Miller, trans. Alan Sheridan [New York: Norton, 1977], pp. 218–19). For Jacques Derrida, the lack whereby being is constituted is originary, which means that the "original" lost object has always already been lost, i.e., it never was completely there anywhere ("The Politics of Friendship"). See also his discussion of "true mourning" in *Mémoires: For Paul de Man* (rev. ed., New York: Columbia University Press, 1989), pp. 30–35, where he writes that "we come to ourselves through this memory of *possible* mourning" (p. 34; Derrida's emphasis). A critical account of the epistemology of lack in Lacan and Derrida both can be found in Madelon Sprengnether: "A beneficial conjunction between feminism and psychoanalysis must take account of the fact (as Lacanianism and poststructuralism fail to do) that a woman's body is the carnal origin of every human subject without desubjectifying the mother herself (as object relations theory tends to do)" (*The Spectral Mother: Freud, Feminism, and Psychoanalysis* [Ithaca: Cornell University Press, 1990], p. 9).

we would all be castrated. We all suffer the finitude of human limitation
and are not gods or even self-sufficient subjects. Yet would not desire
also function in terms of how great, or how meaningful, one's desires
are? Is there not some difference between the desires of common folk
and the desires of an empowered elite? Is the desire of someone who
wishes to earn a few extra million equivalent to the desire of someone
who desperately wants to stay home from another day's work? Lacan
would say, rigorously speaking, that his differential lack can never be
named since it is not this or that specific lack but the "lack of being."
And, rigorously speaking, this may be true since in the logic of desire,
once one thing is satisfied or "named," another comes in its place—as
dis-satisfaction, and dis-places it as such, and so goes the chain of desire
creating new objects of desire as they are (dis)satisfied.

Yet these desires are necessarily *different* desires, predicated as they
are on different lacks, whether or not they are all derived from some
primordial loss, whether or not they continue to register the traumatic
effects of that loss. In any case, these different desires tell us something
about such lacks, that is, how the subject's lacks are accredited or not,
for finally it is not such great news that we are all castrated—religion
has already taught us that. Rather, the question to ask is how and in
whom the fact of castration is assuaged and recuperated, how and in
whom loss is not dismissed but taken seriously, how and in whom lack
is viewed not as a deficiency but as something enabling. For, although
under any symbolic order we may all be equally subject to the finitude
of what Lacan calls castration, some of us, to parody Orwell, are "more
equally" castrated than others.[54] Lacan is unquestionably correct in wanting to call *the* subject—all subjects—into question, but this understanding should not make us forget that subjects are already hierarchically
differentiated (by gender, race, class, ethnicity, and language) according
to the symbolic order under which we live. Hence, *different* kinds of
lack are revealed once we speak about different subjects and no longer
about that one lack that subtends all the lacks. True, all of us have felt
the loss that comes from separation from the mother, but *not all* of us
receive the same social accreditation for that loss. All of us assume this
loss as a lack in our being that constitutes our being, but *not all* of us
are *said to be* lacking, and not all of us are said to be lacking *in the same*

[54] My use of the Orwellian phrase here is inspired by Georges Van Den Abbeele's discussion
of social difference in his introduction to *Community at Loose Ends*, ed. The Miami Theory
Collective (Minneapolis: University of Minnesota Press, 1991).

way, or to the same degree. Here is where psychoanalysis might dovetail with social criticism.

Chief among these differences that encode different symbolic possibilities is gender difference. Joan Kelly has remarked that "femininity" can be understood "as an internalization of inscribed inferiority." To speak about women in this way is to understand the position of "inferiority" *as socially determined* while, at the same time, arguing the need for women to be self-defined: "In short, women have to be defined as women. We are the social opposite, not of class, or caste, or a majority, since we are a majority, but of a sex: men. We are a sex, and categorization by gender no longer implies a mothering role and subordination to men, except as a social role and relation recognized as such, as socially constructed and socially imposed."[55] The concept of woman is in itself a problematic one that indeed can be reduced to the fact of sexual difference, at the same time that "femininity" designates the kind of subject position imposed on women under patriarchy. By "feminine" then, as I have already stated, I do not mean an unchanging essence within *women*; but the social constitution of "woman" by and within patriarchal culture as its traditional object of desire (and disdain).[56]

---

[55]*Women, History, and Theory: The Essays of Joan Kelly*, ed. Catharine R. Stimpson (Chicago: University of Chicago Press, 1984), p. 6.

[56]There has been much debate in feminist circles around the term "essentialism." Diana Fuss (*Essentially Speaking: Feminism, Nature, and Difference* [New York: Routledge, 1989]) has defended Luce Irigaray among others against the charge of essentialism made against her by such feminist theorists as Toril Moi (*Sexual/Textual Politics: Feminist Literary Theory* [London: Methuen, 1985], pp. 127–49), arguing that it is "by no means evident" that "to define 'woman' is necessarily to essentialize her" (p. 56). An alternative is proposed by Teresa de Lauretis, who differentiates between "woman" as "a fictional construct, a distillate from diverse but congruent discourses dominant in Western cultures" and "women" as "the real historical beings who cannot yet be defined outside of those discursive formations, but whose material existence is nonetheless certain" (*Alice Doesn't: Feminism, Semiotics, Cinema* [Bloomington: Indiana University Press, 1984], p. 5). Cf. also her "Feminist Studies/Critical Studies: Issues, Terms, and Contexts," in *Feminist Studies/Critical Studies*, ed. Teresa de Lauretis (Bloomington: Indiana University Press, 1986), p. 10; and "The Essence of the Triangle or, Taking the Risk of Essentialism Seriously: Feminist Theory in Italy, the U.S., and Britain, "*Differences* 1 (Summer 1989), 3–37. This entire issue of *Differences*, "Another Look at Essentialism," includes relevant contributions by Naomi Schor, Luce Irigaray, Diana Fuss, Robert Scholes, Leslie Rabine, and Gayatri Spivak. On the woman/women distinction, also see Marianne Hirsch, *The Mother/Daughter Plot: Narrative, Psychoanalysis, Feminism* (Bloomington: Indiana University Press, 1989), pp. 13 and 25. And lest one think that the critique of essentialism is only a recent, postmodern development, one could consult with profit the words of an early twentieth-century Italian woman writer, Sibilla Aleramo, who writes in her 1906 autobiography: ("In fact *woman* as a concept is a product of male fantasy. When we look at reality we see that only *women* exist" [In realtà *la donna* è una cosa che esiste solo nella fantasia degli uomini: ci sono *delle donne*, ecco tutto]; *Una donna*, 21st ed. (Milan: Feltrinelli, 1989), p. 128; *A Woman*, trans. Rosalind Delmar (Berkeley: University of California Press, 1980), p 126. For an over-

Within the problematic space of women's relation to the symbolic, this book analyzes how questions of "loss" become differently inscribed according to gender. What I am suggesting is that loss and lack—those transcendent Lacanian concepts through which a subject comes to recognize her/his imbrication within the social—are subjected to a cultural determination in terms of who has the most privileged access to the display of loss. In other words, once women and men have entered into the symbolic, a symbolic understood as dominated by a masculine cultural ideal, men and women find themselves in utterly different relations to the representation of loss.

In their *Nostalgia and Sexual Difference: The Resistance to Contemporary Feminism*, Janice Doane and Devon Hodges analyze that peculiar relation to loss called nostalgia in terms of male fears of becoming "feminized." They define nostalgia as "a retreat to the past in the face of what a number of writers—most of them male—perceive to be the degeneracy of American culture brought about by the rise of feminist authority." As the writers further state, nostalgia is "not just a sentiment but also a rhetorical practice. In the imaginative past of nostalgic writers men were men, women were women and reality was real."[57] Nostalgia may indeed be a rhetorical practice, and one need only think of those humanist writers of the Renaissance who melancholically looked to the past, to the classics, to realize that nostalgia as sentiment and as a rhetorical practice has a long history in Western thought; it is not *just* a reaction to contemporary feminism, powerful as that reaction may indeed be. Perhaps it is not so much men's fear of the feminization of men per se that gives way to a rhetoric of nostalgia as it is the fear of an intersubjective male-female relationship such that "feminization" would be seen and understood as an incontrovertible recognition of symbolic castration—that is, of the democracy of lack.

Yet the very fear of such feminization does not necessarily preclude that of another sort of "feminization" that would be totally phallic: an appropriation of women's subjectivities, in the form of a masculinist eros of lack, which would deny to women the very specificity of their being. In other words, the male appropriation of a "feminine" position

---

view of historical changes in the notion of "women," see Denise Riley, *"Am I that name?" Feminism and the Category of "Women" in History* (Minneapolis: University of Minnesota Press, 1988).

[57]Janice Doane and Devon Hodges, *Nostalgia and Sexual Difference: The Resistance to Contemporary Feminism* (New York: Methuen, 1987), p. 3.

under the guise of "sensitivity" or "nostalgia" or "loss" can be utterly concomitant with the restricting of women to a system of motherhood, domestication, and oedipal narrative. As Doane and Hodges point out, women typically appear in the nostalgic fantasy of male writers as domesticated mothers or as dead, in other words as submissive representations that appear as essential to the male, nostalgic view of "true feminine sublimity." Woman is not only a "symptom" for man, as Jacqueline Rose has said,[58] but even more she is a place to occupy whose coded subordination may indeed produce "sensitivity," "passivity," "hysteria," and so on. Nonetheless, such sensitivity would be accredited to a melancholic/nostalgic male since "feminization" is all about a play of differences "between men" that still keeps women in place: the domination of one sex over the other.[59]

Perhaps there is a renewed interest in melancholia because the gendered melancholias with which I take issue in this book can no longer impose their validation in terms of a hitherto explicitly gendered topography. The feminist movement has called into question the limitations imposed on Western thought by patriarchy's domination, but feminism has also radicalized our thinking about subjectivity by refiguring the roles and voices of women in order to enable new social subjects.[60] In turn, this study tries in some way to enable our rethinking of such subjectivities by way of a critique of one *habitus* of cultural empowerment: melancholia.

[58]Rose, "Introduction II," in Lacan, *Feminine Sexuality*, p. 48.

[59]On the collusion between male bonding and misogyny, see most notably Eve Kosofsky Sedgwick, *Between Men: English Literature and Male Homosocial Desire* (New York: Columbia University Press, 1985). On the feminization of men as a masculine strategy in the domination of women, see Christopher Newfield, "The Politics of Male Suffering: Masochism and Hegemony in the American Renaissance," *Differences* 1 (Fall 1989), 55–87. Also see Tania Modleski, *Feminism without Women: Culture and Criticism in a "Postfeminist" Age* (New York: Routledge, 1991).

[60]On the concept of new social subjects, see Teresa de Lauretis, *Technologies of Gender* (Bloomington: Indiana University Press, 1987), and Ernesto Laclau and Chantal Mouffe, *Hegemony and Socialist Strategy* (London: Verso, 1985).

Chapter 1

The Gendering of Freud's "Mourning and Melancholia"

A s Doctor Stanley Jackson writes in *Melancholia and Depression*:
"Twentieth-century thought on the relationship of grief and mourning to clinical melancholia or depression tends to be presented as though it dated from Freud's 'Mourning and Melancholia' in 1917. And, in a manner of speaking, perhaps it did."[1] In spite of his desire to downplay Freud's originality and to place his work within a preexisting medical tradition, Jackson is obliged to admit the prestige and influence of Freud's essay, which has come, in fact, to occupy—whether correctly or incorrectly—the pivotal position for discussions of melancholia not only in psychoanalysis but also in contemporary literary analysis, feminist theory, and cultural criticism. No study of melancholia can begin without a reconsideration of Freud's essay, and rereading that essay may also shed some light on recent feminist interpretations of melancholia.

Ernest Jones tells us that in 1915, at age sixty, Freud "superstitiously" believed that he had only a little over two years left to live. It was also during this year that Freud produced what were to be considered his most important theoretical writings, the so-called metapsychological essays. These comprise five papers begun on March 15, 1915, the last being "Mourning and Melancholia," published in 1917.[2] Also according

---

[1] Stanley Jackson, *Melancholia and Depression: From Hippocratic Times to Modern Times* (New Haven: Yale University Press, 1986), pp. 320–21.

[2] The other four papers are "On Narcissism" (1914), "The Unconscious" (1915), "Instincts

[33]

to Jones, the outbreak of the Great War the previous year "had greatly stimulated [Freud's] working powers."[3] Who knows really whether it was the outbreak of the war or the fear of his impending death (he believed he would die in February 1918) that motivated such an intense production? Nonetheless, it is certainly noteworthy that an essay of such provocative insight into the psychic processes involved in loss, grief, and depression would appear at the same time as the European world's protracted indulgence in global war and destruction *and* as Freud's fatalistic projection of his own imminent death.[4] This anecdotal "co-

and Their Vicissitudes" (1915), and "Repression" (1915). All are included in volume 14 of *The Standard Edition of the Complete Psychological Works of Sigmund Freud*, trans. James Strachey (London: Hogarth, 1953–74).

[3]Jones, *The Life and Work of Sigmund Freud* (New York: Basic Books, 1955) 2: 184–86. The term "metapsychology" seems to have been Freud's invention. By "metapsychology" Freud intended the description of a psychic *process*, which included its dynamic attributes, its topographical features, and its economic significance. This is important to remember, for even today there still are those who think that the psychoanalytic telos would be simply to "reveal" the hidden oedipal drama, the castration complex, etc.—in other words, that psychoanalytic methodology is a hermeneutic whose function is merely to uncover castration anxiety, anal or oral fixations, and so on. In a letter to Karl Abraham, whose own comparative work on mourning and melancholia, "Ansätze zur psychoanalytischen Erforschung und Behandlung des manisch-depressiven Irreseins und verwandter Zustände," was very influential in Freud's discussion of this mental state and who was primarily interested in the difference between melancholia and obsessional neurosis, Freud chastised the good doctor precisely for stopping only at the unveiling of the fixation. He stated: "Your comments on melancholia I found very valuable. I have unhesitatingly incorporated in my essay what I found useful. [Did Freud incorporate Abraham's notion of incorporation and thus the need to distinguish himself from Abraham's studies?] The most valuable point was your remark about the oral phase of the libido; the connection you had made between mourning and melancholia is also mentioned. Your request for criticism was easy to fulfill; I was very pleased with everything you wrote. I will only lay stress on two points: that you do not emphasize enough the essential part of my hypothesis, i.e. the topographical consideration in it, the regression of the libido and the abandoning of the unconscious cathexis, and that you instead put sadism and anal-erotism in the foreground as the final explanation. Although you are correct in that, you pass by the real explanation. Anal-erotism, castration complexes, etc., are ubiquitous sources of excitation which must have their share in *every* clinical picture. One time this is made from them, another time that. Naturally we have the task of ascertaining what is made from them, but the explanation of the disorder can only be found in the mechanism—considered dynamically, topographically and economically." According to Jones, this was written on the day Freud finished his essay (2: 329).

[4]In a letter to Sandor Ferenczi, Freud states: "The superstition that my life is due to finish in February 1918 often seems to me quite a friendly idea. Sometimes I have to fight hard to regain ascendency over myself." But when Ferenczi protested, Freud replied, "You seem to want to believe in an 'eternal recurrence' of the same, and want to overlook the unmistakable direction of fate" (cited in Jones 2: 194). And in a letter to Jones, Freud explicitly draws connections between the new so-called "war neurosis" and melancholia: "The difference between peace and war is that with the former the ego is strong but surprised, with the latter it is prepared but weakened. In this way the war neurosis is a case of internal narcissistic conflict within the ego, somewhat analogous to the mechanism of Melancholy, exposed in the 4th volume of *Schriften*" (Jones, 2: 254). Cf. Abraham's work on war neurosis: "Psycho-Analysis and the War Neurosis," in *Clinical Papers and Essays on Psycho-Analysis* (London: Hogarth

incidence" between the personal and the political might nevertheless serve as an advance warning that the problem of melancholia cannot be so easily isolated within the realm of the private and the imaginary.

While "Mourning and Melancholia" crowned his metapsychological theorizing, the paper was also important on a clinical level. For Jones, in 1955, it was "still the best account available of the psychology of manic-depressive insanity" (p. 251). But whether the melancholia in question is of clinical or of theoretical interest, just what melancholia is comes to be particularly difficult to assess since, as Freud notes at the very beginning of his paper, there does not seem to be any unifying principle behind the symptoms of this particular neurosis. He warns readers against overestimating the value of his conclusions on melancholia because its definition "*fluctuates* even in descriptive psychiatry [and it] takes on various clinical forms the grouping together of which into a single unity does not seem to be established with certainty; and some of these forces suggest somatic rather than psychogenic affections" (p. 243). Such an opening legitimates Freud's recourse here (as well as in the other metapsychological essays) to a "speculative" approach. And by stressing the necessity of speaking of *different* forms of melancholia and pathological depression, the text rejoins the longstanding tradition of treating melancholia as a typology to be classified rather than as a condition to be specified. The paragon of the genre, Burton's *Anatomy of Melancholy*, for instance, uses "melancholia" to describe any number of psychological conditions that range from lycanthropy to religious mysticism to lovesickness. Nonetheless, although Freud says that melancholia cannot be reduced to any fixed concept or symptom, in his attempt to understand what mental processes (dynamic, topographic, economic) are taking place, he proceeds to make some rather clear-cut distinctions. As the title of the essay already suggests, melancholia is defined as distinct from mourning, which, we are soon told, would be the "normal affect" of grief caused by the loss of a loved object, while melancholia is described as a "pathology" that on the surface resembles the painful state of mourning. Such distinctions, as we know from

---

Press and Institute of Psycho-Analysis, 1955), pp. 59–67. On the other hand, as Madelon Sprengnether points out, Freud's refusal to acknowledge any connection between the death of his daughter, Sophie, and the writing of *Beyond the Pleasure Principle* testifies to his persistent "disengagement from an identification with the suffering female body, a strategic gesture that simultaneously sets the parameters of his Oedipal theory" (*The Spectral Mother: Freud, Feminism, and Psychoanalysis* [Ithaca: Cornell University Press, 1990], pp. 127–28 and 33).

Foucault and Derrida, are never "innocent" decisions and entail consequences that remain to be unpacked. Such distinctions inevitably require further and further distinctions that ultimately limit the analyst's scope and reveal his partiality.

Freud's Essay and the Narcissism of Excessive Grief

Freud's discussion of mourning and melancholia could be said to proceed in three moments. The first of these, as I have already said, draws on a comparative analysis of mourning and melancholia; the second focuses on identificatory and narcissistic object relations in both mental conditions, in an effort to distinguish them from hysteria; finally, the melancholic syndrome is what first enables Freud to perceive the workings of a "critical agency" within the psyche, namely, the moralizing conscience or superego. The function of this moral faculty would be further elaborated in Freud's later works, most notably (at least with regard to melancholia) in chapter 11 of *Group Psychology and the Analysis of the Ego* (1921), in chapter 5 of *The Ego and the Id* (1923), and in the *New Introductory Lectures* 31 (1933). The workings of this "critical agency," in Freud's view, are the most crucial dimension of melancholia per se. At the same time, it is his "discovery" of the superego in the course of studying the relation between mourning and melancholia that foregrounds the importance of the 1917 essay within the development of Freud's thought.

But let me turn now to the first of these three moments. The contrastive analogy between mourning and melancholia had already been discussed by Freud as early as 1910 and by Karl Abraham in 1912.[5] In their works mourning, as mentioned earlier, is understood to be a "normal" condition relating to loss, whereas melancholia is described as a "pathology" that mimics the painful state of mourning. As Freud says in "Mourning and Melancholia," "Mourning is regularly the reaction to the loss of a loved person, or the loss of some abstraction which has taken the place of one, such as one's country, liberty, an ideal, and so on. In some people the same influences produce melancholia instead of

[5]See Freud, "Contributions to a Discussion on Suicide," *Standard Edition* (hereafter *S.E.*) 11: 232; Karl Abraham, "Ansätze zur psychoanalytischen Erforschung und Behandlung des manisch-depressiven Irreseins und verwandter Zustände," *Zentralblatt für Psychoanalyse* 2 (1912), 302.

mourning and we consequently suspect them of a pathological disposition" (*S.E.* 14: 243). At the same time, this difference between "pathological" melancholia and "normative" mourning turns out to be a
function of mourning's transparency, a transparency that can be easily
explained: "It is really only because we know so well how to explain it
[mourning] that this attitude does not seem pathological" (p. 244).
Thus, while a distinction is being drawn between normal and pathological forms of mourning, a concession is also being made to the cross-
ing of the boundaries or, as Freud says, the "borrowing" of normal
features by the pathological: "Melancholia, therefore, borrows some of
its features from mourning" (p. 250). The distinction is drawn, it seems,
to be almost immediately blurred. Later in the essay, as we shall see,
Freud makes equally odd distinctions, notably between melancholia and
obsessional neurosis and between melancholia and hysteria.

For Freud, the act of mourning is not only the affective reaction of
grief to a concrete loss such as the death of a loved one; it is also the
very *process* of recuperating the ego's investment of libido in the lost
object through a ritual of commemoration and farewell. What Freud
calls the "work" of mourning (*Trauerarbeit/travail de deuil*) consists in
bringing to consciousness memories of the lost object "bit by bit, at
great expense of time and cathectic energy": "Each single one of the
memories and expectations in which the libido is bound to the object
is brought up and hypercathected, and detachment of the libido is accomplished in respect of it. . . . When the work of mourning is completed
the ego becomes free and uninhibited again" (p. 245). Thus, through
a process of "reality testing" (i.e., the reality principle of Freud's first
topology), the sufferer realizes that the object of love no longer exists;
the ego then decides not to share in the "fate" of the lost beloved but
to break its emotional attachment to it, to "cut its losses" as it were.
And, unlike in some forms of melancholia, as Freud discusses them later
in the essay, after the work of mourning is completed there is no reversal
from the state of woe to a manic phase. This difference leads Freud to
say that even if the economic conditions for mourning are still unclear,
he can nevertheless advance a "conjecture" based on what takes place
when memories of the lost object are checked against the reality of its
having disappeared:

> Why is it that after [normal mourning] has run its course, there is no
> hint in its case of the economic phase of triumph? . . . We do not even

know the economic means by which mourning carries out its task. Possibly, however, a conjecture will help us here. Each single one of the memories and situations of expectancy which demonstrate the libido's attachment to the lost object is met by the verdict of reality that the object no longer exists; and the ego, confronted as it were with the question whether it shall share this fate, is persuaded by the sum of the narcissistic satisfactions it derives from being alive to sever its attachment to the object abolished. (p. 255)

Although the exact workings of this economic process are said to remain obscure, the mourner, according to this scenario, seems to get rid of her or his affective charge in the lost object by rehearsing images of the past, thereby emptying out the affect associated with it through the recollection of memories of the lost object. As I argue later, the work of mourning might be better understood as a *refiguring* of the ego's relation to the object rather than as a simple dismissal or disavowal of it. Far from being insensitive to the lost object after mourning is completed, the ego still remains sensitive to it, but the affective relation is *different* from what it was.

In contrast to this normal, if somewhat uninteresting, psychological labor of mourning is the eminently "pathological"—if not highly romanticized—state of melancholia, wherein a subject acts, as Freud explains, *as if* he or she were mourning some loss whose exact nature remains, nonetheless, and to all concerned, obscure and nameless. Whereas the mourner has no trouble pointing to what needs to be mourned, the melancholic either cannot easily explain the source of her or his feelings or, if one can point to a concrete loss, the melancholic reacts or overreacts to it in an "obsessional" way (pp. 245–51). Accordingly, the painful mental attitude encountered in mourning is transparent, easily comprehended, whereas the equivalent affective state of melancholia is not so clearly understood. In fact, it can be seen as pathological precisely to the extent that, as a state, it is opaque rather than self-evident. Such a binarism between mourning as transparency and melancholia as opacity defines the pathological as something that escapes definition, thereby exceeding the normative or the quotidian. Such a dissymmetry implicitly opens the door for the traditional apotheosis of melancholia as a *culturally* prestigious condition over and beyond its clinical shortcomings. Freud himself can be shown to participate, whether consciously or unconsciously, in this myth of melancholia.[6]

[6]Cf. "Inhibitions, Symptoms, and Anxiety," where Freud characterizes melancholia vis-à-vis other "states of depression" as "the gravest of them" (*S.E.* 20: 90).

All this is exacerbated, as we have already noted, by Freud's insistence on melancholia's irreducibility to any fixed definition or analytic category, except as the mysterious and "pathological" double of mourning. Although later in the essay the differentiating feature of melancholia is found in its "predominantly moral character," at this moment Freud's refusal to define this condition seems to punctuate his own mystification over a psychological condition whose distinguishing features easily dissolve but also produce an entire set of intermediary forms between mourning and melancholia. For example, on the one hand there is "real" mourning signified by the "real" loss of someone "real." But let us remember that Freud said that one can also mourn the loss of "some abstraction which has taken the place of [a loved] one, such as one's country, liberty, an ideal, and so on" (p. 243). (This latter description, of course, raises the question whether the loss of a more ideal kind, hence an abstract loss, could be considered a "real" loss, especially if one way of distinguishing mourning from melancholia might be between "real" and "imaginary" or, if one prefers, between literal and figural losses.) On the other hand, as Freud states, "In one set of cases it is evident that melancholia too may be the reaction to the loss of a loved object" (p. 245). Taking into account this latter qualification, melancholia can psychically ride atop mourning, when it is provoked by an actual loss.

Melancholia's affective tensions, however, exceed what is felt in "normal" mourning. In other words, while both mourning and melancholia can be said to be motivated by either abstract or real loss, the difference between the two seems to depend on the excess of the affect, whose referential status remains unclear. And a condition Freud terms "profound mourning" is said to be identical to melancholia except that in melancholia there is a "disturbance in self-regard" (p. 244). Furthermore, Freud tells us, if the mourner bears an unresolved fixation on the loss, such as the guilt generated by ambivalent feelings toward the object prior to its loss, then "the conflict due to ambivalence gives a pathological cast to mourning and forces it to express itself in the form of self-reproaches to the effect that the mourner is himself to blame for the loss of the loved object, i.e. that he has willed it" (p. 251). As we can see, the distinctions between the syndromes are ambiguous. "The process of detaching the libido bit by bit is to be ascribed alike to mourning and to melancholia; it is probably supported by the same economic situation and serves the same purposes in both" (p. 256). Additionally, in some forms of melancholia, there is an alternation between manic and depressive phases, an alternating whose mechanism escapes Freud even by the end of the essay. In "normal" mourning, however, there is no turn to mania even if (economically speaking) the reabsorption of libidinal energies into the ego should give rise to their ecstatic release. In melancholia, there is thus "something more" (p. 256) than what is found in "normal" mourning, but what this something more is remains to be uncovered. (Returning to the problem in *Group Psychology*, Freud proposes a further distinction between psychogenic melancholias "which occur after the loss of a loved object" and "spontaneous" melancholias. Both of these melancholias, however, can still convert unpredictably to mania: "Thus the state of things is somewhat obscure" [*S.E.* 18: 133].)

From this description of melancholia as something that cannot be subsumed into a fixed category, we might proceed to ask ourselves if melancholia is not some kind of "floating" signifier.[7] To the extent that the very definition of melancholia, in Freud's term, "fluctuates," thereby resisting interpretive closure, every definition or type of melancholia can be replaced by another, thereby explaining its irreducibility "into a single unity." This indefinability even begins to appear as part and parcel of melancholy's symptomatology. For example, at one point, Freud states with respect to the melancholic: "One cannot see clearly what it is that has been lost" (p. 245) and, at another point, he says that it is unclear "what it is that is absorbing him so entirely" (p. 246). Not only do these two examples suggest confusion about where to locate the loss, but confusion also seems to alternate between what is external and what is internal to the melancholic subject: a "what" that moves so far outward that the subject's sight becomes blurred and a "what" that is internal to the subject, consuming or preoccupying him to the point of excluding all exteriority.

Furthermore, the plethora of interpretive meanings that melancholia draws to itself in an attempt to render meaningful (or meaningless) a malady the ancients often termed "sadness without a cause" resembles another phenomenon of melancholia: "The complex of melancholia behaves like an open wound, drawing to itself cathectic energies—which in the transference neuroses have been called 'anticathexes'—from all

---

[7]The term "floating signifier" was initially introduced by Claude Lévi-Strauss to describe the apparently limitless variety of meanings a single word such as *mana* could hold in some languages, serving as a kind of place-holder for unforeseen significances. For a useful critique of the notion, see Jacques Derrida, "Structure, Sign, and Play," in *Writing and Difference*, trans. Alan Bass (Chicago: University of Chicago Press, 1978), pp. 278–92.

directions, and emptying the ego until it is totally impoverished" (p. 253). This "open wound" drains all prowess, like a libidinal black hole absorbing cathectic energies until the ego catastrophically implodes, rendering the sufferer unable to sleep and hence to act. In the same way, the interpreter's energy seems to be drained by the resistance of the condition of melancholia to any unifying description. If, however, the very notion of an "open wound" already seems to evoke the question of castration and thus implicitly that of sexual difference, in the theorist's desire to locate the phallus where it is not, to precipitate meaning onto a condition that seems to be in excess of meaning (and hence to escape the binary logic found within hierarchical systems based on the polarization between feminine and masculine), then we might question just how and why Freud's "open wound" becomes a metaphor of closure, as "anticathexes" that would "empty" the ego "until it is totally impoverished."[8]

And if the positing of this mysterious "anticathecting" "open wound" can come to explain the condition of melancholia as something that cannot be explained, then it should not be too surprising that Freud goes on to postulate that the question to be raised with respect to melancholia is not so much *who* has been lost but *what* in the so-called lost object has been lost. Through the work of mourning the libido is detached from the once loved object of loss, so that "when the work of mourning is completed the ego becomes free and uninhibited again" (p. 245). But in melancholia, it is the fact that the work of mourning remains *unaccomplished* that raises certain considerations as to its genesis. Freud argues: "In one set of cases it is evident that melancholia too may be the reaction to the loss of a loved object. Where the exciting causes are different one can recognize that there is a loss of a more ideal kind." (This statement paradoxically replicates his own earlier remark that the lost object of mourning could also be some lost "ideal." Furthermore, the lines recall his earlier discussion of mourning in a way that suggests

---

[8]The metaphor of the "open wound" appears as early as Freud's unpublished draft article "Melancholia," probably dating from 1895 (*Extracts from the Fliess Papers,* S.E. 1: 200–206). To the extent that this first attempt to theorize melancholia links the condition with sexual disorders in women (from frigidity—which he euphemistically calls anaesthesia—to anorexia to hysteria), its reappearance in the 1917 article with a degendered context once again raises the question of Freud's repression of any identification with the bleeding body of Emma Eckstein, a victim of his friend Wilhelm Fliess's idiotic and incompetent attempt at "corrective" nasal surgery. Both writings imply his repression of the maternal figure in his theoretical production. See Sprengnether, *The Spectral Mother,* esp. pp. 22–38 and 181–86.

that both mourning and melancholia can arise from either a lost object or a lost ideal. The difference for Freud depends on the person: "In some people the same influences produce melancholia instead of mourning" [p. 243].) On melancholia, he continues:

> The object has not perhaps actually died, but has been lost as an object of love (e.g. in the case of a betrothed girl who has been jilted). In yet other cases one feels justified in maintaining the belief that a loss of this kind has occurred, but one cannot see clearly what it is that has been lost, and it is all the more reasonable to suppose that the patient cannot consciously perceive what he lost either. This indeed might be so even if the patient is aware of the loss which has given rise to his melancholia, but only in the sense that he knows *whom* he has lost not *what* he has lost in him. This would suggest that melancholia is in some way related to an object-loss which is withdrawn from consciousness, in contradistinction to mourning, in which there is nothing about the loss which is unconscious. (p. 245)

In mourning the depletion of the ego is thus understood in terms of the work of libidinal decathexis and in terms of the evident relation between the lost object and the resultant sadness. In melancholia what is opaque to observation and to analysis is "what it is that is absorbing [the melancholic] so entirely" (p. 246) since, as Freud has underscored, the object relation in question, that is, the direct loss of the desired object, is controlled by a *what* rather than a *who*. And it is this "what" absorbing the melancholic so thoroughly that signals a difference from mourning, by the tell-tale sign of something repressed, of an affect "withdrawn from consciousness." At the same time, the unconscious "what" also reveals itself in the representation of an impoverished ego: "In mourning it is the world that has become poor and empty; in melancholia it is the ego itself" (p. 246).

Recalling Freud's double "inspiration" in writing the essay—the impoverishment of a world at war as well as his sense of imminent loss in the form of his own death—I suggest that in melancholia both aspects actually exist: that the world does indeed seem impoverished, dull, superficial; and that the ego responds to this betrayal of and by the world with a delusional belittling of the world *and* of itself that makes the ego seem impoverished but that also functions as a pretext through which the ego can represent itself. The melancholic ego, in order to authenticate its conflicted relation between *innen* and *umwelt* inner and outer world, is dependent on loss as a means through which it can represent itself. In so doing, however, it derealizes or devalues any *object* of loss for the sake of loss itself: a sort of suturing between lack and loss, an idealization of loss that paradoxically empowers the ego. Thus, the melancholic ego, I argue, refocuses attention not on the lost *object* but on the loss, on the "what" of the lost object, whose thingness points back to the *subject* of the loss (not the "whom" that is lost in mourning but the "who" that presents himself as losing in melancholia). Hence, the reason the loss in the melancholic is not clear (is opaque to consciousness) is that it is the condition of loss *as* loss that is privileged and not the loss of any particular object. Given this privileging of loss over and beyond any object of loss, perhaps the "what" can be understood as nothing more than the repetition of loss itself.

In tallying the characteristics held in common by both mourning and melancholia, Freud had earlier suggested the phenomenon of a loss that is both in the world and in the ego as what distinguishes melancholia from mourning:

> The distinguishing mental features of melancholia are a profoundly painful dejection, cessation of interest in the outside world, loss of the capacity to love, inhibition of all activity, and a lowering of the self-regarding feelings to a degree that finds utterance in self-reproaches and self-revilings, and culminates in a delusional expectation of punishment. This picture becomes a little more intelligible when we consider that, with one exception, the same traits are met with in mourning. The disturbance of self-regard is absent in mourning but otherwise the features are the same. (p. 244)

The loss of self-esteem in melancholia (so great that it may even produce a desire for and expectation of punishment) thus occurs *in addition to* the loss of a lost object. The exact nature of the connection between the "what" that is lost in the lost object and what the subject loses in himself or herself has yet to be explained.

Taking hold of this underlying structure of loss that unites the various melancholias (whether triggered by a "real" loss, an imaginary loss, or an inexplicable sense of loss), Freud attempts a libidinal economic explication of this impoverishment of the ego (or the loss in addition to the loss of the object) and is accordingly led, in what I have described as the second moment of the essay, to important questions about narcissism and identification. For Freud, in the condition of melancholia (as distinguished at least from hysteria's fixation on an object), an object cathexis is *replaced* by an identification.[9] In other words, the object cathexis is not strong enough to resist the shattering of the object relation due to some interfering factor, so that what follows is not the withdrawal of affection from the object and its subsequent placement onto another one, but rather the retention within the ego of the libido now freed from its investment in the once loved object: "The free libido was not displaced onto another object; it was withdrawn into the ego. There, however, it was not employed in any unspecified way, but served to establish an *identification* of the ego with the abandoned object" (p. 249; Freud's emphasis).

Where once there existed an attachment to some beloved object, a regression takes place such that "the narcissistic identification with the object then becomes a substitute for the erotic cathexis, the result of which is that in spite of the conflict with the loved person the love-relation need not be given up" (p. 249). The economic description of melancholia as regressive identification is its characterization as narcissistic. Now, due to loss or to some kind of interference with this once loved object, "the ego wants to incorporate this object into itself, and in accordance with the oral or cannibalistic phase of libidinal development in which it is, it wants to do so by devouring it" (pp. 249–50).

The incorporation of the lost object of desire into the ego is further complicated when an ambivalent attitude toward the lost object already existed, although the source of that ambivalence turns out to be related to a narcissistic investment in the object. Thus, the "what" that was in the lost object can be understood here in terms of a love felt for the lost object, but an ambivalent one. This narcissistic component not only explains the strongly ambivalent dimension of the love relation but also points back to the subject of loss since the love for the lost object was really self-love to begin with. Such ambivalent love, effected through narcissism, then explains, according to Freud, the ease with which the libido can be detached from the object and transferred back onto the ego. Furthermore, Freud also shows the ambivalence that accompanies

---

[9]The word "cathexis" [Besetzung] literally means investment or occupation, and serves in psychoanalytic theory as an "economic" concept that refers to "the fact that a certain amount of psychical energy is attached to an idea or to a group of ideas, to a part of the body, to an object, etc." (J. Laplanche and J.-B. Pontalis, *The Language of Psycho-Analysis*, trans. D. Nicholson-Smith [New York: Norton, 1973], p. 62). According to Laplanche and Pontalis (p. 62), the term first occurs in Sigmund Freud and Joseph Breuer, *Studies on Hysteria*, S.E. 2.

melancholia to be the expression of a repressed and displaced aggressivity arising from wounded narcissism:

> An object-choice, an attachment of the libido to a particular person, had at one time existed; then owing to a real slight or disappointment coming from this loved person, the object-relationship was shattered. The result was not then a normal one of withdrawal of the libido from this object and a displacement of it onto a new one, but something different, for whose coming-about various conditions seem to be necessary. The object-cathexis proved to have little power of resistance and was brought to an end. But the free libido was not displaced onto another object; it was withdrawn into the ego. There, however, it was not employed in any unspecified way, but served to establish an *identification* of the ego and the latter could henceforth be judged by a special agency, as though it were an object, the forsaken object. (P. 249)

> Melancholia, therefore, borrows some of its features from mourning, and the others from the process of regression from narcissistic object choice to narcissism. It is on the one hand, like mourning, a reaction to the real loss of a loved object; but over and above this, it is marked by a determinant which is absent in normal mourning or which, if it is present, transforms the latter into pathological mourning. . . . In melancholia, the occasions which give rise to the illness extend for the most part beyond the clear case of a loss by death, and include all those situations of being slighted, neglected or disappointed, which can import opposed feelings of love and hate into the relationship or reinforce an already existing ambivalence. This conflict due to ambivalence, which sometimes rises from more real experiences, sometimes more from constitutional factors, must not be overlooked among the preconditions of melancholia. (pp. 250–51)

Freud is at pains to distinguish this narcissistic and regressive identification of melancholia from what might seem to be a similar process in hysteria: in the former the object cathexis is abandoned and in the latter it persists and manifests its influence (p. 250). While in both neuroses there is an identification with an object, in melancholia an object choice is effected though a narcissistic identification that implies a withdrawal of libido from the object and its transference back into the ego, whereas in hysteria the libidinal investment in an object *cannot* be relinquished: "The difference, however, between narcissistic and hysterical identification may be seen in this: that whereas in the former the object-cathexis is abandoned, in the latter it persists and manifests its influence, though this is usually confined to certain isolated areas and innervations. ... Narcissistic identification is the older of the two and paves the way to an understanding of hysterical identification, which has been less thoroughly studied" (p. 250).

It certainly seems strange that one of the foremost theorists of hysteria should point to that malady's lack of study, especially when, as we shall see, crucial portions of his theory of melancholia and narcissistic identification in fact derive from his work on hysteria. In any case, further study of hysteria will have to be deferred indefinitely if we agree with Freud's statement that narcissistic identification is "the older of the two and paves the way to an understanding of hysterical identification." The primariness of narcissism makes it foundational for psychoanalysis. Freud's initial theorizing in the direction of psychoanalysis was unleashed by his work on hysteria. Yet, in a strange turn of events, hysteria is now presented as derivative of narcissism, and the study of hysteria must now patiently await the further results of Freud's analysis of narcissism. In other words, the analysis of melancholia takes precedence over the study of hysteria. Because of this priority, the melancholic foregrounds not only something considered to be psychically more primordial, but also something that seems psychically much more recent and more developed, namely the moral conscience or superego. It is through this discovery that we enter the third moment of Freud's analysis: melancholia, conscience, and the "split" subject.

This melancholic subject helps us understand how the ego is constituted through identification and object choice as well as how the ego in turn becomes objectified as a libidinal position:

> Thus the shadow of the object fell upon the ego, so that the latter could henceforth be criticized by a special mental faculty like an object, like the forsaken object. In this way the *loss* of the object became transformed into a *loss* in the ego and the conflict between the ego and the loved person transformed into a cleavage between the criticizing faculty of the ego and the ego as altered by the identification. (p. 249; emphasis added)

> If the love for the object—a love which cannot be given up—takes refuge in narcissistic identification, then the hate comes into operation on this substitutive object, abusing it, debasing it, making it suffer and deriving sadistic satisfaction from its suffering. (p. 251)

Again, we need to keep in mind that what is at stake is not so much the lost object per se as the "what" of the lost object. In other words, it is what is represented in the lost object that determines the melancholic neurosis on the level of object relations, which will in turn elucidate the cultural category of a moral conscience. The identification of the ego with the abandoned object and the "shadow" of this lost object—the shadow to be understood as the unconscious "what" that the subject lost in the lost object—now divides the ego. This shadow thus draws apart a portion of the ego into an identification with the lost object, over and against which the remaining portion of the ego can rage to assuage the narcissistic wound of its abandonment. The melancholic could accordingly be said to be someone who suffers from unrequited love but who then finds satisfaction by abusing part of the self *as if* that part of the self were the disappointing object. But the object itself has of course already been derealized through the "what" that was lost when loss triggered the regression to narcissism, which then points back to the melancholic self as the subject of the loss. Over and beyond this circumstance, the cleavage of the ego wrought by the incorporated (de-realized) object works to produce within the melancholic psyche a certain moral satisfaction: "The ego may enjoy in this the satisfaction of knowing itself as the better of the two, as superior to the object" (p. 257).

Set in these terms, therefore, the once loved object has been incorporated into the ego in order to maintain a tie with it because of a previous strong attachment having to do with primary narcissism. This narcissistic source of libidinal energy thus explains why this loss can be an ideal as well as a person, for what is invested in it is therefore still a form of the self. But if it is not so much the object of loss that is unconscious in the melancholic but rather the loss of understanding *what* in the object has been lost (i.e., the repressed narcissistic compo-nent), then does this not produce a fetishizing of the loss itself in the economics of melancholia? In other words, the melancholic's very display of loss requires the repression of its narcissistic dimension if the melan-cholic is to be seen (and pitied!) as mourning for something or someone besides the self. Like the fetish, the affect of melancholia both affirms and denies loss, insisting on there being a loss while denying the loss of the "what" in the object. In other words, loss itself becomes the dominating feature when the "content" of loss has been emptied (re-pressed). Or put another way: the positing of the loss acts like an apotropaic defensive screen in order to protect the ego from loss itself. It thus acts like a fetish object or like the positing of the "open wound" at the point of closure just where the theory cannot complete its explanation, where theory itself suffers an open wound in its totalizing desire. And if the reproduction of loss thus works fetishistically, then does not this "fetishistic" work of melancholia also imply a denial of "femininity," or at best manifest a highly ambiguous relation to the "feminine"? Melancholia's "open wound" is that which must be covered over by the phallus, if this *horror vacuus* is not to remain sorely problematic to the male imaginary. The melancholic becomes like a fetishist who accumulates signs of loss, in order to both affirm and deny the fact of castration, to make a gain out of loss itself.[10]

This denial and affirmation can be understood in terms of another trait Freud recognized in the melancholic, "an insistent communicativeness which finds satisfaction in self-exposure" (p.247). Because of the melancholic's inchoate source of unhappiness, we can assume that analysis and therapy are needed to lift the subject's repression and allow him consciously to articulate what is troubling him so. (The classic scenario would be a morbid fixation on the mother, whose primal phantasmic loss can never be avowed by an ego who internalizes that loss into the very definition of its being, who thus perpetually "mourns" a self that never was, and hence borders on a state of pathological narcissism.) The psychoanalytic cure thus seems to be hampered and complicated in the melancholic situation by one of the peculiarities of this neurosis: the very garrulousness of the patient, whose nearly limitless capability for self-criticism and abnegation subtends a "satisfaction in self-exposure." Clearly, the famous "talking cure" comes up against an unusual obstacle here in this pathological verbosity, for if the talking forms part of the etiology how can it form part of the cure?

In point of fact, Freud proposes no treatment of any kind for the melancholic. What he does say is that "it passes off after a certain time has elapsed" (p. 252). Admitting his lack of "*any* insight into the economics of the course of events" (p. 253; emphasis added), Freud then proffers the previously mentioned hypothesis (or theoretical fetish) of melancholia as an "open wound" that "anti-cathects" the ego "until it is totally impoverished" (p. 253). And yet in some strange and miraculous way, with the passage of time, the condition disappears and the ego is restored and revalued "without any gross changes." The positing of a lack seems to lead to a renewed gain. This miraculous shift (Freud

---

[10]On the relation between fetishism and melancholia, see Giorgio Agamben, *Stanze: La parola e il fantasma nella cultura occidentale* (Turin: Einaudi, 1977), pp. 26–27.

then concludes his essay by rehearsing his inability to explain the prevalence of the mood shift from melancholia to mania), as well as the melancholic's discursive plenitude, can be said to rejoin the longstanding tradition of melancholia understood as a source of intellectual and artistic creativity, precisely through its conversion of emotional loss into creative productivity and gain.

For example, the excessive verbalism in, let us say, a Tasso, or in the character Hamlet, draws our attention and curiosity not only to the subject in question but beyond him. It does so because these men or these literary representations have often been analyzed in terms of the *moral* nature behind their illness and hence in terms of their subjectivities as privileged or inspired. Thus the melancholic subject, according to the scheme I am analyzing, is considered to be unaware of the origin of his illness but belies this unconscious aspect by the fact that he is speaking some kind of truth since he is aware of his self-exposure. The dilemma is not unlike the traditional problem Shakespeareans face in deciding whether Hamlet is "feigning" his madness or whether he is mad *because* he pretends to be. Freud well understood the fact that "feelings of shame in front of other people" are lacking in the melancholic. Such self-exposure suggests that the melancholic is at least conscious (if not hyper-conscious) of speaking something meaningful about something.

But why, one might ask oneself, does this sort of chatter take on a meaningful and moral distinction? Why does Freud underscore the truthful content of the melancholic's loosened and harsh tongue? In effect, for Freud, the issue is to determine *at what level* the truth is to be found and not whether the melancholic's "self-criticism" is true or not. Here too the answer is multiple. To contradict the melancholic's accusations against his ego is called "fruitless" since "he must surely be right in some way and he describes something that is as it seems to him to be": "Indeed, we must at once confirm some of his statements without reservation. He really is as lacking in interest and as incapable of love and achievement as he says" (p. 246). Nevertheless, such truths are only "secondary" to "the internal work which is consuming his ego." In this way, another level of "self-accusations" may be "justified" as the sign of a self-understanding that is deeper than that achieved by others: "It is merely that he has a keener eye for the truth than other people who are not melancholic. When in his heightened self-criticism he describes himself as petty, egoistic, dishonest, lacking in independence, one whose sole aim has been to hide the weaknesses of his own nature, it may be,

so far as we know, that he has come pretty near to understanding himself"
(p. 246). Freud then reiterates the traditional view of melancholia as a
creative (and enabling) impairment when he asks "why a man has to be
ill before he can be accessible to a truth of this kind" (p. 246). Concludes
Freud: "There can be no doubt that if anyone holds and expresses to
others an opinion of himself such as this . . . , he is ill, whether he is
speaking the truth or whether he is being more or less unfair to himself"
(pp. 246–47). This is not the alternative it appears to be. For if the
melancholic does not speak the truth, then it is because he is speaking
falsely of himself (only), and that falsehood is less false than it is "unfair"
to him. We thus seem to be encouraged to offer sympathy and support
to this self-effacing modesty.

Furthermore, the melancholic's self-accusations (whether unfair or
not) gain a certain credence by virtue of their taking place on the level
of *moral* criticism: "In the clinical picture of melancholia, dissatisfaction
with the ego on moral grounds is the most outstanding feature. The
patient's self-evaluation concerns itself much less frequently with bodily
infirmity, ugliness or weakness, or with social inferiority" (pp. 247–48).
While such a moral dissatisfaction could be understood as being both
true and unfair to the ego, Freud offers an even more sweeping recuperation of the truth content in the melancholic's "unfair" self-
assessment: "If one listens patiently to a melancholic's many and various
self-accusations, one cannot in the end avoid the impression that often
the most violent of them are hardly at all applicable to the patient himself,
but that with insignificant modifications they do fit someone else, someone whom the patient loves or should love. Each time one examines the
facts this conjecture is confirmed" (p. 248). We can thus revise Freud's
earlier alternative between truthfulness and unfairness as follows: either
the melancholic speaks the truth about himself, or if he speaks unfairly
about himself, it is because he is really speaking the truth about others.
It is therefore only a small step from this interpretation of the melancholic's self-reproaches as a disguised critique of others "on moral
grounds" to a romanticized view of the melancholic as the misunderstood and self-abnegating but truthful "moralist" critic of society; in
other words, as a disagreeable but justified rebel:

> Their complaints are really "plaints" in the old sense of the word. They
> are not ashamed and do not hide themselves since everything derogatory
> that they say about themselves is at bottom said about someone else.

Moreover, they are far from evincing towards those around them the attitude of humility and submissiveness that would alone befit such worthless people. On the contrary, they make the greatest nuisance of themselves, and always seem as though they felt slighted and had been treated with great injustice. All this is possible only because the reactions expressed in their behaviour still proceed from a mental constellation of revolt, which has then, by a certain process, passed over into the crushed state of melancholia. (p. 248)

Such an ironic description, still accredits the melancholic's complaints as "plaints" in the legal sense of the word, suggesting that this attitude of revolt contains both a civic and a social dimension. This position of defiance implies anger at some hurt or perceived injury whose source is not solely narcissistic (at least from the melancholic's point of view). And if the ego is divided between the critical agency and the incorporated object, source of the dissatisfaction, then the melancholic psyche is both plaintiff and judge. In this way, the melancholic can also be understood as he who speaks out the repressed relation between individual and society, but with such authority that the listener or spectator "forgives" him his transgression of speaking some impolite secret. Perhaps the melancholic should thus be situated as a version of the king's fool, since the emblematic figures of melancholia (Tasso, Hamlet) coincide chronologically with the popularity of court and literary fools." A certain pathos also appears in the defeat of the revolt "which has then, by a certain process, passed over into the crushed state of melancholia" (p. 248). The tragic outcome of this "certain process" (which Freud never describes) is the repressed aggressivity of the melancholic, which would not make his "criticisms" any less "true."

One wonders, though, if such a status is equally available to all subjects. At the end of his article, Freud summarizes what he comes to see as the three "preconditions" of melancholia: "loss of the object, ambivalence, and regression of libido into the ego" (p. 258). Once again, the value of the distinction between mourning and melancholia is, for the moment, at risk as Freud acknowledges that "the first two are also found in the obsessional self-reproaches arising after a death has occurred":

"In *A Social History of the Fool* (New York: St. Martin's Press, 1984), Sandra Billington traces a continuous line of development from the earliest medieval court jesters to the rise of the modern comedian or clown, but she also acknowledges and describes the special popularity of the fool during the sixteenth and very early seventeenth centuries (pp. ix–x, 32–50).

In those cases it is unquestionably the ambivalence which is the motive force of the conflict, and observation shows that after the conflict has come to an end there is nothing left over in the nature of the triumph of a manic state of mind. We are thus led to the third factor as the only one responsible for the result. The accumulation of cathexis which is at first bound and then, after the work of melancholia is finished, becomes free and makes mania possible must be linked with regression of the libido to narcissism. (p. 258)

But if narcissism is the distinctive component of melancholia, if it is what produces the excessive grieving or the inability to name "what" has been lost, then what does this say about the *subject* of melancholia? How can this regressive identification and the subsequent split between (critical) ego ideal and (criticized) ego take place unless a sufficient store of narcissistic libido is available? Such questions are elided by the return of the wound metaphor, whose discursive function once again seems to be that of suturing a theoretical gap, a suturing that then allows Freud to "call a halt" to his essay: "The conflict within the ego, which melancholia substitutes for the struggle over the object, must act like a painful wound which calls for an extraordinarily high anti-cathexis. —But here once again, it will be well to call a halt and to postpone any further explanation of mania until we have gained some insight into the economic nature, first, of physical pain, and then of the mental pain which is analogous to it" (p. 258).

So, while "Mourning and Melancholia" is remarkable for having isolated the importance of narcissism in distinguishing melancholia from mourning, on the one hand, and from hysteria on the other hand, it nevertheless stops short of understanding melancholia as a narcissistic fixation on the loss, wherein a certain kind of satisfaction is gleaned in the idealization of loss *as* loss, in the perpetuation and even capitalization of that sense of loss. Just as the positing of the "open wound" paradoxically conditions a transparent suturing of a conceptual hole, so too does the melancholic display of loss paradoxically increases the value (hence accumulating to the gain) of the subject of loss. As such, the melancholic model can be understood not simply as the "incorporation" of a lost object of desire, but also as an introjection of loss that needs to be endlessly reproduced as loss to sustain its myth.[12] In other words,

---

[12]On the "incorporation" of a lost object as theorized by Freud, see "Mourning and Melancholia," esp. pp. 248–50. For theoretical eleboration on the difference between incor-

the greater the loss, the greater the wisdom or "truth" claimed by the loser, who then profits from this turn of psychic events by gaining from the loss. To the extent that the melancholic takes pride in his "moral dissatisfaction," it thus seems once again that it is not so much the lost object that is in question in the melancholic psyche as the melancholic's display of himself as a legitimator or spokesman of the dominant order by virtue of his overdeveloped conscience. Furthermore, the melancholic's position within that order must be maintained through the reproduction of loss as *that* loss which generates the mechanisms (pleasurable or unpleasurable) of a self-reflective ego, which then reflects critically on an other.

As Freud argues, it is the overdeveloped critical faculty that positions the melancholic as morally superior. Freud's moralizing conscience is consonant with the Law of the Father since the conscience or superego is derived from the culture that the parents stand for, which in the West means the patriarchal culture of the father. Given the social and historical situation of the parent with which the child identifies, the "terrrible" conscience of which Freud speaks is necessarily different from "ethics" in all ways except in the most culturally specific and normative sense. This conscience rests on and is dependent on a split between a valued moral agent (superego) and a devalued (immoral?) one that can only reproduce the existing organization of values within the culture.

Now what becomes especially interesting is that inasmuch as the melancholic is in possession of this hyperconsciousness, of a stern and severe superego that judges itself and hence an other (or others), Freud implicitly reserves this particular characteristic for the male, given what he says in "On Femininity" about the "undeveloped" superego of women (*S.E.* 22: 129ff.). The dimension of revolt would remain as exclusively male, if not decidedly oedipal, to the extent that a strong superego is

---

poration and introjection, see Maria Torok and Nicolas Abraham, *The Wolf Man's Magic Word: A Cryptonomy*, trans. Nicholas Rand (Minneapolis: University of Minnesota Press, 1986); and Esther Rashkin, "Tools for a New Psychoanalytic Criticism: The Work of Abraham and Torok," *Diacritics* 18 (Winter 1988), 31–52. On the relation between desire and the lost object, see Agamben, *Stanze*, pp. 1–43, who argues that what is at stake in melancholia is a phantasmic capacity to make it seem *as if* an object of desire had been lost (p. 26). While I agree with Agamben on this latter point, Agamben himself, like the melancholic, seems to place an extraordinary value on the hypostatization of a lost object of desire as a way to eroticize the loss. What Agamben fails to take into account is the way in which such fantasy implicitly belies an eros dependent on the negation of women's subjectivities since the figure of the "feminine" is always, in some way, at stake in these kinds of object relations. Furthermore, in so doing, Agamben occludes the political and social realities of disempowerment by arguing that in melancholia the object is neither lost nor appropriated (p. 27).

dependent on an identification with the father (cf. *The Ego and the Id*, S.E. 19: 31). The question to be raised then, is whether this particular splitting of the ego and consequent moral (dis)satisfaction happens to women, and if so, what or who is the lost object? Can this moral (dis)satisfaction happen to women, for instance, if (or only if?) they are identified with the mother?

The overestimation of the ego (or that part of the ego that judges the other half), so well displayed in the melancholic subject, is, I think, part of a larger cultural process whereby the feminine or the mother or the woman is devalued in the name of the father. The question of gender difference, therefore is indeed significant if one is to understand the implication of there being *different* melancholias. For example, if the primordial lost object can be understood simply as the mother (assuming, of course, that the mother was actually present in one's life during the early phases of the castration complex), then a difference between female and male melancholia seems in doubt. If the loss, however, is understood to be suffered *through* the mother or in spite of her—that is, if the loss were due to some factor that either overdetermines or undermines her value within dominant symbolic structures and so blocks the possibility of narcissistic identification, which is in turn required for the construction of a superego—then we need to question how an apparently universal psychological category such as melancholia might be gendered.

Furthermore, we must also recognize the hierarchical determination of *who* can legitimate loss and recuperate it, *whose* laments are heard and whose are not. If, as some feminists argue, women are a group determined by a presumed "biological" difference,[13] then the questions of loss and lack are legislated according to a hierarchy by which, as I hope to demonstrate later on, different melancholias also are legislated. If, as Freud notes with a grain of perplexity, "in some people the same influences produce melancholia instead of mourning" (p. 243), then the determination of *who* such "people" are is of more than merely clinical interest. In other words, the distribution of lack and loss in melancholic terms legislates a hierarchy within the interpretation of melancholia that encodes "higher" and "lower" forms of depression. Seen in this way, melancholia as a gendered category can subvert women's own claims to

[13]With regard to defining what is meant by feminine difference, see my Introduction, pp. 26–32 and note 56. Also see Joan Kelly, *Women, History, and Theory: The Essays of Joan Kelly*, ed. Catharine R. Stimpson (Chicago: University of Chicago Press, 1984), p. 6.

loss and difference by making of women a group unable to translate these claims into artistic, philosophical, political, or psychological empowerment.

If the melancholic was fashioned from a Renaissance ideal of Renaissance man who nostalgically looks toward the past in order to reinvent and reassess a place of origin, a nostalgia whose desire for origin was also linked to a metaphysical quest for a transcendent union with the lost object of desire (Ficino's Neoplatonic split between body and soul), how could women create a narrative of loss for themselves that was not a rewriting of (male) master myths? Why does a woman's plaint (lament), as we shall see with *Hamlet*'s Ophelia and Freud's "conscientious" women, typically come across as mere chatter and thus as less dignified than the ranting of a Hamletian nobleman (or Tassian poet), whose maddened vituperations are attended to and readily given a status of truth? And why aren't there more women speaking out this "truth" then, and why is it that when a melancholic woman speaks, her loosened tongue is not granted the same extraordinary virtue and wisdom as a man's? Or, at least, why isn't her "unfairness" to herself forgiven?

Perhaps such a suspicion of gender relations can help explain some of Freud's moves. As we have already seen, in "Mourning and Melancholia" Freud distinguishes between melancholia and hysteria by asserting that in the former the object cathexis has been abandoned and the libido has regressed to an identification based on narcisissm. In hysteria (a "female" malady), however, the object cathexis has been retained as well as some identification with it. The separation of hysteria and melancholia seems especially odd given the existence among Freud's early papers of an unfinished draft of an article titled "Melancholia" that begins by noting "striking connections between melancholia and (sexual) anaesthesia,"[14] one of the most prominent features of hysteria. Freud notes in particular "the existence of a type of women, very demanding psychically, in whom longing easily changes over into melancholia and who are anaesthetic" (p. 200). He further reveals "the nutritional neurosis parallel to melancholia" to be "the famous *anorexia nervosa* of young girls" by drawing a correlation between loss of appetite and loss of libido (pp. 200–201). Melancholia, in this early draft, is then the name given for the process of mourning a loss of libido, and it accordingly appears

---

[14]*Extracts from the Fliess Papers, S.E.* 1: 200.

as a psychical condition whose interconnectedness with hysteria is explicitly drawn.[15]

Rejecting this early correlation in his later work, Freud creates an
ever-greater distance between hysteria and melancholia by turning them
into examples of an insuperable dichotomy between the "transference
neuroses" and "narcissistic disorders."[16] And in radically distinguishing
melancholia from hysteria, Freud implicitly makes the former a male
malady, as well as an older form of "pathology" than hysteria to the
extent that narcissism is the "older" of the two forms of identification.
We can further assume that men would have more "narcissistic reserves,"[17] making them more susceptible to melancholia, because, following Freud's logic, narcissistic identification would be effected by the
child through its identity with an ego ideal, whose paradigmatic case is
that of the boy identifying with the father. On yet another level, the
melancholic would and could be a "loner," a master whose supposed
self-sufficiency and distinction from others are conditioned by an already
privileged access to narcissistic mirroring. Nevertheless, this excess of
narcissistic reserves is only built up from the demand of the Other (the
ego ideal/culture/Law of the Father), whose very calling forth of the
subject precipitates *him* into a position of "hyper-normality." In other
words, this *écoute* of the Other can be understood as a calling based on
a lack that is *also* designated as sufficient. Lack as sufficiency would indeed
be an empowering legitimacy, also represented as a split within man
that would meaningfully frame his search for significance.[18]

---

[15]Also see his letter to Fliess of January 16, 1899, where he writes that "there really is
such a thing as hysterical melancholia" (*Extracts from the Fliess Papers, S.E.* 1: 277).

[16]Cf. "Two Encyclopaedia Articles," *S.E.* 18: 249; *The Ego and the Id, S.E.* 19: 51; and
"Neurosis and Psychosis," *S.E.* 19: 152.

[17]Kaja Silverman, *The Acoustic Mirror: The Female Voice in Psychoanalysis and Cinema*
(Bloomington: Indiana University Press, 1984), p. 156.

[18]The concept of "hyper-normality" as referring to melancholia is developed by Arthur
Tatossian in *Phénoménologie des psychoses* (Paris: Masson, 1980). Recapitulating the argument
made by Michèle Le Doeuff in "Women and Philosophy," Toril Moi writes that "female lack
is never truly philosophical lack. Woman is an inferior thinker, not because of her lack but
because of her lack of a lack" (in *The French Feminist Reader*, ed. Toril Moi [Oxford: Blackwell,
1986], p. 10. My argument for male melancholia as opposed to female melancholia is not to
be seen only in a clinical sense, for I would never deny that women are and have been depressed.
But what I see as fundamentally different is the way melancholia as a discourse (and even as
a clinical discourse, if one remembers the relation of the ego ideal to melancholia) favors male
subjectivity in terms of a poetics of depersonalization. After all, the ego ideal is formed by a
masculine economy, and even the male melancholic has the advantage in these terms; it is thus
a relation of sameness: male eros striving to represent its longing for the father in male terms.
Thus the melancholic male subject is favored by culture, for the melancholic draws on the
male eros, which idealizes that philosophical lack as creative lack. The melancholic male ap-

Freud's analysis of melancholia thus seems to preclude the possibility of women falling ill from it (or should we say, gaining access to it?). Indeed, the melancholic's narcissistic relation to lack (the "open wound") seems to qualify the condition as a male strategy to assuage the fact of castration, that is, to deny the fear of sexual difference. The hysteric, on the other hand, since "she" is still dependent on an object cathexis, is less individuated (although we could turn this around precisely as the positive value of women's sense of alterity and collectivity, of the rites of mourning). What is also interesting in Freud's case histories is that at times he suggests that the hysteric also suffers depression. The insertion of depression within the history of a hysteric (as in Fräulein Elisabeth Von R.) begs the important question of whether depression is or is not different from melancholia.[19] Or is depression merely a less valued form of melancholia? Is melancholia a privileged representation of male narcissism and hence patriarchal culture?

If so, then the Freudian relation between "hysterical identification" and "narcissistic identification" is a hidden gendered one. An implicit gendering also seems to be at work in Freud's effort to separate melancholia's "something more" from mourning, especially during the long final section of the essay where he tries to link melancholia with mania. There the linkage would take place through an oscillating condition whose interconnection, however, he cannot explain. At the same time,

---

propriates those lacks and losses to which women are entitled, fetishizes them in terms of cultural production—and thus subverts their possible subversion of the dominant ideology.

[19] Cf. the unnamed "young woman" in "A Case of Successful Treatment by Hypnotism," *S.E.* 1: 118–19; Frau Emma, who complains that the cold baths prescribed for her hysteria make her "melancholy for the rest of the day" while Freud repeatedly insists on calling her affect depression: "Was it really the cool bath that depressed you so much?" (*S.E.* 2: 68n; also 71, 81, 90, 92); Miss Lucy R., *S.E.* 2: 106–7, 118; Fräulein Elisabeth von R.'s mother, *S.E.* 2: 161; Fräulein Mathilde H.: "She had become depressed to the point of a *taedium vitae*, utterly inconsiderate to her mother, irritable and inaccessible. The patient's picture as a whole forbade my assuming that this was a common melancholia" (*S.E.* 2: 163); Frau P., *S.E.* 3: 175–76, 179; the woman dreamer in part VI of *The Interpretation of Dreams*, *S.E.* 4: 332; Dora, *S.E.* 7: 24, 26, 30n, and 54n: "A supervalent thought of this kind is often the only symptom, beyond deep depression, of a pathological condition which is usually described as 'melancholia', but which can be cleared up by psychoanalysis like a hysteria" (p. 54); the "Wolf Man's" sister, *S.E.* 17: 21; and finally, at the end of "Analysis Terminable and Interminable," he locates the impossibility of transference in the penis envy of women, which is also "the source of outbreaks of severe depression" in them (*S.E.* 23: 252). On the other hand, Freud seems a little nonplussed that the seventeenth-century documents about the painter Christoph Haizmann's illness speak "only of the state of depression" while Haizmann "actually calls [it] a melancholia," and throughout the rest of his analysis Freud consistently terms Haizmann's distress "melancholia" ("A Seventeenth-Century Demonological Neurosis," *S.E.* 19: 80–81, 83, 87, 103, 105).

the statement of the condition repositions the neurosis of melancholia (from melancholia to mania and vice versa) once again within the Ficinian tradition by mania's recalling of the form of "divine frenzy."

Finally, what remains striking about Freud's account of melancholia is his choice of examples. On the one hand, Freud describes the illness on three occasions with female examples. First, there is "the case of a betrothed girl who has been jilted" (p. 245), which is supposed to illustrate "a loss of a more ideal kind" where "the object has not perhaps actually died, but has been lost as an object of love" (p. 245). To call the betrayal and abandonment felt by a deserted bride "a loss of a more ideal kind" seems to belittle the force of the resulting grief, whose "exciting cause" is, Freud notwithstanding, extremely precise and constitutes a rather obvious and "real" loss. From a traditionally psychoanalytic point of view, of course, the ideal that has been lost should be easily decodable as the phallus itself.[20] Similarly, the case Freud mentions of the self-deprecating wife euphemistically frames her lament as an accusation of impotence, hence again of the phallus as lost: "The woman who loudly pities her husband for being tied to such an incapable wife as herself is really accusing her *husband* of being incapable, in whatever sense she may mean this" (p. 248, Freud's emphasis). The unquestioned and absolute desirability of the phallus structures these two examples as what a woman's loss would mean. Moreover, no particular depth of "self-understanding" is foregrounded in these cases.

On the other hand, the only named figure who appears in Freud's analysis of melancholia is Hamlet, whose entrance on this theoretical scene is underscored by the *moral* basis of his illness:

> When in his heightened self-criticism he describes himself as petty, egoistic, dishonest, lacking in independence, one whose sole aim has been to hide the weakness of his own nature, it may be, so far as we know, that he has come pretty near to understanding himself; we only wonder why a man has to be ill before he can be accessible to a truth of this kind. For there can be no doubt that if anyone holds and expresses to others an opinion of himself such as this (an opinion that Hamlet held both of himself and of everyone else), he is ill, whether he is speaking the truth or whether he is being more or less unfair to himself." (p. 247)

---

[20]In his discussion of women melancholics, Robert Burton also links their condition to the lack of a good husband and thus predictably locates them most particularly among "maids, nuns, and widows" (*Anatomy of Melancholy* [London: Dent, 1932], 1: 412–19).

In a footnote to the text, Freud adds without further comment the following quote from *Hamlet*: "Use every man after his desert, and who shall scape whipping?" (act II, scene ii). Spoken by Hamlet to the gullible Polonius in an offhand way, the rhetorical question can be easily interpreted as an example of the prince's melancholic madness. At the same time, it can also be read as the statement of a universal truth in which the implicit response to the question would be that no man "shall scape whipping," that we all deserve punishment for some offense. The truth, then, of the melancholic's moral criticisms would be in their universality, whether they refer to the speaker or to others. The generalizability of such truth when uttered with such outspoken "sincerity" motivates, without a doubt, the melancholic's (and Hamlet's) cherished sanctum in the annals of humanism—and of psychoanalysis. As Jacqueline Rose has remarked, Hamlet "is always given the status of a truth, and becomes a pivot for psychoanalysis and its project."[21] Thus for Freud, in references such as the one above, Hamlet appears as a speaker of truths, here the very *porte-parole* of the ego ideal, the critical faculty of the conscience, whose biting accusations are leveled against all, questioning (and invalidating) the morality of each. The interests of patriarchal ideology and of psychoanalysis are both served by the mad prince, whose melancholy gives him truly visionary powers, a "keener eye for the truth." When Freud refers to Hamlet, he signals the fact that a well-known *male* character such as Hamlet is indeed a *nameable* subject, and a subject of literary and psychoanalytic interest precisely because the canon legitimizes his "neurosis" as something grand, or treats it ironically as the experience of nothing (which amounts to the same thing).

With Freud, therefore, we read the two sides of this celebrated illness, that is, melancholia as a clinical form of depression but also melancholia as something that points beyond its clinical form to a *cultural* apotheosis of its victims, those governed by the "heightened self-criticism" and "keener eye for the truth." And along with the father of psychoanalysis, "we" are invited only to "wonder why a man has to be ill before he can be accessible to a truth of this kind" (p. 246). And while it is interesting to note that Freud states in the third example of a female melancholic that a "good, capable, conscientious woman" may also fall ill of this disease, such a "good, capable, conscientious woman" does not quite seem on a par with the gloriously tragic figure of Hamlet. The word

---

[21]Jacqueline Rose, *Sexuality in the Field of Vision* (London: Verso, 1986), p. 133.

"conscientious" ascribed to the "good, capable" woman implies mere dutifulness rather than a "conscience," even as leaving her unnamed relegates her case to a mere *type* in dramatic contradistinction to the attribution of so grand a name as that of Hamlet to the male condition. Not only does a dialectic occur on the level of type and name but there is also a split here between a woman's "practical" nature (bride, house-wife, "good, capable, conscientious") and Hamlet's impractical one. For, if we know anything about the character Hamlet, we know that he is not practical in any ordinary sense; he is after all a petulant prince.

So, if Freud does attribute to this solid woman type who has fallen ill of melancholia a conscience and by implication a superego, given that one of the characteristics of the melancholic is an overdeveloped mor-alizing conscience, then why does he say in "On Femininity" that women do not have a strong superego, that it is undeveloped?[22] Here I think one can read a slippage in Freud's argument: (1) to be ill of melancholia implies a relation to conscience that transcends the normative; (2) both women and men have to suffer this illness before they can be legitimated with a superior understanding about the world; and (3) the illness is different for men and women since they have different relations to the superego. Should we then infer that there are two kinds of melancholia: one like Hamlet's and one like that given to the solid woman who falls ill? And if we study the language Freud uses to talk about this melan-cholic woman, does not the term "conscientious", in this case, imply a servitude to social custom, that is, her dutifulness to the law (of patriar-chy) rather than to her *identification with* the Law of the Father? Ap-parently unable to rise to the critical magnitude of a Hamlet, this woman, says Freud, "will speak no better of herself than one who is in fact worthless; indeed, the former is perhaps more likely to fall ill of the disease than the latter, of whom we too should have nothing good to say" (p. 247).

Who is this "we" who "should have nothing good to say," and why suddenly does the moral issue of "worthlessness" displace the psycho-logical one of "unfairness" to self and the epistemological one of "truth-fulness"? Not only is the "worthless" woman "perhaps less likely" to become melancholic, but neither she nor the "good, conscientious" woman speaks the truth as does Hamlet. The juxtaposition between

---

[22]Cf. Kaja Silverman, who also demonstrates the "extravagance" of Freud's gender politics in denying women a superego (*The Acoustic Mirror*, p. 157).

"conscientiousness" and "worthlessness" suggests that if a woman is not conscientious, hence dutiful, then she is "worthless." Freud himself seems to be playing the role of a Hamlet as he judges who is moral and who is not, speaking for that "superior" conscience of a very male superego: "Get thee to a nunnery." And to whom is the worthless woman without worth? *Who* again is the "we" who has "nothing good to say," if not the phallocratic superego itself, for whom the woman not dutifully bound to the phallus (i.e., not susceptible, like the deserted bride or the self-deprecating wife, of mourning its loss or absence) is of no value, is worthless?

Another word for the loss of value is depression, and such is the term more commonly applied today to the clinical cases—all women—described by Freud. As an editorial note in the *Standard Edition* remarks, "Freud habitually uses the term 'melancholia' for conditions which would now be described as 'depression'" (18: 109; see also 22: 60). "Melancholia" today seems an archaism in Freud's text, one that hearkens back to those great male avatars of Renaissance humanism: Ficino, Dürer, Tasso, the character of Hamlet, Burton. These names (and it is a question of names) have been marked and noted in the Western canon as of value, as "worthy" of note in the representation of loss. As such, they contrast with the "depressed," unworthy, or worthless quality of countless unnamed sufferers, whose devaluation is stereotypically linked with women: those considered "just depressed," "mere hysterics," or banal, faceless mourners. From this standpoint, Freud's text appears on a historical cusp: the (depressed) cases are women but the (melancholic) name is Hamlet. Perhaps this cultural or symbolic acknowledgment of the name is the "something more" that is supposed to distinguish melancholia from mourning, hysteria, and depression.

Melancholia's status as an extraordinary (male) cultural condition can thus be seen to displace and devalue the situation not only of (feminine) hysteria and depression but also that of mourning, a cultural practice that in the West has long been the privileged province of women. Interestingly enough, it was in his case study of the hysteric Fräulein Elisabeth Von R. that Freud first discovered the work of mourning that underpins his theory of melancholia *and* that he discovered that work to be "feminine," to be women's work. As such, we have a double gendering, for the hysteric is a woman who expresses her loss (or losses) in terms of mourning rather than melancholia. Fräulein Elisabeth Von R., a nurse whom Freud characterizes as a "highly gifted lady who suffers

from slight nervous states and whose character bears evidence of hysteria," is analyzed in terms of a nervous disorder that clearly models the
process of the work of mourning and that is curiously enough described
as a quotidian act of repetition, as a daily activity. Her work of mourning
is here called a work of recollection, as she literally gathers together
memories:

> There would begin in her a work of reproduction which once more
> brought up before her eyes the scenes of the illness and death. *Every day*
> she would go through each impression once more, would weep over it
> and console herself—at leisure, one might say. This process of dealing
> with her impressions was dovetailed into her *everyday* tasks without the
> two activities interfering with each other. The whole thing would pass
> through her mind in chronological sequence. I cannot say whether the
> work of recollection corresponded *day by day* with the past. I suspect that
> this depended on the amount of *leisure* which her *current household* duties
> allowed. (*Studies on Hysteria*, S.E. 2: 162; emphasis mine)

Thus, clearly this woman's work of mourning accommodates the imagination to reality and not vice versa (as it would for the great melancholic); her memories, insofar as they are part of the imagination, are
("dovetailed into" reality and brought back to the everyday. This work
of mourning is literally an *oikonomia*, a woman's work that brings everything back into the home, a home economics regulated precisely by
"current household duties." As such, melancholia is itself a discourse
that superimposes a transcendental lack over women's own losses by
devaluing or "depressing" this feminine work and by re-encoding or
inflating male loss as the sign of genius and moral sense, as the very
signifier of cultural superiority. So, if we read the Freudian text's fixation
on the figure of Hamlet within the Ficinian tradition, we realize that
Hamlet also emblematizes the way in which psychoanalysis and literature
devalues women's losses by considering them to be less substantial than
those of a man. And why is it that Hamlet is accorded now the role of
melancholic and elsewhere that of hysteric,[23] whereas women are merely
hysterics and depressed, unless melancholia could be said to appropriate
from women their own specific claims to loss and disempowerment,
relegating women to the prosaics of mourning while celebrating the

---

[23]Hamlet is a hysteric in *The Interpretation of Dreams*, S.E. 4: 265; and a melancholic in
"Mourning and Melancholia," S.E. 14: 246.

melancholic in man as the very essence of the poetic: "To be, or not to be" is not the question. The question, rather, is *who* is meaningfully empowered to ask the question and in asking it to receive the laurels?

The Question of Female Melancholia (Irigaray, Silverman, Kristeva)

In a very provocative chapter in *Speculum of the Other Woman*, Luce Irigaray argues that all the symptoms which Freud describes as melancholic (such as "profoundly painful dejection," or "abrogation of interest in the outside world") typically occur in the little girl when she enters the oedipal phase.[24] In other words, once she has entered into the world of the symbolic and has understood the way in which she and her mother are devalued (castrated) in that world, the little girl experiences the same symptoms as those met in melancholia, with the difference that her "withdrawal" is not said to follow the path of that neurosis. Irigaray shrewdly juxtaposes Freud's comments on the symptoms of melancholia with the question of how the castration complex affects the young girl. She then describes what the young girl might experience once she discovers the shared castration with her mother:

> Unlike the little boy —"who exhibits, therefore, two psychologically distinct ties: a straightforward [?] sexual object cathexis towards his mother and an identification with his father which takes him as a model"— the little girl takes her mother as her first object of love and also as her privileged identificatory reference point for her "ego" as well as for her sex. In point of fact, if all the implications of Freud's discourse were followed through, after the little girl discovers her own castration and that of her mother—her "object," the narcissistic representative of all her instincts—she would have no recourse other than melancholia. (p. 66)

Irigaray writes this paragraph under the rubric of "symptoms almost like those of melancholia." The "almost," however, is also a "not quite":

> In fact the little girl will not choose melancholia as her privileged form of withdrawal. She probably does not have the capacity for narcissism great enough to allow her to fall back on melancholia, and that capacity

[24]Luce Irigaray, *Speculum of the Other Woman*, trans. Gillian C. Gill (Ithaca: Cornell University Press, 1985), p. 66.

is too depleted to build up such a complex defense against castration anxiety and the "catastrophe" brought upon her by the "accomplished fact" of castration. The economy of female narcissism and the frailty of the girl's or woman's ego make it impossible for the melancholic syndrome to establish a firm and dominant foundation.... It is not that she lacks some "master signifier" or that none is imposed upon her, but rather that access to a signifying economy, to the coining of signifiers, is difficult or even impossible for her because she remains an outsider, herself (a) subject to their norms. (p. 71)

What does Irigaray mean by all this? Does she mean that women cannot become depressed—even severely depressed? Certainly not. In fact, what she is accurately describing is depression, understood as feelings of disempowerment, dejection, and "abrogation of interest in the outside world." But I think the problem arises in deciding how women have been able to express their depression or their loss. Although Irigaray's theoretical paradigm, does imply that women have a certain narcissistic reserve built up from the first phase of the oedipus complex, that capacity for sufficient narcissism is also said to become depleted, *once* the little girl recognizes the fact of castration. This "fact," however, is perhaps less the horror of anatomical lack than the horror that she has been *designated as* lacking—and that both men and women have supported that fiction of anatomical lack, translating it into an incapacity for self-definition: "She functions as a *hole*—that is where we would place it at its point of greatest efficiency, even in its implications of phobia, for man too—in the elaboration of imaginary and symbolic processes. But this fault, this deficiency, this 'hole' inevitably affords woman too few figurations, images, or representations by which to represent herself" (p. 71). In economic terms, it is women's lack that has been appropriated and turned against them and against any claims they may make for a lack that is productive, i.e., symbolic.

As Lacan has argued, symbolic castration is shared by all since we have all lost some primary object. The difference lies in the fact that recognition of this "common ground" is often denied in the play of power whereby patriarchy already situates the little girl outside the signifying economy of loss and of gain. Seen in these terms, melancholia is in itself a particular form of narcissistic desire for origin that excludes women because they are designated as the "hole" through which loss and lack are recuperated for the male subject. We have already had occasion to note the efficiency such a "hole" has for male theory in the case of Freud's "open wound."

In Freud too, the primary characteristic of the melancholic is the harsh critical function of the superego, an agency patterned on the father (as stated in *The Ego and the Id*) and from which "one" then derives, "religion, morality and social sense . . . the chief elements in the higher essence of man." (19: 35). The humanist bias of this statement is evident, suggesting Freud's own imbrication in those Western philosophical paradigms typically associated with the Renaissance.

What Irigaray is demonstrating is not, as Freud elsewhere suggests, that women have no superego: if this were the case, then we would not have depressed women. What I think is the crux of her argument is that the superego "in this history" of Freud's is constructed to benefit the little boy, whose fear of castration is assuaged by his alliance to what the superego implies, namely, identification with the same sex in terms of the Law of the Father: "So he will have to arm his penis with laws and ideals . . . reassured by identification with the all powerful law-giving father, supply it with a severe super-ego" (p. 86). Understood in these terms, then, the superego of the male subject in melancholia has the advantage of recreating loss in terms of a superego that is also a noncontradictory ego ideal based on representation. Thus Hamlet would be of a certain type of melancholia while the good conscientious woman is of another category. Seen in these terms, melancholia is indeed gendered, and Irigaray's analysis of why women cannot become melancholic can be better understood.

According to Irigaray and following Freud himself, melancholia's conflict between ego and ego ideal presupposes a certain amount of narcissistic libido, which is a prerequisite to representing subjectivity, that is, to representing oneself as a subject who is the subject of *her* loss. For Irigaray, the little girl cannot be this subject because she is already subjected to the "norms" of patriarchal discourse. It is indeed hard to have enough narcissistic reserves built up if at the moment she enters the symbolic, a young girl realizes not only that she is sexually and socially devalued but also that her feeling of loss at this recognition finds little in the way of means to express itself. The implication, of course, is that to become melancholic one would need some kind of access to cultural production, that is, what Irigaray calls "access to a signifying economy" whereby the subject in question—here, the little girl—could represent loss, could create out of the feeling of loss some valid way to articulate that loss, that "painful dejection," meanfully.

For Irigaray, the "what" that has been lost in the lost object remains structurally opaque to the consciousness of the young girl, who does not even know "*what* she is losing in discovering her castration": "It is really a question for her of a loss that radically escapes representation . . . whence the impossibility of mourning that loss" (p. 68). Although the unrepresentability (or repression) of the "what" that is lost in the lost object seems the same as in Freud's own description of melancholia, there is an important difference in the representability of the loss itself according to gender. While the Freudian melancholic may not know "what" he has lost, he is more than able to display, even ostentatiously, that there is a loss (which is inevitably to his credit). For Irigaray, women's loss is radically "unrepresentable" because its representation has been given short shrift by master discourses, which have belittled women's own losses and discursive practices and have designated as the only recognizable losses the ones men incur. The question of representation, then, is a question of who holds the means to assuage the fact of loss itself—a question, that is, of who controls the "coining of signifiers." Also implied here is that the little girl has lost a sense of community with other women because of the isolation that results from the devaluation not only of herself but of *all* women, including the mother.

Given the impossibility for women to mourn the loss or to represent the "what" that has indeed been lost, Irigaray posits hysteria as a transcendent and transhistorical site of feminine articulation. But not only is hysteria a (particularly devalued) mode of women's representation, it is also a determinately historical one. Just as one needs to historicize melancholia, one also needs to historicize hysteria and read this "female" malady not only negatively as a function of women's exclusion from the public sphere (as Irigaray also suggests), but also positively as a mode of resistance to the specific domestic and religious enclosures of nineteenth-century Europe. Instead of being hypostatized as an essential feminine space, hysteria needs to be understood as a particularized and historicized means that women have had to articulate loss.[25]

Also to be understood in a social context is the narcissism that would precondition the possibility of melancholia, for where would the "narcissistic reserves" come from, if not from precisely the same symbolic order

---

[25]On such interpretations of hysteria, see note 37 in the Introduction.

that accredits the male in his narcissism and devalues the female for her "castration"? Is it the "fault" of the little girl that she "lacks" a "sufficient" reserve of narcissism, or is that lack not demonstrably a function of her lack of social "mirroring"? Isn't the possibility of investing (narcissistically) in one's ego linked to whether or not one sees oneself invested in and by the gaze of others, again to one's "access to a signifying economy"? One needs to go beyond the Lacanian assertion of the determining role of the other in the constitution of the ego and to discuss the very *different* ways in which different egos are constituted in relation to different others, who interpret the other. The patriarchal "norms," for example, to which the little girl is subject prefigure her in an essentialized relation of lack to the phallic order (again in ways that *differ* from the little boy's subjection to those same norms). As such, a libidinal analysis of her "object relations" cannot be separated from a consideration of social, symbolic relations. Only by breaking with the psychologizing tendencies that continue to haunt Lacan himself can we begin to see to what extent "object" relations *are* social relations. Such indeed appears to be Irigaray's move when she analyzes the "economy of female narcissism": "It is not that she lacks some 'master signifier' or that none is imposed upon her, but rather that access to a signifying economy, to the coining of signifiers, is difficult or even impossible for her because she remains an outsider, herself (a) subject to their norms" (p. 71).

To the extent that Irigaray here takes the view of melancholia (and narcissism) not as a psychological syndrome but as a gendered practice, she correctly re-situates the problem on the level of the symbolic. For it is on that level (and not by the often-prescribed return or retreat to some inarticulate, regressive state like the "pre-oedipal"[26]) that the order

---

[26]Here, I do not wish at all to desubjectivize the figure of the "pre-oedipal" mother but rather to resist the kind of desubjectivization that happens to her, even in some feminist theory, and that inevitably works in league with a misogynist position that reinforces the kind of self-hatred and unexpressed depression I would like to break out of. As Shirley Nelson Garner, Claire Kahane, and Madelon Sprengnether conclude in their Introduction to *The (M)other Tongue: Essays in Feminist Psychoanalytic Interpretation* (Ithaca: Cornell University Press, 1985): "To link the potential for reproduction in all women with the capacity for cultural production is to transform not only the figure of the mother but the very bases of psychoanalytic theories in their preoedipal orientation" (p. 29). In a paper read at the Modern Language Association convention in 1990 and titled "Like a Film: Reopening the Case of the Missing Penis with Rainer, Silverman, and Torok," Timothy J. Murray has convincingly and provocatively argued the issues in the Irigaray-Silverman debate from a Torokian point of view that understands the acquisition of language not as paternal metaphor but as instantiation, let us say *nom de la mère*. The paper will appear in his *Like a Still: Ideological Fantasy on Screen, Camera, and Canvas* (forthcoming from Routledge).

of the symbolic can be effectively challenged in terms of the symbolic itself. The *extent*, though, of Irigaray's pursuit of this politico-theoretical agenda seems to remain limited to these allusive remarks. So, if Irigaray means that women cannot become melancholic, then she is, to a degree, correct, *if* (and it is not entirely clear from her analysis) she is taking melancholia as a *discursive and cultural practice* that has given men a cultural privilege in displaying and representing loss so as to convert it into a sign of privileged subjectivity. The symbolic, or Law of the Father, indeed provides for men a discourse that ensures the positive represen- tation of their loss: they can create narratives from it, go to war over it, even create nations out of it.[27] As if to underscore the ways men are accorded the symbolic means to generate imaginary narratives from their social and psychological "exiles," Irigaray insists that women do not have "access to a signifying economy, to the coining of signifiers," a formulation from which one can infer that melancholia—as a discursive practice—does not give to women an access to the coining of that particular signifier (p. 75).

Melancholia could be understood as a particular discourse that en- codes male subjectivity in terms of the history of great men and great deeds. In this light, then, it is not so much that a melancholic syndrome cannot establish itself vis-à-vis the young girl, but that the syndrome is in itself part and parcel of a melancholic *discourse* that has in effect privileged male subjectivity in terms of loss itself. One could thus state that depression is the failure of melancholia—or that melancholia is a culturally valued form of depression and has devalued other kinds of losses such that depression itself becomes hierarchized into "higher" and "lower" forms. Again, it is imperative to distingush between depression and melancholia, depression as the common version of "melancholia" and melancholia as the culturally privileged version of despair. From this point of view, Irigaray is then correct in saying that the little girl does not choose melancholia as her "privileged form of withdrawal." Thus, although melancholia could be read as a pathological state, it is nevertheless a state that allows the male subject to represent his stakes in the game of cultural legitimation. It is a privileged cultural form of

[27]The consequences of a nationalism built on nostalgia have become most apparent in twentieth-century fascism. On this question see especially Alice Yaeger Kaplan, *Reproductions of Banality: Fascism, Literature, and French Intellectual Life* (Minneapolis: University of Min- nesota Press, 1986); Jean-François Lyotard, *The Differend: Phrases in Dispute*, trans. Georges Van Den Abbeele (Minneapolis: University of Minnesota Press, 1988).

depression. Women, therefore, are not melancholic per se; they are depressed. In this way, "painful dejection" is nothing more than painful dejection, since the young girl is trapped within a symbolic order that designates her being as essentially lacking and thus neutralizes her capacity for the representation and politicization of loss.

But if Irigarary is correct in concluding that melancholia is not a preferred form of withdrawal for women given what we understand about the category of melancholia as a complex that authenticates an oedipal trajectory, then why not see women's depression as something that can profoundly radicalize the way depression is understood? In other words, I am not proposing a return to some origin as a way to undermine the oedipal trajectory (i.e., the uncritical celebration of the pre-oedipal). Rather, I propose to see women's capacity to change the symbolic from women's own perspective on the ways that discursive practices such as the melancholic have subverted women's own claims to loss, and thus to legitimate other modes of feminine self-representation.[28]

Taking issue with Irigaray's premise that women cannot be melancholics, Kaja Silverman has recently argued for the existence of female melancholia, not as a "pathology" but as "a psychic condition which is somehow endemic to the female version of the positive Oedipus complex."[29] If, in the male version of this complex, the little boy must renounce his desire for the mother (negative moment) by identifying with the father (positive moment), the little girl, according to Silverman, must not only identify with the mother *but also* renounce the child's primordial desire for the mother. As Silverman explains, "It is possible to conceive of that complex beginning with a period of time during which she would both desire the mother and identify with her, and in

[28]While there has recently been a strong reaction against French feminists as being too polarized and reproducing in their analyses the very same paradigms of Western metaphysics that do not take account of women as social subjects, I suggest that if one wants to avoid the essentialism of recreating women out of the void, and if one then has recourse to deconstructing the ruses of patriarchal supremacy, such a risk is almost inescapable. Such is also the case in a discussion of melancholia and of the discourses that legitimate this prestigious form of neurosis. Assuredly, it is not "unfeminist" to practice the delegitimation of such discourses. In this regard, I think it is imperative to understand Irigaray's aims; her book must be read as a critique of a certain Western philosophical tradition from Plato to Freud that has ascribed an essential practicality to women, a practicality that has nothing to do with the kind of lack that inspires empowered representation in, let us say, a "dispossessed," melancholic male subject. On the debates surrounding French feminism, see especially Alice Jardine, *Gynesis: Configurations of Woman and Modernity* (Ithaca: Cornell University Press, 1985).
[29]Silverman, *The Acoustic Mirror*, p. 152.

which considerable narcissistic reserves would be built up. With the advent of the castration complex, the mother would undergo a devaluation, and the girl would be encouraged to displace her desire onto the father. She would at the same time feel enormous cultural pressure to continue to identify with the mother, and it is here that melancholia enters the picture" (p. 156). The complex dynamics involved in "deinvesting" from a culturally devalued object with which one is nonetheless *also* expected to identify lead to the familiar melancholic symptoms of despair and self-deprecation, and thus help "to explain the rigorous system of internal surveillance with which the female subject so frequently torments herself" (p. 157).

Silverman pursues her analysis of female subjectivity and of melancholia through a rereading of Freud (especially *The Ego and the Id*, "Female Sexuality," and "On Femininity") that underscores the "continuity" rather than "discontinuity" of the little girl's love for her mother (p. 120). In order to demonstrate this thesis, she cites *The Ego and the Id*, where Freud significantly revises the Oedipus complex to show how the child straddles the line between two moments, one seen as a normal outcome and the other as perverse:

> One gets the impression that the simple Oedipus complex is by no means its commonest form, but rather represents a simplification or schematization which to be sure, is often enough justified for practical purposes. Closer study usually discloses the more complete Oedipal complex, which is twofold, positive and negative, and is due to bisexuality originally present in children: that is to say, a boy has not merely an ambivalent attitude towards his father and an affectionate object-choice towards his mother, but at the same time he also behaves like a girl and displays an affectionate feminine attitude to his father and a corresponding jealousy and hostility towards his mother. (*S.E.* 19: 33; cited in Silverman, p. 120)

For Silverman, this passage from *The Ego and the Id* is crucial since it raises the question of what this negative moment means for the little girl, the question Freud skirts in his later essays by rewriting the negative oedipal in terms of a pre-oedipal: "I intend to hold Freud to his much earlier formulation, and to attempt to demonstrate that 'the pre-Oedipal phase' has improperly replaced 'the negative Oedipus Complex' as the appropriate rubric with which to designate what, in the early history of the female subject, conventionally precedes her desire for the father" (p. 120). For, as Silverman points out, both in "Female Sexuality" and in

"On Femininity" Freud insists that the love the little girl transfers from the mother to the father originates in the girl's love for the mother (p. 121). Such a reading of the little girl's relationship to the mother at the negative phase of the oedipal complex leads to a reconsideration of how the little girl enters into the positive Oedipus complex. "To resituate the girl's libidinal investment in the mother firmly within the Oedipus complex is also to force a serious reconsideration by means of which the male subject is made to *exit* from the Oedipus complex, but the female subject to *enter* it. However, once the mother is included within the general equation, the castration crisis becomes the impetus whereby the little girl enters only onto the *positive* Oedipus complex, and not the Oedipus complex *tout court*"(p. 122).

At this moment of the "negative" oedipal complex, that is, prior to the moment of the castration complex, Silverman argues, the child must separate itself from the mother, a separation that also leads to desire, and especially desire for the mother:

> To situate the daughter's passion for the mother within the Oedipus complex...as I think we are obliged to do, is to make it an effect of language and loss, and so to contextualize both it and the sexuality it implies firmly within the symbolic...Finally and most important, it is not to foreclose upon what might be called a "libidinal politics" but to make it possible to speak for the first time about a genuinely oppositional desire—to speak about a desire which challenges dominance from within representation and meaning, rather than from the place of a mutely resistant biology or sexual "essence." (pp. 123–24)

What Silverman has uncovered in her readings of Freud is the moment of symbolic castration, the moment where the child enters into language and desire. That moment is specifically relevant for the girl because it situates her in a relation to the mother, to femininity: "Identification with the mother during the negative Oedipus complex is at least in part an identification with activity. The equation of femininity and passivity is a consequence only of the positive Oedipus complex, and the cultural discourses and institutions which support it" (p. 153). Thus symbolic castration gives women a way to rethink their position in terms of loss, to challenge the status quo of woman's installment within castration proper since her relationship to her mother during the negative oedipal phase is also one of activity. In this regard, Silverman cites Freud himself from "Female Sexuality": "The little girl's preference for dolls is probably

*evidence of the exclusiveness of her attachment to her mother, with complete
neglect of her father object"* (cited in Silverman, p.153; Silverman's emphasis). Furthermore, this play not only situates the girl in an active
role vis-à-vis the mother and activity per se, but also points to the way
in which imitation of the mother, the playing with dolls, indicates a
desire to beget a child with the mother, since the father "figures as the
object neither of desire nor of identification" (p. 153). Thus, during the
negative Oedipus complex the little girl has invested her libido into her
mother, and it is therefore the narcissistic investment that the girl child
has in her mother that leads us into the question of female melancholia
at the onset of the positive oedipal complex.

The mother thus appears as the first object choice for the little girl
(as well as for boys), and identification with and separation from this
object choice is what constitutes the negative oedipal phase, one that
implies an active rather than passive relation to the object of love and
to the little girl's desires. But the problem for little girls arrives at the
onset of the "positive" phase of the Oedipus complex and "with the
cultural discourses and institutions which support it." The arrival of the
positive Oedipus complex ushers in melancholia for the little girl, and
with it the typically Freudian symptoms of "profoundly painful dejection," "abrogation of interest in the outside world," and "fall in self-
esteem," symptoms Irigaray has shown to align themselves with female
subjectivity. Silverman, at this point, takes issue with Irigaray's argument
in *Speculum* that women cannot become melancholic for lack of narcissism. Silverman argues that if we see the little girl only from the theoretical perspective of the positive Oedipus complex, then "it is also
impossible under these theoretical conditions to imagine the girl having
sufficient narcissistic reserves to become a melancholic, since the only
identification with the mother which would be available to her would
be one predicated upon lack, insufficiency, and self-contempt" (p. 156).
According to Silverman's analysis, however, the little girl *has already
built up* sufficient narcissistic reserves during the negative oedipal phase.
The melancholic basis for female subjectivity, therefore, comes at the
moment of the positive Oedipus complex. It is at this point, and only
at this point, that the young girl perceives the mother as devalued. And
not only is the mother now a devalued object of love but the young girl
is pressured to identify with the mother in order to displace her desire
for her onto the father. Thus the Oedipus complex proper would be
the moment when the female body is anatomically differentiated from

the male thereby positioning the little girl in terms of lack, "by means of which woman is made to assume the burden of male lack as well as her own" (p. 123).

Caught within a culturally imposed dilemma, the little girl not surprisingly becomes ambivalent in her relation to the mother—who has been loved and then devalued, and with whom the girl child must still identify, all of which means that the incorporation of the now devalued love object can only come at the cost of an enormous struggle within the young girl's own self. For as Freud has shown, in melancholia, the self-reproaches of the melancholic can be understood in terms of the ego warring against the incorporated object of love. Silverman thus insists that the lost object of desire is not so much "surrendered as relocated within the subject's own self" (i.e., introjected or encrypted), an analysis Freud had sketched in "Mourning and Melancholia," stressing that in order for the love object to be incorporated it must have once been very much idealized.

Thus the young girl's anger and self-deprecation are directed toward the incorporated object—the imago of the mother. Her superego is, moreover, responding to the same law of culture as that of the boy, the law that deems the mother, or by extension any woman, inferior. The situation is further complicated for the little girl because the mother is the object with whom she can most strongly identify, but the imposed ego ideal in a patriarchal culture would be modeled after the father. Thus, in melancholia, the paternally identified ego ideal "wars against" the maternal object, which is also her own ego, therefore casting her "self" into crisis. It is this moral conscience that presents an especially difficult task for the depressed woman. For if we read Freud correctly, we see over and over again the value placed on the conscience, on the superego, which is supposed to have its original source in the love for the father. Rather than credit the Freudian notion of women's lack of a superego, I would like instead to stress how much more severe this moral conscience is for women than for men. For if the etiology of the moral conscience is indeed the father, that is, a stand-in for cultural value, then the woman's relation to this superego is further complicated by her alienation from the value inherent in the Law of the Father, since it is precisely that law which inscribes both her and her lost object of desire (the mother) in terms of a double indemnity, that is in terms of an absolute lack. Thus feminine subjectivity and melancholia would derive from an ego devalued both in terms of the social position of

woman (i.e., a devalued subject) and in terms of the ambivalent internalization of the mother (a devalued object). The superego, an agency
of the father, inherited at the Oedipus complex as one assumes one's
position in the ordering of sexuality, works to maintain and reinforce
the dominance of the father over the mother. It is no wonder, then,
there are so many depressed women! Thus, according to Silverman, the
woman is forced to assume a divided position: "In effect, the female
subject is punishing the mother (and consequently herself) for being
inferior and insufficient, unworthy of love" (p. 158).

While Silverman has thus argued remarkably for an etiology of female
melancholia in a strict clinical sense, I would like to suggest a possible
realignment with Irigaray's statement that women cannot become melancholic. On the one hand, Irigaray states that this is so because of a
lack of sufficient narcissism; Silverman has, however, shown us how
women through the negative oedipal phase are sufficiently narcissistic
to fall ill of melancholia. And on this point, I strongly agree with her
since women are indeed depressed (a term I prefer to use for women
rather than "melancholic" for reasons that I hope will become increasingly apparent). On the other hand, Irigaray has stated that women
cannot become melancholic because there is no adequate signifying economy at their disposal. To requote Irigaray: "It is not that she lacks some
'master signifier' or that none is imposed upon her, but rather *that access
to a signifying economy, to the coining of signifiers, is difficult or even impossible
for her* because she remains an outsider, herself (a) subject to their
norms." Interestingly, Silverman does not take these lines into consideration when she heaves her attack at Irigaray, even though the lack of
a signifying economy for women as subjects that Irigaray stresses is
perhaps the most significant moment in her understanding of why
women are not melancholics per se. This "signifying economy" that
Silverman fails to confront is based on the way cultural discourses have
traditionally underscored women's limitations in participating within
the formation of discourse itself. One must see melancholia not simply
as a psychological construct but also as part of a cultural order, one that
has en-gendered the male subject in terms of a loss that he can represent—and that represents him—as a legitimate, if not privileged, participant in the Western tradition. While I agree with Silverman's basic
analysis, once again I feel that a distinction between depression and
melancholia would be helpful. Thus, while Silverman is correct in saying

that women can fall ill of "melancholia," it is the function and value of the term "melancholia" that consistently needs to be reexamined and re-situated in historical and cultural terms.

While Silverman may be attempting to realign women's subjectivity with melancholia in order to find a way for women to reject their participation within oedipal structures, I think that to understand how melancholia has functioned one needs to understand the way melan-cholia as a discourse has been read as a special prerogative for male subjectivity. In other words, melancholia is considered to be in excess of a purely normative state of depression; its discourse encodes male eros and male subjectivity. Silverman herself is sensitive to this issue when she states: "That essay, 'Mourning and Melancholia,' provides a chilling account which may be pathological for the male subject, but which represents the norm for the female subject—that condition of melancholia which blights her relations with both herself and her cul-ture" (p. 155). It is here that I see a stake in the differences between male and female melancholia. For men, the melancholic position is path-ological but dominates Western thought as a special prerogative for representing the alienated and creative individual, whereas for women it is normative, thus reducing women to the category of an essentialized and therefore inconsequential lack. Women, I think, are excluded from melancholia not because they cannot become or have not been painfully depressed, but because melancholia as a traditional discourse has always implied a masculine economy that favors cultural production by de-realizing the mother and recuperating the feminine from a male position. I think this idea is what Irigaray, conscious of historical (and philo-sophical) discourses in Western culture, aims at when she says that women do not have the adequate "signifying economy" available to them to express their melancholias. It is not that they cannot do so, but that the way they can do it falls short of the hermeneutic codes implied in or imposed by the patriarchal discourses of the West.

On the other hand, Silverman's origination of "female melancholia" in terms of a *specific* object of loss, the mother, more vividly evokes mourning than classic male melancholia. Indeed, I suggest not only that women's depression is representable but that women have also char-acteristically represented their losses through a language that approxi-mates a mourning for their barred or devalued status within the symbolic rather than a melancholic fixation on the tomb as the imaginary return to the womb. What I am suggesting is that if what Silverman calls after Lacan "aphanisis of being"[30] happens for women through a separation from and loss of the mother in conjunction with an identification with her devalued status, and if she consequently finds herself at a loss to express herself within a system of symbolic exchange that positions her as an object of the male gaze, then might we not see her resultant "depression" as the onset of a mourning for the mother, a mother whose loss is also the devaluation of the female self, a mother whose devaluation is introjected by the daughter as the fundamental sense of lack or loss that characterizes her "identity"? To be sure, it is not altogether clear exactly *what* in the mother is lost: the mother as maternal presence? the mother's cultural potential? the daughter's selfhood as modeled on the mother's (lack of) self? But no matter what the precise mode of identification with the mother—whether grief, or guilt, or resentment, or anger—the daughter's identity is necessarily already a communal one to the extent that the mother is *within* her.[31] As Silverman says, "The lost object is not so much surrendered as relocated within the subject's own

---

[30] Silverman, *The Acoustic Mirror*, p. 156; see Jacques Lacan, "The Subject and the Other: Aphanisis," in *The Four Fundamental Concepts of Psycho-Analysis*, ed. Jacques-Alain Miller, trans. Alan Sheridan (New York: Norton, 1978), pp. 216–29.

[31] This persistence of the maternal image within the child's psyche, not as the sign of morbid degeneracy or as pathological fixation but as a positive kernel in the formation of feminine agency, is an unusual one for psychoanalysis, one that reconceptualizes some of its basic paradigms. For Sprengnether, the attempted repression of the mother in psychoanalytic theory situates her resurgences within that theory as uncanny: "Freud's focus on Oedipal masculinity effectively obscures his vision of the preoedipal mother. Her presence, for precisely this reason, will haunt his texts" (*The Spectral Mother*, p. 38). By critically rereading the mother within the Freudian opus ("the loss that precipitates the organization of a self is always implicitly the loss of a mother" [p. 9]), Sprengnether is able to propose an "elegiac" understanding of the ego for whom the pre-oedipal mother is "both origin and Other," thus saving her from "the equally devastating effects of idealization and erasure" and "allowing for the possibility of maternal discourse as well as a nonphallocentrically organized view of culture" (p. 9). In a different but complementary critique, Marianne Hirsch charges psychoanalysis—even feminist psychoanalysis—with being "profoundly child-centered" to the point of being unable to "theoriz[e], beyond childhood, the experience of adulthood: But, so long as the figure of the mother is excluded from theory *psychoanalytic feminism* cannot become a *feminist psychoanalysis*" (*The Mother/Daughter Plot: Narrative, Psychoanalysis, Feminism* [Bloomington: Indiana University Press, 1989], p. 12). For Hirsch, far from connoting some primal identity, the figure of the mother is *the* locus of gender difference and of differences within gender itself: "The multiplicity of 'women' is nowhere more obvious than for the figure of the mother, who is always both mother and daughter" (pp. 12–13). It is in this necessary *intersubjectivity* of the maternal that I would locate a feminist dynamics of mourning as the inception of a community of *differences* and the concomitant possibility of a symbolics that would undo the phallocentric one of Lacan or of Freud. As Jessica Benjamin specifies, such intersubjectivity "refers to experience *between and within* individuals, rather than just *within*" (*The Bonds of Love: Psychoanalysis, Feminism, and the Problem of Domination* [New York: Pantheon, 1988], p. 125).

self—which is precisely where the mother's imago must be situated if the girl is to identify with her" (p. 157).

The loss that is mourned is, thus, not merely the mother's absence, nor simply the daughter's devalued sense of self, but also and more generally the structured denial of privilege for *all* women within patriarchal societies. As such, the individual and apparently contingent case of the depressed woman finds its correlative in the traditional and *communal* practice of women's mourning. But this is, then, also to pinpoint a locus of women's resistance, and by thus realigning depression with mourning, we might be able to articulate loss and lack in terms of a feminine symbolic that offers a counter-discourse to the melancholic tradition. Perhaps such a counter-discourse is what is glimpsed when Silverman argues that "memories will inevitably retain their cathexis, and assert the mother's desirability even in the face of the most violent detraction on the part of both culture and the super-ego" (p. 158). In other words, the mother is not given up as a lost object but is rediscovered *through* depression and mourning as an object of love and identification. Through depression and mourning, the mother's imago resurfaces from the interstices of the oedipal to assert her desirability as refigured by her identification and solidarity with other women.

If such a refiguring is possible, then we can read women's depression not as a failed expression of loss—as prosaic grief—but as an *incipit* to a mourning of both daughter and mother's devalued status in a symbolic governed by a masculine economy of self-recuperation. Such a depression then is not a static category but rather part of a feminine symbolic that may indeed be a way to re-inscribe women's losses through another type of representation.

Silverman's politics of female melancholia requires a positive encrypting of the mother within the daughter, but Julia Kristeva instead analyzes the pathological dimension of depression instead in terms of an incomplete or unsuccessful *detachment from* the mother. If Silverman wants to mobilize a matriphilic discourse to assuage the self-denegration of women that results from their having to identify with the mother who is also the devalued parent, Kristeva (in *Black Sun: Depression and Melancholia*) states the necessity of psychical "matricide" as the only effective "counter-depressant." When such a killing off of the mother is not achieved successfully in childhood, psychoanalysis (but also religion and literary creation) is able to carry out this "counter-depressive" function by properly channeling what Kristeva terms the "matricidal drive" rather than making use of antidepressant drugs such as lithium (to which Kristeva nonetheless gives a disturbing amount of consideration and credit).[32]

For Kristeva, the problem of melancholia thus comes down to a problem of differentiation: the lack of separation from the mother implies an inadequate integration into the symbolic, evidenced by such depressive symptoms as slowness of rhythm, lack of concentration, and minimal or poor use of speech. Unlike for Freud, the "object" whose loss provokes this behavior does not bear any mysterious "what" for Kristeva: that lost object, for her, is purely and simply the mother. Even in the case where the melancholic points to another loss, the loss of the mother is what stands behind that loss (and even behind all other losses) as a sign of the melancholic's disproportionate affect. This excessive quality of the melancholic's sense of loss points not only to the lack of an adequate reckoning with the loss of the mother but also to her continued presence in the psychic life of a subject who is unwilling to recognize that she is lost. And the mother is not simply a lost "object" but that pre-objectal "thing" whose loss (in the sense of the ego's differentiation into a separate entity) precipitates one into risky, heterogenous (and decentering) possibilities in which objects can be lost—or found:

> For man and for woman the loss of the mother is a biological and psychic necessity, the first step on the way to becoming autonomous. Matricide is our vital necessity, the sine-qua-non condition of our individuation, provided that it takes place under optimal circumstances and can be eroticized—whether the lost object is recovered as erotic object (as in the case for male heterosexuality), or it is transposed by means of an unbelievable symbolic effort, the advent of which one can only admire, which eroticizes the *other* (the other sex, in the case of the heterosexual woman) or transforms cultural constructs into a "sublime" erotic object (one thinks of the cathexes, by men and women, in social bonds, intellectual and aesthetic productions, etc.). (p. 28)

Although one cannot help but agree that a loss of the mother as object of infantile attachment does (and most probably should) take place, and that it is precisely that loss (and/or an extraordinary sense of loss) that

[32]Julia Kristeva, *Soleil noir: Dépression et mélancolie* (Paris: Gallimard, 1987); English citations from *Black Sun: Depression and Melancholia*, trans. Leon S. Roudiez (New York: Columbia University Press, 1989), p. 24.

structures the subject's entrance into the world of difference and tex-
tuality under the aegis of a symbolic lack, what is *not* immediately obvious is why this separation should take the psychically violent form of
what Kristeva calls a matricide.[33] Indeed, in the light of Silverman's
analysis of "female melancholia," it seems very problematic for women,
in particular, to "kill off" the mother without destroying their own
subjectivities (egos?) in a process of ultimate accommodation with a
phallic order of male dominance. For Silverman, the "cure"—the giving
up of the mother—through which the female melancholic completes
the work of mourning can only aggravate her depression and intensify
her self-deprecatory tendencies to the extent that she must identify with
a mother she must also reject. Kristeva, on the other hand, sees the
violent rejection of the mother signified by the term "matricide" as the
only viable alternative to the self-destructive tendencies of an ego under
the sway of the death drive: "The lesser or greater violence of matricidal
drive, depending on individuals and the milieu's tolerance, entails, when
it is hindered, its inversion on the self; the maternal object having been
introjected, the depressive or melancholic putting to death of the self is
what follows, instead of matricide. In order to protect mother, I kill
myself while knowing—phantasmatic and protective knowledge—that
it comes from her, the death-bearing she-Ghenna" (p. 28).

The passage continues in this first-person discourse. The Kristevan
melancholic thus kills himself or herself in place of having killed off the
mother and in this way finds some sort of recompense, becoming a
Dostoevskian figure not of parricide but specifically of matricide. For
the melancholic, according to Kristeva, the lost object (the mother) is
not lost, or at least not lost enough. Lost enough to be mourned, the
mother *qua* "death-bearing" is not lost enough for the ego to overcome
her morbid presence.[34] Sidestepping the traditional and complex psy-

---

[33]As Cynthia Chase remarks, "If a term such as 'matricide' or 'abjection' is imported into
an account precisely *not* of specific cultural manifestations but of universal linguistic structures
or of intralinguistic activities, the question arises as to whether the writer is not *enforcing* the
misogynistic gesture—is not killing the mother by finding her already dead. Such writing may
enact the performative gesture on which it seeks to comment. It thereby confronts the reader
with a problem of *ethical* as well as critical judgement" ("Primary Narcissism and the Giving
of Figure: Kristeva with Hertz and de Man," in *Abjection, Melancholia, and Love: The Work of
Julia Kristeva*, ed. John Fletcher and Andrew Benjamin [London: Routledge, 1990], p. 133).
Also see her "Desire and Identification in Lacan and Kristeva," in *Feminism and Psychoanalysis*,
ed. Richard Feldstein and Judith Roof (Ithaca: Cornell University Press, 1989), pp. 65–83.

[34]The "spectral mother" whom Madelon Sprengnether sees as haunting the text of Freud
returns with a vengeance in Kristeva's version of the psychoanalytic parable of the trauma of
separation. At the same time, however, the switch from a threatening mother who is repressed

choanalytic dynamics of incorporation and/or introjection, and mobilizing in its place what can only be called a murderous rhetoric of violence against women, Kristeva argues that the only way to complete the work of mourning the lost—but not sufficiently lost—object that is the mother is by her execution: "I make of Her an image of Death so as not to be shattered through the hatred I bear against myself when I identify with Her, for that aversion is in principle meant for her as it is an individuating dam against confusional love. Thus the feminine as image of death is not only a screen for my fear of castration, but also an imaginary safety catch for the matricidal drive that, without such a representation, would pulverize me into melancholia if it did not drive me to crime. No, it is She who is death-bearing, therefore I do not kill myself in order to kill her but I attack her, harass her, represent her" (p. 28). Not only is the choice, as indicated by one of Kristeva's chapter titles, between "killing and being killed," but in a strange turn of events, mourning is what comes *before* the death of a loved one. In fact, mourning is the sign that the mother as the love object continues to live within an ego whose world is consumed by the beloved (mother). Thus, the "ego" lives life as its own death agony.

Only in the next paragraph does it become clear that the voice that is speaking is emulating a male position. To kill off the mother in order not to become a melancholic or a depressive would mean to assume the same oedipal position as the boy who needs to kill off the father, or pretend to do so, in order to preserve his own ego from destruction. The "counter-depressive" strategy of matricide offers only a transposed or transvestitized oedipal drama. For Kristeva, women not up to this ego-preservative "crime" can only turn into depressives, essentially linked to the maternal in a way that imposes a barrier to artistic and intellectual creativity: "For a woman, whose specular identification with the mother as well as the introjection of the maternal body and self are more immediate, such an inversion of the matricidal drive into a death-bearing maternal image is more difficult, if not impossible" (pp. 28–29). Suddenly the option of killing off the mother becomes by implication ex-

to an explicitly aggressive one leaves the maternal figure in the same abject place, as a disturbing entity to be gotten rid of, and raises the question of Kristeva's gender politics, which appears in *Black Sun* to be much more congruent with phallocentrism than in her earlier works. Even a relatively late text such as *Histoires d'amour* (Paris: Denoël, 1983) still views the phallocratic conflation between motherhood and abjection as no less than the origin of misogyny (p. 45). Also see Cynthia Chase's crucial reading of this text in "Primary Narcissism and the Giving of Figure," esp. p. 127.

clusively male. Often insisting on the "immense" difficulty of heterosexual object choice in women as well as on the virtual "impossibility" for women to kill off the mother, Kristeva comes close to assigning an *essentially* depressive status to women. How indeed can a woman turn either herself or her mother into a "bloodthirsty Fury, since I am She (sexually and narcissistically), She is I? Consequently, the hatred I bear her is not oriented toward the outside but is locked up within myself. There is no hatred, only an implosive mood that walls itself in and kills me secretly, very slowly, through permanent bitterness, bouts of sadness" (p. 29).

But it seems that Kristeva has here betrayed her recourse to a traditionally masculine economy of misogyny: the hatred for and matricide of the mother, which is then textualized as a categorical difference in biological natures and as the essential quality of women's depression. Kristeva seems to succumb much too easily to the phallocratic ideology that judges the mother (and by extension, all women) as inferior, as dangerous (whether castrating or mortiferous), and that accordingly prescribes either her domestication and internal surveillance within the "home" or her systematic expulsion and exclusion outside society. Given this ideological bent, it is not too surprising that Kristeva also includes the male homosexual, without further ado and with no argumentative justification, within the category of the essentially depressed, although with the exception—also unexplained—of gay sadism: "He is an exquisite melancholy person when he does not indulge in sadistic passion with another man" (p. 29; translation modified) [C'est un mélancolique exquis quand il ne se livre pas à la passion sadique avec un autre homme] (p. 40).

And, in general, Kristeva's appropriation of clinical, even biological, descriptions of depressive behavior works to situate her analysis within the received Kristevan theses concerning the role of the drives in artistic production, the relation between primary and secondary processes, the semiotic and the symbolic, the inarticulate expressiveness of the *chora*, and the repressive articulation of cultural form. But if this theoretical matrix served the anarchistic politics of libidinal liberation in her early *Revolution in Poetic Language*, in *Black Sun* the same categories seem called upon to promote the normative value of the symbolic through a descriptive pathology that prescribes by implication an oedipal solution to the melancholic's overly close attachment to the maternal.

Whereas, for example, Freud refers to the talkativeness of the melancholic, Kristeva insists on the taciturn quality of depression, on its inarticulateness as well as its "repetitiveness" and "monotony": "Faced with the impossibility of concatenating, they utter sentences that are interrupted, exhausted, come to a standstill. Even phrases they cannot formulate. A repetitive rhythm, a monotonous melody emerge and dominate the broken logical sequences, changing them into recurring, obsessive litanies" (p. 33). Kristeva articulates this physiology of melancholia as speech pathology into an oedipal drama described as an unaccomplished mourning for the mother (or the denial of the necessity of relinquishing her). This Kristevan double bind positions the "ordinary" depressive subject as inarticulate and therefore incapable of negotiating with the symbolic order. The only outcome can be an incomplete relation to the symbolic order, hence to its primary system: language.

> Melancholia then ends up in asymbolia, in loss of meaning: if I am no longer capable of translating or metaphorizing, I become silent and die. (p. 42)

> The spectacular collapse of meaning with depressive persons—and, at the limit, the meaning of life—allows us to assume that they experience difficulty integrating the universal signifying sequence, that is, language. In the best of cases, speaking beings and their languages are like one: is not speech our "second nature"? In contrast, the speech of the depressed is to them like an alien skin; melancholy persons are foreigners in their maternal tongue. They have lost meaning—the value—of their mother tongue for want of losing the mother. (p. 53)

> As the time in which we live is the time of our discourse, the alien, retarded, or vanishing speech of melancholy people leads them to live within a skewed time sense. It does not pass by, the before/after notion does not rule it, does not direct it from a past toward a goal. Massive, weighty, doubtless traumatic because laden with too much sorrow or too much joy, *a moment* blocks the horizon of depressive temporality or rather removes any horizon, any perspective. Riveted to the past, regressing to the paradise or inferno of an unsurpassable experience, melancholy persons manifest a strange memory: everything has gone by, they seem to say, but I am faithful to those bygone days, I am nailed down to them, no revolution is possible, there is no future. . . . A dweller in truncated time, the depressed person is necessarily a dweller in the imaginary realm. Such a linguistic and temporal phenomenology discloses, as I have often emphasized, an unfulfilled mourning for the maternal object. (pp. 60–61)

Caught in the pre-oedipal web of the maternal, the Kristevan melancholic remains a prisoner of his or her imaginary, forever seeking an (unrealizable) denial of difference and thus incapable of negotiating the complex networks of differences that are language, time, and society. Although the "positive" oedipal moment of identification with the father (necessary for the construction of a superego, whose biting criticisms, we remember, were a prominent feature of Freud's etiology of melancholia), is never mentioned, Kristeva's paradigm remains firmly oedipal. But she condenses the "classic" version, whereby the mother is relinquished as an object of desire and the father killed off so the son can take his place, into one in which the father absolutely disappears from the scene and the mother must be *both* relinquished *and* murdered so that the child can take her place by killing her off instead of being killed by her. To be killed by her can then only point to the ego's destruction, which is characteristic of melancholia. In other words, the source of depression in the child's denial of difference turns out to be the exclusive fault of a murderous mama. Taking the side of difference in such a schema is tantamount to placing oneself unreservedly on the side of the phallic and accrediting an entire literature of male paranoia emblematized by such figures as the *vagina dentata*, the Hydra, the Medusa, the wicked stepmother of fairy tales, or even *Hamlet*'s Gertrude. As we shall see later on, such figures in fact do not point so much to a debilitating indifference as to a proliferation of differences unleashed by the (mis)understanding of that primal difference that is gender.

But if Kristeva wants to analyze melancholia as a pathology of inadequate differentiation from the mother, she, like Burton or Freud, cannot pursue the point without introducing other differences into her account of the "disease," differences whose ultimate outcome is to separate out some superior, implicitly male, aesthetic or cultural possibility from the field of what can only be seen as sick women.

Among the first of such differences is Kristeva's assertion early on that melancholia is "not French." For her, the "Gallic . . . tone" would be given over to "levity, eroticism, and rhetoric" (p. 6). She notes three obvious exceptions to this rule in the "sorry figure[s]" of Pascal, Rousseau, and Nerval, and without further reflection makes those exceptions prove the rule, without qualification. While one could quibble by naming any number of Frenchmen writing under the aegis of melancholia (LaRochefoucauld, Chateaubriand, Baudelaire, Proust are equally obvious examples or "exceptions"), a more subtle cultural distinction is being drawn here. Succinctly put, the fun-loving French do not get depressed, but when they do, they become great melancholics whose contributions to philosophy, social theory, or literature are truly unparalleled. On the one hand, the French are not melancholic; but on the other hand, their melancholia is extraordinary.

Even more telling is Kristeva's differentiation between the categories of melancholia and depression: "I shall call *melancholia* the institutional symptomatology of inhibition and asymbolia that becomes established now and then or chronically in a person, alternating more often than not with the so-called manic phase of exaltation. When the two phenomena, despondency and exhilaration, are of lesser intensity and frequency, it is then possible to speak of neurotic depression" (p. 9). The final adjective tells us that the gradation in degree of "intensity" between the two poles of milder depression and graver melancholia reproduces the classic psychoanalytic distinction between neurosis and psychosis. In fact, in the next few pages, Kristeva explicitly draws the connection between the more serious condition of the disease (i.e., melancholia) and that favorite of *Tel Quel* as well as of Deleuze/Guattari: schizophrenia. The semi-scientism of Kristeva's "clinical" approach makes of depression the milder, more mundane (neurotic) version of the more virulent and grave (psychotic) condition of melancholia; and in so doing, Kristeva implicitly grants to melancholia the greater privilege of psychic intensity and cultural radicality. In other words, for Kristeva, melancholia may be the clinically more serious form of depression, but it is also, as it has been for theorists of melancholia from Ficino through Freud, graced with the aura of artistic or creative genius.

In fact, Kristeva's distinction between depression and melancholia comes on the heels of a, for her, crucial differentiation between clinical and artistic forms of the disease, whereby the artist takes on a heroic status: "A written melancholia surely has little in common with the institutionalized stupor that bears the same name. . . . The artist consumed by melancholia is at the same time the most relentless in his struggle against the symbolic abdication that blankets him" (p. 9). In order to legitimate this heroicizing of the artist, Kristeva has to admit, later on, in seeming contradiction to her insistence on the reduced speech and slow rhythm of depression, that what may also occur is an "accelerated, creative cognitive process—witness the studies bearing on the very singular and inventive associations made by depressed persons starting from word lists submitted to them. Such hyperactivity with signifiers reveals itself particularly by connecting distant semantic fields and recalls the puns of hypomanics" (p. 59). For speed and creativity to be suddenly foregrounded in relation to language use points less to a contradiction in the diagnosis of depression than it does to the special status she wishes to grant the artist. The artist (and especially the artist *qua* poet and thus creator of words) would be an individual courageously in quest of sublimation (*à l'amor heroycus*) who stubbornly resists the "symbolic resignation" otherwise known as melancholic depression. While the artistic melancholic may suffer from the same sense of lack and loss as other melancholics, there is, according to Kristeva, a disavowal of that sense that would psychoanalytically encode the work of art as a fetishistic production to the extent that it both posits and denies the existence of the lack: "If loss, bereavement, and absence trigger the work of the imagination and nourish it permanently as much as they threaten it and spoil it, it is also noteworthy that the work of art as fetish emerges when the activating sorrow has been repudiated" (p. 9). For Kristeva, this state of affairs is "an enigmatic paradox that will not cease questioning us" (p. 9). In fact, it is a paradox, for the melancholic artist is totally *unlike* any other depressive. And unlike the entropic imaginary of the depressive that leaves him or her sluggish, inarticulate, and undifferentiated, the melancholic's symbolic achievement signals a dynamic and energetic mastery over linguistic, temporal, and societal differences. As such, the triumph of the artist *qua* melancholic seems to be the triumph of difference and the symbolic (i.e., the oedipal) over the depressive's fall into indifference and the imaginary (pre-oedipal).

To the melancholic's successful fetishism corresponds what Kristeva names as the depressive's hystericism. This hystericism is a suffering due to an unfelt or "senseless" affect, the defining symptom being the somatic one of inarticulate speech. The conscious (and successful) articulation of this affect thus remains the analyst's aim, which cannot be achieved, requires a certain "tact":

> The meaning of melancholia? Merely an abyssal suffering that does not succeed in signifying itself and, having lost meaning, loses life. That meaning is the weird affect that the analyst will be looking for with utmost empathy, beyond the motor and verbal retardation of the depressed, in the tone of their voice or else in cutting up their devitalized, vulgarized words—words from which any appeal to the other has disappeared—precisely attempting to get in touch with the other through syllables,

fragments, and their reconstruction. Such an analytic hearing implies *tact*.
(p. 189)

A corollary to the analyst's tact can be found in the aesthetic (and
"orthodox Christian") activity of pardon, "which identifies with abjection in order to traverse it, name it, expend it" (p. 190). For Kristeva,
the prime example of such an analytical tact or "pardon" is Feodor
Dostoevsky. His work would successfully (fetishistically?) sublate or
sublimate the hysteria of the melancholic who is trapped in his/her
imaginary and morbid identification with the mother into a reconciliation with what now turns out to be a benevolent and loving paternal
order: "Whoever is in the realm of forgiveness—is capable of identifying
with a loving father, an imaginary father, with whom, consequently, he
is ready to be reconciled, with a new symbolic law in mind" (p. 207).

These sorts of formulations already point us back in the direction
of the "gendered" division within melancholia, which I have been noting
elsewhere. For if artistic or fetishistic melancholia seems to be a victory
for the father and its clinical (hysterical) counterpart a submission to
the mother, the results of this theoretical division are to be reaped in
the "case-study" portion of Kristeva's book. There a single chapter titled
"Illustrations of feminine depression" recounts the psychoanalysis of
three depressed women, whereas each of four other chapters, is completely devoted to a great melancholic artist. If one also includes the
case study of "Anne" scattered through an earlier chapter, one cannot
help but notice that three of the four women are explicitly characterized
as "hysteric." Of the four melancholic artists, three are classical men
(Hans Holbein, Gérard de Nerval, Dostoevsky) and one is a contemporary woman writer (Marguerite Duras).

At least two of the three men are represented as significant recuperators of loss rather than "melancholic," and certainly not all are
viewed as depressed: to Holbein's resurrectional iconography ("Seeing
the death of Christ is thus a way to give it meaning, to bring him back
to life" [p. 137]) corresponds Dostoevsky's previously mentioned "hypostatization" and "pardoning" of suffering. The argumentative weight
of the book thus seems to fall onto the reading of Nerval, and in fact
onto the reading of a single Nerval poem, "El desdichado." The poem's
importance for Kristeva is underscored by her taking the title of her
book from the final words of the poem's first quatrain: "the black sun
of melancholy" [le soleil noir de la mélancolie]. And while her close

reading of Nerval's text gives us some of the best exegetical pages in the volume, often brilliant in their explication of this extremely opaque text, one cannot overlook the critic's desire to "fit" every detail of the poem into the pre-oedipal paradigm that guides her interpretation of melancholia. This hermeneutic desire is especially betrayed by a constant shifting and slippage between literal and figural modes of reading. While Kristeva is at pains to analyze the melancholic *representation* carried out by Holbein, for example, without psychologizing the painter himself as a melancholic, she insists on reading the pronoun "I" in "El desdichado" as referring unproblematically to the historical person of Gérard de Nerval. And this she insists on in spite of the fact that few poets (even the Rimbaud of "I am an other" [Je est un autre]) have such an alienated relation to the use of the first person.

One need only glance at a few pages from *Sylvie* or *Aurélia* to see that Nerval *problematizes* autobiographical narration in ways that make it tempting but very difficult to draw any direct parallels between the authorial "I" and the narrative "I." In "El desdichado," the "I" is qualified in different ways, making it unclear whether there is only one "I": "I am the somber one, the widower, the unconsoled one" [Je suis le ténébreux, le veuf, l'inconsolé] (p. 140; translation modified). Kristeva, of course, is not completely unaware of the possibility of such a fragmented subjectivity: "The proper names gathered . . . work more as signs of various identities. If the "persons" that have been named belong to the same world of love and loss, they suggest—through the poet's identification with them—a dispersal of the "I," loving as well as poetic, among a constellation of elusive identities" (p. 157). But then a sentence later, she reinterprets this disintegrative "accumulation," reducing it to instances of the unsuccessfully mourned maternal "Thing": "The litaneutical, hallucinatory gathering of their names allows one to suppose that they might merely have the value of signs, broken up and impossible to unify, of the lost Thing." Thus the problematic differentiation of the self, which Nerval foregrounds, is suddenly turned into Kristeva's paradigm of pre-oedipal indifferentiation.

In order to maintain this interpretation, Kristeva reads the genealogical thematics of the poem which seem to concern an anxiety about lost lineage and paternal abandonment (hence the title "El desdichado," the disinherited one), as a *figural* displacement of the loss of the mother. In support of such a reading, Kristeva proceeds with marvelous hermeneutic acumen to locate the many instances where the poet identifies himself with various women; she does so presumably to show that such an identification with female figures (or any such identification?) points to a deep-rooted identification with and indifferentiation from the mother—the precondition, we must assume, for the melancholia and eventual suicide of Gérard de Nerval. But if, as Kristeva argues though-out, the manipulation of language as a symbolic system points in theory to an overcoming of the pre-oedipal entrapment within the imaginary that would precipitate depression ("poetic writing mimics a resurrec-tion" [p. 171]), then why does Nerval's poetic "success" lead to his psychological undoing?

Let us play havoc with Kristeva's schema and suggest instead that perhaps the poetic "I" should be read figuratively and the genealogical anxiety taken more literally. Given the scenario of paternal abandonment could we not also argue that the poet tries on (or appropriates) a number of identities, most notably feminine ones, even the maternal one, as if to present himself as a potential love object for the lost father? Such a rhetorical transvestism (inevitably in league with a fundamental miso-gyny) and "patri-eroticism" can be found, as we shall see, in an entire tradition of melancholic texts from Tasso's "Canzone al Metauro" through Shakespeare's *Hamlet* and Rousseau's *Les solitaires*. Once again, Kristeva sees this possibility in Nerval's text only to pass by its signifi-cance: "The series of names attempts to fill the space left empty by the lack of a sole name. Paternal name, or Name of God" (p. 163). By insisting on the religious over the paternal theme in the Christic narrative as metaphor of Nerval's poetic situation, Kristeva is able to bring her discourse back to her schema via the figure of "the universal mother, Isis or Mary" (p. 169). Again, however, what one could call a "blame-the-mother" motif which may illuminate several aspects of Nerval's dif-ficult writing, nonetheless fails to capitalize on the same text's inscription of a patriarchal desire that could be said to condition the poet's social reception and symbolic success in the representation of loss itself. Even his death—the loss of the writer's very body—is symbolically recuper-ated as part of the myth of a poetic genius, of a creative inspiration, the proof to be found in the artist's worldly ineptitude. And yet, whoever or whatever is meant by "the mother" in Nerval, her anonymity is as sealed as the proper name of the son is celebrated.

This social and sexual differential of the proper name is clearly made in the case histories of the "depressed" women. There Kristeva uses the clichéd artifice of the first name (Anne, Hélène, Marie-Ange, Isabelle), a rhetoric that supposedly protects anonymity but in this gendered context glaringly points to the women's lack of symbolic representation when bereft of a patronymic supplement. What is perhaps the surprising outcome of this rhetorical move, however, is that it (unwittingly) reveals how the lack of adequate integration into the symbolic that Kristeva associates with depression turns out *not* to be the psychic fault of the women involved but rather the fault of the extra-psychic structure found in the social hierarchy of a male-dominated symbolic order which can only create oppressive effects on the psyche itself. For Kristeva, the women she analyzes are troubled by their femininity, by their role as women, and for her this has to do with not having killed off the mother, not having created of her an object of eros in a textualized form.

What surfaces here in the tone of her discussion is anger, Kristeva's anger that women have not created à la Holbein an alternative Christ out of their mothers, have not made of their lack some transcendental signifier, have not recuperated their egos in terms of a (male) fetishistic model of artifacts that point to the denial and asseveration of the loss of the mother. The women Kristeva portrays in this chapter are horribly bound to their depression—I would say pornographically so—for they represent the essential impossibilty for women to get beyond their sadness and their anger. They remain forever clinical cases, mere hysterics whose treatment at the hands of their unnamed analyst (presumably Kristeva herself) seems neither particularly "tactful" nor empathetic and pardoning. Kristeva, in fact, ends the first of the three overt case histories with the introduction of yet another suspect differentiation within the now delimited field of "feminine depression," namely, a gender difference within gender difference that divides women between those who experience clitoral and those who experience vaginal orgasms. For Kristeva, there is no question of the superiority of vaginal orgasm and of its access only to "real" women who, having successfully murdered the mother, can become mothers in turn via an "other jouissance" (p. 79). The maternally identified/depressed woman, on the other hand, for reasons Kristeva does not care to specify, is said to be locked into "competition with the symbolic power of her [male] partner" and thus can only obtain the "jouissance phallique" of the clitoris (p. 89).

This final hierarchical difference in the economy of depression/melancholia speaks of a female misogyny in Kristeva that may do much to explain the inclusion of Marguerite Duras within her list of great melancholic artists. For the literary and cinematic works of Duras portray the mother in terms consonant with Kristeva's theory: sometimes heroic, often castrating, devouring, or "mortiferous," always dominating. Even the women characters' relations with men and with other women, their unending doubling of roles, are reduced in Kristeva's analysis to an "echo to death-bearing symbiosis with the mothers" (p. 250). She who lurks as the source of the violence, longing, and despair found in Duras's writing is none other than that "archaic rival" that is the pre-objectal mother. This "uterine" core (cf. pp. 260, 263) of Durassian fiction suggests that the writing is the outcome of a successful reckoning with the maternal—a symbolic matricide: "It displays the same painful, deadly passion (a constant with Duras), conscious of itself and held back" (p. 230)—and should thus situate Duras as a vaginal orgasmic type, one able to have literary as well as biological offspring. On the other hand, the melancholic violence of Duras's writing also "evokes" what we saw earlier on to be the essential condition of women, that is, an unaccomplished mourning for the mother: "Suffering, in Duras' work, in a mannered way and with empty words evokes that impossible mourning, which, if its process had been completed, would have removed our morbid lining and set us up as independent, unified subjects. Thus it takes hold of us and carries us to the dangerous, furthermost bounds of our psychic life" (pp. 257–58). Is it this seductive power (or maternal pull?) that leads Kristeva finally to dismiss the Durassian opus in the last section of the book?

For if Duras is *the* woman writer to achieve the symbolic status of male melancholic artists, this symbolic success is attenuated by the use of a historicizing context that is absent from Kristeva's readings of the three male authors (whose works incidentally span three hundred years). According to Kristeva, the "blankness of meaning" and "rhetorical clumsiness" (p. 264) of Duras appeal to a specifically modern sensibility shaken and formed by the traumas of Hiroshima and Auschwitz. Supposedly such a historical context would transcend any claim to gendered loss (whether male or female) by the radical and terrifying specter of species loss. In other words, the general "crisis of signification" (p. 230) ensuing from this historically determined absolutization of loss seems to give women (or at least one woman, Marguerite Duras) access to the symbolics of melancholic grief. Although Kristeva does not consciously articulate this heretofore singular historical situation in gender terms, it does seem that the need to treat Duras in this historicizing context already begs the question.

In any case, Kristeva on the very last page of her book suddenly decides that this modernist "malaise" is out of fashion,[35] since it is now challenged by what she considers (in apparent contradiction to other theorists) to be postmodernism's "desire for comedy" (p. 258). In other words, if women now have access to the symbolics of loss, loss suddenly seems to be no longer of interest or value: Duras has come too late in an intellectual and aesthetic climate wherein, says Kristeva, one remembers the "shades of Marivaux and Crébillon" (p. 259). This evocation of two male French writers of comedy at the conclusion of her analysis of melancholia in turn recalls Kristeva's beginning remarks about how melancholia is so very un-French. After all, as Kristeva points out, Duras's "personal sensitivity to suffering" is not unrelated to her childhood in Indochina: "the strange experience of having been uprooted, a childhood on the Asian continent" (p. 238). As she aggressively distances herself from any such subjectivity of melancholia (decodable now as foreign, modern, and feminine), Kristeva thus concludes her book with a bubbly prediction that "a new amatory world comes to the surface" (p. 259) thanks to an unmitigated faith in a law of "eternal return" that guarantees a seemingly endless fund of "divertissement," "agréments," and "émerveillement" [distraction, amenities, and wonderment] (p. 259).

It also becomes very difficult not to read Kristeva's book in terms of her own ambivalence, if not hatred, toward women. While Holbein, Nerval, and Dostoevsky incur sympathy and admiration, the case of Duras is finally as dismissable as that of the "depressed women" analyzed earlier in the book. Such a misogyny that repeats the traditional paradigms of the discourse of melancholia seems all the more disturbing for being written under a woman's name, the name, no less, of a woman considered to be one of the premier voices of French feminism. Furthermore, the reactivation of the gendered categories of melancholia in conjunction with Kristeva's own particular rhetoric of violence against the feminine in general and against the maternal in particular betrays in her case an uncritical overestimation of the male term and a self-hatred generalized to all those of her own sex, who are perceived as abject and essentially inferior. If the essential nature of women is to be caught in their incapacity to kill off the mother and if the male appropriation of

---

[35]This "malaise" of modernity is marked for Kristeva not only by the popular success of a female melancholic writer but by "a fascination, not to speak of a flirtation, with Judaism" and its rhetoric of reserve (p. 231).

female subjectivity (as most overtly demonstrated in Nerval) is full of cultural significance, then as a woman reading Kristeva, I find myself angrily and inevitably positioning Kristeva herself as the evil mother, whose misogynistic domination I must either submit to at the cost of my own subjectivity or resist by killing her off as author. Either I allow her theory to essentialize me as inarticulate and insufficiently differentiated, or I am set up by her so that, transferentially speaking, I must be the aggressor toward her *qua* phallic mother who tells me she would rather have had a boy than a girl child. More unfortunately, however, does not this dilemma itself replicate the very narrow set of possibilities available to women under patriarchal law, namely silent subservience or a reactive violence whose target always seems to be another woman? Such a choice is nothing more than an alternative between different modes of complicity with a male order. Can I not mourn my mother, mourn her hatred of herself and her hatred of me, without seeking to destroy her, that is, without in some way destroying a crucial part of *my own* subjectivity?[36]

It would be too easy then to fall into the trap of analyzing Kristeva's position as evil mother, to denounce in her case a repressed identification with the mother, who would have been introjected for lack of an adequate separation or differentiation. Kristeva could then be diagnosed as a repressed melancholic, and one whose repression is signaled by her "postmodern" desire for the comedy written by French men.

More important, however, the apparent dilemma between killing

[36]On the maternal body, Kristeva says in "Motherhood According to Bellini": "The maternal body slips away from the discursive hold and immediately conceals a cipher. . . . This ciphering of the species, however, this pre- and transsymbolic memory, makes the mother mistress of neither begetting nor instinctual drive . . . ; it does make of the maternal body the stakes of a natural and "objective" control, independent of any individual consciousness. . . . The maternal body is the module of a biosocial program. Its jouissance, which is mute, is nothing more than a recording, on the screen of the preconscious" (in *Desire in Language: A Semiotic Approach to Literature and Art*, ed. Leon S. Roudiez, trans. Thomas Gora, Alice Jardine, and Leon S. Roudiez [New York: Columbia University Press, 1980], p. 241). See Elizabeth Grosz's critique of Kristeva's notion of maternity as a "process without a subject" whereby women would not have a "special link to the maternal body either as a specifically female child. . . . or in her position as mother" ("The Body of Signification," in *Abjection, Melancholia, and Love*, ed. Fletcher and Benjamin, pp. 97–98. For Kristeva, any relation between daughters and mothers must be predicated on an *essentially* depressive one as is foregrounded in her *Black Sun*. Such a reduction of their relationship to one of mutual enslavement belies Kristeva's own view of maternity as necessarily inarticulate and unable to signify unless it is positioned as the ground for repression, as the signification underlying art and religion. Hence women and maternity, daughters and mothers stand in a relation to each other that is mutually essentialist but becomes the necessary material for creative work. Women remain but the other, and Kristeva thereby reinforces the patriarchal basis of hierarchical production.

and being killed by the mother should be understood not only in terms of the patriarchal positioning of women against other women, all competing for access to the phallus, but also, as partaking in the binary logic characteristic of the imaginary. In fact, the main pitfall of Kristeva's reading is in her continued insistence on situating the problem of melancholia, as in Freud and even in Ficino, within the field of the imaginary. At best, women's melancholia or depression is thought of as a problematic access to a phallic order that is fundamentally (and uncritically) viewed as desirable. In order to escape this complicity with patriarchy and the subsequent misogynist rivalry with other women, melancholia needs to be thought out, as suggested by my earlier readings of Irigaray and Silverman, *at the very level of the symbolic*, where and only where a *collective* rearticulation of women's loss can take place. Only the radical construction of a feminine symbolic can give value and legitimacy to the voicing of women's depression, not as some personal failure to "differentiate" but as the very site of mourning, of expression, and of community.

Given such a sociocultural and political horizon, the traditional category of melancholia can be distinguished from what we now call clinical depression, but not as Kristeva does in terms of a slight degree of difference in intensity. Rather, melancholia and depression must be seen as differently constituted and legitimated *in the cultural field* according to gender. As it stands now, melancholic loss remains part of a cultural ideal predicated on lack, but a lack that is phallic even when it takes the socially extensive form of Lacan's "symbolic" castration, or when, as in Kristeva, it stipulates a violent strategy of killing off the mother in order to assume one's place in the symbolic. Such a complicity with the current (male) symbolic order and its unspoken claim to a universalizing discourse based on a patriarchal hierarchy organizes a universe of imaginary individuals, separate from community and unified only in their nostalgic quest for the lost object. Typically, when the loser is male, the loss *can* be idealized into the enabling condition of his individualistic and otherwise inexplicable "genius"; when the loser is female, loss becomes but a contingent circumstance in an essentialized and devalued depression. One task of the feminist analysis of melancholia is precisely to redeem the cause of depression, to give the depression of women the value and diginity traditionally bestowed on the melancholia of men.

In "Melancholy and Melancholia," Jennifer Radden considers the modern displacement of the term "melancholia" by that of "depression."[37] In tracing the history of the term "melancholia" and in discovering that "melancholy" was considered a fashionable illness in Renaissance England, Radden argues that in modern terms "melancholy" corresponds to "depression," and "melancholia" to "depressive illness or reaction," and that these terms "permit—and encourage—the class of those suffering melancholia or clinical depression to be set apart from the person who is merely depressed or melancholy" (p. 240). The differentiation Radden is making is an important one, since "clinical depression" is by far the most frequently used term for a condition related to behavioral rather than psychological characteristics, and therefore "melancholia" is an outmoded term for the description of a pathological condition. In discussing the differences between melancholia as a psychological description of mood and behavioral descriptions of clinical depression, Jennifer Radden states: "Clinical depression, then, unlike the earlier melancholy, is characterized as much or more by certain behavioral manifestations as by the moods and feelings it involves: by a slowing or agitation of movement, by fatigue, loss of appetite and insomnia" (p. 243). And later she adds: "The history of medicine suggests that women have long been subject to ideologically colored diagnoses and forms of treatment and these have apparently differed extensively from period to period. But one theme remains constant: medicine's prime contribution to sexist ideology, as Ehrenreich and English put it, has been 'to describe women as sick, and as potentially sickening to men'" (p. 246).

What needs to be clarified, however, is that the term "melancholy" in sixteenth-century England is but the English translation of Latin *melancholia* and the distinction was subject to considerable slippage and blurring. Whether one suffered from "melancholy" or "melancholia" prior to the replacement of these terms by "depression" or "clinical depression," the former or "outmoded" terms were the continuing legacy of the Aristotelian and specifically Ficinian reading of the *homo melancholicus*. What is important here is that "melancholia" with all its diverse spellings at different historical moments means not only a type of disease but also a form of cultural empowerment. Although Radden correctly shows how melancholia was previously a category for men ("Another

[37]Jennifer Radden, "Melancholy and Melancholia," in *Pathologies of the Modern Self: Postmodern Studies on Narcissism, Schizophrenia, and Depression*, ed. David Michael Levin (New York: New York University Press, 1987).

difference between the earlier melancholy and today's clinical depression is that the latter is a woman's complaint" [p. 243]), what needs to be stressed is that melancholia as a *cultural* category for the *exceptional* man appears concomitant with a denial of women's own claims to represent their losses within culture. Perhaps nothing more poignantly corroborates the shifting force of cultural values than the simultaneity with which the substitution of "melancholy" by "depression" is doubled by the switch in gender attribution. The glory of male melancholia becomes but the commonality—or even oblivion—of women's depression. The change in social positioning is qualified when Radden states that while the melancholic of old was "an ordinary, familiar and everyday figure, the depressive of today is increasingly rendered remote and alien, *her* condition unrelated to ordinary experience" (p. 245). Again, while the melancholic of the past may have circulated more freely within society, he who cultivated his melancholia aspired to a status *above* the commonplace. The melancholic of the past was an accredited figure of alienation and very much desirous of accentuating *his* difference from the everyday. The difference that, I think, needs to be stressed, is that women have not had the same cultural tradition, one that would enable them to express feelings of disempowerment and loss in a "non-alienated" way. The melancholic of the past was a "great man"; the stereotypical depressive of today is a woman.

Thus, what we know today as clinical depression is a form of melancholia—or melancholy—but without the romanticized discursive apparatus, that is, without a discourse suggesting that to be ill of this disease is also to be granted a privileged status. The historical disappearance of the category of melancholy has left only its devalued and quotidian counterpart, depression—which, as Radden has remarked, is now viewed as a "woman's complaint." This is perhaps why today so many women are clinically depressed, and this is why to speak of female melancholia is to speak of something that is historically mute. This is not to deny, however, that women have historically found ways to represent their loss and grief. But I argue that loss must be rethought in terms of modes of mourning and depression, which differ from the melancholic tradition. Mourning and depression have been devalued forms of loss, and it is through those categories that we can begin to read the repressed history of melancholia, or if one prefers, the repression that is the history of melancholia. And it is to some avatars of that history that I now turn.

Chapter 2

Black Humor? Gender and Genius in the Melancholic Tradition

Jennifer Radden's contention, following Barbara Ehrenreich and Deirdre English, that Western medical and philosophical practices have contributed to sexist ideology by describing women as "sick" or as "potentially sickening to man" is borne out by the tradition of humoral medicine. In particular, the impairment brought on by the melancholy humor is described as either a privileged state of inspired genius from which women are implicitly or explicitly excluded, or a pathological state—a disease—whose onset in men often refers back to some intrusive "femininity." And on the few occasions when melancholia afflicts women, it is said to occur because of the essentialized frailty and inadequacy of their "nature" (as that melancholic prince *per eccellenza*, Hamlet, says of his mother: "Frailty thy name is woman"). Indeed, melancholia in women is often diagnosed in terms of lack in regard to the phallus, a condition known as erotomania.[1] The divergence, however, between

[1]William Shakespeare, *Hamlet*, ed. Cyrus Hoy (New York: Norton, 1963), I, ii, 146. Gertrude's "frailty," as condemned by Hamlet, is that of erotomania. He accuses her of marrying too soon after his father's death: "O God, a beast that wants discourse of reason would have mourned longer" (I, ii, 150–51). Ophelia too would have been diagnosed as erotomanic. Cf. Elaine Showalter, "Representing Ophelia: Women, Madness, and the Responsibilities of Feminist Criticism," in *Shakespeare and the Question of Theory*, ed. Patricia Parker and Geoffrey Hartman (New York: Methuen, 1985), pp. 77–105; and Jacqueline Rose, *Sexuality in the Field of Vision* (London: Verso, 1986), p. 139. Sappho, of course, appears on many lists of melancholics but precisely to the extent that she represents erotomania. On melancholia and female erotomania, see Jacques Ferrand, *A Treatise on Lovesickness*, trans. and ed. Donald A.

what we could call the inspirational or philosophical and the pathological
or medical traditions of melancholia should not blind us to the misogyny
that subtends them both. When the medical tradition, for example, does
not locate in woman a source if not *the* source of the disease, the philosophical tradition's glorification of melancholia (as the condition of
genius) seems to do away altogether with women and sets apart an elite
community of men bound in their common descent from the fatherly
figure of Saturn.

With respect to the medical tradition, the Hippocratic writings were
the first to consider melancholia in terms of a clinical diagnosis by
isolating a category of disease caused by an excess of black bile, which
supposedly led to a *physiological* imbalance among the bodily fluids, or
"humors."[2] Melancholia was associated with fear, restlessness, sorrow,
lethargy, and a general moroseness of the mind and spirit. Galen later
systematized and revised this humoral theory of physiological harmony
into the fourfold schema of *psychological* complexions, whereby each
person's character was determined by the dominance of one of the humors over the others: blood, which was considered warm and moist;
yellow bile, warm and dry; black bile, cold and dry; and phlegm, cold
and moist. Blood eventually became characterized as "sanguine," and it
was generally perceived that the person in whom this type of humor
predominated maintained a stable and healthy physical and mental disposition. Grief was associated with black bile, considered to be (as
Klibansky, Panofsky, and Saxl describe it) a "noxious degeneration of
yellow bile, or alternately of the blood."[3] And therefore it happened that
medical writers began to conceive of the atrabilious person as both

Beecher and Massimo Ciavolella (Syracuse: Syracuse University Press, 1990); Massimo Ciavolella, *La "Malattia d'amore" dall' Antichità al Medioevo* (Rome: Bulzoni, 1976); and Donald
A. Beecher, "Des médicaments pour soigner la mélancolie: Jacques Ferrand et la pharmacologie
de l'amour," *Nouvelle Revue du XVIe Siècle* 4 (1976), 87–99. And for a typically traditional
and sympathetic reading of Hamlet's melancholia as the sign of an exceptional nature, see
Bridget Gellert Lyons, "La malinconia di Amleto," in *La malinconia nel Medio Evo e nel
Rinascimento*, ed. Attilio Brilli (Urbino: Quattro Venti, 1982), pp. 99–145.
²The best source for material on the history of melancholia as a clinical and interpretive
category remains Raymond Klibansky, Erwin Panofsky, and Fritz Saxl's *Saturn and Melancholy*
(New York: Basic Books, 1964). I have also drawn on Lawrence Babb, *The Elizabethan Malady:
A Study of Melancholia in English Literature from 1580 to 1642* (East Lansing: Michigan State
College Press, 1951); Rudolf Wittkower and Margot Wittkower, *Born under Saturn: The
Character and Conduct of Artists: A Documented History from Antiquity to the French Revolution*
(New York: Random House, 1963); Brilli, *La malinconia*; and Stanley W. Jackson, *Melancholia
and Depression from Hippocratic Times to Modern Times* (New Haven: Yale University Press,
1986).
³Klibansky et al., *Saturn and Melancholy*, p. 14.

physically and psychologically disturbed by a variety of (often contradictory) symptoms including sleepfulness, sleeplessness, mania, irasci-
bility, excessive lust, and impotence, but especially fear and depression:
"Constant anxiety and depression are signs of melancholy," says an
ancient Greek source.[4] Thus, from a purely physiological category, the
humors evolved into a complex system of character and mental types,
with melancholia as the most dramatically pathological and negative
type. It was certainly the medical tradition of Galen that later influenced
the patristic literature on melancholia—which Saint Hildegard of Bingen, for example, would consider a sign of man's fall into sin. The
accompanying theological concept of *acedia* (sloth) was understood as
a most grave sin, one that especially afflicted monks and was believed to
be a temptation from the devil. Later still, the notion of *tristitia* (sorrow)
entered the typology of sin, and from that concept eventually grew the
understanding that sorrow was not necessarily related to a sinful disposition but, as Giorgio Agamben has argued, to an impasse between
the desire for union with God and the feeling of hopelessness deriving
from the *taedium vita* that endlessly deferred this goal.[5]

    In late medieval romance, Tristesse and Merencolyie appeared as
threatening female figures wreaking allegorical havoc on poor young
knights and lovers. And as Klibansky, Panofsky, and Saxl point out, the
personification of melancholy stood out as being particular from "mere"
'Tristesse,' as something more menacing and at the same time more
active" (p. 222). Perhaps the most complex of these figures is the Dame
Merencolyie of Alain Chartier's *Traité de l'espérance*, who is described
as an old woman, "leene, drye, ryvelid, with a pale colour bloo as leed
and swollen," with a "downwarde" look, a troubled voice, a heavy pace,
a head wrapped in a "kerchief like as it had been through suotte and
asches," and her body clothed in the rags of "a threadbare mantille."[6]
Coming upon the poet in his "hevy and sorowfall thought," wherein

---

    [4]*Aphorismata* [attributed to Hippocrates], cited in Klibansky et al., *Saturn and Melancholy*,
p. 15. For an extended analysis of the incredibly heterogeneous symptoms of melancholia, see
Babb, *The Elizabethan Malady*.
    [5]On the question of *acedia*, Giorgio Agamben's *Stanze: La parola e il fantasma nella cultura
occidentale* (Turin: Einaudi, 1977), pp. 5–35, is indispensable; on *tristitia*, see pp. 5–19, and
Klibansky, Panofsky, and Saxl, pp. 221–28.
    [6]*L'esperance ou consolation des trois vertus, c'est à scavoir Foy, Esperance & Charité*, in *Les
oeuvres de maistre Alain Chartier*, ed. André du Chesne (Paris: Thiboust, 1617), pp. 263–64.
I cite from Margaret S. Blayney's excellent and useful edition, *Fifteenth-Century English Translations of Alain Chartier's "Le traité de l'esperance" and "Le quadrilogue invectif"* (London: Early
English Text Society/Oxford University Press, 1974), pp. 4–5.

he "aboode as a mane confusid, the visage blemishid, the wittis troubled and the bloode medlid in the body," Malencolye "sodeinly" takes him in a tight embrace, covers him with her "unhappy mantelle," and leads him off to "the lodging of infirmite, and then I was caste on a bedde of anguish and maladye." For the male poet, melancholia occurs as the sexual violence of an old hag (whose physical attributes are but the systematic negation of the idealized woman of courtly love literature[7]), a phantasmic castration in the encounter with sexual difference: such a castration is suggested when the poet is blinded by the mantle Melancholia casts over him as well as when his heart is crushed by her embrace "as in a vicegrip."

The figure of Dame Melancholy not only recalls the traditional misogynist topos of the *vagina dentata* but also acquires phallic features of her own: *Male*ncolia (as the fifteenth-century English translator interestingly spells her name) "torments" the poet's brain "with hir harde handis" as he lies "revercid upon that noyouse couche... with a faade mouth and a fayled appetite." This obviously penetrating activity leads to the opening up of the "parte that was in the myddis of my hede in the regyon of ymaginatyffe, which some men call fantasye." At that moment, from the "darkest place of my bedde," spring forth three more "horrible semblaunces and fygurys of women passing feerful to loke vpon." These "thre abhominable monstres," whose phallic menace is punctuated by the translator's orthographic fidelity to the French (ab-*homin*-able) as well as by the "sharpe whippe" held by one of them, allegorically represent "Deffyaunce," "Indignacyon," and "Desesperaunce"; they proceed to berate the poet one by one in a series of monologues culminating in Desesperaunce's admonishing the poet to commit suicide. In fact, it is only the timely awakening of his young male companion, Undrestondynge, that saves the poet from this feminine onslaught. Those dangerous female figures of destruction are then driven off and replaced with the more docile and idealized feminine (and theological) figures of faith and hope. Male reason seems to be the cure for the crippling affliction brought on by "Dame Mérencolyie."

Besides representing melancholia as a terrifying figure of phallic femininity, woman also served in medieval culture as the *cause* of that malady.

[7]Cf. Alice Colby, *The Portrait in Twelfth-Century French Literature* (Geneva: Droz, 1965); and Barbara Spackman, "Inter musam et ursam moritur, or Folengo and the Gaping 'Other' Mouth," in *Refiguring Woman: Perspectives on Gender and the Italian Renaissance*, ed. Marilyn Migiel and Juliana Schiesari (Ithaca: Cornell University Press, 1991), pp. 19–34.

And she was especially implicated in a variant form of melancholia, one associated with *amor hereos*. In a work titled *Lilium medicinale* and under the paragraph heading "amore qui hereos dicitur," Doctor Bernard of Gordon (1258–1318) discusses melancholic illness:

> The illness called *hereos* is melancholy anguish caused by love for a woman. The *cause* of this affliction lies in the corruption of the faculty to evaluate, due to a figure and a face that have made a very strong impression. When a man is in love with a woman, he thinks exaggeratedly of her figure, her face, her behavior, believing her to be the most beautiful, the most worthy of respect, the most extraordinary with the best build, in body and soul, that there can be. This is why he desires her passionately, forgetting all sense of proportion and common sense, and thinks that, if he could satisfy his desire, he would be happy. To so great an extent is his judgment distorted that he constantly thinks of the woman's figure and abandons all his activities so that, if someone speaks to him, he hardly hears him. And since this entails continuous contemplation, it can be defined as melancholy anguish. It is called *hereos* because noblemen and lords of the manor, because of plenty of pleasures and delights, often were overcome by this affliction.[8]

How then can the suffering lover be healed and once again achieve mastery and judgment over this precarious situation? Gordon suggests, as Ioan Couliano recounts in of *Eros and Magic in the Renaissance*, that one should "stage a dramatic scene" with an old woman who "should wear a rag soaked in menstrual blood" and hurl invectives against the woman who caused the melancholy: "If that proves useless, she should remove the rag from her bosom, wave it under the nose of the unhappy man, and shout in his face: 'Your friend, she is like this, she is *like this!*'" suggesting that she is only—as the *Malleus Maleficarum* is to say—'a bane of nature.' "[9] Here the old hag serves not as the disease but as its cure. This is a reversal only to the extent, however, that the hag reveals

[8]Cited in Ioan P. Couliano, *Eros and Magic in the Renaissance*, trans. Margaret Cook (Chicago: University of Chicago Press, 1987), p. 20.

[9]Couliano, *Eros and Magic*, pp. 20–21. There is a similarity between Freud's critical faculty in the melancholic and Gordon's desire to restore this faculty to the ill man. Where Freud's analysis of melancholia suggests a binary relation—which has been internalized—between the critical faculty and the incorporated object of desire, Gordon suggests that the cure for the melancholic—so that proper judgment can be restored—depends on looking at a hag, which would then reveal the truth of woman and thus expel her image from the psyche. It is the proximity of these two modes of looking—of specularizing the object of libidinal investment—that is striking, whether such "looking" is internalized as in Freud's model or externalized as in Gordon's.

the repulsive truth behind woman's dangerously seductive appearance. This function of revealing the "truth of woman" is typically performed by such figures, as Barbara Spackman has argued, in late medieval and early Renaissance misogynist literature.[10] The epistemological dilemma of gender difference is resolved by the male fantasy (both fear and desire) that behind every beautiful damsel lurks a decrepit old hag. The hag's toothless jaw, as Spackman also reminds us, is the negative sign of that other mouth, the castrating *vagina dentata*,[11] that would define all women as the "bane of nature" connoted by the bloody rag waved in the melancholic's face. As such, woman is not only made to appear "sick" or "sickening to men" but she is also the cause of the sickness in men (of the sickness that is in man?) as well as the very icon of disease itself. And with regard to melancholy, perhaps no text is more direct than Filidor's late seventeenth-century *Debate between Melancholy and Mirth*: "Melancholy... is an old woman, dressed in filthy rags with her head shrouded, seated on a stone beneath a dead tree" [Melankoley... ist ein altes Weib in verächtlichen Lumpen gekleidet mit verhülleten Haupt Sitzet auff einem Stein unter einem dürren Baum].[12]

All of this debilitating femininity seems to disappear (at least overtly) whenever the disease is given a positive value. This is what happens in the text that initiates the tradition of connecting melancholia with genius, Aristotle's *Problems* xxx, 1, and also in the influential revival of that topos in the fifteenth century at the hands of the humanist philosopher and doctor Marsilio Ficino. Before turning to a detailed examination of these two texts, I want to note that a positive reevaluation of melancholia does not *ipso facto* imply a positive reappraisal of women. In fact, as we shall see, the texts of Aristotle and Ficino proceed to a repression of the figure of woman. Her disappearance from the scene of melancholia nonetheless leaves traces of a fundamental misogyny.

Aristotle and the Humor of Outstanding Men

Subtitled "Problems connected with Thought, Intelligence, and Wisdom," Aristotle's thirtieth book of *Problems* opens with a "fact" asserted

[10]Spackman, "Inter musam et ursam moritur," p. 23.
[11]Ibid.
[12]Cited in Walter Benjamin, *The Origin of German Tragic Drama*, trans. John Osborne (London: Verso, 1977), pp. 154–55; and in Klibansky et al., *Saturn and Melancholy*, pp. 227–28.

in the form of a question: "Why is it that all men [andres] who have become outstanding [perittoì] in philosophy, statesmanship, poetry or the arts are melancholic [melancholikoi] and some to such an extent that they are infected by the disease arising from black bile [melainhs cholhs], as the story of Heracles among the heroes tells?"[13] Revising the pre-Galenic problem of the relation between the psychological "temperament" of melancholia and the physiological disease brought on by an excess of black bile, Aristotle resituates the entire problem in terms of melancholia as a condition of "greatness," as an elite affliction, in those for whom black bile "naturally" predominates, and as a diseased condition in those not so blessed. Although Aristotle begins by asserting that all uncommon or extraordinary men [pantes perittoì andres] are melancholic, he ends his discussion by stating that all melancholics are uncommon or extraordinary [perittoì], and closes the interpretive circle in a way that links being extraordinary and being melancholic in a relation of mutual identity.

Aristotle's ability to perform this logical feat is nonetheless predicated on his ascribing to melancholia an extraordinary variety of symptoms, enough to daunt even a Freud with his multiple categories. The symptoms of Aristotelian melancholy range from such physiological problems as epilepsy, apoplexy, torpor, skin sores, and varicose veins to all kinds of psychological characteristics including desire for solitude, excessive lust, fear, despondency, sluggishness, stupidity, cleverness, talkativeness, self-control, inexplicable cheeriness, mania, overconfidence, despair, madness, and suicidal impulses. "The melancholic temperament is in itself variable," says Aristotle, "just as it has different effects on those who suffer from the disease which it causes" (p. 163). To illustrate his point, Aristotle compares the effects of melancholia with those of wine, which "when it is drunk produces a variety of qualities, making men ill-tempered, kindly, merciful or reckless" and thereby "produces every sort of character": "So, just as a single individual changes his character by drinking and using a certain quantity of wine, so there are men corresponding to each character" (p. 157). The similar abilities of wine and melancholia to produce such dissimilar states suggests something more

---

[13]Aristotle, *Problems*, trans. W. S. Hett (Cambridge: Harvard University Press/London: Heinemann, 1953–57), 2 vols., 2: 155. The authorship of this text remains disputed and is only attributed to Aristotle. From our perspective, however, the correctness of the attribution makes little difference since we are interested in the *historical* effects of this text during a period when it *was* attributed to Aristotle.

than an analogy between the two: "It is evident that wine and nature produce each man's characteristics by the same means" (p. 159); "red wine above all things produces the characteristics found in the melancholic" (p. 161). The only difference turns out to be one of duration: "Wine endows man with extraordinary qualities [polun peritton] not for long but only for a short time, but nature makes them permanent for so long as the man lives" (p. 159).

At the same time, he argues that the changeability of the symptoms is nothing more than a variation in body heat: "[The] melancholic humor is already mixed in nature; for it is a mixture of hot and cold; for nature consists of these two elements. So black bile becomes both very hot and very cold" (p. 161); "like water, sometimes [the melancholic temperament] is cold and sometimes hot" (p. 163). As a passing disease that ends in due time (one to which the melancholic by natural temperament is no less subject than others), excessive black bile is cold and "produces apoplexy or torpor, or despondency or fear, but if it becomes overheated, it produces cheerfulness with song, and madness, and the breaking out of sores and so forth" (pp. 161–63). Black bile may be just a temporary disturbance for those people who fall ill of this disease, but it becomes the determining influence on the character in "those with whom this temperament exists by nature" (163). It thereby becomes a determination that can be calculated according to temperature:

> Those for instance in whom the bile is considerable and cold become sluggish and stupid, while those with whom it is excessive and hot become mad, clever or amorous and easily moved to passion and desire, and some become more talkative. But many, because this heat is near to the seat of the mind, are affected by the diseases of madness or frenzy, which accounts for the Sibyls, soothsayers, and all inspired persons, when their condition is due not to disease but to a natural mixture. Maracus, the Syracusan, was an even better poet when he was mad. But those with whom the excessive heat has sunk to a moderate amount are melancholic, though more intelligent and less eccentric, but they are superior to the rest of the world in many ways, some in education, some in the arts and others again in statesmanship. (p. 163)

Out of this new variety of character effects, which range from sluggish stupidity to the mad frenzy of the sibyls, emerges once again the figure of the great man, "more intelligent and less eccentric," "superior to the rest of the world in many ways." Not just a sub-variety of the melancholic temperament, this thermodynamic equilibrium represents the quintessence of melancholia: "Those with whom the excessive heat has sunk to a moderate amount *are melancholic*." For that "eminent" or "uncommon" being who is the melancholic by nature, the excesses of sluggish stupidity (like the Christian *acedia*) and maddened frenzy are psychological risks brought on by the heating or cooling of the black bile:

> To sum up what we have said, the melancholic are not equable in behavior, because the power of the black bile is not even; for it is both very cold and very hot. But because it has an effect on character (for heat and cold are the greatest agents in our lives for the making of character), just like wine according as it is mixed in our body in greater or less quantity it makes our dispositions of a particular kind. Both wine and black bile are full of air. But since it is possible that even [a] varying state may be well attempered, and in a sense be a good condition, and since the condition may be warmer when necessary and then again cold, or conversely, owing to the presence of excess, all melancholic persons are out of the ordinary [perittoi], not owing to disease but by nature. (p. 169)

Melancholia thus appears as a privileged but also perilous condition. And in their references to the Aristotelian text, it is certainly as a peril that the medical tradition from the Stoics through Scholasticism viewed it.[14] Inasmuch as it could humble the condition of eminent men, melancholia was undesirable and a disease in need of a cure. In fact, this medical/philosophical tradition echoed Aristotle's words as a warning in, for example, Chartier's depiction of Dame Malencolye: "Hir doctrine haue ben and oftintymes by the high wittis and the grette vndirstonding of persones and excellent men gretly troubled and made derke aftir the havntyng or exercyse of to depe and diuerse thoughtis" (p. 5). As Klibansky, Panofsky, and Saxl have demonstrated at length in their history of the phenomenon, it was not until Ficino that the privileged dimension of the melancholic temperament was revived.

But if Aristotle does not yet encode the perils of melancholia in terms of the feminine, his description of it does suggest a masculine prerogative, the specifically *androcentric* privilege of "all uncommon *males*" [pantes perittoi andres]. Indeed, Aristotle's choice of eminent melancholics seems to bear out this gendering of melancholia: Heracles, Lys-

---

[14]Cf. Klibansky et al., *Saturn and Melancholy*, pp. 67–97; and Agamben, *Stanze*, pp. 5–24.

ander the Syracusan, Ajax, Bellerophon, Empedocles, Plato, Socrates, Maracus the poet, Archelaus the king of Macedonia. As much later in Freud, the only mention of a female melancholic is not to a *named* woman but to a generic category, the Sibyls, who exemplify the "madness or frenzy" [manikois o enthousiostikois] brought about by the over-heating of the black bile. Aristotle underscores a doubtful eminence to be attributed to this excessive condition by the qualifying and self-contradictory remark that "many, because this heat is near to the seat of the mind, are affected by the diseases of madness or frenzy, which accounts for the Sibyls, soothsayers, and all inspired persons, when their condition is due not to disease but to a natural mixture." In order to substantiate the notion of an inspirational madness that would be "nat-ural" rather than accidentally brought on by "disease," Aristotle at this moment brings forward the case of "Maracus, the Syracusan, [who] was an even better poet when he was mad [ekstaih]." The heightened ability of the mad poet—a topos whose legacy in Western culture would be-come quite prominent—is thus positioned as an unambiguous example of melancholic genius over and against the cases of "Sibyls, soothsayers, and all inspired persons," for whom moments of prophetic vision may be due only to an occasional disease. This category of the disease serves to call into doubt, if not to exclude, the possibility of there being a melancholic woman. In other words, if a woman happens to express all the manic-depressive characteristics of uncommon inspiration, it is be-cause she is sick and not because she bears the "natural" relation to genius that marks the mad poet. (True to the ensuing tradition of West-ern medicine and philosophy, woman appears as an object to be treated but not as a *subject* of knowledge.[15]) This is not, by any means, the last time we will see the figure of the mad poet displace— or repress—the possibility for an *accredited* (as opposed to a disparaged) feminine melancholia.

This masculinization of melancholic genius is not restricted to what some readers might view as my tendentious use of Aristotle's "examples." (And if I belabor this text of Aristotle's, it is not simply to discover the truth of the author's personal misogyny, which should surprise no one. Instead, it is to unpack the far-reaching influence of this essay on the crystallization of an affective paradigm, melancholic genius, that at first

[15]The lack of attention given women in medical studies has become increasingly apparent. See Mary Lake Polan, "Research That Ignores Women's Health Problems," *Sacramento Bee*, 9 March 1991, B7; rpt. from *Los Angeles Times*.

glance would not seem to be the effect of an en-gendering discursive practice.) Aristotle's descriptions of other gender-specific features of melancholia include his "explanation" of male tumescence as well as of the thermodynamic consequences of ejaculation. The former occurs within Aristotle's extended analogy between wine and melancholia, where both are considered to be "full of breath": "this is why physicians say that diseases of the lungs and chest are due to black bile. And the power of wine is due to air. So wine and the atrabilious temperament are similar in nature. Froth shows the wine contains air. . . . And for this reason wine makes men inclined to love, and Dionysus and Aphrodite are rightly associated with each other; and the melancholic are usually lustful. For sexual excitement is due to breath. The penis proves this, as it quickly increases from small to large by inflation." (p. 159) Ejaculation (which is physiologically "due to the impulse of the breath" [p. 161]) leads to cheerfulness in men when a large amount of semen is expelled, "for they are relieved of waste product and of breath and of excessive heat" (p. 169). Furthermore, those who emit a small amount of semen "are usually rather depressed; for they are chilled by sexual intercourse because they are deprived of something important" (169). The thermodynamics of the black bile thus define melancholia not only as male, but as downright phallic. And a concomitant fear of woman is also inscribed into the risk of losing too much heat during sexual intercourse, that is, of being "deprived of something important." We even have a prefigurement of the enchantress-turned-hag motif suggested in the analogy with drunkenness, where Aristotle says that a man is led "to kiss one whom no one would kiss, if he were sober, either because of appearance or age" (p. 159).

The extent of this phallic essence of melancholia, however can only be appreciated if we briefly widen our view to consider the general place of woman in Aristotelian physiology. According to Aristotle, the female is the result of a generative event not carried through to its final conclusion,[16] she is less fully developed than a man, is colder and moister. In fact, the physiological thermodynamics we have seen at work in the analysis of melancholia, far from being value-neutral or simply quirky, undergird the Aristotelian theory of gender difference. This coupling of the opposition between male and female with that between hot and cold

---

[16]Ian MacLean, *The Renaissance Notion of Woman: A Study in the Fortune of Scholasticism and Medical Science in European Intellectual Life* (Cambridge: Cambridge University Press, 1980), p. 8.

runs throughout the entire Aristotelian corpus but becomes most explicit in book IV of *The Generation of Animals*. Furthermore, feminine coldness is there understood as an *essential incapacity*—not even as coldness per se but as a fundamental *lack* of heat:

> But the male and the female are distinguished by a certain capacity and incapacity. (For the male is that which can concoct and form and discharge a semen carrying with it the principle of form—by "principle" I do not mean a material principle out of which comes into being an offspring resembling a parent, but I mean the first moving cause, whether it have power to act as such in the thing itself or in something else—but the female is that which receives semen, but cannot form it or discharge it.) And all concoction works by means of heat. Therefore the males of animals must needs be hotter than the females.[17]

The hot male's "concoction" of semen is set against the cold female's overabundance of blood. Through such a juxtaposition, Aristotle both "explains" the phenomenon of menstruation and is constrained to argue against the traditional association of blood with heat: "Females, owing to inability to concoct, have a great quantity of blood, for it cannot be worked up into semen" (p. 1186). In the same way, the embryo that does not achieve a sufficient temperature results in a female offspring: it "is female because of its inability to concoct and of the coldness of the sanguineous nutriment" (p. 1186). The inferiority of women—their essence as lack—is the unsurprising conclusion of this theory of temperament: "For females are weaker and colder in nature, and we must look upon the female character as being a sort of natural deficiency. Accordingly while it is within the mother it develops slowly because of its coldness (for development is concoction, and it is heat that concocts, and what is hotter is easily concocted); but after birth it quickly arrives at maturity and old age on account of its weakness, for all inferior things come sooner to their perfection, and as this is true of works of art so it is of what is formed by nature" (p. 1199)

In the ninth book of *The History of Animals*, some further "psychological" consequences of this inferiority are drawn:

> The female is softer in disposition, is more mischievous, less simple, more impulsive, and more attentive to the nurture of the young; the male, on

---

[17] *The Complete Works of Aristotle, the Revised Oxford Translation*, ed. Jonathan Barnes (Princeton: Princeton University Press, 1984), 1: 1184.

the other hand, is more spirited, more savage, more simple and less cunning. The traces of these characteristics are more or less visible everywhere, but they are especially visible where character is the more developed, and most of all in man.

The fact is, the nature of man is the more rounded off and complete, and consequently in man the qualitites or capacities above referred to are found most clearly. Hence woman is more compassionate than man, more easily moved to tears, at the same time is more jealous, more querulous, more apt to scold and to strike. She is, furthermore, more prone to despondency and less hopeful than the man, more void of shame, more false of speech, more deceptive, and of more retentive memory. (1: 948–49)

Many of these "female" characteristics evoke the emotional symptoms of melancholy, not only in Aristotle's account but also at the other end of the historical spectrum, in the Freudian elements of dejection and abrogation of interest in the outside world, including the melancholic's shamelessness before others and incessant talking. The similarity—in fact—is striking and seems to suggest that women are particularly prone to melancholy. On the other hand, the essential coldness of women, their "incapacity" to heat up sufficiently to produce the frothy semen that we earlier saw linked with melancholia, seems to limit them to the "cold" version of melancholia, to the symptoms of "torpor, despondency and fear": "Woman is . . . more easily moved to tears, . . . more prone to despondency and less hopeful than the man." Yet the idea that, constitutionally speaking, woman is subject only to the cold-depressive features of melancholia contradicted by Aristotle's sole example of melancholia in women, that of the overheated, manic Sibyls. If we keep in mind the phallic foundations of melancholia as described by Aristotle as well as the thermal threat to men that women represent for him, we should view the example of the Sibyls (an example whose value, as we saw earlier, is already undermined by its possible roots in the accident of disease rather than in the essential nature of temperament) as a sign that betrays the text's misogynist motivations rather than as some simple logical inconsistency. For if women can attain the extremely hot as well as the extremely cold boundaries of melancholia, why should they not find their place *per eccellenza* among the uncommon eminences, the *perittoi* of melancholic genius?

A rather disturbing answer can be found if we shift registers from what Lacan would term the Aristotelian "imaginary" of thermal physiology with its binary thinking to the "symbolics" of eminence as described in the *Politics* I, 13. In discussing the quality of excellence, Aristotle there raises the question of "whether there is any excellence at all" in slaves, women, and children—as opposed to the implicit, natural excellence of the freemen who rule over them. Aristotle then justifies this hierarchy by making an analogy with a split in the soul that prefigures the psychic division we saw earlier in Freud's melancholic subject: just as in the soul "one part naturally rules, and the other is subject, . . . the one being the excellence of the rational, and the other of the irrational part," so do the "excellences of characters" vary between the rational rule of the freemen and the irrationality of the ruled: "All should partake of them [these excellences], but only in such manner and degree as is required by each for the fulfillment of his function. . . . Clearly, then, excellence of character belongs to all of them; but the temperance of a man and of a woman, or the courage and justice of a man and of a woman, are not, as Socrates maintained, the same; the courage of a man is shown in commanding, of a woman in obeying" (p. 1999). Aristotle concludes by citing the verse that "Silence is a woman's glory" but adds, "This is not equally the glory of man" (p. 2000).

Here we can discern the workings of a double bind. If a melancholic woman achieves uncommon excellence, it can only be the excellence of the good, dutiful wife and mother, who stays at home and remains silent, chaste, and virtuous.[18] Interestingly, such a good wife, as we have already noted, is also described by Freud over two millennia later as "perhaps more likely to fall ill" of melancholia than the woman of whom "we would have nothing good to say" ("Mourning and Melancholia," *S.E.* 14: 247). But if feminine eminence is tantamount to silence (if the "bad" woman, the woman of "ill repute," is the one of whom there is "nothing good to say," the "good" woman under the patriarchal arrangement would be one of whom there is *nothing at all* to say), such an eminence can hardly be called eminent. Indeed, to define the uncommon woman as the common wife is precisely the exclusionary move of a phallocracy that attempts to deny women's access to the symbolic order as anything other than objects of exchange between men. Just as the perfection of woman lies in her being imperfect, so too her "eminence" implies her oblivion.

[18]See my "In Praise of Virtuous Women? For a Genealogy of Gender Morals in Renaissance Italy," *Annali d'Italianistica* 7 (1989), 66–87.

The Aristotelian interpretation of melancholia allows for its possible reevaluation as a cultural value at the same time that it patriarchally implies the exclusion of women. Such an implicit casting out of women from melancholia as empowerment should be read against the prevalent devaluation of melancholia as disease which is all too often coded by its representation *as* woman. The Aristotelian model would be significantly upgraded and expanded by Ficino, to whom we now turn, but its effects lingered covertly, as we have seen, as late as in Freud and are openly renewed in the contemporary thought of Giorgio Agamben:

> A bringing up to date of the list cited by Aristotle in *Problems* xxx (Heracles, Bellerophon, Heraclites, Democritus, Maracus) runs the risk of being very long. After a first reappearance among the love poets of the thirteenth century, the great return of melancholia began with humanism. Among artists, the cases of Michaelangelo, Dürer and Pontormo remain exemplary. A second epidemic is in Elizabethan England: the exemplary case is that of John Donne. The third epoch of melancholia is in the nineteenth century; among the victims figure: Baudelaire, Nerval, De Quincey, Coleridge, Strindberg, Huysmans. In each of these three epochs, melancholia was interpreted, with a daring polarity, as something at once positive and negative. (*Stanze*, p. 16)

Certainly, looking at this list, one would wonder again if any women have ever been melancholic. Yet a relation to femininity reappears in Agamben's discourse of the history of melancholia, a relation that not only reconnects the two traditions we have delineated (i.e., the overtly misogynist and the implicitly exclusionary) but that also pinpoints the specificity of Ficino's influential revision of the discourse of melancholia. Perhaps this arrangement throws light onto why Irigaray chooses to speak about hysteria as the site of feminine empowerment. Perhaps it is a measure of defense—one that some feminists would see as "essentialized." But if we consider the way melancholia has been assumed by culture as an empowering form of male eros, then I think we can also understand the position of anger from which Irigaray speaks and why she speaks of female hysteria. In hysteria at least women *have been* historically represented. If we study, however, the way melancholia has been given a particular symbolic status, we discover that melancholia as a discourse exceeds the clinical in a strict sense when it encodes a form of male "greatness" and eros, whether it be Aristotle's discussion of heroes or Freud's discussion of Hamlet. Historically in between the two,

Marsilio Ficino is important for having foregrounded the sentiment of lack and loss as the subjective condition of melancholia, a view that stands in dramatic contrast to the Aristotelian and Galenic traditions' multiple and contradictory symptomatology. Although the abstract physiological notion of heat "loss" is implicit in Aristotle's melancholia, without Ficino's privileging of the concept of loss as the sign of the philosopher's "divine frenzy" in the positive Platonic sense Freud's later libidinal economics of melancholia is unthinkable.

Having analyzed the relation between melancholia and love and having seen them as historically conjoined, Agamben also concludes that what is at stake is the melancholic's relation to a lost object of desire. Now in the theological literature of the Middle Ages, as we already know, this lost object is God.[19] In the literature of troubadour poetry and later of the *dolce stil nuovo*, it is precisely the figure of woman that comes to stand for the place of desire. In both cases, a way is found to speak about a desire that cannot be consummated. Desire for God or for a woman would be a way to prolong desire to the extent that to live in desire is to exacerbate it: "In this perspective, melancholia would not so much be the regressive reaction to the loss of an object of love as it would be the fantasmatic capacity to make an inappropriatable object seem lost. If the libido behaves *as if* a loss had taken place, even though *nothing* in reality has been lost, this is so because it stages in this way a simulation where what was not able to be lost because it had never been possessed because, perhaps, it was never real, can be appropriated as though it were a lost object" (pp. 25–26). For Agamben, melancholia is a privileging of absence in order for the desiring fantasy to take hold. As Agamben describes it, the deferral inherent in this form of subjectivity is grounded in an absence that has everything to do with an ideal—with the longing for a union with God, or, as I will argue, with a de-corporealized (idealized) woman—an ideal of which the melancholic is aware and which empowers his fantasy in terms of the absence itself as the source of *his* emotional state.[20] If we reinterpret Agamben, then we must add that it is not simply a question of a lost

[19]See also, on the relation between God as lost object and the rise of mysticisim in late medieval Europe, Michel de Certeau, *La fable mystique, XVIe–XVIIe siècles* (Paris: Gallimard, 1981).
[20]A similar analysis of the absence of women as a stand-in for male lack can be found in Jacques Lacan, *Feminine Sexuality: Jacques Lacan and the Ecole Freudienne*, trans. Jacqueline Rose, ed. Juliet Mitchell and Jacqueline Rose (New York: Norton, 1982), pp. 141, 149–61. Cf. Rose's introduction, pp. 48–49.

object to be somehow reappropriated or "incorporated" but of an ambivalent relation to loss that empowers itself as fantasy to the extent that the idealized absent object is kept present in the very attention paid to its absence. Agamben is thus able to draw together the Freudian text of "Mourning and Melancholia" with the ancient and medieval traditions.

In reading "Mourning and Melancholia," Agamben insists on the elusiveness of the neurosis to clinical analysis: there exists an ambivalence toward the lost object, and one is never quite sure in melancholia what the loss really is. Melancholia, for Agamben, becomes then not merely a metapsychological problem, but a metaphysical one coextensive with the history of Western philosophical thought. Far from comprising a resistance to Western metaphysics, melancholia is complicitous with it, for finally melancholia is a way for men to talk about their exile, about their losses, and about their desire for a union that cannot be had but that points to some kind of truth. What Agamben does not go on to say is how this metaphysics of melancholia interlocks with its gendering, with the *masculine* subjectivity that bemoans an absent object.

If men cultivate melancholia as the site of a certain form of male eros, would it not work to maintain women at a distance, to define the moral basis for melancholia as one in which woman functions merely as a detour or strategy whereby the purity of the "sufferer" is measured in terms of the *pathos* of his abstention from women?[21]

Ficino's Philosophical Celebration of Loss

The revival of the classics in humanist Italy led to the rediscovery of melancholy as the possible inscription of genius in men and therefore rescued it from the criticism it had received from medical literature and from the church fathers. As Klibansky, Panofsky, and Saxl have argued, "Out of the intellectual situation of humanism—that is to say out of the awareness of freedom experienced with a sense of tragedy—there arose the notion of a genius which ever more urgently claimed to be emancipated in life and works from the standards of 'normal' morality

---

[21]For a discussion, on a very different set of texts, of such suffering as a masculinist strategy, see Christopher Newfield, "The Politics of Male Suffering: Masochism and Hegemony in the American Renaissance," *Differences* 1 (Fall 1989), 55–87.

and the common rules of art."²² And as they have also underscored, it was above all the Florentine philosopher Marsilio Ficino, a self-described melancholic, "who really gave shape to the idea of the melancholy man of genius and revealed it to the rest of Europe," and who defined the affliction as the privileged subjectivity of the lettered, a subjectivity with its own set of risks and with its own rewards.²³ In the first of the three books of *On Life* (1489), Ficino details a strict and elaborate regime for scholars wishing to negotiate the perils of phlegm and black bile, "as if they were sailing past Scylla and Charybdis."²⁴ Black bile is the more extensively discussed of the two "occupational hazards" faced by men of letters, but melancholia is also reinterpreted, above and beyond Aristotle's *Problems* xxx, as the very condition of intellectual achievement.

The motivation—even the urgency—of this reinterpretation of melancholia and the elaboration of a set of guidelines for harnessing the ambiguous qualities of the affliction to the scholar's benefit can be glimpsed in the famous exchange of letters between Ficino and his "unique friend" Giovanni Cavalcanti, wherein Cavalcanti upbraids the translator of Plato for bemoaning the "malign influence" of Saturn, the planet presiding over Ficino's birth. Traditionally, Saturn was considered an unlucky and malicious planet, and it was generally thought that those born under its auspices were unhappy and taciturn men prone to melancholic torpor. Reminding Ficino that Saturn also "looked down on the divine Plato's arising," Cavalcanti admonishes Ficino to "beware of transferring your blame to that supreme star which has caused you to be heaped up with almost infinite and very great gifts."²⁵ After detailing Ficino's myriad achievements, Cavalcanti asks, "Will you therefore accuse Saturn, he who purposed that you should rise above other men as far as he himself rises above other planets?" (2: 32). In closing, Cavalcanti requests that Ficino sing a "hymn of recantation" to the highest planet, much-maligned Saturn. Accepting his friend's criticisms, Ficino none-

²²Klibansky et al., *Saturn and Melancholy*, p. 254.
²³Ibid., p. 255.
²⁴Marsilius Ficinus, *De vita libri tres*, ed. Martin Plessner (Hildesheim: Georg Olms Verlag, 1978). Since this facsimile edition is not paginated, all page numbers as well as English translations are from *Marsilio Ficino: The Book of Life*, ed. and trans. Charles Boer (Irving, Tex.: Spring Publications, 1980). See also the more recent *Three Books on Life*, ed. and trans. Carol Kaske and John R. Clark (Binghamton, N.Y.: Medieval Texts and Studies in conjunction with the Renaissance Society of America, 1989).
²⁵*The Letters of Marsilio Ficino*, trans. Language Department of the School of Economic Science, London, American ed. (New York: Gingko Press, 1985), 2: 31. Hereafter cited in the text by volume and letter number alone.

theless insists on his melancholic temperament: "I accuse a certain melancholy disposition, a thing which seems to me to be very bitter unless, having been softened, it may in a measure be made sweet for us by frequent use of the lyre. Saturn seems to have impressed the seal of melancholy on me from the beginning" (2: 33). Realizing that he is again about to blame the heavenly body for his woes, Ficino suggests an alternative: "But where have I so heedlessly fallen? I see that you are again, not unjustly, urging me to sing another hymn of recantation to Saturn. So, what shall I do? I shall seek a shift; either I shall say, if you wish, that a nature of this kind does not issue from Saturn; or, if it should be necessary that it does issue from Saturn, I shall, in agreement with Aristotle, say that this nature is a unique and divine gift" (2: 34).

The reference to the passage in Aristotle's *Problems* is also an interpretation of it, one that replaces the physiological cause that makes some men uncommon, eminent, or out of the ordinary [perittoì] by a "divine gift," which implies an *unambiguously* positive closeness to God and which positions the melancholic as the privileged recipient of a heavenly gift. Not just out of the ordinary, the Ficinian melancholic is decidedly *above* the ordinary. Nor does Ficino remain content with the alternative that closes his letter, between Saturn's non-influence on the melancholic temperament if it is destructive, and its influence if melancholy is divinely beneficial. For one of the concerns of *De vita*, published over a dozen years after this letter, is to situate the influence of the astral bodies on our health and character. In that work, Saturn remains along with Mars as the most negative of planetary forces, with the outstanding exception of the "contemplative mind" for whom it is a friend and for whom "alone Saturn is propitious" (p. 165). Harmful to all others, Saturn is the scholar's best friend since he is *the* astral source for a melancholic temperament that sets the scholar above and apart from the common crowd, the *vulgus*.

Depression for "qualified" men becomes a sign of spiritual greatness which allows such men to capitalize on difference by making it a difference that counts. Ficino not only turned melancholia into an inscription of something extraordinary for men but, more specifically, he made the Saturnine man—the melancholic man—an emblem of the mentally creative man, more specifically of the *literarum studiosi*. But while as Ficino's rereading of Aristotle rescued melancholy from characterization as a wholly negative illness, he also rewrote the melancholic man in terms of his own Neoplatonism. What is underscored in Ficino, then, is not so much the debilitating effects on the person in question but rather the way the melancholic is poised for the quest for truth, as a nostalgic desire to return to an original state. Whereas the Aristotelian picture of melancholy afflicting all great men implied, as Klibansky and company point out, a maxim of "be different" rather than "be virtuous" (*Saturn and Melancholy*, p. 41), with Ficino the two collapse into each other such that to be different is also to be virtuous. In other words, difference from the common *vulgus* is the sign of the melancholic's virtue and intellect. Intellect emblematizes virtue since, for Ficino, intellect is itself a virtuous striving for knowledge and self-knowledge. The one, therefore, who most perfectly embodies virtue is the one who loves excessively the "heavenly Venus," who in turn signifies the desire for truth and knowledge. Hence, not only is Socrates Ficino's hero but he also becomes emblematic of what heroism stood for: (h)eros or love. Already described by Aristotle as a melancholic, Socrates is seen by Ficino as both the perfect lover *and* the perfect melancholic. Thus from the system of humors in Galen and Aristotle, in Ficino we come to a *platonizing* of the melancholic genius, a new vision of the melancholic man as one whose quest for knowledge is inspired by an eros that fuels his desire for a relationship with the transcendent.

Ficino's discussion on melancholic genius takes place as the unprecedented articulation of humoral medicine with Plotinian cosmology, of Aristotelian physiology with the Platonic ethics of "divine frenzy," of pharmacological prescriptions for corporeal good health with the psychology of desire as a dialectic of lack. To understand this reworking of the philosophical tradition that issues in *De vita libri tres*, we need to consider the emergence of the melancholic being as a crucial category in his earlier *De amore* (1469), a book on the art of love written by way of a commentary on Plato's *Symposium*. Probably Ficino's most influential work, *De amore* was widely received and admired throughout the European aristocratic court milieu, and its ideas spawned the Neoplatonic poetry so predominant in that milieu from the late fifteenth through the mid-seventeenth centuries. Historically coincident with the economic decline of the feudal hierarchy, Ficinian Neoplatonism describes an eros whose content was the nostalgic one of recapturing a lost ideal. Furthermore, the act of falling in love displayed the elite condition of its sufferer, propelled to the heavens by his amatory anguish. The elite character of this eros (and its popularity among the social and cultural elite of the Renaissance) was guaranteed by Ficino's categorical opposition between *two* types of eros, or as he calls them, two Venuses, the "heavenly Venus" [la celeste Venere] and the "vulgar Venus" [la vulgare Venere].[26] Whereas the heavenly Venus leads us to "understand superior things," the vulgar Venus allows us to "procreate inferior ones" (p. 117); the heavenly Venus "raises" us "above the nature of man and passes [him] into a god" (p. 168) [inalza l'uomo sopra l'uomo e in Dio lo converte] (p. 211), but the vulgar Venus "brings men down to the level of the beast" (p. 168). The heavenly Venus allows us to transcend the corporeal and to ascend back to the "one" from which we all descend; the vulgar Venus aggravates the fall into the state of multiplicity that in Ficino's Neoplatonic system is also the state of the body.

For Ficino, "the relation between cause and effect is one of necessary decline" (p. 138) [come suole ogni effecto essere meno degno che sua cagione]" (p. 164), the ultimate cause being that originary "one." From this singular wholeness derive the multiplicity and materiality of the cosmos, which remains nonetheless permeated by that "one" as its pro-creative soul [anima mundi]. Birth is nothing more than the moment when the soul is "depressed into a body" (*Letters* 1: vii), an incorporation that has the immediate effect of blocking the soul's hitherto unhampered knowledge. Knowledge, then, can never be the acquisition of "new" insights; it can only be the remembering of what was once known but has been forgotten. Contemplative study is defined by the recuperation of the epistemological loss that occurred in our birth as embodiment, that is, in the degenerative materiality we call life. This situation of loss to be overcome is also the origin of love, which Ficino rigorously views as a dialectics of desire grounded in the inability to overcome lack.

This is the lesson of the allegory of Porus and Penia, whose names "mean plenty and poverty respectively" (p. 116). It is from their inter-course, as Plato described it, "on the birthday of Venus, while the gods were feasting," that love was born. Comments Ficino:

> Why is love partly rich and partly poor? Because we are not accustomed to desire that which we completely possess or that which we completely lack. For since everyone seeks that which he does not have, if a person possesses the whole thing, what more can he want? But also, since no one wants things which are unknown to him, anything that we love must

[26]Marsilio Ficino, *El libro dell'Amore*, ed. Sandra Niccoli (Florence: Olschki, 1987), p. 129. English translations are from *Commentary on Plato's Symposium on Love*, ed. and trans. Sears Jayne, 2d rev. ed. (Dallas, Tex.: Spring Publications, 1985), p. 117.

necessarily have been known to us beforehand in some way. . . . Therefore anyone who loves something certainly does not yet possess it completely in itself, but through the activities of his soul he knows the thing, judges it pleasing, and believes that he can attain it. This knowing, judging, and hope are a kind of present anticipation, as it were, of an absent good. For he would not desire it unless it pleased him, and it would not please him unless it had been pre-tasted in some way. Therefore, since lovers certainly partly have what they desire but partly do not have it, love is not inappropriately mixed of a certain poverty and plenty. (p. 117)

Again, love occurs as a desire for something already known and already partly possessed. In fact, this partial possession is the condition for the generation of the desire. There needs to be a certain lack of possession, in other words, to sustain the desire, since overcoming the lack eradicates the desire.

What is particularly interesting about Ficino's version of this traditional logical dilemma is his articulation of the fable with its allegorical sense. Porus, for him, is not just the figure of satiety, but "the ray of God" [el razzo di Dio], which brings, "as though in a kind of seed, the Reasons of all things" into the darkness and ignorance of Penia. While Porus is associated with Saturn and Jupiter,[27] Penia is connected to "the power of understanding, which we think is Venus": "This power is of its own nature formless and dark unless it is illuminated by God, like the eye's power before the arrival of the sun. This darkness we think is *Penia*, a lack, as it were, or deficiency of light. Finally, that power or understanding, turned by a certain natural instinct toward its parent, receives from Him the divine ray, which is *Porus*, or plenty" (p. 116). The seminal light of Porus enters Penia as a phallic illumination, by whose "flames" Penia's "natural instinct is kindled." This natural instinct is what turns that power of understanding "which we think is Venus" toward its parent, the supreme God, identified here with the masculine figures of Uranus, Saturn, and Jupiter: "It is certainly for this reason that that heavenly Venus, aroused by her first taste of the divine ray, is carried by love toward the complete plenitude of the whole light" (p. 117).

This copulative allegory eroticizes knowledge, portraying it as an

---

[27]While Plato has the meeting between Prous and Penia take place in the "garden of Jupiter," Ficino's apparently gratuitous addition of Saturn betrays his own agenda, which we earlier glimpsed in the letter to Cavalcanti; Ficino emphasizes the central importance melancholia has for the inspired genius of the lover of knowledge.

insemination that reveals what was already known but has been forgotten. For Ficino, then, there is no such thing as a desire for the
unknown. What can be called "knowledge" is nothing more than the
aftereffect of the mind's recuperative "ascent" to God whereby the mind
retrieves all that was lost at the moment of its descent or "depression"
into the body. At the same time, we should not overlook the obvious
gendering of this relationship, which posits a phallic godhead in relation
to which the "lower" term is always feminized. The other name in Ficino
for body or matter or multiplicity is "woman," the essentialized lack
that is Penia and that waits for the "fulfillment" of Porus, the "masculine"
principle of unity, clarity, and intelligence.

For the lover, then, it is not the body of the beloved that is loved
but what is perceived beyond the body, "for he does not desire this or
that body but he admires, desires and is amazed by the splendor of the
celestial majesty shining through bodies" (p. 52).[28] For Ficino, the whole
point is not to get fixated on the beloved's body or to fall prey to what
is the necessary ignorance of the vulgar Venus: "Lovers do not know
what they desire or seek, for they do not know God himself. . . . We
rightly do not know what we are desiring or suffering" (p. 52). In
Freudian terms, the cathexis of the beloved occurs as an unconscious
pull toward fulfillment in that other, but the fulfillment of that libidinal
impulse remains impossible since the unknown or unconscious force of
the drive is conditioned by a longing for something incorporeal. Hence
the "vulgar" lover always misses his object, and so can never achieve
satisfaction. As we shall see, this repression described in Ficino's schema
would be precisely that which causes the melancholic disturbance, although Ficino himself does not posit his own melancholia in these terms.
What we are here discovering, however, is the fictionality of the lost
object as cause of a melancholic disturbance, since the lost object is
already a myth about origin and thus creates in the person desirous for
fusion with a mythological ideal an irrevocable sense of loss. This loss,
it is true, is also the condition for desire and for knowledge. Herein we
see a startling prefigurement of Freud's own reading of the melancholic

---

[28]Bizarrely, Ficino's discussion of the beloved body is similar to Lacan's statement that
"it isn't the lack of this or that but lack of being whereby being exists" (*Seminar II: The Ego
in Freud's Theory and in the Technique of Psychoanalysis, 1954–1955*, ed. Jacques-Alain Miller,
trans. Sylvana Tomaselli [New York: Norton, 1988], p. 223). The question remains as to
whether or not there is a metaphysical slippage into a lack that transcends all lack or a celestial
body that transcends all earthly ones.

as one who does not know "what" it is he has lost but whose loss is signified by his very suffering from this unknowability, which as we know is not so much unknown as unconscious, as repressed.

And just as the specificity of narcissism was crucial to Freud's elaboration of the distinction between mourning and melancholia, so too (and much earlier) does Ficino offer narcissism as the important theoretical discovery of his inquiry into the psychology, or rather, the metaphysics of love. Just as all knowledge is reduced to anamnesis, so too what one loves in the beloved is also what the beloved *recalls* in the lover: "This is how it happens that everyone loves most, not those who are the most beautiful, but those who are his own, that is similarly born, even if they are less beautiful than many others. . . . The soul thus stricken recognizes the image before it as something which is its own" (p. 114). This amatory narcissism is excused, however, as a positive regression toward the "one" or God by the reduction of differences, that is, by circumventing the corruption called multiplicity. To love ourselves in the body of the beloved is acceptable if and only if "we shall not really be loving these things, but God in them" (p. 144). And here, in the conclusion to speech VI, is where the recuperation of loss represented as theological redemption overcomes the threat of castration understood as desire for the body (for woman):

And anyone who surrenders himself to God with love in this life will recover himself in God in the next life. Such a man will certainly return to his own Idea, the Idea by which he was created. There any defect in him will be corrected again; he will be united with his Idea forever. For the true man and the Idea of a man are the same. For this reason as long as we are in this life, separated from God, none of us is a true man, for we are separated from our Idea or Form. To it, divine love and piety will lead us. Even though we may be dismembered and mutilated here, then, joined by love to our own Idea, we shall become whole men, so that we shall seem to have first worshipped God in things, in order later to worship things in God, and to worship things in God for this reaon, in order to recover ourselves in Him above all, and in loving God we shall seem to have loved ourselves. (p. 145)

But if the body of the beloved is only a transitional moment in this narcissistic ascent to unity with God, and if the cosmological hierarchy is metaphorized as proceeding not only from higher to lower but also from masculine to feminine, then we should not be too surprised to find the narcissistic transcendence buttressed by a privileging of the homoerotic[29]: "Perhaps someone will ask, by whom especially, and in what way, lovers are ensnared, and how they are freed. Women, of course, catch men easily, and even more easily women who display a certain masculine character. Men catch men still more easily, since they are more like men than women are, and they have blood and spirit which is clearer, warmer, and thinner, which is the basis of erotic entrapment" (p. 165). Along with this correlation of attractiveness and masculinity is the recurrence of the phallic ray motif earlier noted in the allegory of Porus and Penia: "But among males those attract men or women most quickly who are predominately sanguine but partly choleric, and who have large eyes, blue and shining; and especially if they live chastely, and have not, through coitus, exhausting the clear sap of the humors, disfigured their serene faces. For these qualities are required in order for the arrows themselves which wound the heart to be sent out properly, as we have explained above" (p. 165). Love is a visual wounding and penetration implicitly situating gazer and gazed in a relation of masculinity and femininity respectively and regardless of physiological gender.[30]

It is also the triumph of a logic of identity, wherein "narcissism" signifies the transcendence of difference and corporeality, the overcoming of matter and *mater* ("because *mother*, to the physicists, is *matter*" [p. 53]). Such a narcissism is to be differentiated, of course, from the perversity of narcissism that would by mistake identify the love object with the body itself:

[29]I am less interested in unraveling the relations between homosexuality, homoeroticism, homosociality, etc., than in detailing the very *different* problem of how a certain masculinist appropriation of the trope of sensitivity and suffering is exclusive of women and a means to power and legitimacy with other men. Once again, see Eve Kosofsky Sedgwick, *Between Men: English Literature and Male Homosocial Desire* (New York: Columbia University Press, 1985), and Christopher Newfield, "Politics of Male Suffering," *Differences* 1 (Fall 1989), 55–87. On the question of homosexuality in Renaissance Italy, see Guido Ruggiero, *The Boundaries of Eros: Sex Crime and Sexuality in Renaissance Venice* (Oxford: Oxford University Press, 1985); and Michael J. Rocke, "Il controllo dell'omosessualità a Firenze nel XV secolo: gl: Ufficiali di Notte," *Quaderni storici* 66, anno 22, n. 3 (1987). On the Plotinian sources of Ficino's notion of eros, see Al Wolters, "Ficino and Plotinus' Treatise 'On Eros,' " in *Ficino and Renaissance Neoplatonism: University of Toronto Italian Studies I*, ed. Konrad Eisenbichler and Olga Zorzi Pugliese (Ottawa: Dovehouse, 1986), pp. 189–97. On Platonic eros in Ficino, also see Michael J. B. Allen, *Marsilio Ficino and the Phaedran Charioteer* (Berkeley: University of California Press, 1981); and Paul Oscar Kristeller, *Renaissance Thought and Its Sources* (New York: Columbia University Press, 1979).

[30]Ficino's insistence on the visual foundation of love is, of course, indebted to (among others) Petrarch and the style of lyric poetry associated with his name.

Only our soul, I say, is so captivated by the charms of corporeal beauty that it neglects its own beauty, and forgetting itself, runs after the beauty of the body, which is a mere shadow of its own beauty.

... For it does not really desire the body itself; rather, seduced, like Narcissus, by corporeal beauty, which is an image of its own beauty, it desires its own beauty. And since it never notices the fact that, while it is desiring one thing, it is pursuing another, it never satisfies its desire. (pp. 140–41).

Such narcissism leads the soul to its own death "since it now seems to be a body rather than a soul" (p. 141). Instead, the selfsameness that is the source of love must be one that elides the material, differentiated, feminine realm of the body and that resounds in a supra-corporeal mirroring of likeness, whose dynamics are spelled out most eloquently in letter 129:

Whoever loves passionately in some way takes himself from himself and gives himself up to his beloved, so the beloved, if he be right minded, cherishes the lover as his own. For everyone should hold dearest what belongs to him. The beloved also knows that if like is to be rendered for like, man must be given for man, and, of course, will for will.

Now the lover fashions in his mind the image of the one he loves, and so his mind becomes, as it were, a mirror in which the form of the beloved is reflected. Since the beloved recognises himself in the lover, he is compelled to love him. But if we seek the truth of that proverb from nature, she will perhaps teach us this: likeness always begets love. But likeness is a quality that is the same in more than one person, for if one man is like another the other is necessarily like him. And so the same likeness that compels one man to love another also leads the other to love him. (1: 129)

Yet a crucial dissymmetry underlies this Ficinian version of the mirror stage by way of the fundamental masochism that defines Neoplatonic love as the eros of dispossession, that is, of being possessed by another, if not by the other. The sadomasochistic thrill of that mirroring relation that is called love is described in detail in a long passage from the sixth speech of the *De amore*:

Who would not hate one who took his soul away from him? For as liberty is more pleasant than anything else, so servitude is more unpleasant. And so you hate and love beautiful men at the same time; you hate them as thieves and murderers; you are also forced to love and revere them as mirrors sparkling with the heavenly glow. What can you do, O wretch? Where to turn, you do not know; alas, O lost soul, you do not know. You would not want to be with this murderer of yourself, but you would not want to live without his blessed sight. You cannot be with this man who destroys you, who tortures you. You cannot live without him, who, with wonderful enticements, steals you from yourself, who claims all of you for himself. You want to flee him who scorches you with his flames. You also want to cling to him, in order that by being very near him who possesses you, you may also be near yourself. You seek yourself outside yourself, O wretch, and you cling to your captor in order that you may sometime ransom your captive self. You would certainly not want to love, O madman, because you would not want to die. You would also certainly not want not to love since you think that service must be rendered to an image of heavenly things. (p. 129)

Affect seems to be all on the side of the interpellated subject of passion, a soul whose dispossession would bring it closer to something that resembles itself, that transcends itself and is only found outside of itself in the "heavenly glow" [el celeste lume] of its male tormentor/seducer. The pain and loss of self experienced by the impassioned soul place that self in the phallocratically determined position of a feminized victim, who suffers the scorching flames of the beloved's beauty and the pene-trating wound of the beloved's phallic gaze (be that beloved male or female). In fact, what the Neoplatonic discourse of love seems to cho-reograph over and over again is a male fantasy of rape (one need only think of all those sonnet cycles detailing the exquisite woes of some male poet at the hands of some cruel, unfeeling, that is, phallic woman whose penetrating gaze is what first awakens his desire). But in this fantasy what is lost and hurt—what dies—is the lover's material bodily self, his feminine self, to the benefit of the incorporeal soul, whose liberated flight to God points to its likeness with the divinity's fatherly face: "Not only because the image of the paternal countenance pleases us, but also be-cause the appearance and figure of a well-constructed man correspond most closely with that Reason of Mankind which our soul received from the author of all things" (p. 91). And as we know also from *De amore*, "man is the soul alone [l'uomo solo è l'anima]; the body is merely a work and instrument of Man [dell'uomo]. The more especially because the soul...understands incorporeal things through the intelligence, whereas through the body only corporeal things are known.... But when God infused His own light into the soul, He adapted the light above all to this: that it might lead men to bliss, which consists in the possession of Him" (pp. 75,77). Thus, the superego in Ficinian terms is understood in terms of the virtues of prudence, courage, justice, and temperance, and it is through these virtues that one returns to heaven: "For no one returns to heaven except who have pleased the King of the Heavens. They please Him who love Him exceedingly.... Therefore what restores us to heaven is not knowledge of God but love" (p. 79). Love would then be the drive leading man toward God, toward the truth of the "one," through a transcendence of matter that returns us to our incorporeal or pre-corporeal origin.

What place is left in all this for women? Not much, if we consider the one exception in Ficino to the eroticized identification with the female victim. This exception is not the procreative pleasure of the vulgar Venus, which remains singularly unerotic for the Florentine philosopher, but the sublimated propagation that is called pedagogy: "Once the soul is mature, the love of procreation inspires it with a burning desire to teach and to write, so that by propagating its knowledge, either in writings or in the mind of students, the wisdom of a teacher may remain among men eternally" (p. 131). Like its literal counterpart, the erotics of pedagogy nonetheless puts a premium on physical beauty, for which a philosophical justification is necessary: "Certainly we cannot see the soul itself. And for this reason we cannot see its beauty. But we can see the body, which is the shadow and image of the soul. And so, judging by its image, we assume that in a beautiful body there is a beautiful soul. That is why we prefer to teach men who are handsome" (p. 132). And again, the homoerotic relation is privileged over what I would call the heteroerotic as male is over female, identity over difference, and the pure ideality of the one over the corrupt heterogeneity of the multiple:[31]

> But some, either by nature or by education, are better fitted for progeny of the soul than of the body, and others, certainly the majority, the opposite. The former follow heavenly love, the latter, vulgar. For this reason the former naturally love males and certainly those already adult rather than women or boys, since in them sharpness of intellect flourishes more completely, which, on account of its more excellent beauty, is more

[31]Given the bias for understanding the libido as masculine and for the explicit privileging of the male term over the female, I use the term "heteroerotic" to name an eros that is "other"-directed regardless of physiological gender.

suitable for receiving the learning which they wish to procreate... And it often happens that those who associate with males, in order to satisfy the demands of the genital part, copulate with them. Especially those at whose birth Venus was in a masculine sign and in conjunction with Saturn, or in the house of Saturn, or in opposition to Saturn. (p. 135).

And so by way of Ficino's pedagogue we return to melancholia as the sign of one's belonging to a philosophical elite, an elite whose sign is also the celestial one of Saturn (notice that the mere presence of the "highest" planet seems sufficient, its relative location in the heavens— conjunction, opposition, or ascendency—being apparently indifferent). No longer identified with a feminized victim, the maleness of the melancholic teacher is certified by his homoerotic attraction via the "heavenly" Venus to male students eager to be impregnated by his semen, if not by his seminal ideas. The more "mature" soul of the philosopher is thus one that rises above the base, material, bodily differentiation that is the feminine, a decidedly misogynistic arrangement wherein this masculine ego is protected from the difference of woman as the instance of a corporeality scrupulously understood by the NeoPlatonist as inferior.

But while the melancholic philosopher appears as a kind of supermale desiring and inseminating other men as other men do women, he too remains implicitly feminized vis-à-vis the superior, paternal instance with which he seeks reunification. Thus, both like and unlike Freud's oedipal theory, in Ficino's rewriting of the melancholic man, loss and separation are understood as a loss and separation from fathers—mother and woman appear only as the abject realm into which separation from the father has exiled the son. At the same time, this nostalgic desire for the father posits him as the source both of the separation (in psychoanalytic terms, castration) and of its transcendence. The figure of Saturn is just such a father, a castrator of his father only to be castrated by his son: "Saturn, however, separates you from your earthly life, from which he is himself separated, but returns you to heavenly and eternal life" (*De vita*, p. 67). Saturn is also the god of all kinds of separations and divisions, including that inescapable differentiation which is time ("chronos" from Kronos, the Greek name for Saturn) and without which there could be no such phenomenon as nostalgia. It is then also not surprising that he turns out to be the god of uncommon men, of all those who are different from others: "Saturn takes the separated ones" [usurpavit segregata Saturnus] (*De vita*, p. 166). "Highest" of the planets according to the Ptolemaic cosmology, old man Saturn is the closest to that "paternal countenance" of the One. And it is precisely in the likeness of the One that the philosopher erotically finds himself again as he once was before "depression" into the body. As such, all those who share the sign of Saturn share the traits of a secret resemblance to each other, a resemblance that in turn guarantees their common triumph over the differentiated world of matter/*mater*. Furthermore, Ficino and his friends, including Lorenzo de Medici and Pico, found the "proof" of their Saturnine eliteness in their common (homosocial) bond with the highest planet, a bond they understood themselves to share with the originators of philosophy, Socrates and Plato.[32] No wonder the astrological determinates of the planet had to be indeterminate enough to meet this obvious social demand, that is, flexible enough to connect all true "men of genius" with Saturn as well as implicitly flexible enough to exclude all others from Saturnine influence, which as we remember was malign to all who were not situated among "his own" (*De vita*, p. 166).

If one's reunion with the godly father, with God the Father, is to take place in the mode of knowledge reacquired as a function of eros ("what restores us to heaven is not knowledge of God but love"), then we should not be too surprised to see the figure of the perfect lover connected with that original philosopher or lover of knowledge, Socrates, the great melancholic. In fact, Ficino in *De amore* writes that "when Plato pictures love itself, he paints the whole likeness of Socrates, as if true love and Socrates were exactly alike" (p. 155). Socrates was the true lover: "Consider now; recall to your soul that picture of love. You will see in it Socrates pictured. Put the person of Socrates before your eyes. You will see him *thin, dry* and *squalid*, that is, a man melancholy by nature, it is said, and hairy, thin from fasting, and filthy from neglect" (pp. 155–56). In spite of what appears to be a physical dissipation, "Socratic" love "benefits Socrates himself for recovering the wings with which to fly back to his homeland" (p. 172). This angelic flight, which historically foreshadows Dürer's winged figure of melancholy, takes place as the unfolding of one's wings that love inspires, "for true love is nothing other than a certain form of flying up to divine beauty, aroused by the sight of corporeal beauty" (p. 172). Furthermore, it is via the figure of Socrates that the relation between impairment and transcendence, between dissipation (physiological loss) and inspiration, is spe-

[32]Klibansky et al., *Saturn and Melancholy*, p. 273.

cifically coded as melancholia: "Choleric and melancholy men pursue as
the only remedy and solace of their vexatious complexions, the pleasures
of song and beauty. And it is for this reason that they are more susceptible
to the charms of Venus. And Socrates, whom Aristotle judged a melancholic, confessed that he was the most inclined to the art of love of
all men" (p. 122).

In the extended commentary on Diotima's discourse on love that
leads up to this Socratic allusion, the physiological effects of being in
love are explicitly shown to lead to melancholia in its traditional sense
as a disease caused by an excess of black bile. Nevertheless, what Ficino
is at pains to show is that this excess of humor is induced by an irre-
pressible economy of *loss*, the ultimate risk being that of suicide. Because
"the entire attention of a lover's soul is devoted to continuous thought
about the beloved" (p. 121), there is an incremental lack of sustenance
going to the body:

> For this reason the food in the stomach is not digested perfectly. Whence
> it happens that the greater part is eliminated as superfluous wastes; the
> smaller part, and that indeed raw, is drawn to the liver. There, too, for
> the same reason, it is badly digested. For this reason only a little crude
> blood is dispersed from there through the veins. As a consequence, all
> parts of the body become thin and pale because of the scarcity and crudity
> of food.
>
> Moreover, wherever the continuous attention of the soul is carried,
> there also fly the spirits, which are the chariots, or instruments of the soul.
> The spirits are produced in the heart from the thinnest part of the blood.
> The lover's soul is carried toward the image of the beloved planted in his
> imagination, and thence toward the beloved himself. To the same place
> are also drawn the lover's spirits. Flying out there, they are continuously
> dissipated. (p. 121)

The beloved acts as a drain on the lover's spirits, emptying him while
restorative nutrients are blocked, leading to starvation. This scarcity is
most extreme in the blood, that humoral source of the sanguine
temperament.

> Therefore there is a need for a constant source of pure blood to replace
> the consumed spirits, since the thinner and clearer parts of the blood are
> used up every day in replacing the spirits. On that account, when the
> pure and clear blood is dissipated, there remains only the impure, thick,

dry, and black. Hence the body dries out and grows squalid, and hence lovers become melancholics. For from dry, thick, and black blood is produced melancholy, that is, black bile, which fills the head with its vapors, dries out the brain, and ceaselessly troubles the soul day and night with hideous and horrible images. This, we have read, happened to the Epicurean philosopher Lucretius on account of love; shaken first by love and then by madness, he finally laid hands on himself. (p. 121)

The "lack of sanguine heat" [difecto di caldo sanguigno] (p. 135) leads to an overabundance of black bile, whose effect is the portrait of Socrates as corporeally deficient when it is not the extreme one emblematized by Lucretius's suicide: "You will see him thin, dry and squalid, that is, a man melancholy by nature, it is said, and hairy, thin from fasting, and filthy from neglect."

Not only is the state of lack associated with melancholia, an extreme state brought on by love, but—again as in the case of Socrates—those who are "melancholy by nature" (and not just as a contingent or accidental effect of love) are said to be more prone to falling in love: "When ancient physicians observed these things, they said that love was a passion very close to the disease of melancholy. And the physician Rhazes taught that it was cured by coitus, fasting, inebriation, and walking. And not only does love render men thus but conversely those who are thus by nature are more susceptible to love" (p. 122). Although cholerics are said to fall more quickly in love "because of the force of the fiery humor," "melancholics love more slowly because of the sluggishness of the earthly humor, but because of the stability of that humor, after they have been caught, they continue for a long time. Therefore Love is rightly described as dry and squalid" (p. 122).

Just as in Aristotle's *Problems*, the opposition between natural melancholy and the disease of excessive black bile is that which favors the uncommon qualities of those who suffer from natural melancholy as exemplified most especially in a man of letters—like Socrates—whose corporeal loss is his transcendental gain. Natural melancholics are also more prone to the melancholia called love; and the "amatory madness" that propels the lover on his flight to Saturnine oneness must not be confused with the humorally induced madness that *physiologically* afflicts "those who are desperately in love" [amore perduti]. This distinction is sketched out in the course of a very loose commentary on Plato's *Phaedrus*:

In the *Phaedrus*, our Plato defines madness as an alienation of the mind. But he teaches two kinds of alienation. One he thinks comes from human illnesses, and the other from God. The former he calls insanity, the latter, divine madness. In the sickness of insanity, a man is brought down below the species of man and in some degree is changed from a man into a beast. There are two kinds of insanity. One rises from a defect of the brain, the other from a defect of the heart. The brain often becomes too much occupied with burned bile, burned blood, or sometimes black bile. Hence men are sometimes rendered insane. . . . And these three kinds of insanity certainly result from a defect of the brain. For when those humors are retained in the heart, they produce distress and anxiety, but not insanity; they cause insanity only when they oppress the head. Therefore these are said to occur through a defect of the brain. We think that the madness by which those who are desperately in love are afflicted is, strictly speaking, caused by a disease of the heart, and that it is wrong to associate the most sacred name of love with these. (p. 158)

Driven on by the vulgar Venus, these disease-ridden types can never achieve satisfaction, and in fact can only lead lives of exacerbated frustration. Whether divine madness or divine gift, melancholia is, on the other hand, associated with the heavenly Venus *cum* Saturn, and its chosen recipient or privileged victim finds satisfaction in desire itself:

Whoever has truly thirsted for this source for a long time, seems also to have drunk from it, for the very price at which this liquid is bought is the thirst itself. And, from a certain offering of drink, the parched spirit has this very thing for which it thirsts. Drinking more fully from that, it is satisfied so that it thirsts for nothing more. . . .
. . . The desire of him, who strives for anything other than love, is often totally frustrated by the event. But he alone who loves nothing more than love itself, by desiring immediately attains, and in always attaining continues to desire. (*Letters* 2: 21)

If love reaches its height in the melancholic sense of loss, then loss itself becomes the sign of a superior gain, of a divine gift, and one not available to all. Indeed, it turns out that such profound love would be harmful to all those who are not chosen to receive it.

This is precisely the working hypothesis of the three books of *On Life*, which focus most especially on the special problems *qua* gifts that melancholia imposes on scholars, now revealed as the privileged children of Saturn. Written under the sign of his "two fathers" (the doctor Dietifeci Ficino and Cosimo de Medici), Ficino's discussion of why scholars are especially susceptible to melancholia ends by giving them an elite status, one that makes them not only different but also intrinsically superior to other mortals. Assuming the authoritative stance of a doctor, Ficino lists three causes of melancholia: "The first is heaven-caused, the second is natural, and the third is human" (p. 6). With regard to the first, heavenly cause, we find Mercury, traditionally the god of writing and scholarship, as well as Saturn, whose expected but incidental reference here will, not surprisingly, be subject to considerable expansion as the *De vita* progresses. In any case, the "cold and dry" natures of these two planets (strange as this may seem for such unlike orbits) is nonetheless in analogy with the cold, dry condition of the melancholic physiology. Analogy is also at the heart of the second, so-called natural cause of melancholia: "The natural cause seems to be that because the pursuit of knowledge is so difficult it is necessary for the soul to remove itself from external things to internal things, as if moving from the circumference to the center. While one is looking at this center of man (of which more later), it is necessary to remain very still, to gather oneself at the center, away from the circumference. To be fixed at the center is very much like being at the center of the earth itself, which resembles black bile" (p. 6).

While black bile "provokes the soul" into concentration, *causes* this concentration, it is also *like* concentration. In other words, black bile functions as both cause and analogy in its capacity to condense or contract the soul. And as black bile "drives the student to the center of each thing," or *causes* this movement to reach the core of what is being contemplated, so too is that center "*very much like* being at the center of the earth itself, which *resembles* black bile." Not only is melancholia spurred by this centripetal force whereby the soul "remove[s] itself from external things to internal things, as if moving from the circumference to the center"; it also "moves [the student] to understand the highest things, since it is in accord with Saturn, the highest of planets" (p. 6; cf. p. 11). The impetus to the cosmological center (of the earth) is at the same time a passage to the universal circumference (the orbit of Saturn, then thought to be the outermost planet). Yet we know from *De amore* that the Saturniane circumference is also the closest to the divine center of transcendent oneness. In other words, center and circumference are—without further explanation—joined together in the concentrated understanding of the divinely gifted melancholic, thus closing the interpretive circle. This lack of logic points to the melancholic's inspired vision of the true oneness to be discoverd behind the falseness of multiplicity. As we will see in the reading of *De vita*, the analogical delirium that motivates the text finds the proof of its truth content in the logic of identity that reveals an essential sameness behind every difference. (And as we shall also see, the political consequences of such a thought, sketched out for the benefit of the Medici rulers of Florence, are not to be forgotten.) If the "nature" of the cosmos, the *anima mundi*, is an essential oneness from which stem all things in their multiplicity, then we should not be too surprised to find the "natural cause" of melancholy elaborated, in this convoluted manner, as both cause and analogy.

The third or "human" cause of melancholia closely replicates Ficino's discussion on amorous melancholia. Too much agitation and exertion lead to a physiological destitution that leaves the body, in analogy with the qualities of Mercury and Saturn, cold and dry:

> The human cause is through ourselves. Because with frequent agitation the mind often violently dries up and a great part of its moisture is consumed (which is nourishment of its natural warmth), much of its warmth is also extinguished. The condition of the brain then turns dry and cold, which is why this quality is called earthly and melancholy.
>
> Furthermore, because of the frequent movement involved in thinking, the spirit also is continually broken by such movement. The spirit thus broken, it is necessary to repair it with some thinner blood. Since the thinner and clearer parts of the blood are usually consumed, however, the remaining blood by necessity runs dense, dry, and black.
>
> It all comes down to this, that with the mind and heart bent on contemplation, the stomach and the liver fail. Then, especially if you are eating rich or hard foods poorly cooked, the blood becomes cold, thick, and black. Finally, with an excessive swiftness of the limbs, and with neither the remaining stuff nor the hard glutinous stuff being separated, dusky vapors are exhaled. All these make for a melancholy spirit, a sad and fearful soul. Since these darknesses are much more inside than outside, they seize the soul with sadness and wear it out. (p. 7)

Too much attention to other things, whether it be through love or scholarly contemplation, leads to an incapacity to take in nutrients and to replenish the blood which destructively consumes the body and "wears out" the soul. Too much concentration, it seems, leads to total dissipation; a paradox resolved by a quick gloss of "our dear Plato": "This is in fact what our dear Plato meant in the *Timaeus*, when he said that the soul, in frequent and intense contemplation of the divine, grows on such nourishment and becomes so powerful that it departs the body, and its body, left behind, seems to dissolve. It is as if it abandoned its bodily nature, fleeing sometimes with great agitation, and sometimes with none at all" (p. 7). True to the Neoplatonic scheme of *De amore*, the body's loss is the soul's gain.

And no one, lover or scholar, loses and gains more than that lover of knowledge, the philosopher: "Of all scholars, those devoted to the study of philosophy are most bothered by black bile, because their minds get separated from their bodies and from bodily things. They become preoccupied with incorporeal things, because their work is so much more difficult and the mind requires an even stronger will. To the extent that they join the mind to bodiless truth, they are forced to separate it from the body. Body for these people never returns except as a half-soul and a melancholy one" (p. 7). It seems that for the philosopher, for whom separation from the body is the sign of his proximity to the truth, melancholia is not just a job hazard but a terminal condition. As Charles Boer remarks, "For the neo-Platonist, the soul does not want to be in the body, and melancholy is the cry for escape."[33] Thanks to Ficino, melancholia is reconceived as a kind of wisdom; it is the knowledge of what we have lost through our "depression" into the body, that is, the reality of the incorporeal oneness that transcends the material world of multiplicity. Melancholia is the knowledge of a loss, one that is recaptured by the cognition of that loss. In like manner, the philosophical stigmata of physiological deprivation are the signs of a proximity to God.

From the Neoplatonist perspective, then, nothing could be more euphoric, than the loss of the body. Hence no one is more dismissive or critical of the act of mourning than the great renovator of melancholia, Marsilio Ficino, whose correspondence is riddled with such remarks as "What is it that you mourn in a friend's death?" and "But why should I lament the death of Piero, our Cardinal?" (*Letters* I: 97, 117). If melancholia is the privileged intuition of a nameless and transcendental "what" that has been lost, it also appears concomitant with a denial of the "what" that is explicitly represented as lost in the ritual of mourning. As I also argue, the politics of this hierarchy between mourning and melancholia are not without motivation and consequences.

---

[33]Charles Boer, Introduction to *Marsilio Ficino: The Book of Life*, p. xiii.

Finally, the repeated distinction between "natural" and accidental melancholia serves to bestow all beneficial and illuminating effects onto those elect ones whose condition is created by melancholia *per natura*. In fact, it would not be stretching matters at all to say that the natural melancholic who is the philosopher is really an utterly different—and even physiologically different—species of human being. The melancholia that afflicts this child of Saturn has nothing to do with the common medical category of *melancholia adusta*, a condition brought about by the burning or "combustion of either natural melancholy, pure blood, bile, or phlegm": "When the burning kind occurs, it is harmful to judgment and wisdom, for when this humor rises and burns, it makes you upset and angry, what the Greeks call Mania, what we call madness. But even when it is extinguished, and its subtler and clearer parts broken, and all that is left is a foul soot, it makes you dull and stupid. This is why they call the melancholy disposition madness and insanity" (*De vita*, p. 8). This madness produced by "the burning kind" of melancholia is no more like the true, philosophical melancholia than the "diseases of the heart" are like true love.

The "natural type" of melancholia is described as "nothing other than a part of the blood getting thicker and dryer"; it is "conducive to our judgment and wisdom" (p. 8). "But not always" [neque tamen semper], adds Ficino, who at his most Aristotelian then details the contradictory effects of this "natural" melancholia and even draws an analogy with wine, another unpredictable modifier of behavior:

> Melancholy has a power just as extreme. It is stable when in a certain unity and of a fixed nature. This is the situation when extremity does not reach to the other humors. When greatly heated up, it moves to great boldness, even ferocity, and when it gets very cold, it moves to extremes of fear and cowardice.
>
> There are middle stages between cold and heat, various stages of incompleteness, where it produces various effects, not unlike what happens with wine, especially with strong wine. Wine can make some drinkers drunk, or some just a little loosened up—wine has different effects on people.
>
> It is good, therefore, to keep black bile in moderation. (p. 10)

This last sentence points to Ficino's particular contribution to the discussion. For Ficino, there is what we can call an *art* of melancholia, that is, a set of techniques that allows the scholar—and only the scholar—

to avoid the pitfalls of excessive black bile and at the same time to benefit from it: "We must seek and nourish as much black bile, even bright bile, as is best, and we must avoid as much black bile, as we have said, as works against itself" (p. 11).

What follows in the remainder of book 1, appropriately titled "On Caring for the Health of Men of Letters," is an elaborate regime designed to guide the scholar in managing his humoral condition, especially with respect to black bile. The underlying assumption, of course, is that this different kind of human being, the Saturnian creature, the scholar himself, has a completely different set of bodily needs from other human beings. In addition, the elite quality of the care for the scholar's health is further underscored by the numerous exotic and undoubtedly expensive spices that Ficino prescribes. Hardly the starving student or ascetic monk, the ideal Ficinian scholar needs enormous wealth, power, and prestige. For example, Ficino's favorite remedy, to be liberally imbibed by the scholar, is theriaca, a pharmaceutical compound of over fifty ingredients whose "preparation was considered so difficult and requiring such skill that in fifteenth-century Venice its preparation officially required the presence of the *Priori e Consiglieri*." In Ficino's own Florence, a civil statute "required that it be made with all the pharmacists and physicians together, and that it could not be sold without the approval of the Consuls."[34]

While humanist scholars (Charles Boer, Paul Oscar Kristeller) have tended, laudably perhaps, to emphasize the commonsensical and practical advice Ficino gives scholars who wish to maintain their health,[35] it seems important to keep in mind that such humanist pearls of wisdom as keeping regular hours and getting plenty of sunshine appear next to such strange injunctions as pouring "heated silver" into one's drink or smearing "oil of violets" on one's face to cure insomnia. Even Boer ironically suggests that "the Food and Drug Administration should attach a warning label to this book, should a reader be found to try some of Ficino's formulas."[36] But then we are discussing formulas for the divinely inspired scholar, for whom what is toxic for the rest of us may be just what the doctor ordered. Like Plato's *pharmakon*, at least as Derrida has analyzed it, the Ficinian drug's ability to work as medicine

[34]Both citations are from Charles Boer's notes to *The Book of Life*, p. 194.
[35]Boer, *The Book of Life*, pp. iii–xviii; Paul Oscar Kristeller, *The Philosophy of Marsilio Ficino*, trans. Virginia Conant (New York: Columbia University Press, 1943).
[36]Boer, *The Book of Life*, pp. xvii–xviii.

or as poison may have more to do with who one is than with how one uses the drug.[37] Remember, the most noxious of planets, Saturn, "does not harm those in his house, his domestics, but only outsiders" [Saturnus non laedat domesticos, sed externos] (*De vita*, p. 166). And certainly, following his Neoplatonic aspirations, would not the death of the patient be the ultimate remedy, the final release from the depressive body that would allow for the winged flight back up to celestial oneness and bliss?

On a more serious level, perhaps, the regime of the body that comprises book 1 is finally directed to an elision of the body, to its being forgotten so that the disappearance of the body implies its disappearance as an obstacle to philosophical contemplation:

> When someone purges his eyes and looks at that light, he suddenly finds its splendor pouring in, shining grandly with the colors and figures of things. It is the same when through moral discipline the mind is first purged from all the disturbances of the body, and directed by a religious and most ardent love to divine truth, that is, to God himself. Suddenly, as the divine Plato says, a divine truth flows into the mind, and happily explains true reasons, which are contained in it, and in which all things exist. It surrounds the mind with as much light as the joy that it pours so happily into the will. (p. 36)

This paragraph of book 1 once again recalls the theological eros of *De amore*, but this time with its modality fixed on philosophy as the true art of love.

This time, though, the predominant distinction that guides *De amore*, namely the distinction between the vulgar and the heavenly Venus, is replaced by one between Venus (in her unqualified entirety) and Saturn. The old man, in other words, has replaced the ethereal woman as the figure of divine rapture in a cosmos where love literally makes the world go round:

> The astrologers say that Venus and Saturn are enemies of each other. Nonetheless, in heaven, where all things are moved by love, where there is no fault, there can be no hatred. When they say enemies, therefore, we must interpret this as meaning that they differ in their effect.
> Let us put aside for now the other aspects of this. Imagine Saturn now as in our center, giving pleasure, and Venus at the circumference,

giving pleasure. Pleasure is really a kind of food for the spirits. So, from opposite sides, Venus and Saturn chase after the flight of our spirit. She lures us to external things through her pleasure, while he, meanwhile, through his pleasures, calls us back to the innermost things. So they distract and dissipate the spirit if they both move at the same time.

This is why there is nothing more harmful to the business of being contemplative or curious than Venereal activity, and nothing more contrary to Venereal activity than careful contemplation. (*De vita*, p. 69)

Not only is the centripetal force from Saturn ethically superior to the Venusian seduction by external things, but some are more drawn toward one than the other: "A man, therefore, should know which way he is, and be his own self-regulator. A man should be his own doctor" [Unusquisque igit se cognoscat, suique ipsius moderator, ac medicus esto] (p. 70). The medical advice nonetheless echoes an ethical difference, expressed as follows in a speech by Mercury, the god of medicine, that once again privileges the Saturnian:

"The insidious Venus, however, fabricates her enticements through marvelous favors which slowly destroy your life as if you were secretly caught on a hook.

"Why, therefore, do you attack Mars? Why attack Saturn? Mars hurts you rarely, and only in public! And Saturn, too, at least shows you his face is your enemy, and only hurts you slowly, and never denies anybody the time for remedies.

"Only Venus comes on openly as your friend, and is secretly your enemy." (p. 66)

And later:

"Yet just as I warn you to beware the crafty Venus' delights of touching and tasting, I must tell you to beware, also, Saturn, with too much of his busy and secret delight in the contemplative mind, for he frequently devours his own sons in this. He seizes them with the enticements of his more sublime contemplations, and knows that he is in the meantime cutting them off from the earth with a kind of scythe if they are lingering too long there. He often kills the earthly life of these unwary people.

"In this, at least, he is a little easier than Venus, because Venus, when she takes your life away, gives it to someone else, and does not give you anything in exchange. Saturn, however, separates you from your earthly life, from which he is himself separated, but returns you to heavenly and eternal life." (pp. 66–67)

Under a friendly and enticing guise, Venus lures one into that false
material-bodily realm of "external things" that draws one outside the
self toward destruction in the same way as do "the lethal songs of the
Sirens" [letales syrenum cantus] and "the poisons of Circe [Circes huius
veneficia] (p. 66). This classic misogynistic fear of women as devourers
of men is probably most evident in Ficino's later allusions to the "lamias":
"those lewd and Venereal daemons who disguised themselves as beautiful girls and lured beautiful men. Luring them as a serpent does an
elephant with its mouth, they sucked them with vulva as well as mouth,
and emptied the men out" (pp. 158–59). Interestingly, the obvious
situation of loss in such male fantasies/fears does not bear any relation
in Ficino to the high philosophical category of melancholia, understood
as the true sign of love at the hands of Saturn *qua* heavenly Venus. In
fact, Ficino does away with a simple misogynistic view of woman as the
cause of male melancholia as she was figured in the medieval romance
genre. (This view—paradoxically enough— would at least somewhat
improve the position of woman in his Neoplatonic theory to the extent
that she would still have some role to play, albeit a disturbingly negative
one.) Instead, Ficino establishes a different kind of erotic relation for
melancholia, one that excludes the role of women. In fact, that exclusion
allows for more of the paranoid view of feminine difference seen in his
depiction of Venus. This exclusion is, in fact, the key to understanding
the substitution of Saturn for the Heavenly Venus, and let there be no
mistaking the erotic force of this "non-vulgar" side of the opposition:
"Venus fertilizes the body, and stimulates fertility. Saturn presses the
mind, pregnant by his seed, to give birth" [Sed haec quidem faecundat
corpus, stimulatque faecundum. Ille mentem suo femine gravidam urget
ad partum] (p. 67). Showing his face openly as an enemy, Saturn nonetheless reveals a strange friendship for the privileged man of letters.

Although Ficino elsewhere depicts Saturn as a malevolent force ("a
very great stranger to the common life of man" [p. 166; cf. p. 114]),
Saturn is here cast as propitious toward his own: the privileged, isolated
and nocturnal world of scholars (p. 165). And, among these, he behaves
favorably only to the *true* scholar, while remaining an enemy to those
who are false or uninspired: "There is no Saturn more unfeeling than
the one for men who only pretend to the contemplative life, not really
doing it" (p. 165). Saturn's disadvantages for the "common life of man,"
for whom the outermost planet is a "very great stranger," are advantages
for those who are his "kinsmen," those isolated men of genius whose

Saturnian intellect allows them to penetrate to the core of "the innermost secret things" (p. 173).

This penetrating ability is also the distinctive feature of the "heavenly rays" that are the basis of Ficino's cosmology. These rays metaphorize a phallic universe wherein the coupling of sexual opposites is never egalitarian but always hierarchical in terms that privilege the male:

> The wise men of India say that by this same kind of attraction the world is bound to itself, saying that the world is sometimes a masculine animal, sometimes a feminine one, and that it is everywhere copulating with itself out of this mutual love of its own limbs. They say that it exists in such a way that the bonds that hold these limbs together are inside its own mind, which, going through its limbs, works the whole mass and mixes with the great body itself.
>
> Orpheus called this nature of the world, and Jove's world, both masculine and feminine. It is so because the world is everywhere hot to make love to its own mutual parts. Everywhere it is mixed between the masculine and feminine sex, as the order of signs declares, where, in perpetual order, the masculine goes first, the feminine follows. The trees and herbs prove this too, which have both sexes the same as animals.
>
> I will pass over the fact that fire goes to air, and water goes to earth, like man to woman, because there is nothing surprising in the fact that the world's limbs, among themselves and all its parts, lust for copulation with each other. (p. 179)
>
> The sky is married to the earth but does not touch it (in most people's opinion, anyway). He does not copulate with his wife, the earth, but he beholds his wife through the pits of the stars, as if with the rays of eyes that are everywhere, and beholding her, he impregnates her and creates living things. ("Apology of Marsilio Ficino," De vita, p. 188)

The metaphysical-mythological eros of De amore has here been projected onto the cosmos with the phallic gaze of the beloved superimposed on the sources of celestial light as well as on the astrological influences of heavenly bodies. In fact, the "heavenly Venus" of De amore has become literalized as light itself. On the other hand, the superiority of the male or impregnating elements recalls the masculinity attributed to the superior term in the erotic relation described in De amore and suggests once again the superiority of the "highest" planet in the Ficinian scheme. Saturn does indeed come off as the macho planet: its toxic rays can be turned to advantage only by that superior race of men, the philosophers, with their penetrating intellects.

In fact, the point of the last of the three books, titled "On Making One's Life Agree with the Heavens" [De vita coelitus comparanda], is to recognize under whose celestial influence one belongs and to act accordingly. As the heading to chapter 23 reads, "In order for you to live and work prosperously, above all know your mind, your star, your Genius, and a place that is fitting for them. Live here, and follow your natural profession" (p. 168). Unhappiness and misfortune result from one's taking "a daemon who is different from his own Genius" [diversum a genio subit daemonem] (p. 172), that is, from not following one's astrological encoding. The grand order of cosmological copulation stipulates that everything and everyone has its place within that order. Wisdom, that is, the "duty of a wise man" [solius sapientis est officium] (p. 160), is to find and keep one's place in that order. "Seizing by imitation" is the Ficinian road to success. One's "good health" means a certain mirroring of the cosmos, a reproduction of what is inscribed in the heavens. Images are what are reproduced when the phallic gaze of the *anima mundi* impregnates the earth; and the construction of various images of stellar objects in order to capture this power and energy occupies much of Ficino's time in the central chapters (13–21) of book III.[38]

The political consequences of this mimetic ethics point to an imperative of accommodation and imitation whereby one makes one's life

---

[38]Chapter 13, "On the Power of Images According to the Ancients, and on Acquiring Medicines from the Heavens" [De virtute imaginum secundum antiquos, atque medicinarum coelitus acquisita], begins thus: "Ptolemy said in the *Centiloquium* that the images of lower things are subject to the celestial faces. Ancient wise men used to fabricate certain images, therefore, similar to the faces of the planets when they are in the sky, as if these faces then entered into examples of the lower things" (p. 126). Here is where analogical delirium pretends to a demiurgic prestige, as various kinds of figures or representations are cast to attract or repulse the practical effects of celestial powers. Again, as in *De amore*, the power of likeness legitimates the underlying logic of identity. Speculation finds its end in the reduction of the universe to a mere *speculum* (for Luce Irigaray, this self-mirroring of speculation is not an innocent operation in the general context of Western phallocentrism; *Speculum of the Other Woman*, trans. Gillian C. Gill [Ithaca: Cornell University Press, 1985]). Chapter 19 is dedicated to that ultimate Borgesian representative feat, the reproduction of "a universal image, that is, an image of the universe itself" [universalem ipsam idest universi ipsius imaginem] (p. 151), which Ficino recommends setting up in the room "where you spend most of your time" [ubi plurimum vigilet] (p. 153). Mimetism, concludes Ficino, in a manner more Platonic than Plato himself, is the way back to the universal oneness lost at the moment of our birth and "depression" into the body: "If, therefore, this is what heaven's life is—a mind that is grasped through thought, which could not know that such a form exists in heaven, and a most excellent body, which goes around always with a perfect motion, giving life to everything—then and more our own life should naturally approach nearer to this likeness of itself, and each day expose itself more fittingly to heaven's influxes" (p. 155).

"agree" with the powers that be. At the same time, an exception is made for the philosopher himself, that phallocratic master of identities. This kind of politics is made explicit in letter 53 (vol. 2), addressed to Cherubino Quarquagli: "The duty of the private individual is to obey the magistrate's commands so willingly that he seems to be led by his own will." This formulation sheds light on the ethics of *making* your life agree with the heavens. The logic of this formulation is paradoxical: that of choosing freely in order to accommodate oneself with what already determines an individual. Put in other words, how can one choose to be what one is forced to do? More insidiously, however, the paradox points to the early Renaissance invention of the superego, as the introjection into the ego of authoritarian institutions—not just the family father of nascent bourgeois liberalism but the paternal figures of prince and God as represented by the cultural institutions of state and church. A successful introjection of these patriarchal figures would reduce the ego to nothing more than the perfect mirror of what rules from above, which would be in accordance with the kind of phallic hierarchy of reflection that Marsilio Ficino so intricately describes. As this philosopher-son of Cosimo de Medici specifies, the duty of a son is to "revere" his father "as a second God"; the duty of a teacher is "to beget a learned and good disciple as if he were bringing to birth a child of his own mind." And finally, the phallocratic hierarchy of impregnation *cum* imitation is completed by the figure of a "virile" man who "should beware of being effeminate in any way," while a woman "should strive to have the spirit of a man in some measure, but above all to be modest"—words that recall Aristotle's similar disqualification of feminine distinction and to which the same criticisms apply. In other words, a woman cannot be distinguished and can only be celebrated by being unknown.

The philosopher, on the other hand, is freed from this mimetic subservience precisely to the extent that he personifies its very principle. In fact, only the philosopher is not obliged "to hazard his life for his country." Why? Because, continues Ficino, "a philosopher is a philosopher against the will of the state in which he is born and in spite of its active resistance; and he is a son of heaven, not of earth." The philosopher transcends the state and all duties to it because he is, as we learn elsewhere, an image of something much superior: "Philosophy is a gift, a likeness, and a most happy imitation of God" (*Letters* 3: 18). Being "born under Saturn," we remember from the letter to Cavalcanti, is the source of this divine gift called philosophy. The philosopher thus becomes an intermediary between God and men, and therefore a leader of all other men. This position of go-between is so sacred that the name of its founding figure shall not be taken in vain: "Profane men not only must not slander Plato in any way, but even, under the pretext of praise, they should not dare to utter his holy name through their profane mouths" (*Letters* 3: 19). The reconciliation of Christianity with Greek philosophy, attempted by Augustine and Aquinas, is achieved by Ficino in his sacralization of Plato and in the Christ-like function of the philosopher as intermediary between God and his creatures: "For, lower than the human race, those who have no part in philosophy degenerate rapidly, as it were, into beasts. Those, however, who give moderate service to philosophy will without doubt go forth as men fit to teach the learned and rule the rulers. Yet he who, throughout an entire life, devotes himself wholly to her alone, once the body has been laid aside, as it were, will go straight and free to the upper regions and will ascend beyond human form, having become a God of life-giving heaven" (*Letters* 3: 13). To boot, the devalued category of melancholia as a physiological affliction is now philosophically reinterpreted as the call back to the heavenly and thus as the sign of the philosopher's transcendence, not just in spiritual but also in temporal matters. Happiness is by necessity impossible on this earth except as error or stupidity (the ignorant bliss, for example, of following one's nature as predetermined by an "inferior" planet). It follows then that "happiness" is what results when one fails to recognize the temporal finitude of this world and the truth of what lies beyond life: "Since man *cannot live content* in earth, he should realise that he is indeed a citizen of heaven, but an inhabitant in earth" (*Letter s* 2: 53). In other words, if you are not melancholic, you must be dumb.

What can such a political and philosophical self-justification mean in the world of fifteenth-century Italy? According to Sears Jayne, the Medicis needed an "intellectual elitism to reinforce [their] financial elitism" and to legitimate their rule against the "genealogical elitism" of the old aristocratic families. For this purpose, they needed the prestige of a philosophical mind able to translate and popularize the as yet untranslated works of Plato, a task that could circumvent the Aristotelian hegemony of contemporary educational and ecclesiastical institutions through the establishment of an esoteric alternative linked to the Florentine court.[39] Ficino was "their man" for this job of cultural revisionism, a most successful one if we can judge by subsequent intellectual developments in the cinquecento, and even by our contemporary received ideas about the "rebirth of letters" during what has come to be known as the "Italian Renaissance."

Diabolical Melancholia
in Hildegard of Bingen

To measure the impact of the Ficinian reinterpretation (and hence the socio-symbolic reevaluation) of melancholia, I turn to the writings of a medieval nun, Saint Hildegard of Bingen, whose own take on this privileged affliction presents a very different and even radical possibility. Not only is she the only woman of pre-modern times known to have engaged the medical and philosophical discussion of melancholia, but she also appears, as far as I have been able to ascertain, to be the only theorist of melancholia to have confronted (critically) the question in terms of gender difference. For her, melancholia is neither, as it is for Ficino, the blessed gloom that signals one's transcendent membership in an (implicitly male) intellectual elite, nor is it, as in the medical tradition, a distressing disease that men (especially "great men") incur through some phantasmic encounter with a threatening femininity.

In almost every respect, Hildegard's is the most negative assessment of melancholia, and she sees almost nothing redeemable, desirable, or recuperable about that condition. Perhaps this negative assessment is not surprising in and of itself, given her obvious (and historically determined) entrenchment in the psycho-physiology of humoral medicine and in the dichotomized categories of scholastic logic.[40] As we have seen, the physiological approach most often entails a view of melancholia as an unfortunate disease, one to which, in accord with the Aristotelian tradition, "great men" are especially prone—although this does not necessarily make their condition an enviable one. For the recuperators of melancholia, among whom Ficino stands in a pivotal but certainly

---

[39]Sears Jayne, Introduction to Ficino's *On Love*, p. 18. For a recent discussion of the importance of Aristotelianism in the Italian academy, see Luce Giard, "L'Aristotélisme padouan: Histoire et historiographie," *Les Etudes Philosophiques* no. 3 (1986), 281–307.
[40]On scholastic notions of woman, see MacLean, *The Renaissance Notion of Woman*.

not isolated position, the "problem," as Walter Benjamin has so eloquently put it, "was to separate sublime melancholy, the *melencolia 'illa
heroica'* of Marsilius Ficinus,... from the ordinary and pernicious
kind."[41] What is presupposed in this "ennoblement of melancholy,"
which Benjamin correctly identifies as "the principal theme" of Ficino's
De vita,[42] is the separation from as well as the debasement of the physiological affliction brought on by an excess of black bile. And if, according
to the Western medical and philosophical tradition, the physiological
state of disease is stubbornly linked with the figure of woman (whether
as its cause or its icon), the often vague and contradictory symptomatology of melancholia is also what allows it to be manipulated by an
Aristotle, and *a fortiori* by a Ficino, in the creation of an elite psychological condition implicitly or explicitly associated with the genius of
"great *men*."

By contrast, Hildegard's attempt to delineate the physiological causes
of psychological afflictions (the sense of the title to her work *Causae et
curae*), appears incredibly precise in her descriptions of personality types
engendered by humoral complexions.[43] Compared with the vague, almost willfully indefinite features found in humoral literature, Hildegard's
types are striking for their coherence and plausibility. She describes their
causae and *curae* from a number of perspectives, but most notably from
that of gender. And it is precisely here that Hildegard's most daring
revision of the humoral tradition lies. Not only does her conceptual
rigor firmly eschew any privileging of some psychological apotheosis
over physiological baseness, but also and more important her delineation
of gendered types suggests the radical notion that the relation between
(physiological) *causae* and (psychological) *curae* may *not*, for whatever
reason, be the same in women as in men. In Hildegard's work, the
melancholic woman, for instance, appears as an explicit and necessary
category and not as some kind of aberrant or noteworthy exception to
an elite masculine order: for even Ficino can manage to find room for

[41]Walter Benjamin, *Origin of German Tragic Drama*, p. 151.
[42]Ibid.
[43]Hildegard von Bingen, *Causae et curae*, ed. Paul Kaiser (Leipzig: B. G. Teubner, 1903).
All translations are my own. On Hildegard's life and work, see Barbara Newman, *Sister of
Wisdom: St. Hildegard's Theology of the Feminine* (Berkeley: University of California Press,
1987); and Sabina Flanagan, *Hildegard of Bingen, 1098–1179: A Visionary Life* (London:
Routledge, 1989). Also see the shorter commentaries by Denise Riley, *"Am I that name?"
Feminism and the Category of "Women" in History* (Minneapolis: University of Minnesota Press,
1988), pp. 21–22; and Peter Dronke, *Women Writers of the Middle Ages* (Cambridge: Cambridge University Press, 1984), pp. 180–81.

Sappho as that exception in his otherwise phallocratic ideal of the philosopher as melancholy eros.[44] What is unprecedented in Hildegard, however, is that there *are* melancholic women *as a matter of course and as a logical consequence, indeed as a necessity, of humoral psycho-physiology.* These women, in fact, are not the dread icons of male paranoia but *subjectivities* in need of both care and understanding, an attitude that makes Hildegard's text, anachronistically or not, a feminist or proto-feminist one.

Let us look at some of Hildegard's categorizations and how they work. In describing male melancholia, she begins with a purely physiological description that follows the tradition of medieval portraiture by moving from top to bottom[45]:

> There are other males, however, whose brain is plump [pingue], and the skin over their brain and their veins are in turmoil. Their faces have a morose hue, such that their eyes even have something of fire and of vipers in them. They have hard and strong veins, which contain black and thick blood. Their flesh is thick and hard and they have big bones, whose marrow is of only a moderate size but heats up so strongly that around women they are incontinent and act like animals and like vipers [velut animalia et ut̜ viperae]. And wind exists in their loins in three ways, so that it is fiery or windy or mixed with the fumes of melancholia. (p. 73)

From the fatty quality of the atrabiliac's gray matter (the word *pingue* refers primordially to well-fattened livestock and could imply here either the intelligence of a big brain or, in a common figurative sense, the "thick-headedness" of an idiot), the male melancholic's body is not inscribed with the enabling lacks so dear to Ficino and his legacy, but with a malignant excess. In fact, this male melancholic is by no means inscribed with a loss of the flesh but rather with a vicious—and massive—corporeality. Hildegard does not attempt to minimalize the melancholic's link to the body by focusing on some kind of transcendent flight to higher spheres; instead the big-boned, big-brained, big-veined, and mighty melancholic is brought down to the level of bestiality by the clumsiness of his overwhelming physique.

The bestiality of melancholia is shown by the patient's viperous eyes (from which darts not love but hate) and by his animalistic behavior

[44]*De amore*, p. 138; *On Love*, pp. 122–23.
[45]Colby, *The Portrait*, pp. 6–7 and passim.

around women. Writing some three hundred years before Ficino, Hildegard finds in the categories of vision and desire not the recuperative signs of superhuman transcendence that propel Ficino's inquiry but the marks of a subhuman depravity. Her radical reinterpretation of melancholia as devolutionary regression is amplified in the following psychological depiction of male melancholic behavior:

> And for this reason, they have no proper delight in or affection for anything; but they are bitter, greedy, and foolish. With women, they are like asses [velut asini], exceedingly desirous and without moderation: whence if they should take a break from this desire, they readily fall into mental insanity, in such a frenzy are they. And when they follow through on this desire in intercourse with women, they do not suffer mental insanity; however, their embrace, which in moderation they owe women, is tortuous, hateful, and mortiferous like that of impetuous wolves [velut rapidorum luporum]. Now, some of these guys, because of strong veins and because of a marrow burning strongly, do cheerfully follow human nature in their contact with women, but nonetheless they hold these women in contempt [eas odio habent]. And some of these guys may shun women, because they neither love them nor want to have them, but in their hearts they are as enraged as lions and share the habits of bears [tam acres sunt ut leones, et mores ursorum habent]. (pp. 73–74)

Once again, the bestial regression of the male melancholic is signaled by his asinine sexual attentions, wolfish embraces, repressed feline rage, and bearish behavior. And, in a manner that anticipates a key strategy of Freudian psychoanalysis, Hildegard quickly shifts her psychological discussion from static moral concepts such as bitterness and greed to the intersubjective workings of a male libidinal economics predicated on a fundamental misogyny. Indeed, the melancholic's hatred of women becomes the defining trait that gives the affliction its coherence. Misogyny, however, as the unifying trait of the male melancholic is not for Hildegard an essential quality of male behavior in general. For example, in her discussion of the sanguine temperament, one "that flees and evades the bitterness of melancholia" [quem acerbitas melancoliae fugit et devitat] (p. 72), the sanguine man is one who in the absence of women is like a day without sunshine [velut dies qui sine sole est] and who in their presence becomes pleasant like a clear day [velut dies cum sole clarus est] (p. 73). The misogyny that is coextensive with melancholia, on the other hand, is what brings man down to the level of the beast.

Indeed, perhaps misogyny itself points to that perplexing "what" that Freud can never seem to uncover from a purely libidinal point of view. If one follows Hildegard's analysis, however, the melancholic man is, libidinally speaking, caught in an impossible situation. The very first remark she makes in shifting from physiological description to psychological analysis is to note what Freud too, much later, would note, namely that the melancholic suffers from a seeming inability to cathect his emotions [rectam dilectionem ad nullum habent]. To the extent that the libido is *not* cathected, however, there is logically an excess of libido in dire need of discharge. Consequently, one finds the (for Freud unexplainable) manic, or in Hildegard's terminology, frenetic moment of the melancholic syndrome, a frenzy whose repression according to her precipitates the subject into insanity: [si de hac libidine interdum cessaverint, facile insaniam capitis incurrunt]. So far, all of this can be transcribed into the received theses of psychoanalysis. Melancholia implies a libidinal economics wherein satisfaction can only take place for a short time at the same time that the repression of these minimal cathexes would provoke a psychosis. In contradistinction to Hildegard, but within this same framework of libidinal investments, Freud can be said to have thought of melancholia in terms of an initial problem of decathexis from the object (thus his recourse to the analogy with mourning) rather than in terms of an inability to cathect at all in an other.

But a close reading of Hildegard's text will allow us to go even further in revising Freud (as well as Ficino and others), for she raises the question—impossible to raise from within the intrasubjective frame of most psychoanalysis[46]—of what happens to the "love object" on whom the libido is discharged. Yes, she says, in a reversal of Aristotle's advice on the question, the male melancholic will save *his* sanity in the course of being with a woman, in intercourse with her: [in convictionem mulierum]. But what happens to *her*? And what is this *convictionem* really all about? In classical Latin, the substantive *convictio*, derived from the verb *con-vivere*, referred to a variety of forms of social interaction from feasting together (from which we have the *convivium*, a banquet such as the one Plato describes and which Ficino formally reproduces as the commentary *On Love*), to living together, to whatever the writers of

---

[46]Lacanian psychoanalysis is, of course, the most critical of this frame, especially as interpreted by theorists such as Juliet Flower MacCannell (*Figuring Lacan* [Lincoln: University of Nebraska Press, 1986]) or Jessica Benjamin (*The Bonds of Love: Psychoanalysis, Feminism, and the Problem of Domination* [New York: Pantheon, 1988]).

Latin dictionaries euphemistically call "intimate association." In the ecclesiastical Latin of the Middle Ages, which Hildegard would certainly have known, there is another sense of *convictio*, this time derived from *con-vincere*, to overcome, and thus, in legal terms, to convict. In ecclesiastical rhetoric, a *convictio* is a refutation, the act of convincing others through the force of one's own convictions that they are in error and thus stand "convicted." The implicit verbal aggressivity of such an agonistic approach might suggest another, less "convivial" reading of Hildegard's line about male melancholics "following through upon their desire in intercourse with women" [cum hanc libidinem in convictionem mulierum exercent], for it would also be possible to construe the same line to mean that they "exert their libido in convincing women." And what would women need to be "convinced of," if not that they should acquiesce to male desire, to having intercourse with this melancholy *convictor*?

Of course, this convincing evidence, being a piece of convicting evidence—the exhibit A of American court trials—is also a staging of the convincing process itself, a theater play about conviction. In this case, what is staged as convincing is the old misogynist myth—enormously comforting to the male ego—that women inherently do not enjoy sex, need to be convinced to have it, and certainly have no desires of their own. It is thus no surprise that the Western male has celebrated his rhetorical prowess in the "art" of seduction, with its militarist metaphors of besieging, penetrating, and possessing a resisting enclosure, from Roman elegy through troubadour lyric, *amor courtois*, the *Roman de la rose*, and on up through Petrarch and Renaissance Neoplatonism. And as all readers of this masculine cultural production well know, the intended addressee is never the "lady" to whom the text is supposedly directed but the *convivio* or circle of male readers whose function is either to approve and celebrate the seductive poet's "technical" achievement or to commiserate in his lack of "success." From Plato to Ficino, the *convivium* is an all-male gathering (presided over by that greatest of lovers and melancholics, Socrates). There, women may furnish the after-dinner entertainment, not by their all too threatening corporeal presence, but through their absent presence as the topic of male discourse.[47] Thus

[47]Cf. the similar discussion that takes place in the fifth part of Baldessar Castiglione's *Il Libro del Cortegiano*, in *Opere di Baldassare Castiglione, Giovanni della Casa, Benvenuto Cellini* ed. Carlo Cordié (Milan: Ricciardi, 1960), where women are for once physically present but determinately silent while the men discuss the virtues and faults of women.

"woman" figures as the occasion for a rhetorical exercise that is itself focused on male desire as a rhetorical problem: how to convince women to satisfy that desire or, better yet, how men can convince themselves that they do not really need women to satisfy that desire.[48] Either way, woman not only appears as the object of the convincing force of male verbiage but also and more distressingly, woman stands *as convicted*: a cruel and castrating femme fatale if she says no and remains "unconvinced," or a "vulgar" and "degrading" (i.e., also cruel and castrating) whore if she says yes too easily or, worse yet, immoderately displays her lack of needing to be convinced (once again, ostensibly threatening the male with castration).

Hildegard's text is necessarily eccentric to such a tradition and is not concerned with that perennial subject of male discourse, the unsated lover, whose castration (according to any of the above scenarios) is prosaically dismissed by Hildegard as a loss of mind, *insaniam capitis*. This "decapitation" is nothing more than a clinical madness whose "frenetic" energy is certainly not a pretext for its recuperation as the kind of divine frenzy or inspired insanity that so enthralls the Western male imaginary from Plato to Artaud and Pasolini. As Hildegard remarks, lack of satiety may lead to madness in men, but their libidinal satisfaction, whether through convincing women or having intercourse with them, or by having intercourse with them "because" they have convinced them to agree to it, means that these men do not suffer [non patiuntur] such debilitation. The question she raises is what happens to the women who have been convinced and who thus "convivially" associate with these men, who offer a feast to the victors of this rhetorical battle, a victory feast where the women are not dear friends or associates who eat together (*cum* + *panis*) but the spoils to be devoured.

The eloquence of Hildegard's *sed tamen* follows right on the heels of the *non patiuntur* of men: "but nevertheless"! Someone suffers from the *convictionem*, someone who appears as the victim of that conviviality, a victim devoured by a bestiality now characterized as specifically carnivorous: wolves, lions, bears.[49] The Freudian metaphor of incorpora-

---

[48]See my "In Praise of Virtuous Women?" and my "The Domestication of Woman in Cantos 42 and 43 of the *Orlando Furioso*: or, a Snake Is Being Beaten" *Stanford Italian Review* (Fall 1991).

[49]Hildegard's description of the dehumanization of the melancholic also forestalls any idealizing of men turned into beasts, especially with respect to that particular bestialization known as lycanthropy and frequently associated with melancholy.

tion (one of the most intriguing and important aspects of Freud's theory
of melancholia) has never seemed so literal as it now does in Hildegard's
description of cannibalism. If the melancholic is somehow incapable of
cathecting his libidinal energy onto an object, then he will become
literally insatiable, rapacious in his devouring of women who will never
be able to give him enough, to give him what he wants. (Perhaps the
real secret of psychoanalysis is not in its inability to describe what
"woman" wants—Freud's *Was woll das Weib?*—but in the even more
mysterious "what" that men want and for which they do all sorts of
things from repression to sublimation to incorporation to foreclosure.)

What the woman who suffers the male melancholic's embrace feels
is not love but hate [odiosa], Hildegard says, not the life-giving force
of copulation (whether understood carnally or, as in Ficino, cosmolog-
ically) but a draining of energy that brings death [mortifera]. And if the
libidinal economics of Freudian metapsychology is supposed to be a
theory of energy flows, why is it conceived in intrasubjective terms—
especially if so many of the same processes of energy transfer, displacement, and so on, happen so overtly in our day-to-day social lives?[50]
People who are a drain on our energy, for example, depress us (we view
them as depressing and they cause us to feel depressed); others radiate
an energy we find uplifting. Not that these sorts of processes are easy
to describe. In fact, the works of Jacques Lacan (especially his work on
transference as the key intersubjective event) are a testimony to both
the difficulty and the urgency with which even psychoanalysis with its
much touted "Copernican revolution" must think beyond the limits of
the subject.[51]

Following Hildegard, male melancholics, because they cannot cathect, suck all the life out of the women they are with. They cannot find
satisfaction in the company of women, so either they remain with them
while holding them in contempt, or else they reject women altogether
and secretly nurture their repressed anger against women. Melancholics
can never get enough and thus long for some heavenly Venus (or Saturn)
that does not present herself corporeally, that is, as "vulgar" Venus.
Since they long for this something beyond woman, they cannot love
her for herself [quia feminas non diligunt] but only for this something
beyond herself that she may represent but, of course, can never em-

[50]See Jessica Benjamin, *Bonds of Love.*
[51]See MacCannell, *Figuring Lacan.*

body.[52] All of this is to say finally that the melancholic man cannot love, has no *caritas*: [nulla opera caritatis et amplexionis in eis sunt] (p. 74). In fact, this inability to be generous points back to the truly sinful and diabolical dimension of the male melancholic, who, for Hildegard, in turning away from God is *also* turning against women: "The suggestion of the devil [suggestio diaboli] so rages in the libido of these men that, in marriage, if they could, they would put the woman to death" (p. 74).[53]

The social consequences of male melancholia are not limited to this form of domestic violence, for Hildegard also considers (and is apparently once again the only person to consider) what happens to the children of the melancholic. Such children "often receive a diabolical insanity in their vices and customs, for they are raised without love" [multotiens diabolicam insaniam in vitiis et in moribus suis habent, quoniam absque caritate emissi sunt] (p. 73). Victims too of melancholic ungenerosity, they are described as unhappy, tortured people, unable to enjoy the company of other human beings or even to live under the same roof with them. They "are fatigued by many fantasies" [multis fantasmatibus fatiguntur], and if they remain among human beings they have "no joy" [nullum gaudium], and are full of hatred, envy, and perversity. In many ways, this description of the melancholic's offspring sounds much more like conventional descriptions of melancholia than the insatiably sexualized rage of their fathers. Yet here too Hildegard resists the standard lines of recuperation. For her, this daydreaming misanthrope (or highly imaginative and misunderstood loner?) is not destined for any kind of greatness or special recognition—even should such persons be "prudentes et utiles": "But nevertheless [sed tamen] they display such serious and contrary manners that they can be neither prized nor honored, like worthless stones that have no glitter and are all worn out and that are not chosen from among shiny stones because they do not have a beautiful shine" (p. 74). The selfishness of the melancholic father translates into the death of the mother and the deter-

---

[52]Once again one need only think of Petrarch's Laura as well as other figures of women represented in male poetic texts who have stood for that something beyond. The eros of it is thus predicated on a safe inaccessibility. In other words, they can be loved because they are safely unreachable.

[53]Hildegard's acerbic criticisms of men's treatment of women are echoed some five hundred years later by another nun, Suor Arcangela Tarabotti, in her *La semplicità ingannata o la tirannia paterna*, in *Donna e società nel seicento: Lucrezia Marinelli e Arcangela Taraboti*, ed. Ginevra Conti Odorisio (Rome: Bulzoni, 1979), pp. 199–214.

mined ignominy of the children. It is hard to find a more sweeping condemnation of one of the West's most cherished psycho-cultural categories.

But there is also another category in Hildegard's schema that is not the grave *sed tamen* by which she usually unveils a brutal reality behind the mystifying illusions of melancholia. For Hildegard does not describe a state of depression that would spur conceptual or artistic insight but uncovers an ego structure dependent on the devaluation of others, here women and children, in order to give the ego a value in spite of the fact that it can never feel secure about itself. Here, one is once again reminded of Freud's split in the psyche, wherein one part of the ego feels superior to the other. *Sed tamen!* There is, however, a completely different category of melancholia, that of female melancholia. And through this category, Hildegard does not refer either to the female victims of male melancholia (why should they be particularly melancholic?) or to a female version symmetrical to the male condition (which is impossible under a patriarchal symbolic order and could certainly not have the same extended consequences).

Hildegard's discussion of female melancholia at first seems to follow—but then breaks down—the neat distinction she makes in her analysis of the male type: a physiological characterization was followed by a psychological assessment leading into a consideration of the melancholic's sexual and familial relations. True, the first sentence paints a physiological portrait, and the second offers some psychological correlatives: "But there are certain other women, who are lean in flesh with big veins, moderate-sized bones, and blood that is more livid in color than blood, and their faces are mixed with a greenish and black coloration. Their thoughts are also flighty and unstable, and they wearily languish in distress and affliction; and they are also of a nature to faint easily since they are also often tired out from the black bile" (p. 89). As distinct from the brawny male melancholic, the melancholic woman is emaciated and weak from the abundance of black bile that flows through her veins and thus gives her a livid hue. This overabundance of the black bile in the blood is also a source of fatigue, fainting spells, and difficulty in concentration. With the exception of the difficulty in concentration, Hildegard's picture resembles that of the melancholy lover in Ficino (the Ficinian scholar, we remember, had a heightened ability to get to the core of things); but again (*sed tamen?*) any horizon of transcendent beatitude is denied. Far from being some wondrously wounded lover carried on the wings of desire, the melancholy woman suffers from acute difficulties in sexual relations for both physiological and psychological reasons.

In order to carry out this analysis, however, Hildegard must ground herself in the physiological. Given her historical epoch, this grounding requires a questionable recourse to the Aristotelian theory of female physiology. Because of the influx of black bile and her large veins, the melancholy woman suffers from an unusually heavy menstruation, which is, according to Aristotle, the sign of woman's inherent infertility and inability to "concoct" (as the Cambridge translation puts it). Says Hildegard: "But they suffer from much blood in the menstrual period, because they have a weak and fragile womb. Whence, they are unable either to conceive or to retain or to heat up the male semen" (p. 89). And while she does not question the "cold-blooded" theory by which Aristotle simultaneously explains the physiological phenomenon of menstruation and denies to women any role in the reproductive process other than providing a receptacle for germination, Hildegard locates the cause of excessive menstruation and infertility in the effect of the same black bile that the Greek philosopher had linked with outstanding achievements in males. If melancholia helps men excel, its effects on women are completely debilitating, again corroborating my thesis here about the gendering of melancholia. This gendered dissymmetry is manifested, as I have also been arguing, in the symbolic register as the social accrediting of male lack and the concomitant discrediting of female loss. In other words, the castrated male is recuperated as transcendent genius while the infertile female is categorically rejected as one whose inability to be a mother deprives her of the only role patriarchy cares to assign her.

But here is where the physiological and the psychological are not just propped one on top of the other but are complexly intertwined in a way that suggests that the question of a woman's body *cannot* be separated from her social and hence psychological situation. Under canon law, one of the few reasons a husband could divorce his wife was if she failed to give him an offspring, and a male offspring at that. One can imagine the personal situation of medieval women who for whatever reason were unable to conceive. One can well imagine the mental and physical debilitation brought on by the prolonged anxiety associated with the fear of abandonment and loss of social status for not being able to force one's body to do something it refused to do. No wonder

Hildegard says that melancholic women are "saner, stronger and happier when without husbands than with them, because if they were with husbands they would become debilitated" [saniores, fortiores et laetiores sunt absque maritis quam cum eis, quoniam, si cum maritis fuerint, debiles redduntur] (p. 89).

On the other hand (as if Hildegard were positing a dialectical correlative on the psychological level), it turns out that melancholic women are only somewhat attracted to men and men are not at all attracted to them: "But men turn away from them and flee them, for these women do not address men affably and because they love men only moderately. And if these women would have had carnal pleasure with the men they love, nevertheless this pleasure quickly ceases in them" (p. 89). More reasons it would seem for women, or at least melancholy women, not to lock themselves into long relationships with men. Yet here again, Hildegard gives another response: "But some of these women, if they are with robust and sanguine husbands, after a certain time when they have come to an advanced age such as fifty, give birth to at least one child. If, however, they are with other husbands whose nature is feeble, then they will not conceive from them but will remain forever infertile" (p. 89). If we recall Hildegard's positive words about the sanguine male who lights up in the presence of women and is gloomy in their absence, we can read this alternative as an allegory of love (not, of course, in the transcendent and misogynist Ficinian sense but in a practical way as a comment on that rare event of an affection that is other-directed[54]). If we read a little between the lines of Hildegard's text, as I think we should, female melancholia is a psycho-physiological condition brought about by the anxiety of making one's body meet the (quite impossible) demand of a patriarchal symbolic order to be nothing more than a reproductive device. Under such conditions, anxiety and its psycho-physiological effects can only be alleviated by the tropism of a husband who lives for his wife, and not in spite or beyond her. Such a type, in Hildegard's analysis, would not be the melancholic, choleric, or phlegmatic husband, whose effect on the wife could only be the chilling one of a permanent infertility, especially if the husband's principal aim was to have a son. The sanguine husband, on the other hand, through his long-term assiduous attentions would actually bring about a slow re-

---

[54]Or what Juliet MacCannell calls "otherly" love (*Figuring Lacan*, p. 72).

versal in his wife's melancholic condition, thus allowing her to begin conceiving at an age when other women cease to do so.

Interestingly too, the sanguine male (whose temperament is characterized by an excess of blood in his body) has this positive effect on a condition in which one of the symptoms is stated to be an overly abundant menstrual flow. On the other hand, the lack of sanguinity in the male is as pernicious to the wife as is a precocious cessation of menstruation. Taking on her most doctorly and concerned tone, Hildegard diagnoses an obstruction by something "corrupt and fetid, which ought to have been purged out of their bodies through menstruation" [quoniam tabes et foeditas illa, quae per menstrua in corporibus earum purgari debuit] (p. 89). Such a woman is in dire need of help from "God or medicine" [per adiutorium dei seu per medicinam] (p.89) and is at risk of any number of severe ailments from swollen limbs, gout, back pains, and insanity ("stirred up by the black bile" [quam melancolia excitat]," p. 89) to death.

Female melancholia thus appears as a specifically gynecological malady that is inextricably physiological and psychological in nature. And, as such, it requires the particular concerns and attentions Hildegard directs to the suffering woman afflicted by this otherwise invisible or nonexistent category of humoral medicine. By rejecting any possible positive benefits of the disease in *either* of its gendered forms, she responds to this malady as an unfortunate affliction that needs to be diagnosed and treated. What Hildegard's text implicitly suggests is the need in medieval society for a radical revision of gender relations, that is, for an overturning of a symbolic order that positions the safety, happiness, and sanity of women in a precarious dependency on their bodies' (re)productive capacities. Furthermore, her critique of melancholia is also a criticism of a society that would allow the ruin of an entire family for at least two generations if the hierarchically superior father (on whom wife and children are made to depend) falls ill from a disease—melancholia—that leads him to devalue and devour those who should be most dear to him. So far, it seems that the principal lesson to be drawn from Hildegard's remarkable analysis—and all the more remarkable for its significant departures from the norms of humoral theory—is that a psychological category such as melancholia cannot be understood in purely psychological terms but that it also requires an understanding of its socio-sexual context.

In fact, such a context is precisely the point missed by Klibansky,

Panofsky, and Saxl in their ludicrously brief discussion of Hildegard of Bingen. Although they grant the "absolutely convincing inner unity" of her "pictures," they see her conceptual force as merely the effect of her stating everything "invariably in terms of sexual behaviour."[55] What they implicitly dismiss as "this very singular and entirely individual viewpoint" is also they say, "painted in the liveliest turns of phrase."[56] With apparent condescension and unwillingness to credit the intellectual force of this medieval woman's radical critique of melancholy, they quickly turn away from her, thus crediting the male-dominated history that has so unfairly buried her work and thought in quasi obscurity. Instead, they turn back to those unquestioned "greats" of melancholia: the male philosopher and the male artist, Ficino and Dürer.

Not everything, of course, is progressive or proto-feminist in Hildegard. Her correlation between heavy menstrual flow and infertility is one example we have seen. Another is her (not surprising) recourse to a theological frame within which to situate her analysis of melancholia. But even here, attention to nuance reveals a notable shifting of registers. In conjunction with the predominant moral and scholastic literature, Hildegard understands male melancholia as a sinful condition related to *acedia* or sloth, which designates the soul's laxity with respect to its spiritual duties to God. But when she discusses the female version of melancholia, the theological dimension is decidedly absent. Instead, we find a clinical emphasis on the psycho-physiological determinants of melancholia. Some explanation for this difference can be found in terms unrelated to gender if we turn to other dispersed comments she makes on the question of melancholia in general. For example, she often links the origin of melancholia with the fall of Adam himself, with the work of the devil's tongue: "Melancholia['s] beginning in the seed of Adam originated from the serpent's breath [de flatu serpentis], since Adam followed through on the serpent's advice regarding food." And "this melancholia is natural, however, in all men from the devil's first suggestion, since man transgressed the precept of God in eating the apple. And from this eating, this same melancholia has grown in Adam and his entire race, and it has roused every pestilence in men" (p. 38). In a more developed passage entitled, "On the Fall of Adam and Melan-

[55]Klibansky et al., *Saturn and Melancholy*, pp. 110–11. Oddly, they quote Hildegard on male melancholia but only briefly allude at the end of a long footnote to her discussion of female melancholia. Cf. also Agamben's dismissive treatment in *Stanze*, p. 20.

[56]Klibansky et al., *Saturn and Melancholy*, pp. 110–11.

cholia" [De Adae casu et melancolia], Hildegard not only pinpoints the origin of melancholia in Adam's original sin but seems to suggest a correlation between melancholia, or the workings of the black bile in the human body, and sin itself:

> For when Adam knew good and committed evil by eating the apple, in the vicissitude of his change melancholia rose up within him (which without the devil's suggestion is more dormant than wakeful in men), because sadness and despair which Adam got on account of his transgression arise from melancholia. For when Adam violated the divine precept, in that very moment melancholia coagulated in his blood, just as brightness recedes when a light is extinguished and as the hot and smoking candlewick remains with its foul smell. And so it was with Adam, because when the brightness in him was extinguished, melancholia coagulated in his blood, from which sadness and despair arose within him, since the devil kindled [conflavit] the melancholia in him which henceforth provides man with doubt and incredulity. (p. 143)

Given that within Hildegard's theological frame, the fall of Adam, [casus Adae] is the ultimate *cause* of our *curae* (cares), it is not surprising that she should devote such an effort to understanding the psychophysiological dynamics of this event. The metaphor of a blown-out candle seems most helpful if we are to unpack her interpretation. Although Adam is already stated in the first sentence to "know" the difference between good and evil, the moment of his transgression—the blowing out of the light of his soul—is simultaneous with his succumbing to the force of the devil's breath [flatus serpentis] and to the coagulation of black bile within his blood, a coagulation that is said to be "kindled" [conflatus] by the devil. The burn-out of his soul is doubled by the burning of the blood that produces black bile [melancolia adusta], which Hildegard likens to the smelly and smoldering residue of the blown-out candle. An onslaught of emotions such as sadness, despair, doubt, incredulity accompanies this surfacing of black bile. Without the devil's suggestion, melancholia remains dormant in the body and is only aroused by the act of turning against God that is sin. Melancholia thus is not simply a cause of sinful behavior but is the very presence of sin in the human being. It is the presence of the devil in man whose "viperous" eyes and suspect behavior speak of the internalization (introjection) of the evil serpent. The emotions associated with melancholia can therefore be understood as signs of the sinful state man falls into in the absence of God. Thus, the melancholic is not just depressed (i.e., sad and despairing) but also skeptical, producing an affective nexus that leads the sufferer farther and farther away from God. In another passage, Hildegard writes that the melancholic's doubt is such as to refuse any and all forms of consolation [dubietatem totius consolationis parat] (p. 38). Certainly not a gain in insight of any kind, Adam's fall and resultant melancholia are a plunge into a very dark ignorance: "When Adam transgressed, however, the brightness of innocence was darkened in him, and his eyes which previously could see the heavens were put out" (p. 145).

Hildegard's Adam, however, is not just some kind of unconscious Oedipus (i.e., one who suffers the same punishment but without the corresponding heightening of consciousness); he is also a misguided Prometheus seeking deliverance from the wrong hands: "But because the human form is bound [ligata est] such that it cannot raise itself upward, man fears God and is sad, and often in this sadness so lacks faith in God as to despair that God might be watching him" (pp. 143–44). As in Freud, the melancholic is haunted by the judgmental gaze of a superior entity. Hildegard, however, denounces this particular super-ego, which already resembles the fearsome panoptic God later cherished by Protestant reformers, as a fundamental misrecognition that forgets that humankind is supposed to be formed in the image of God [homo ad imaginem dei formatus est] (p. 144). It is only by denying the *formal* resemblance between God and the human creature (the divinity in humankind or even the humanity of God) that one could "fear God more than the devil" [quod homo deum tamen plus timet quam diabolus] p. 144). But then who or what is the devil? Is he not the negative other or sinister double (*dia-bolus*) of God, he who instead of blowing life into the body blows out the candle of the soul? Melancholics, in mistaking God for the devil and vice versa, end up blowing or burning themselves out: "But the suggestion of the devil so often twists itself [se intorquet] into this melancholia and makes men sad and despairing, such that in this way men suffocate and consume themselves out of desperation" (p. 144).

This conclusion suggests that melancholia is an essential and inescapable condition of all post-lapsarian human existence, a condition of sin itself. And in fact, in addition to sadness, despair, and doubt, Hildegard is thereby able to connect melancholia with numerous other *curae*, including lethargy, impiety, and even wrath: "For wrath is born of sadness, just as humans contracted sadness and wrath and everything injurious from our first parent" (p. 146). (Compare her entire section titled "De tristitia et ira," (p. 146.) There is, however, a resistance against this all-encompassing determinism that makes melancholia coextensive with the work of the devil, sin, and what appears to be the entirety of human misery (or *curae*): "Many, however, resist this evil to themselves such that they are like martyrs in this battle" (p. 144).

In other words, resistance to melancholia is resistance to sin. The struggle to maintain hope and a sanguine temperament is heroic and even saintly for Hildegard, who also incidentally differentiates God from the devil in terms of the former as the source of hope: "Man finds hope in God, the devil however has none for him" (p. 144). As we saw in the discussion of the female melancholic and marriage, feisty sanguinity had already been foregrounded as a model of positive benefit just as the incrementally negative and sinful consequences of melancholia had been demonstrated in the masculine version of the syndrome. All of this brings us to raise the question of gender in Hildegard's general theory of melancholia as a condition that emanates from the fall of Adam. In fact, Hildegard's repeated allusions to Adam emphasize an absence so glaring it cannot be ignored: that of Eve, who in the text of Genesis is *first* seduced by the serpent's words and *first* tastes the forbidden fruit before Adam himself follows suit. There should be no need to point out the importance of this sequence in the Judeo-Christian tradition: it legitimates the view of Eve as the cause of Adam's downfall, as the gullible or foolish woman who listens to the devil's sweet talk and then manages to convince a presumed-to-be skeptical husband.

Now, Hildegard's departure from the biblical script attributes the sole agency and responsibility for the transgression to Adam and thus obviates *any* possibility of pinning the cause of melancholia onto a female agent (as the late medieval romance misogynously does), just as she has foreclosed any hint of privileged being in the melancholic subjectivity (whether in an Aristotelian or in a Ficinian vein). It is for this reason that I have placed the discussion of her text *after* the other principal points of the melancholic tradition. While there is, to my mind, a (very small) risk of chronological confusion in this sequence of presentation, it also allows one, I think, to see even more dramatically how radically different this woman's text is from the canonically male lineage of melancholia.

Indeed, the resistance to melancholia, which Hildegard posits as a

moral strategy over and beyond the psycho-physiological determinism
of humoral medicine, also pinpoints an ideological and political struggle
against a male hegemonic construct. By attributing the origin of melancholia to the fall of Adam, she unmasks the fundamentally phallocratic
allegiance of the melancholic tradition. Her willful revision of the biblical
text *is* (anachronistically or not) a feminist gesture that still teaches
feminist theory today the urgency as well as the possibility of deconstructing male myths, and especially male myths of origin. It is this
critical dislocation of the phallocratic construction that signals the value
of her project over and beyond any possible "essentialism" of gender
categories or any entrapment in Christian narrative.

Let me go one step further. In addition to delineating a theory of
female melancholia, Hildegard points to an unveiling of desire at work
in its male version. In Satan's blowing out of Adam's candle, we have
a ready metaphor of what Lacan calls primary castration, which Hildegard would thus connect with the origin of melancholia as a universal
human predicament (i.e., one with which we must all come to terms).
The melancholic, however, who mistakes the devil for God, seeks to
deny his castration by appealing for salvation to the very agent of the
castration. Such a masochistic relation cannot help but recall Ficino's
Saturnian elitism, in which the malevolent, devouring, and castrating
Saturn was also the friend and inspiration of the melancholic philosopher. Structurally, Ficino's Saturn seems to occupy the same position
as Hildegard's *diabolus*, with the difference that Hildegard would reveal
the promise of heightened insight, and so on to be a dangerous mystification. There are some reasons—iconographic as well as alliterative—
to place Saturn and Satan together: devouring mouths, black cloak,
sickle, dragon-drawn chariot, etc.[57] Furthermore, in psychoanalytic
terms their mythical and structural proximity suggests that the origin
of melancholia has something to do with a vexed relation to a castrating
father who would also be an object of affection and desire.[58] The duplicity (or doubleness) of the *diabolus* suggests the imagistic ease with
which both possibilities can be played out: God and the devil are mere

[57]See the images of Saturn in ibid., plates 10–59, although the authors do not make the
connection. On the devil as a figure of the father, see Freud, *A Seventeenth-Century Demonological Neurosis*, S.E. 19: 83–92.
[58]For a suggestive analysis of melancholia as the affect produced by a cultural (heterosexual)
prohibition that would deny the son's love and access to the father, see Judith Butler's *Gender
Trouble: Feminism and the Subversion of Identity* (New York: Routledge, 1990), pp. 57–65.

doubles of each other, like the "good" and the "bad" fathers in Freud. Desiring and fearing the father's love is certainly a problem for feminine subjectivity, but it is constructed as an insuperable contradiction for a masculine one in the context of Western patriarchy: either the little boy must renounce à la Oedipus both desire and fear, or he must seek to take the place of a woman in the father's heart. Whence the beatified feminization of the melancholic in Ficino, but also the viperous rage against women depicted by Hildegard.

Hildegard also traces a crucial difference when she speaks of those who resist melancholia as potential "martyrs." Yet nothing seems to emblematize the ruses of male melancholia as a discursive practice better than the figure of the martyr, whose woeful suffering is merely the price to be paid for entrance into the immortal pantheon of heroes, philosophers or artists. But in Hildegard's revisionist sense, the martyr's suffering is not the call of something higher but the call to struggle for something better. Suffering is not something to withstand or passively "enjoy" but something to alleviate and overcome. Melancholia is not a blessed curse; it is just a curse, one that we must all work to overturn. Not to work against this affliction would be to indulge in a narcissism that can only separate human beings from each other in vicious rivalry. Such is the crucial lesson, both clinical and cultural, to be learned from the too-quickly forgotten text of this medieval nun.

Chapter 3

Appropriating the Work of Women's Mourning: From Petrarch to Gaspara Stampa, and from Isabella di Morra to Tasso

W hile he was still alive the fame of Marsilio spread throughout almost the whole world." So spoke Giovanni Corsi in his 1506 biography of the great melancholic philosopher Ficino.[1] By the time Ficino died in October 1499, his celebrity and institutional importance warranted the pomp of a public funeral. Corsi's description of this funeral is brief but telling: "All his friends attended the funeral as well as many of the nobility. Marcello Virgilio made the funeral speech away from the general gathering. Marsilio was buried in the church of the Santa Reparata in the sepulchre reserved for canons. The people of Florence attended, with grief and tears" (p.148). While Corsi's account depicts the dead philosopher as *both* a notable citizen and a popular hero, it also sketches powerful social and symbolic differences. The eulogy made by the humanist scholar Marcello Virgilio Adriani, then chancellor of Florence, takes place distinctly *apart* from the "general gathering," presumably made up of the same grieving and tearful *populo* who attend the burial. In other words, humanist and neo-Latin eloquence pronounced in the company of noblemen and friends of the philosopher contrasts with and takes place in a space exclusive of the inarticulate

---

[1] " 'The Life of Marsilio Ficino' by Giovanni Corsi," in *The Letters of Marsilio Ficino*, trans. Language Department of the School of Economic Science, London, American ed. (New York: Gingko Press, 1985), 3: 147.

expressions of popular sorrow. Class difference thus seems to subtend
a difference in mourning practices.

While such a social hierarchy seems consonant with the general
framework of Ficinian philosophy especially as expressed in the letter
to Cherubino Quarquagli, it is nevertheless ironic that this philospher
of melancholia who repeatedly rejected the act of mourning became
upon his death such an accredited object of mourning and grief. "Tell
me," writes Ficino in a letter to Bernardo Bembo,

> what is it that you mourn in a friend's death? is it death? or is it the person
> who is dead? if it is death, mourn your own, Bernardo. For as surely as
> he is dead will you too die; or rather, you are dying; for from moment
> to moment your past life is dying. If it is the dead person you mourn, is
> it because he was bad, or because he was good? If he was bad, you are
> well rid of such a companion; and you should not grieve over your
> blessings. If he was good, which I prefer to think since he is loved by a
> good and prudent man, surely for him it is good to live removed from
> the continuous death of the body. It is not right to grudge a friend such
> great blessings. (*Letters* 1: 97)

Elsewhere Ficino asks, "But why should I lament the death of Piero,
our Cardinal? Immortal God will not desert us, even if a mortal man
has done so" (1: 117). For Ficino, death was but the threshold through
which man's melancholy soul would return to an originary oneness.
Only the *vulgus* could be taken in by the lure of mourning, while the
wise, and no doubt melancholic, humanist elite could find consolation,
if not downright celebration. This split is what at first seems to explain
the double crowd attending Ficino's funeral: the friends and nobles
calmly listening to speeches on the inside, the wailing and tearful rabble
on the outside.

While Ficino's neo-platonism could celebrate death as life, other
humanists of the early quattrocento, such as Bruni and Salutati, had
already been modeling a relationship to death that was predicated on
control of outward expressions of grief. Humanism ushered in a new
code of public decorum, especially for those who held public office. As
historian Sharon Strocchia explains, "Bruni's chancery reforms of 1436
denied signs of public mourning to members of the Signoria, principal
communal officials, and their notaries. By the time Bruni died in 1444,
his eulogist Manetti offered such decorum as a more generalized model

for citizenship and manhood as well."² Yet, as Strocchia has further shown in a series of important articles, the humanist revision of funerary practices was not innocent and must be understood in terms of what it was revising. According to Strocchia, trecento funerals in Florence were occasions for displays of "conspicuous consumption" on the part of the city's ruling families. The more sumptuously the corpse and mourners were bedecked, the more persuasive were that family's claims to prestige and power. Within this corporatist mentality the funerals of women were as much the occasion for this self-aggrandizing ostentation as the funerals of men; the symbolic gains accrued to the family as a whole. Moreover, as Strocchia's study of sumptuary permits shows, "women frequently exploited funeral occasions through the manipulation of mourning routines and clothing."³ It is against the exhibition of such finery and ornamentation that the humanist prescription of restraint and understatement should be placed.

More important, as Strocchia also shows, there is a gender politics at work in this humanist critique, whose appearance in the early quattrocento coincided with a move from a corporatist to a patrilinear social order. Perhaps what needs to be understood is the way grief and mourning became reconceived through humanist discourse, which explicitly "masculinized" the affect of grief at the same time that the ideology of masculinization (along with the ideology of citizenship) came to restructure and dominate the public sphere precisely through a reconceptualization of death. The rise of civic humanism meant the establishment of funerary practices whereby public praise and eulogies no longer extended to dead women. Furthermore, Strocchia argues that if (male) humanists sang the praises of dead women, it was explicitly done in

²Sharon T. Strocchia, "Funerals and the Politics of Gender in Early Renaissance Florence," in *Refiguring Woman: Perspectives on Gender and the Italian Renaissance*, ed. Marilyn Migiel and Juliana Schiesari (Ithaca: Cornell University Press, 1991). Also see her "Remembering the Family: Women, Kin, and Commemorative Masses in Renaissance Florence," *Renaissance Quarterly* 42 (Winter 1989), 635–54; and "Death Rites and the Ritual Family in Renaissance Florence," in *Life and Death in Fifteenth-Century Florence*, ed. Marcel Tetel, Ronald G. Witt, and Rona Goffen (Durham, N.C.: Duke University Press, 1989), pp. 120–45. On the tradition of ritual mourning in Mediterranean culture, see Ernest de Martino, *Morte e pianto rituale nel mondo antico: Dal lamento pagano al pianto di Maria* (Turin: Einaudi, 1958); Alberto Tenenti, *Il senso della morte e l'amore della vita nel rinascimento* (Turin: Einaudi, 1957); and Moshe Barasch, *Gestures of Despair in Medieval and Early Renaissance Art* (New York: New York University Press, 1976). On women and ritual, see Christiane Klapisch-Zuber, *Women, Family, and Ritual in Renaissance Italy*, trans. Lydia Cochrane (Chicago: University of Chicago Press, 1985).
³Strocchia, "Funerals and the Politics of Gender."

private and through the genre of consolatory letters, which thus served to mark even more the privatization of women. This privatization, Strocchia shows, could also be seen in the restrictions placed on women's public (and collective) expressions of grief. Not the least "visible" of these restrictions was the imposition of dress standards with the spread of sumptuary laws in the quattrocento that eventually led in the following century to the adoption, "under Spanish influence," of the notorious black dress.[4] Such an ideology of the containment of grief and affect is concomitant with the defeminization of the public sphere and, as such, the repression of women's public mourning. The class difference foregrounded at Ficino's funeral is thus also a gender difference.

One of the most explicit statements of this ideology is made by one of the foremost figures of early Renaissance humanism, Francesco Petrarca, in a letter of 1373 titled "How a Ruler Ought to Govern His State" and written to Francesco da Carrara, then lord of Padua. In this letter of political pedagogy, Petrarch in no uncertain terms commands that grieving women should no longer be allowed to gather in the streets.

> Therefore, I will tell you what I am asking. Take an example: Some old dowager dies, and they carry her body into the streets and through the public squares accompanied by loud and indecent wailing so that someone who did not know what was happening could easily think that here was a madman on the loose or that the city was under enemy attack. Now, when the funeral cortege finally gets to the church, the horrible keening redoubles, and at the very spot where there ought to be hymns to Christ or devoted prayers for the soul of the deceased in a subdued voice or even silence, the walls resound with the lamentations of the mourners and the holy altars shake with the wailing of women. All this simply because a human being has died. This custom is contrary to any decent and honorable behavior and unworthy of any city under your rule. I wish you would have it changed. In fact, I am not just advising you, I am (if I may) begging you to do so. Order that wailing women should not be permitted to step outside their homes; and if some lamentation is necessary to the grieved, let them do it at home and do not let them disturb the public thoroughfares.[5]

---

[4]Ibid., and "Death Rites and the Ritual Family." On the adoption of the "Spanish" black dress, see Charles Boer, ed. and trans., *Marsilio Ficino: The Book of Life* (Irving, Tex.: Spring Publications, 1980), p. xiv. Also see Diane Owen Hughes, "Sumptuary Laws and Social Relations in Renaissance Italy," in *Disputes and Settlements: Law and Human Relations in the West*, ed. John Bossy (Cambridge: Cambridge University Press, 1983), pp. 69–99.

[5]Francesco Petrarca, "How a Ruler Ought to Govern His State," in Benjamin G. Kohl and Ronald G. Witt, eds., with Elizabeth B. Welles, *The Earthly Republic: Italian Humanists*

This passage merits comment. What we have before us is a scene, the public thoroughfare of Padua where a funeral cortege is taking place. But the scene is explicitly gendered, for not only are the mourners women but the person they are mourning is a deceased woman, more precisely a dowager, hence a wealthy dead woman. But her name is unimportant to Petrarch since she is merely an example, just "some old dowager." (I cannot help but be reminded here of Freud's women melancholics who too are mere types of women.) Her name thus can be implicitly disparaged as *any* old dowager, as anybody who is not somebody because that body is the body of a woman. Thus, in this particular scene, her death attains meaning to the extent that she is the cause for the "loud and indecent" lamentations of the mourning women who carry her body. Furthermore, as Petrarch informs us, if we did not know what was happening, we would think that "a madman [was] on the loose or that the city was under enemy attack." Madness, indecency, and war are all here linked by Petrarch to women's voices in his appeal to clean up the streets of Padua and to rid them of such unruly behavior. We might even suggest that these "unruly" women who rule the public streets at such times with their ritualized laments are Petrarch's occasion for grief. Thus, his grievance is with the ruler of the state who would still allow women to gather together in public to grieve. Surely it is no coincidence that Petrarch's desire to territorialize the public sphere as masculine, as clean, sober, and silent (or silenced by the expulsion of women) appears in a text on how a ruler should govern his state. As Carole Pateman argues in another context, but one that nonetheless seems to apply transhistorically, "The disorder of women means that they pose a threat to political order and so must be excluded from the public world."[6] And yet, one may ask, were these women's ritualized expressions of grief really disorder? How could they be disorder when mourning was part precisely of a symbolic order? I think what we need to see is that in the transition from a feminized symbolic (or one at least in which women had a more central role) to a masculinist symbolic, the "disorder of women" becomes part of an ideological apparatus that would empower men to hegemonize the public sphere, hence to phallicize the symbolic.

But Petrarch's desire to rid the streets of Padua of grieving women

---

on Government and Society (Philadelphia: University of Pennsylvania Press, 1978), pp. 35–78, quotation from p. 78.

[6]Carole Pateman, *The Disorder of Women* (Stanford: Stanford University Press, 1989), p. 4.

in favor of a masculine ideology of moral stamina signified by silent grief is situated not only in a text attendant to notions of citizenship and the state, but also in a text in which political correctness and political order turn around issues of death. Petrarch maps out for the ruler of Padua the ways different rulers in history died and how their deaths affected their subjects.[7] What is thus at stake in this text is precisely death and who or what group defines the ideology of living and dying properly. It is here in the symbolic definitions of death and life that we read how notions of loss and of lack are inscribed within ideologies that gender subjects according to hierarchical schemas of empowerment and disempowerment. And it is ironic that Petrarch, as *poeta vates* or seer poet, phallicizes grief through a poetics of loss and absence, that is through Laura as the absent object. Laura is the woman who has disappeared from the public sphere only to reappear as the epitome of "femininity," the idealized woman whose absence allows the poet to fetishize absence while women are systematically domesticated and privatized.[8]

Diane Owen Hughes too has shown that—in Italy—as modern communes were formed, women were systematically excluded from retaining any central role in what had been part of a feminine symbolic, such as the rites of mourning.[9] And in her now classic "Did Women Have a Renaissance?" feminist historian Joan Kelly argues that the early

---

[7]Petrarca, "How a Ruler Ought to Govern," pp. 46–47.

[8]While Strocchia does discuss alternative modes of women's empowerment in the private and their ways of finding access to the public sphere (i.e., through church rituals such as the requiem mass), these alternatives scarcely pertain in the world of letters, and not at all in terms of access to public office, etc. It should also be mentioned that although Strocchia is talking about Florence, the letter Petrarch wrote is addressed to the ruler of Padua, which suggests that the tendency to masculinize the sphere is really a *humanist* move regardless of region and has its consequences in other parts of Europe. On mourning and the meanings of death in Renaissance Florence, see the excellent essays in Tetel, Witt, and Goffen, *Life and Death in Fifteenth-Century Florence*, especially, with regard to Petrarchan humanism, William J. Kennedy, "Petrarchan Figurations of Death in Lorenzo de' Medici's Sonnets and *Comento*," pp. 46–47; and John McManamon, "Continuity and Change in the Ideals of Humanism: The Evidence from Florentine Oratory," pp. 68–87. On Venice, see Margaret L. King, "The Death of the Child Valerio Marcello: Paternal Mourning in Renaissance Venice," in *Renaissance Rereadings: Intertext and Context*, ed. Maryanne Cline Horowitz, Anne J. Cruz, and Wendy A. Furman (Urbana: University of Illinois Press, 1988), pp. 205–24.

[9]Diane Owen Hughes, "Invisible Madonnas? The Italian Historiographical Tradition and the Women of Medieval Italy," in *Women in Medieval History and Historiography*, ed. Susan Mosher Stuard (Philadelphia: University of Pennsylvania Press, 1987), p. 31: "The ordering of the commune, an exclusively male corporation whose earliest laws not only excluded women from membership but also sought to limit their dominance in the private sphere, restrict[ed] those marriage festivities, mourning ceremonies and birth celebrations that had accorded women a central role."

consolidation of city-states in Italy's urban north, the precocious capitalism of those city-states, and the ideological import of contemporary writings on family life and education did much to create a split between public and private, relegating women more and more to the latter. However, as Kelly remarks, it is within such a framework that we can more easily chart some of the complexities of women's subject positions in terms of art, literature, and philosophy, "the symbolic products of society." As Kelly says, we can measure these responses in terms of "loss or gain."[10] But while the social space defined by women's right to mourn became increasingly restricted and while women became more and more ensconced within the home, some women of the Italian cinquecento resisted and found ways to reformulate loss, I argue, by writing out a poetics of mourning in lieu of a poetics of melancholia.

Before turning to the particular cases of Gaspara Stampa and Isabella di Morra, I would like to consider more generally the situation of women writers of the Italian Renaissance in confronting and rewriting a poetic inscription of eros dominated by a masculine economy of desire that situates loss within an aesthetic privileging of woman as the mere object of the male gaze, a poetics best known by the name of the same Petrarch who advocated the suppression of public mourning by women. These women writers faced a male economy of desire that recuperates loss by denying it to women, even or especially when woman is aesthetically privileged as the very metaphor of loss. What I am proposing is a way to read those women poets of the Renaissance who revise that melancholic tradition by rejecting the metaphysical figure of woman as a mere icon of male desire. If there are discourses on melancholia (such as Ficino's) predicated on loss and privileging a masculine aesthetic that would represent "his" loss (Ficino and Petrarch), it should also be understood that women too have represented loss but not necessarily in terms of a melancholic poetics. Instead of a mere mimesis of melancholic eros certain women writers reaffirm *mourning* as an intersubjective space within which loss is represented. Within a symbolic structure governed by the phallus wherein lack would be sutured through the figure of woman, the explicit acknowledgment of loss that mourning carries out points in these women's texts to a refusal of such positionings.[11]

[10]Joan Kelly, *Women, History, and Theory: The Essays of Joan Kelly*, ed. Catharine R. Stimpson (Chicago: University of Chicago Press, 1984), p. 20.
[11]Strocchia, "Funerals and the Politics of Gender." On this type of intersubjectivity, see

Within the specific context of cinquecento Italy, we thus need to understand how women manipulated the Petrarchan language and its traditions and how they came to challenge that same language and tradition by rewriting the poetic voice in terms of a gendered self that exposes the Petrarchan poetics of lack as a cultural and metaphysical recuperation of male eros. It is well known that Petrarch's *Canzoniere* became the model that dominated poetic expression in the Renaissance. In fact, his poetics could be said to be the institutionalized eros of the Italian Renaissance. Petrarch's glorification of Laura became the means through which Petrarch attained glory and through which woman as the specular object for erotic self-recuperation became institutionalized. The ecstasy and despair of Petrarch's lyric eroticized lack in terms of a lost object, the bemoaning of whose loss also erected the poetic subject.[12] As Klibansky, Panofsky, and Saxl have also argued, Petrarch, although never naming himself a melancholic, did indeed pave the way for a melancholic poetic pathos to emerge.[13] And one could further their claim by stating that Petrarch modeled and legitimated male desire in terms of a specifically *nostalgic* quest for "truth." The "feminine" became ensconced in the beyond and became the pretext for a poetic trajectory, and as such, the "feminine" became the representational place of loss. Through such a representation of loss, Petrarch enfranchised his eros for the ipso facto derealized, idealized, specularized Laura. As Nancy Vickers has shown, " 'I' speaks 'his' anxiety in the hope of finding repose

---

Jessica Benjamin, *The Bonds of Love: Psychoanalysis, Feminism, and the Problem of Domination* (New York: Pantheon, 1988), esp. pp. 19–24, 125–31, and 211–24.

[12]While it is, of course, possible to reread Petrarch so as to show how the subject erected in his poetry is also rhetorically undone—see for example, John Freccero, "The Fig Tree and the Laurel: Petrarch's Poetics," *Diacritics* 5, 1 (1975), 34–40; and Marguerite R. Waller's more ambitiously deconstructive *Petrarch's Poetics and Literary History* (Amherst: University of Massachusetts Press, 1980)—that is not the "Petrarch" that subsequent writers and especially women poets have had to confront. On the contrary, Petrarch's self-representation as a "scattered" self does not prevent—indeed I would argue that it promotes—the association of the poet with a powerfully inspired subjectivity. The point is that psychological loss is recuperated as aesthetic and cultural gain. Therefore, rather than reread Petrarch to recuperate his lyric from a misogynist image, my analysis here takes the risk of a certain "unfairness" to show how some women poets (Gaspara Stampa, Isabella di Morra) rewrite Petrarch's poetry and Petrarchism. I choose to read Petrarch's poem "Weep, ladies, and let Love weep with you" not out of some arbitrary malice toward its author but because Stampa's shrewd revision of that poem dramatizes by way of contrast precisely the narcissistic subjectivity and conceptual binarisms (including gender binarism) that have historically been received as the hallmarks of Petrarch's poetry. As I argue later, reconceiving the noncanonical status of these female *petrarchisti* is an issue for a feminist literary history.

[13]Raymond Klibansky, Erwin Panofsky, and Fritz Saxl, *Saturn and Melancholy* (New York: Basic Books, 1964), p. 248.

through enunciation, of re-membering the lost body, of effecting an inverse incarnation—her flesh made word. At the level of fictive experience which he describes, successes are ephemeral, and *failures become a way of life*" (my emphasis).[14] It is precisely the fictionality of failures that idealizes the loss of Laura as the artistic triumph of the poet, whose "inspired" words monumentalize his loss as the absolute gain of poetic immortality. She is a mere pretext for a melancholic voice that needs her ensconced in the far away in order to represent a trajectory whose difficulty signifies that voice as extraordinary.[15]

What happens, though, if we have a woman writing in the Petrarchan tradition and the roles are reversed, that is, the "I" that speaks is the "I" of a woman? As Ann Rosalind Jones has argued, the poet Gaspara Stampa (like her contemporary Tullia d'Aragona) takes on her role as a woman poet/lover, but in such a way as to refute the pastoral, solipsistic melancholy of previous writers such as Petrarch or Sanazzaro through a rewriting of Ovid's tales of Echo and of Procne and Philomel as "fable[s] of troubled feminine identity, eased through woman-to-woman solidarity." Jones has shown how Stampa, for example, establishes a "relationship of willed empathy with mythological heroines" whom "she invites into a *chorus* of laments."[16] What Jones demonstrates is that in Stampa we read a willful refusal to accept the solitary male figure as the only possible utterance of loss. Instead, her sonnets often point to a communal mourning. Through a Stampa, then I think we can see a recasting of loss in terms of a feminine symbolic, that is, in terms of a collective mourning for the expropriation of women's subjectivities, their appropriation through a poetics of nostalgia that has historically devalued the potential for women to make viable claims in terms of loss and grief. Whereas male melancholia can be understood as an eroticized lack of the object that builds up the subject (as in Petrarch), Stampa is, in

[14]Nancy Vickers, "Diana Described: Scattered Woman and Scattered Rhyme," in *Writing and Sexual Difference*, ed. Elizabeth Abel (Chicago: University of Chicago Press, 1982), p. 105. For a reading that analyzes Petrarch's poetic subjectivity and the eros of dispersion in terms of an anxiety about the passage of time, see Teodolinda Barolini, "The Making of a Lyric Sequence: Time and Narrative in Petrarch's *Rerum vulgarium fragmenta*," *MLN* 1–38.

[15]For the reduction of the lover to a hypostatized lost object of desire in the Arabic and Provençal poetry that so influenced Petrarch, see Ioan Couliano, *Eros and Magic in the Renaissance*, trans. Margaret Cook (Chicago: University of Chicago Press, 1987), esp. p. 20. Also see Jacques Lacan's remarks on courtly love in *Feminine Sexuality: Jacques Lacan and the Ecole Freudienne*, trans. Jacqueline Rose, ed. Juliet Mitchell and Jacqueline Rose (New York: Norton, 1982), p. 141.

[16]Ann Rosalind Jones, "New Songs for the Swallow: Ovid's Philomela in Tullia d'Aragona and Gaspara Stampa," in *Refiguring Woman*, ed. Migiel and Schiesari, pp. 263–77.

fact, mourning the loss of women's own subjectivities, the loss of the ability to speak as a libidinalized voice, while at the same time she defies that appropriation by the act of writing out a strategy for women to mourn their loss *together*. It is thus not that the object of loss (let us say, women's voices) cannot be represented. It is just that the subject of the lament has not been sufficiently empowered to represent it.

According to the long-standing tradition of male literary criticism, the women writers of the Italian Renaissance (with the possible exception of Vittoria Colonna) have never been or could never be Petrarchan enough.[17] What Stampa is mourning is the deprivation that disallows women's voices from being accredited. It is not that loss cannot be represented or mourned for; it is just that the loss is appropriated by discourses that give to men an accredited loss. It can thus be argued that instead of writing a poetics of lack, some *cinquecento* women poets have written a poetics of the "prosaic" by recasting loss in terms of an ironic recapitulation of male desire. I use the term "prosaic" not to diminish the artistic value of their work but by way of polemical affirmation in the face of male literary critics such as Eugenio Donadoni, who in attempting to value Gaspara Stampa's work devalue it (and by extension that of other women poets) by suggesting that her work is a mere outlet for passion, a mere expression of life, that "rarely become[s] art."[18]

If a woman's lack is never lacking enough, and her poetry never Petrarchan enough, Stampa, I argue, rewrites the poetics of metaphysical and artistic lack and refashions the voice of the "victim." The mourning for a lost object in her poetry may be at times an explicit reference to her lover. But it is mourning *not* merely for a particular lost object, but also for the generalized loss of possibilities women suffer under patriarchal dominance by their lack of an accredited lack. Even if she appropriates certain of its conventions, Stampa thus rejects the Petrarchan metaphysics of lack that would inscribe her as inferior. In sonnet XXVIII, "when I come before those beautiful eyes" [quando innanti ai begli

---

[17] Cf. among other choice examples, Jacob Burckhardt, *The Civilization of the Renaissance in Italy*, trans. S. G. C. Middlemore (New York: Harper & Row, 1958), 2: 390; and Giulio Ferroni's introductory note on Isabella di Morra in his anthology *Poesia italiana del Cinquecento*, ed. Giulio Ferroni (Milan: Garzanti, 1978), pp. 249–50. On the traditional treatment of Gaspara Stampa's poetry as of merely epistolary or documentary interest, see Fiora Bassanese, *Gaspara Stampa*, Twayne's World Authors 658 (Boston: Twayne, 1982), p. 99 and passim.
[18] Cited in Bassanese, *Gaspara Stampa*, p. 40. See also, in a more sympathetic vein, Bassanese's own remarks on the "prosaic" in Stampa, p. 45.

occhi], Stampa's persona is represented as one for whom language fails whenever her lover's gaze is upon her: "the style, the tongue, desire and wit, thoughts, concepts and feelings remain all oppressed or all spent, I become as if stupid and mute" [lo stil, la lingua, l'ardire e l'ingegno / i pensieri, i concetti e i sentimenti / o restan tutti oppressi o tutti spenti / o quasi muta e stupida divengo].[19] Such an unabashedly negative positioning of a woman in terms of her inability to articulate can be read as an ironic and conscious displacement of the male gaze, for the eloquence of her text contradicts this statement.[20]

Unlike the Petrarchan model, Stampa is clearly (and ironically) articulating both the way women were often perceived—as less able to create "exceptional" verse—and also the way women can rearticulate such a disempowered status, charting another form of literary concern that refuses the totalizing view of metaphysical lack. For example, in her sonnet XVII, "I do not envy you at all, holy angels" [io non v'invidio punto, angeli santi], Stampa refuses to buy into the erotic metaphysics of lack.[21] In this sonnet, she ironically overturns the Petrarchan and Ficinian metaphysics by brashly saying that she does not envy the many glories and goods that the angels enjoy in the heavens because her own delights are so plentiful [perche i diletti miei son tali e tanti]. In fact, she depicts a sort of competition between heavenly pleasure and her own earthly pleasures, and finishes the sonnet by saying that the angels will win only in the fact that their joy in beholding God is eternal and established while hers will end: "In this alone will you win over my joy. Yours is eternal and established and my joy can soon end" [In questo sol vincete il mio gioire / che la vostra à eterna e stabilita / e la mia gioia può tosto finire]. What she is proposing is not an infinitude. Rather in turning around the metaphysical desire for eternal joy, Stampa very clearly remarks on the *finite* nature of her life and her love. Such an acceptance of the finiteness of all pleasure—and the concomitant eventuality of pain—implies a recognition of the self within the other, that

[19]In *Gaspara Stampa-Veronica Franco, Rime*, ed. Abdelkader Salza (Bari: Laterza & Figli, 1913), p. 19. All citations from the *Rime* are referred to by roman numerals in the text. Translation mine.

[20]In a forthcoming piece titled "Gaspara Stampa: Petrarchan Authority and Gender Revisions," William J. Kennedy offers a detailed analysis of the ways Stampa overturns Petrarch's rhetoric, especially with regard to her reappropriation of gendered figures from mythology. I thank William Kennedy for allowing me to see an advance copy of his manuscript.

[21]For a lengthy discussion of the differences between Petrarch's metaphysical preoccupation with death and moral rectitude and Stampa's accent on finitude, see Bassanese, *Gaspara Stampa*, esp. pp. 75–81.

is, it implies a recognition of one's limitation which in turn implies an impressive recognition of alterity and of community in the very finitude of joy itself without any transcendental quality of desire. Here the consciousness of loss, of finitude, is not one of a nostalgic quest for a transcendent eros but one in which loss is clearly understood as finitude and which is self-conscious. This sonnet—one among others—allows us to rethink the ways in which women writers of the Italian Renaissance made use of a Petrarchan framework to create another tradition in women's poetry that is non-Petrarchan.[22]

Certainly the addressee of many of her love sonnets, Count Collatino di Collato, was also a "cause" of her poetry. And as we know from her sonnets, he was a most unfaithful lover. But the fact that in the sonnets he interacts as both presence and absence in her life rhetorically allows poetics of the "prosaic" and undermines the otherworldliness of a Laura. Stampa's ironic displacement of the metaphysics of male melancholia invites us to think of her poetic expression as one that mourns women's dilemma within the Petrarchan tradition as the necessity of a double-visioned practice that cannot allow one either to pursue a solitary metaphysics of absence made present in the Petrarchan tradition or simply to write outside a cultural practice so dominant as to define what poetry could be at that time. From this contradiction, Stampa is able to refashion out of her loss, her "victimization," a language that points to a continual acting out of the rite of mourning, one that is finally dynamic and collective in the depiction of her finitude and that rejects any claim to an absolute. Grief is thus reformulated and women's losses could be said to appear as a form of mourning, a rite that had been taken from them but is, in turn, reappropriated from the poetic practice of melancholia.

Such a reappropriation of the space of feminine mourning occurs explicitly in her sonnet "Cry, Women, and let love weep with you" [Piangete, donne, et con voi pianga Amore], a poem whose opening line thus repeats the incipit of Petrarch's sonnet 92 of his *Rime sparse*. In Petrarch's poem, a circumstantial work written on the death of Cino da Pistoia, the initial appeal to women to undertake their traditional task of mourning the dead poet turns out to be but the first in a series of appeals to a wider set of entities, whom the poet asks to join in the mourning: "Love" [Amore], "lovers in every land" [amanti, per ciascun

---

[22]Cf. Kennedy, "Gaspara Stampa."

paese], the city of Pistoia and its "perverse citizens" [cittadin perversi], even the "rhymes"[rime] and the "verses" [versi] are enjoined to weep. But this immersion of women's voices within a universal chorus of mourning dissolves their specificity and implicitly converts them into mere metaphors of the poet's own literally inexpressible grief: "For *myself, I* pray *my* cruel sorrow that it not prevent my tears and that it be so courteous as to let *me* sigh as much as is needful to unburden my heart" [*Io* per *me* prego il *mio* acerbo dolore / non sian da lui le lagrime contese / e *mi* sia di sospir tanto cortese / quanto bisogna a disfogar il core] (emphasis added).[23] Not only is more space (an entire quatrain) devoted to the poet himself as a voice of unsure expression but that voice is also implicitly situated as what speaks behind and through all the others. The usurpation of centrality is implied by the very imperatives with which the poet commands all the other voices (including those of women) to express their grief on his behalf.

In Gaspara Stampa's revision of this poem, however, the weeping of women is invoked by way of a call for community and support against the threat of another discourse, no doubt a male one, that would devalue, belittle, discount, forget, or otherwise calumniate the poet herself. Far from assuming the conversion of emotional loss into the infinite gain of poetic immortality, the poet finds in unrequited love only an imminent death and a real risk of ensuing oblivion. Other women and the allegorical figure of Love are asked to weep the fact that her lover does not weep the precipitous departure of the soul from her "tormented body," torments and departure both presumably the effects on her of his insensitivity. Instead of being asked simply to partake in a general chorus of woe, however, the women are also asked, significantly enough, to *write*—as if the scriptural extension of mourning were a feminist response to a male melancholia appropriative of the symbolics of women's loss. The women are specifically asked to write out the cause of the poet's sorrow [la cagion del mio dolore], a cause that will, in all likelihood, not be heard unless it is written down by the mourning women.

What is intriguing about this text is less the concluding epitaph the poet asks the women to write on her tomb (an epitaph that follows the traditional model of "here lies the most faithful lover that ever was")

---

[23]In *Petrarch's Lyric Poems,* trans. and ed. Robert M. Durling (Cambridge: Harvard University Press, 1976), pp. 194–95.

than the explicitness with which the poet states her dependence on the communal solidarity of women who will mourn her death and the urgency of her injunction that this community go beyond its traditional functions by seizing for itself (that is, for all women) the practice of writing. The fragility of the communication is further underscored when the poet precedes the request to write by a long clause beginning with "se mai" (if it so happens that) in reference to the distinct possibility that her final words—these words—will not be heard out by someone else: "if it so happens that this voice in extremity be heard out by someone else" [se mai... l'estrema voce altrui fu essaudita]. What one could call the structural insecurity of this "estrema voce" or voice in the extremity of disempowerment contrasts with the self-assured and self-designating quality of the *poeta vates* of male Petrarchan lyric—even, or especially, when that lyric expresses feelings of loss or sorrow.

But if Gaspara Stampa, like her contemporary Louise Labé,[24] can evoke a community of women (that is, a feminine readership) whose work would be the overcoming of concrete loss through mourning, another cinquecento poet, Isabella di Morra, who also refashions loss in terms of mourning instead of melancholia, phrases the concomitant and dire risk that lies in the impossibility of community. In her canzone, "Since you have clipped the wings of the fine desire" [Poscia ch' al bel desir troncato hai l'ale], di Morra mourns the loss of her status, of her family and of community.[25] Addressing various persons, di Morra's poem appears as a desperate, perhaps unsuccessful search for someone adequate to hear her lament. Di Morra's poem explicitly mourns her loss of voice and status in terms of an injury done to an entire generation. She appeals to a community where she hopes she can be seen and heard and read. What marks her tone as different from a melancholic pathos, however, is that her grief extends to include all those who have been injured by the law. She does not situate her loss of status around an idealized ego of loss but rather through a grievance she shares with others in terms of a lack of a viable community. To be sure, the circum-

---

[24]Louise Labé, Sonnet xxiv, "Ne reprenez, Dames, si j'ay aymé," and Elégie iii, "Quand vous lirez, ô Dames Lionnoises," in *Oeuvres complètes*, ed. Enzio Guidici (Geneva: Droz, 1981), pp. 164, 137–40.
[25]My source for Isabella di Morra's canzone is *Poesia italiana del Cinquecento*, ed. Giulio Ferroni, pp. 250–52. Translations, with some modifications, are from Beverly Allen, Muriel Kittel, and Keala Jane Jewell, eds., *The Defiant Muse: Italian Feminist Poems from the Middle Ages to the Present* (New York: The Feminist Press, 1986), pp. 10–14. Further references are in the text.

stances surrounding di Morra's poetic work are—in the extreme—more
dramatic than Stampa's. Born in 1520, Isabella di Morra was the daughter of Giovanni Michele di Morra of Favale, who was forced to leave
the kingdom of Naples after he had sided with the king of France against
Charles V of Spain. He lost all his rights in Naples and went to live in
France. For reasons that remain unclear, Isabella was kept like a prisoner
by her brothers in their castle of Favale in the Basilicata; she wrote her
poem sometime during this period. She was then murdered by her
brothers in 1546, when they caught her exchanging letters with a certain
Don Diego Sandoval Castro. He too was murdered by the same
brothers.[26]

Isabella di Morra's biography is interesting not only for our understanding of the context of her poem, but also for the intriguing parallels
with Torquato Tasso's fate as textualized in his "Canzone al Metauro,"
written in 1578.[27] Like Isabella di Morra, Tasso wrote his poem in a state
of exile and isolation. But Tasso's poem was written during one of his
self-imposed exiles from Ferrara, one year prior to his incarceration in
Sant'Anna. The poem recalls Tasso's youth, when his father, Bernardo,
had also been obliged to leave the kingdom of Naples for having sided
with the French against Charles V. Eventually following his father into
exile, Tasso left his mother, Porzia, in Naples, where she too, like Isabella,
was kept a prisoner by her brothers and may have been subsequently murdered by them. In fact, Bernardo Tasso believed that Porzia's brothers
had killed her in order to keep the dowry for themselves.[28] Autobiograph-

---

[26]See *Poesia italiana del Cinquecento*, ed. G. Ferroni, p. 249; Giovanni Caserta, *Isabella Morra e la società meridionale del Cinquecento* (Matera: META, 1976); Benedetto Croce, *Isabella di Morra e Diego Sandoval de Castro* (Bari: Laterza, 1929).

[27]For Torquato Tasso's "Canzone al Metauro" see Angelo Solerti, *Le rime di Torquato Tasso* (Bologna: Romanuoli Dall' Acqua, 1900), 3: 104–8. Further references are in the text; the translations are my own.

[28]For a detailed account of this crisis, see Angelo Solerti, *Vita di Torquato Tasso* (Turin: Ermanno Loescher, 1895), vol. 1, chap. 1. See also Margaret W. Ferguson, "Torquato Tasso: The Trial of Conscience," in *Trials of Desire: Renaissance Defenses of Poetry* (New Haven: Yale University Press, 1983), pp. 54–136. Ferguson gives an excellent psychoanalytic reading of the oedipal crisis that runs like a leitmotif throughout Tasso's life and in his major works. Among critics who have discussed the "Canzone al Metauro," see especially Ferguson, pp. 74–77; Antonio Daniele, *Capitoli tassiani* (Padua: Antenore, 1983); Karlheinz Stierle, "Episches und lyrisches pathos: Torquato Tassos Canzone al Metauro," in *Interpretation: Das Paradigma der Europäischen Renaissance-Literatur. Festschrift für Alfred Noyer-Weidner zum 60 Geburtstag*, ed. Klaus W. Hempfer and Gerhard Regn (Wiesbaden: Franz Steiner, 1983); Lynn Enterline, "Armida's Lap, Erminia's Tears: In the Wake of Paternity and Figuration in Tasso's *Gerusalemme liberata*," paper presented at the colloquium "Refiguring Woman: Gender Studies and the Italian Renaissance," Cornell University, April 8–9, 1988.

ical coincidences notwithstanding, the similarity of the two poems leads one to suspect that Tasso read and "imitated" di Morra's poem, especially if one considers that Tasso's library was well stocked and he certainly must have been familiar with the anthologies in which her work appeared.[29] Documented evidence of such imitation is lacking, however. In any case, a comparative analysis of the two texts and their respective receptions reveals the gendered construction of the male melancholic artist as a privileged subjectivity, whose privilege is in turn predicated on the devaluing, if not appropriation, of women's losses.

A cruel Fortune casts her unhappy spell in both poems. "Poscia ch' al bel desir troncato hai l'ale," composed of six stanzas of eleven lines each and a valediction of five lines, is addressed to "cruel Fortune" [crudel Fortuna] (l. 2), who is identified as the source of all the poet's pain. The poet continues: "Thus with loosened reins oh pitiless Fortune / have you always pursued me / beginning from mother's milk and from the cradle" [Così, a disciolta briglia / seguitata m'hai sempre, empia Fortuna / comminciando dal latte e de la cuna] (ll. 20–22). She is "placed here by everyone in blind forgetfulness" [qui posta da ciascuno in cieco oblio] (l. 11). The terrible irony of that phrase is compounded and emblematized by the effective oblivion into which Isabella's poem had fallen, at least until recently. Even though her poem was published in an anthology in 1556, in Venice, it was not until Benedetto Croce rediscovered her in 1929 that some attention was given to it. She had been, therefore, lost to the world, unheard and unread.

Fortune has drawn the poet from her beloved father, the only person who could restore her to her "own or proper state" [proprio stato] (l. 34), the only person who could rescue her from oblivion and restore her to a place within the social framework from which she might be seen and perhaps heard. Indeed it is a community that Isabella di Morra desires. She tells Fortune, "If I had been nurtured in the city, you would have more blame and I more pity" [se nodrita già fossi in cittade, / avresti tu più biasmo, io più pietade] (ll. 54–55). But in the community in which the poet finds herself—"irrational people / deprived of intelligence" [gente irrazional, priva d'ingegno] (l. 8), presumably her brothers and, in general, the inhabitants of the Basilicata—the poet has no

[29]I thank Rinaldina Russell for bringing to my attention earlier anthologies that included poems by Isabella di Morra: *Rime di diversi signori napoletani e d'altri, libro settimo* (Venice: Giolito de' Ferrari, 1556), and *Rime diverse d'alcune nobilissime e virtuosissime donne* (Lucca: Busdrago, 1559).

voice. She also remains unheard by the king of France, the "great king" [gran Re] (l. 71), as well as by the man whom she calls "Cesar," a title she uses negatively for Charles V, whom the pope had proclaimed as an heir to Augustus Caesar and Charlemagne. This new Caesar becomes the interdictive power who does not allow her father to help her: "Caesar forbids him to help me / o thing never before heard / to deprive the father of means to help his daughter" [Cesar gli vieta il poter darmi aita / o cosa non più udita / privar il padre di giovar la figlia] (ll. 17–19). The multiplication of addressees—Fortune, the king of France, the inhabitants of the Basilicata, her father, and Charles V—would inspire one to believe that a viable community exists that would recognize the poet's grief. However, her "inner ill" [interno male] (l. 5) speaks of the forced suppression of her knowledge of her own victimization: by virtue of being a woman, she is denied entry into the world of symbolic exchange as an accredited voice of grief. Her *interno male* libidinally expresses the impossibility of her social determination; that is, relations of power exist without her while they exercise their dominance over her.

Torquato Tasso's "*Canzone al Metauro*," an unfinished sixty-line poem in three stanzas, also attacks Fortune. Tasso says, "Me from mother's breast / impious Fortune, a child divided" [Me dal sen de la madre / empia fortuna pargoletto divelse] (ll. 30–31) and insists on Fortune's persecution of him since the time of his birth: "Alas! From the day that / I first drew in the vital air and opened my eyes / in this light to me never serene / I was the plaything and sign of / unjust and evil Fortune" [Ohime! dal dì che pria / trassi l'aure vitali e i lumi appersi / in questa luce a me non mai serena / fui de l'ingiusta e ria / trastullo e segno] (ll. 21–24). Fortune is in direct conflict with the poet's ego: the *Me* that begins his line of woeful separation from the mother. What is at stake is *his own* persecution, *his own* loss of the mother. And instead of *his* mother, Tasso speaks of *the* mother, turning her into the abstract principle of his loss. That loss is loudly heard and displayed—not only in the fiction of the poem—but also throughout the history of Tasso's work.

While Tasso mourns the loss of his mother as *his* loss, as the loss he experiences of her love, Isabella di Morra mourns the loss suffered *by* her mother (whom she identifies as "unhappy mother" [misera madre] (l. 57) and the loss suffered by a father who is denied the means of helping his daughter. Both poems raise a pressing question: whose loss is it?

For Isabella, the lament frames the scenario within which—as well as through which—she is excluded and forgotten. The psychic economy of loss can be seen in the exclamation : "Oh thing never before heard / to deprive the father the means to help his daughter" [o cosa non più udita! / privar il padre di giovar la figlia.] (ll. 19–20). Loss is everywhere but none of it is hers to claim. She can only lament her condition of disempowerment. Her loss is dependent on her father's power; she sees her loss to be his. As she situates loss elsewhere, she demarcates the way her psyche is implicated as other, as the negative space of loss. Her psychic position must be read in terms of her social position, in terms of the other's (patriarchal) power. Both her psychic and social realities clearly demarcate the relations between dominance and forced submission which she, from her dislocated place, articulates and which paradoxically allow us to read what is at stake in her lament: the economy of gain and loss whose vectors cannot be determined except from without. It is her father's loss, it is the gain of Charles V and the king of France. (Even her father had not lost; we know from her biographers that he went to live happily ever after in Paris with a good pension, wholly uninterested in Isabella's fate.)[30]

After the poet's initial address to Fortune, she writes: "I will tell in this crude and weak style *some part* of the internal ill caused by you alone" [dirò con questo stil ruvido e frale/*alcuna parte* del interno male/ causato sol da te] (ll. 4–6; emphasis mine). Her "internal ill" can remain privatized only to the extent that her voice, her text, has no public arena. Her text thus cannot be externalized or "published" as an artifact of the self. It cannot be externalized as such because the speaking/writing subject is female; were she actually in a public (i.e. court) arena, she still would have another signifying economy than would a male court poet.[31] As if to exacerbate the poet's exclusion from the public sphere, she says that she can only tell "some part" of this "internal ill." The lack of further qualification or explication renders the poet's statement extremely complex: she may be suggesting that her pain is so great that it could never be fully described, or that there is no social space within which her

[30] Cf. Caserta, *Isabella Morra*.

[31] Furthermore, the subtext here suggests that to attempt to represent her loss would be impossible since by virtue of her being a woman and both literally and psychologically locked away, she remains subject to what Jean-François Lyotard (calls) the *différend*, "that something [which] asks to be put into phrases, and suffers from the injustice of not being able instantly to be put into phrases" (Lyotard, "The *Différend*, the Referent, and the Proper Name," trans. G. Van Den Abbeele, *Diacritics* 14 [Fall 1984], 7).

lament could be heard, or she may be suggesting that the language available to her is itself insufficient to communicate such pain.[32] Perhaps it is also her ability to extend her sorrow to include others that makes her pain seem only *partially* representable.

Di Morra says: "Here woman's rightful place I do not experience" [Qui non provo io di donna il proprio stato] (l. 34). Her father's return would, we may assume, enable Isabella di Morra to reclaim the dowry she needed to marry and thus to reclaim her own, proper state [proprio stato]. This proper and independent state is neither, however, since it depends on her positioning by and within a patriarchal order. There, a woman might function merely as an object of exchange whose value is crudely measured by the monetary value of her dowry. Her *proprio stato*, far from being some state proper to her, might be no more than capital for male investment. Or rather, since she desires a position that is by virtue of its construction already prefigured as lacking the full autonomy of male selfhood, her desire becomes inconsequential. In other words, the expression of her "inner ill" cannot surface from the suppression and reclusion she finds herself in, and her social as well as discursive disempowerment would remain, whether or not patriarchy reinstates her in her *proprio stato*, precisely because it is patriarchy that decides.

Yet we could also argue that the *proprio stato* refers less to the poet's symbolic role within society than to her libidinal position as a desiring subject (as an object of desire, and even as one desiring to be desired). She writes, "Blind and infirm, I have done without everything here / without ever knowing praise of beauty" [Tutto ho passato qui cieca ed inferma / senza saper mai pregio di beltade.] (ll. 25–26). Thus, for her, her subjectivity would be constructed over and beyond the comprehension of herself as an object of desire, through her knowing praise for her beauty. A certain narcissism is at stake, but it is a narcissism, as we shall see, decidedly different from Tasso's. Isabella di Morra's narcissism is marked by a desire to return to one of the only "public" spaces available to her—as an object of desire. Such a feminine narcissism is obviously fraught with problems. On the one hand, and from a standard patriarchal position, the poet's narcissistic investment in her own ego cannot fetishize it as the image of autonomous selfhood, since her *proprio stato* designates her within the male world as one who "essentially" lacks.[33]

---

[32]See Elaine Scarry, *The Body in Pain: The Making and Unmaking of the World* (New York: Oxford University Press, 1985).

[33]On the notion of feminine narcissism, see Sarah Kofman, *L'énigme de la femme: La*

On the other hand, her desire to be desired, to be the *subject* of her own desire, that is, to know the "value or praise of beauty" [pregio di beltade] works against her victimization being accepted simply as something essential or "natural" to her condition, since this desire does originate from herself. Her desire to know the *value* of her beauty and to hear *praises* of her beauty is also a desire to be a referent in others' discourse, to oblige someone else to speak of or to her. On the other hand, because she has no symbolic *place of her own*, no truly proper *proprio stato*, she cannot ever fully succeed in presenting herself as a desiring subject. The poet's feminine desirability depends on her being the object of an other's desire, just as her "feminine" loss is ultimately understood as belonging to an other.

In spite of these oppressive effects of patriarchal law, one can never-theless argue that di Morra's canzone indeed resists patriarchal norms—first, because the text *has been written*. Secondly, because by positing a plurality of addressees (Fortune, her father, her mother, the inhabitants of the Basilicata, and the embedded addressee of Fortune, the king of France), di Morra's canzone refuses to accredit any one male figure as the hierarchical center of phallic dominance. If, as Freud has shown, more than one phallus implies castration,[34] then the multiplicity of sub-ject positions figuratively decenters the phallus from its position as the organizing principle behind the distribution of social roles to the extent that the situation of woman is no longer merely that of *not* being man, of not being in a relation of absolute difference from man, of being the other of man.[35] At the same time, in place of a hierarchy where one father stands for another in a series of substitutions ultimately grounded in some symbolically primal or transcendental father (such as God or king), we see rather a dispersion of a shifting historical and political ground of differences in gender and even of differences *within* gender differences. The poet addresses a community that she would have as different than it indeed is but against the conflation of whose differences she nonetheless inveighs.

The invective in her canzone is born of the realization that her

---

femme dans les textes de Freud (Paris: Galilée, 1980); Naomi Schor, "Female Fetishism," in *The Female Body in Western Culture*, ed. Susan Rubin Suleiman (Cambridge: Harvard University Press, 1985), pp. 363–72.

[34]Freud, "Medusa's Head," *S.E.* 18: 273–74.

[35]For a discussion of such subjectivities constituted—engendered—by a multiple, het-erogenous field, see Teresa de Lauretis, *Technologies of Gender: Essays on Theory, Film, and Fiction* (Bloomington: Indiana University Press, 1987), p. 1 and passim.

predicament is the result of the undifferentiating ignorance of those others who, like her brothers, no doubt see themselves as the immediate representatives of patriarchal law, as unthinking metaphors of the father, and hence as the invested protectors of the symbolic order, (self-)empowered to imprison or even murder those who go against that order. Blame, here, is justly placed on the ignorance of those who cannot understand her, that is, on the empowered:

> S'io mi doglio di te si giustamente,
> per isfogar la mente
> da chi non son per ignoranza intesa
> i' son, lassa, *ripresa*. (ll. 50–54)

> If I complain of you so justly
> to relieve my mind
> by those who through ignorance misunderstand me
> alas, I am *reproved*.

This moment of understanding can be seen to be where the "real" is situated, that is, where the censorship of the victim occurs even as it is stated. Contradicting the patriarchal norm that defines her in terms of lack, and accused through the ignorance that stands in for that so-called law, she questions that law which denies her the space of articulation. The anger in her invective against the ignorance of the powerful thus belies any essentialist victim's discourse, as she follows in the tradition of other women writers of that period, as well as those earlier humanist women who inveighed against the injustice they suffered from male authority.[36]

---

[36]Although she is truly locked away, her luckier contemporaries were also, but perhaps more subtly, denied access to the public space. One need only think of the treatises of Leonardo Bruni or even of Baldassare Castiglione who, on the one hand, extol women's virtues and their ability to learn but who, on the other hand, edify the final verdict for women: marriage in order to become the perfect *donna di famiglia* in support of a courtier husband's social affairs. The argument has been made that in the sixteenth century, as the state was being formed as an autonomous entity, women were steadily excluded from the public space and became, as we read in Castiglione's *Il libro del Cortegiano* (*Opere di Baldassare Castiglione, Giovanni della Casa, Benvenuto Cellini*, ed. C. Cordié [Milan: Ricciardi, 1960]), the emblem of the perfect lady, almost a mirror of the courtier (except that she was exempt from arms). The public increasingly became the space for men, and the home, as the locus of the private, the space for women. On this issue so much has been written that I cite only a few representative sources: Joan Kelly, "Did Women Have a Renaissance?" in her *Women, History, and Theory*, pp. 19–50; Lillian S. Robinson, "Woman under Capitalism: The Renaissance Lady," in her *Sex, Class, and Culture* (New York: Methuen, 1978), pp. 150–75; Peter Stallybrass, "Patriarchal Territories: The Body Enclosed," in *Rewriting the Renaissance: The Discourses of Sexual*

Like the texts of those women, di Morra's poem concerns the problematic space of an articulation that constantly risks the fall back into
inarticulateness for lack of an accredited locus in the phallocratic order;
the poem mourns a victimization that is political, social, historical—and
prosaic. By "prosaic," I mean that it evokes neither the special status of
its poet nor an eroticized poetics of lack as melancholic idyll. This is
not to suggest that Isabella di Morra is devoid of eros, for her very
desire to know herself as an object of value and of beauty is in itself an
erotic longing for love and appreciation. But the difference lies in the
way in which erotic desire is recuperated. Her desire for poetic expression
is not a desire to display (whether critically or uncritically) the melancholic ego of loss; it is a desire for a community wherein she can be a
participant—desire not for a pre-oedipal indifferentiation but for the
indefinite exchange of social and discursive differences. The longing for
her father looks toward the father for the future, for liberation from her
status as abject, rather than nostalgically toward any fixated past. For
the father, here, is not a space to occupy but simply, for di Morra, a
possibility of self-determination.[37] This is an ambiguous line that
women have historically had to cross and re-cross, a line between their
imbrication within patriarchal values and their resistance to such
determination.

This ambiguity implies again the problematic nature of the voice of
melancholia. Unlike Isabella's mournful desire to be heard, the melancholic imagination is legitimated by a cultural mythology empowering
male fantasy in terms of a divine illness. The subject of melancholia
assumes a place within the symbolic order where the fixation on loss
can be converted into a representation of the ego that vies both for and
against the father's love. In classic phallocentrism, loss is often linked

---

Difference in Early Modern Europe, ed. Margaret W. Ferguson, Maureen Quilligan, and Nancy
J. Vickers (Chicago: University of Chicago Press, 1986), pp. 123–42; Sarah Kofman, *Le
respect des femmes* (Paris: Galilée, 1982); Margaret L. King, "Book-Lined Cells: Women and
Humanism in the Early Italian Renaissance," in *Beyond Their Sex: Learned Women of the
European Past*, ed. Patricia M. Labalme (New York: New York University Press, 1980), pp. 66–
90. On the issue of women's education, see especially Leonardo Bruni, "De studiis et litteris,"
trans. and ed. William H. Woodward, in *Vittorino da Feltre and Other Humanist Educators*
(New York: Teachers College, Columbia University, 1963), pp. 119–33.
    [37]It is noteworthy that during the Renaissance a strong bond established itself between
young girls and their fathers since it was often the father who took care of his daughter's
education (as it was in Isabella's case; cf. Caserta, *Isabella di Morra*). Margaret King has argued
that as educated girls became learned women, they were often frustrated in their hope for an
extended intellectual *and* public role. As women, they inevitably had two choices: to marry,
or to take vows ("Book-Lined Cells," pp. 66–81).

to the maternal and to death, and functions phantasmically as the expression of desire for a return to something other. For those who see themselves as disempowered, loss is imbued with nostalgia. When articulated from a melancholic "male" position, this loss becomes a pretext for an aesthetic and even political project that continually derealizes the feminine by recasting loss in terms of a golden age, one that I would wager, women themselves have never known.

Such an oedipalized narrative of loss can be found egregiously played out in Tasso's "Canzone al Metauro." As I noted earlier, the poet describes the necessity of having to follow his father Bernardo into exile, leaving his mother, Porzia, behind in Naples. The lamenting hero of this narrative is Tasso, the *me* separated from the mother. He is the one to whom loss and lament are said exclusively to belong: "Now am I not so *rich* of my own woes that I alone suffice for material of grief, that others by me need to be lamented?" [Or che non sono io tanto / *Ricco* de' propri guai che basti solo / Per materia di duolo/ Dunque altri ch'io da me dev' esser pianto?] (ll. 48–50; my emphasis). It is the word *ricco* that points here to the differential economics at work in the gendering of melancholic mourning.

In Isabella di Morra, the feeling of loss extends beyond her own loss, for she also feels the loss of her mother, and even extends pity for her brothers. It is a loss that remains socialized, aware of others. Though this socialization can be seen as a mere negative result of the cultural conditioning of women, I would rather read it in an ambiguous manner. It might indeed be negative if it were seen to be the only capacity—one overladen with sentimental value—ascribed to women's social roles. But one might also read this social libido as a critical one that makes no claim to a nostalgic collapse of difference.

Even in Tasso's poem the oedipal is not resolved as the end to a happy story. Although Tasso movingly describes his traumatic separation from the mother in terms of his having to follow his father, the poet can nonetheless assume a significant role in his narrative. In other words, Tasso, unlike di Morra, is able to insert his loss within the Law of the Father. For Tasso, fathers become the addressees who legitimate his position in regard to them, while "the" mother, the phantasm of the symbolic female, is internalized as the muted figure of alienation, lack, and even death. This position exiles women as other and creates of femininity a negative pole.[38] The notion of the "feminine" can easily

---

[38]Jacqueline Rose states: "As the place onto which lack is projected and through which

appear as Freud's critical object, which "conscience" judges and to whom it can feel morally superior, since access to the male-dominated symbolic order, to patriarchal subjectivity, is dependent on a split from or renunciation of woman. The notion of the "feminine" thus becomes that in contradistinction to which cultural empowerment can measure itself.

For di Morra, fathers function as the representatives of law, as "equivalences of subject positions" on whom her socially constructed identity is literally, prosaically, founded.[39] For her, it is not a question of oedipal narrative, of linearity, but rather of the mere possibility to enunciate. For Tasso, desire is knotted nostalgically to the mother as phantasm; she is evoked not because of her death/murder but because he desires to return to his own birthplace, marked by the tomb of Parthenope. "If only the glorious and nurturing siren, near whose cradle I was born, knows. If only I had had a tomb or grave, at the first blow" [Sassel la gloriosa alma sirena / Appresso il cui sepolcro ebbi la cuna / cosi avuto v'avessi o tomba o fossa / A la prima percossa] (ll. 27–30).[40] Tasso's melancholic mourning is focused on the mother, whose own loss is appropriated as if it were his own. He positions his body and his text under the sign of loss, as the sign of the suffering beloved. The libidinal connection between the poet, the mother and the poet's loss is situated at the nexus between womb and tomb. The mother allows entry into the economics of recuperation, allowing the poet to relive his losses repeatedly. Continuity is thus foremost localized primarily in the desire

---

it is simultaneously disavowed, woman is a 'symptom' for the man" (*Sexuality in the Field of Vision* [London: Verso, 1986], p. 72). Thus the mother is simply the hidden face of a phallic desire wherein the feminine figures as the fearful place of lack and of castration, as "the child's desire for her which does not refer to her but beyond her, to an object, the phallus, whose status is first imaginary (the object presumed to satisfy his desire) and then symbolic (recognition that desire cannot be satisfied)" (p. 62). However, in pathological mourning, it is precisely the deferral of desire that creates an eros of nostalgia, which becomes the sign of the subject's entrapment in the imaginary. "Woman" or "Mother" figures simply as a phantasmic object, as a pretext for a transcendent relation to otherworldliness such that the "feminine" becomes a mere idea for phallic organization and does not imply a social relation between subjects.

[39]The term is borrowed from Ernesto Laclau and Chantal Mouffe (*Hegemony and Socialist Strategy* [London: Verso, 1985]), who intend by it an ambiguous relation between identity and difference: "Two terms, to be equivalent, must be different—otherwise, there would be a simple identity. On the other hand, the equivalence exists only through the act of subverting the differential character of those terms" (p. 128).

[40]See Ferguson, *Trials of Desire*, pp. 71–75. Ferguson argues that the siren is an analogue for Tasso's mother in "being a woman deserted and indirectly killed, and the epic hero is for Tasso always in some sense guilty of murdering Eros" (p. 75). Certainly eros is murdered to the extent that woman is denied, but is this eros not recuperated in Tasso's poem through the reinscription of his mother's death onto his own eros, i.e., as the eros of loss, and through the aestheticization of her death?

to return to some sort of originary state. This originariness is represented through a corporeal tie with the mother: the "knots" that bind him to her.

> "Ch'io non dovea giunger più volto a volto
> Fra quelle braccia accolto
> con nodi così stretti e tenaci.
> Lasso! e seguii con mal sicure piante,
> Qual Ascanio o Camilla il padre errante. (ll. 36–40)[41]

> That I was no longer to reach her face to face,
> held between those arms
> with knots so tight and so tenacious.
> Alas! And I, like Camilla or Ascanius, followed
> with insecure footsteps the wandering father.

Leaving aside the obvious oedipal crisis, engendered by the "cutting" of the knot in consequence of the father's departure which also takes away the son, let us look at how this moment becomes the focal point on which the oedipal narrative is sutured. The "knots" represent a corporeal loss since they are the knots of the mother's embrace; they call attention to the morbidly erotic bond even as they *devalue* the specificity of her loss and victimization. A symbol of permanent lack, she becomes the means through which the poet's "loss" of her is nothing more than a pretext for the aestheticization of loss. Insofar as such an appropriation may indeed produce a discourse based on an ambivalent rivalry with the father, this ambivalence requires recourse to yet *another* discourse, which attempts to reinscribe oedipal narrative in terms of the poet's own desire to be the exclusive object of the father's love, to be the chosen son. For the last stanza of Tasso's canzone plays out Tasso's relation to his father, whom he apostrophizes in the final lines:

> "Padre, o buon padre, che dal ciel rimiri,
> Egro e morto ti piansi, e ben tu il sai,
> E gemendo scaldai
> La tomba e il letto; or che ne gli alti giri

---

[41]These knots, *nodi*, serve to sexualize the male ego in terms of his narrative. They eroticize the woman (in Tasso, his mother's death) and therefore derealize the specificity of her loss and victimization. The victim becomes an instance of aesthetic production. See my "The Victim's Discourse: Torquato Tasso's *Canzone al Metauro*," *Stanford Italian Review* 5 (Fall 1985), 189–203.

Tu godi, a te si deve onor, non lutto:
A me versato il mio dolor sia tutto. (ll. 55–60)

"Father, oh good father, who looks down from the sky,
I cried for you, weak and dead, and well you know it.
And with tears and laments, I warmed the tomb and bed;
now that you in the high circles rejoice,
to you is owed honor, not grief.
Let it be enough for me to have poured out all my pain.

The unfinished canzone ends here, suggesting that the poet's mourning is anything but fully poured out.

Certainly this relation is inspired by the melancholic tradition. By appropriating his mother's death as if it were his own loss and victimization, Tasso becomes the oedipal prince not only of his lyric but also for modern notions of disenfranchised subjectivity. The male subject finds satisfaction in his melancholic voice precisely because this voice incorporates as well as appropriates the dissonances found within patriarchal power relations. Tasso thus becomes the possessor of the voice that expresses both the struggle for dominance and the necessity of submission. Through this voice, he is legitimated in *his* rearticulation of *his* victimization through the prestigious position of he who incarnates *the* alienated and creative subject of literary production. Having incorporated his mother's real victimization, he makes it his own by designating himself as the preferred victim of patriarchy; at the same time, he continues his oedipal dialogue with patriarchy by romancing the father and eroticizing those maternal knots. Lack as a place to be "occupied" serves as an efficacious means to bring the prodigal son back into the folds of established procedures. Incorporating the mother's loss thus saves patriarchy for patriarchy.

Tasso's biographer, Gianbattista Manso, and later Goethe glorified Tasso as the quintessential heroic model for an alienated genius, who suffers from both unrequited love and hostile politics. Countless articles and books have been written on Tasso's poetry. Many of Tasso's critics have been fascinated with his language and metaphors, often remarking on the prevalent erotic feeling that his work evokes. He has been romanticized as the melancholic *per eccellenza* of the late Renaissance, as he who embodies the poetic spirit of alienation and disempowerment, whose suffering modeled an eros of lack: melancholia. Few have raised the question of what there is in his work that privileges lack as the motivation of eros.[42] The cultural acquisition of loss for individual gain helped to forge a newly arising individual subjectivity and to re-encode melancholia as a particular form of male creativity. Not only does this form of exclusive sensitivity build its particular hegemony on notions of loss and lack predicated on the appropriation of the feminine—predicated, that is, on the *devaluation* of women's experiences as historical reality—but such loss is granted a privileged place of recuperation within Western aesthetics when uttered by the disenfranchised male poet. Tasso's discourse of victimization is mediated through the story of women; Porzia's and Isabella di Morra's stories are lived—and forgotten—as historically determined abjection. The stories of these women, like the women themselves, are therefore reduced to the function of the maternal, a position necessarily associated with the abject in classic phallocentrism. Tasso, by appropriating their "position" through an act of pathological mourning, denies, in a sense, *their* historical and sexual difference.

My reading thus suggests that melancholia is not simply a pathological condition of either medical or psychological interest, but a historically specific discursive practice that differentiates along gender lines (or *at least* along gender lines, but perhaps also along those of class, race, and nationality) between those "losses" that are considered significant and those that are not. Furthermore, the "significant" losses of the melancholic are themselves appropriated from what, from *his* standpoint, can only be called "insignificant others." Caught in the bind of an expressive inexpressibility, only to have it expressed by others as if

---

[42]Critics who have dealt with Tasso's compulsion to privilege lack include Mario Fusco, "La question des obstacles dans la *Jérusalem délivrée*," *Les Langues Neo-Latines* 248 (1984), 55–76; and N. Jonard, "L'érotisme dans le *Jérusalem délivrée*," *Bergomum: Bolletino della Civica Biblioteca* 78, nos. 3–4 (1984), 43–62. On the relation between melancholia and loss in Tasso, see Ferguson, *Trials of Desire*, esp. pp. 123–26. In her forthcoming book *White Lies: Genealogical and Poetic Disfiguration in the "Gerusalemme liberata,"* Marilyn Migiel argues that the price Tancredi must pay for Clorinda's death is perpetual sorrow: "He first considers suicide, turning the guilty hand against himself. But he deems this too merciful, because it would bring his grief to an end. The solution left him is to become a 'misero mostro,' for this punishment allows him to reenact repeatedly the horrible act of killing Clorinda and simultaneously punish himself for doing so." In Tancredi, we thus see the melancholic syndrome at work: the murder of Clorinda is recuperated into an eros of lack and loss, and the incorporation of this lost object of desire is reinscribed as the eros of a gendered pathos that legitimates the melancholic in his excessive suffering. See also Lynn Enterline ("Armida's Lap, Erminia's Tears"), who argues that the loss of Tasso's mother is recast into the figure of Armida who then mourns this loss for him. Tasso thereby situates mourning itself in a precise "feminine" register.

it were their own, the latter in their plight point to the suspect quality
of Freud's distinction betwen mourning and melancholia, which implicitly subtends a historical opposition between woman and man,
hushed and garrulous, prosaic and poetic. Such a psychoanalytic reading
of some Renaissance texts thus points to a historicization of the Freudian
categories and undertakes a revisionist and feminist critique of psychoanalysis while, I hope, demonstrating and advancing the critical rigor
and validity of the psychoanalytic approach.

The comparison of the lyric poems by Tasso and di Morra also serves
to illustrate the relationship of women to the canon (at least in the late
Italian Renaissance) as their exclusion from it by a melancholic "male"
pathos. I stress, however, that this lack of representation is not a mere
epistemological gap but a systematic repression that occurs through the
non-attribution of value to the text of women's mourning, the denial
to it of the *culturally empowered* status of melancholia. This is certainly
borne out by one editor of Isabella di Morra's poem, Giulio Ferroni,
who makes a double-edged remark: "Isabella's fame, which in this century was rediscovered by Croce, is completely tied to the drama of her
biographical moment. And in her few verses, we are able clearly to
discern the traces of her scholastic isolation, with the *tiring attempt* to
put together a scholastic language, certainly inadequate to express the
tragedy of a condition without hope" [La fama della poesia della Morra
(che nel nostro secolo è stata riscoperta dal Croce) è tutta legata a questa
drammatica vicenda biografica; e nei suoi pochi versi si possono ben
scorgere le tracce del suo isolamento scolastico, col *faticoso tentativo* di
mettere insieme un linguaggio scolastico, certamente inadatto ad espri-
mere la tragicità di una condizione senza speranza].[43] The last part of
Ferroni's statement is ambiguous. To whom does the *faticoso tentativo*
belong? Is this the editor's tiring task, or is it Isabella's because she
doesn't have language adequate to express her isolation? Does the *faticoso
tentativo* belong to the "traces of her scholastic isolation" that arise in
her verse fragments? Or does this "fatigue" belong to Ferroni, whose
unwieldy prose (as the syntax of the sentence appears to imply) suggests
his unwillingness to deal with a marginalized woman?

[43]See *Poesia italiana del Cinquecento*, ed. G. Ferroni, pp. 249–50 (emphasis mine).

Ferroni's comment regards the "proper" form in which a dilemma may be articulated before it is or can be legitimated. And he is quick to condemn the inarticulateness of noncanonical authors. Isabella di Morra's marginalization is expressed within a language that is codified as Petrarchan but that nonetheless assumes a difference from the Petrarchan register. In Petrarch, language is the means through which the poet determines the register of selfhood and of an ensuing canonization. In Isabella di Morra's canzone, the Petrarchan register for linguistic expression does not imply a reality that perceives her acquisition of language and culture as an exit from her socially determined position. She is damned if she does and damned if she doesn't.

Ferroni then, in a moment of self-reflection, states that language, though "inadequate," is not what is at stake here but "the oppression which weighs upon her, and from which she cannot imagine any other exit except that of the mythical return of her father, of the restoration of her family wealth and of the restoration of the noble dignity of her own family" [l'oppressione che grava su di lei, e da cui essa non può immaginare altra uscita che quella di un mitico ritorno del padre e di una restaurazione della ricchezza e della dignità nobiliare della propria famiglia] Despite this act of critical "noblesse oblige," the implicit message becomes quite clear. The canon legitimates certain linguistic practices without ever examining *what* the conditions for linguistic legitimation are (as, for example, the erotic dimension of Tasso's poetry in contrast to Isabella's "prosaicness").

In the end, the critic's humanist assumptions come to bear even further upon Isabella's text when he says: "Her poor language of scholastic Petrarchism is only the painful echo of an even larger social prison which surrounds the private prison in which she is enclosed: it is a further confirmation of the fact that in feudal society there is no way out" [il suo pover linguaggio di scolastico petrarchismo non è che l'eco penosa di una prigione sociale ancora più vasta, che sta intorno alla prigione privata in cui ella è rinchiusa: è una conferma ulteriore del fatto che nella società feudale non c'è nessuna via d'uscita] (p. 250). Brandishing the name of Petrarch as the inspired original of which di Morra's text would be just an inept imitation, the critic thus reveals the exclusivist discourse of the canon. When the subject concerns, for example, women's experience of disempowerment, then this experience becomes just a singular event, nameless, everyone's and thus no one's. Her "story" becomes simply one among many possible others within "feudal" so-

ciety. In this way, di Morra's experience becomes all too easily neutralized—and forgotten, a mere document for the archives. When the
loss is Tasso's, it is elevated to high aesthetic status and is analyzed because his loss could also be the loss of other men. He becomes a symbol of the alienated and creative individual, he becomes celebrated,
he and his language even become models. Furthermore, the canon, as
an instance of patriarchal authority, legitimates itself through an imaginary literary historicity precisely because it does not recognize certain
articulations of disempowerment. Thus a "victim," such as Isabella di
Morra, is denied a legitimate voice of pathos and mourning in literary
form.

I would like to end by suggesting that Isabella's canzone is interesting
not only because it allows us to expose the legitimating power behind
melancholic texts but also because her lament offers a strategy for feminist criticism. Through Isabella's "prosaic" lament, and through her
mourning, we can discern how her experience charts a different but
hopeful space in which one can rethink the diversity of subject positions
entailed in the experience of women in its complexity. From her position
of extreme marginalization, Isabella di Morra (like Stampa and others)
rewrites Petrarchan language, the institutionalized poetic eros of her
age. Even if in Renaissance Italy one cannot speak of a feminist movement per se, women did appropriate their own subjectivities, thereby
refiguring feminine possibilities and resisting the structured bias of gender difference within Western patriarchy.[44] To rethink the specificity of
Isabella's canzone and of her desire for a space in which she can be heard
and seen is to rethink a place beyond the Petrarchan, a space not prefigured on lack as a metaphor for the phallic economics of fetishized
self-recuperation. Rather, a feminine social space allows one a way to
think of lack *not* in terms of a transcendental signifier, but in terms of
a consciousness of self *and* otherness, that is, in terms of subjects en-
countering others, in terms of a plurality of addressees and addressors,
in terms of a proliferation of social and ethnic differences, all of which
make it possible to think of overturning the very basis of gender, class,
and racial hierarchies.

What I suggest then, by way of a conclusion, is that in speaking of

---

[44] As Teresa de Lauretis has argued, "The specificity of a feminist theory may be sought
in that political, theoretical, self-analyzing practice by which the relations of the subject in
social reality can be rearticulated from the *historical perspective of women*" (*Alice Doesn't: Feminism,
Semiotics, Cinema* [Bloomington: Indiana University Press, 1984], p. 186; emphasis mine).

women's depression and the possible representation of such depression, we must first come to terms with the practice of a melancholic voice as one that historically has been the culturally empowered expression òf loss and sorrow by men. And although I do not exclude the existence of concrete male mourners or women melancholics,[45] I think that in order to describe women's depression and the ways women have historically represented loss, we might look away from the over-laden melancholic model and rethink the possibility of women's loss as represented and re-situated in terms of mourning, a mourning for the lost object that is the mother—and by extension all women—which is recathected and can be refigured as a new object. Such a revision entails a rereading and a re-situating of loss in terms of a practice, a practice that understands itself as a dynamic process of introjection and projection, a sort of mourning, let us say. Through mourning women can represent and have represented their poetic, political, social, and cultural selves in terms of a "community at loose ends,"[46] one whose articulation is found in the mutual recognition of finitude (as in those mourning rituals whose "disorder" displeased the humanists) but whose finitude is also affirmatively marked by a determined refiguring of the fragility— and power—of women's political and social roles.

[45]On the need to establish and affirm a practice of male mourning, see Douglas Crimp, "Mourning and Militancy," *October* 51 (Winter 1989), 3–18; and Michael Moon, "Memorial Rags" (forthcoming). See especially Crimp's discussion of Moon's paper in "Mourning and Militancy," pp. 6–7.
[46]The term is taken from the conference "Community at Loose Ends" held at Miami University, September 1988, and inspired by Jean-Luc Nancy's *La Communauté Désoeuvrée* (Paris: Christian Bourgois, 1986).

Chapter 4

Soverchia maninconia:
Tasso's Hydra

Tasso never completed the "Canzone al Metauro." Instead, he left the protective court atmosphere of Urbino to wander about Italy dressed "in the clothing of an unknown pilgrim" [in abito di sconosciuto peregrino].[1] Not content with the textual representation of loss in the canzone, Tasso did not mourn but literally reenacted the traumatic separation he posited as the origin of his (lack of) being. Sending himself into exile, he mimed the status of the "pilgrim in flight" [fugace peregrino] which the canzone had described as *his* state at the time of his boyhood departure from Naples. This new period of exile ended about a year later when Tasso returned to his earlier patron and benefactor, Duke Alfonso of Ferrara, only to have the duke incarcerate him in the prison-hospital of Sant'Anna for behavior diagnosed by the court physicians as the effect of melancholy. This dramatic moment sent a ripple of shock through educated Europe and would leave its mark on future writers.[2] For example, the biographer Gianbattista Manso in the early seventeenth century and the poet Goethe in the following century read this moment in Tasso's life as the outward manifestation of a travesty committed against the alienated and creative individual who suffered not only from

---

[1] *Il padre di famiglia*, in Torquato Tasso, *Prose*, ed. Ettore Mazzali (Milan: Riccardo Ricciardi, 1959), p. 76.

[2] See note 33, Introduction.

unrequited love but also from a hostile and despotic court.[3] In due time, Tasso became romanticized for his celebrated melancholia, often understood to be aggravated mercilessly by the putative injury done to him by his patron, Duke Alfonso. In this chapter, I reexamine some of the texts surrounding this celebrated event in order to disclose the way the losses exhibited in the case of Torquato Tasso redound to his gain as one of the key modelings of the misunderstood, mad, and melancholic genius. In fact, by his reappropriation of melancholic madness as a condition he characterizes as uniquely his own, he can be said to be *the* subject of the ideology of melancholia.

Tasso's oscillating exiles and returns, self-concealments and self-revelations, acts of naming and unnaming, betray more than an unstable personality; they also describe a highly ambiguous relation to the symbolic. In the interconnected world of the northern Italian courts, his repeated assertions or enactments of loss (of home, of name, of identity, . . . and of sanity) are always *public* and ask for a response from authority. For this narcissistic subject, what is felt and displayed *as* loss is the discovery that its own being is not full or autonomous but necessarily lacking. This narcissistic wound then leads the melancholic subject both to blame powerful figures and humbly to request their protection, aid, and love. Tasso's princely patrons are rejected and recalled just as he enters and departs their towns. Both hurling and seeking accusation, he also compulsively seeks absolution and forgiveness.

One example of this ambivalence is Tasso's departing Urbino and leaving his "Canzone al Metauro" unfinished at the moment when the text becomes a prayerlike invocation to his father, Bernardo, who is conflated with the divine father in heaven and by implication with the political father who is his patron, the duke of Urbino. But it is precisely at this moment of imminent success when all the fathers literal and symbolic are conflated into a single one capable of being addressed and capable, therefore, of taking the poet into his protective arms that Tasso breaks off, leaves the poem unfinished, and leaves town, reverting to the "anonymous" garb of the pilgrim. It is as if he desired "failure" and the emergence of new obstacles. One critic has in fact noted a similar

---

[3]On the novelization of Tasso's biography as well as on Manso's mistake in understanding the "reasons" for Tasso's melancholia, see Donald McGrady, "On the Origins of the 'Telltale Mirror' in the Legend of Torquato Tasso," *Italian Culture* 5 (1984), 67–75. Also see Edwina Vittorini, "Montaigne, Ferrara, and Tasso," in *The Renaissance in Ferrara and Its European Horizons*, ed. J. Salmons (Cardiff: University of Wales Press, 1984), p. 156.

pattern in the narrative arrangement of the poet's epic, *Gerusalemme
liberata*. According to Mario Fusco, the narrative of that epic is organized
not by the overcoming of obstacles but by the relentlessness with which
they frustrate and delay the conclusive conquest of Jerusalem. But if, as
Fusco also argues, the notion of failure determines the way characters
and plots evolve, what does this say about the poet's own desire for
limitations rather than liberation?[4] Similarly, having established a courtly
home, Tasso puts himself in a self-imposed state of exile, from which
he can beseech various princes and rulers to save him by taking him into
their courts. Loss and exile are publicly displayed to the paternal figures,
who are alternately blamed for these conditions or beseeched as possible
saviors from them. In either case, these figures incarnate a superego
whose satisfaction is impossible.

For such a psyche, the distinction between persecution and self-
persecution becomes increasingly blurred. For example, we know that
during the years 1575–1577 Tasso's sense of persecution intensified: he
was living under the constant fear that both his enemies and his servants
were robbing him of his writings. And he was later convinced that his
enemies wanted to poison him. He began seeing enemies in every nook
and corner, and this continued fear led him to outbursts of fury as
exemplified by his attacking a servant with a knife.[5]

Extending his criticisms of others to himself, in July 1577 the poet
accused himself of heresy to the inquisitor of Ferrara. We know from
Solerti's biography that the inquisitor kept Tasso for a few days and
then absolved him (1: 263–64). Tasso was dissatisfied with his absolution, angered that he was acquitted on medical grounds for reasons
pertaining to his "melancholia" when he himself wanted to be absolved
of heresy. This need for absolution was compounded by Tasso's un-
founded fears that a certain Montecatini was whispering into the in-

[4]See Mario Fusco, "La Question des obstacles dans la *Jerusalem délivrée*," in *Les Langues
Neo-Latines* 248 (1984), 54–76 and esp. 70–72. For Tasso's oedipalized relation to father
figures, see of course Margaret W. Ferguson, *Trials of Desire*: Renaissance Defenses of Poetry
(New Haven: Yale University Press, 1983); and Sergio Zatti, *L'uniforme cristiano e il multiforme
pagano: Saggio sulla "Gerusalemme liberata"* (Milan: Saggiatore, 1983). My own work aims to
expand this psychoanalytic paradigm of oedipal rivalry to show how that paradigm legitimates
and models a melancholic eros that remains tributary to a patriarchal masculinism that is
exclusive of women. At the heart of Tasso's "oedipal conflict" is an overweening desire for
approval from the father.
[5]Angelo Solerti, *Vita di Torquato Tasso* (Turin: Ermanno Loescher, 1895), 1: 257–59.
Solerti's *Vita* is still the canonical biography of Tasso's life, and much of my information is
drawn from his work. Further references are in the text. Also see the more condensed biography
by C. P. Brand, *Torquato Tasso* (Cambridge: Cambridge University Press, 1965).

quisitor's ears that the poet had maintained and proffered heretical thoughts and acts. (Montecatini continued for years to be the poet's preferred imagined enemy [1: 290–91].) This suspicion led Tasso to write a letter "Ai Cardinali della Suprema Inquisizione" in Rome in which he denounced his absolution: "He was absolved for being a sinner of melancholic humor rather than as one suspected of heresy" [fu assoluto più tosto come peccante di umor melancolico che come sospetto d'eresia].[6]

At the same time, Tasso's anxieties were heightened by the polemics ensuing on the completion of his *Liberata* (1575). His increased preoccupation with the magnum opus not only coincided with his many revisions but more interestingly, and probably connected to the revisions, coincided with the polemical controversy between *Ariostisti* and *Tassisti*.[7] The derision that Tasso encountered during this controversy, as well as the explicit condemnation by Lionardo Salviati and Silvio Antoniano, the latter an extreme Counter-Reformist, probably did contribute to Tasso's anxiety over the question of his religious as well as literary legitimacy.[8] One of the major results, on Tasso's part, was the *Apologia* written on behalf of his *opus* and including a perfunctory defense of his father, Bernardo.[9] In the meantime, while Tasso was oscillating between feelings of heresy and his fears of being poisoned, the duke of Ferrara and others became more acutely aware that Tasso's mental stability was slipping. As a result, the duke, on the advice of his physicians, withheld from the poet his manuscripts and forbade him to continue working until he had regained a measure of self-control. According to Solerti, this was done not out of malice or caprice but out of a "paternalistic" desire to protect the poet from exhaustion, since the court doctors believed that the poet's melancholia was due to nervous

[6]See Torquato Tasso, *Lettere*, ed. Ettore Mazzali (Turin: Einaudi, 1978), 1: 88.

[7]See Solerti, *Vita* 1: 252–327. Also see Bernard Weinberg, *A History of Literary Criticism in the Italian Renaissance* (Chicago: University of Chicago Press, 1974), 2: 954–1073; and Marziano Guglielminetti, preface to Torquato Tasso, *Gerusalemme liberata* (Milan: Garzanti Editore, 1982), 1: xxiv–xxx. Among Tasso's most severe critics was Lionardo Salviati, who wrote *De gli accademici della Crusca Difesa dell'Orlando Furioso dell'Ariosto contro 'l Dialogo dell' Epica Poesia di Camillo Pellegrino* (Florence, 1584).

[8]For an accessible collection of many of the letters pertaining to this controversy, see Tasso, *Prose*, pp. 331–731. Also see Tasso, *Lettere*, ed. Cesare Guasti (Florence: Successori Le Monnier, 1852–55), vol. 5. On Salviati, see the preceding note.

[9]See Tasso, *Prose*, pp. 411–88. Also see Margaret Ferguson's analysis of Tasso's defense of his father in *Trials of Desire*, pp. 98–102.

exhaustion because of overwork and distress related to his opus.(1: 281–82)

Tasso often fled from his courtly home of Ferrara from August 1577 to June 1578, when he sought shelter from his peregrinations at the court of Urbino. There he wrote his "Canzone al Metauro" before fleeing again (1: 306–9). Tasso eventually decided to return to Ferrara for the same reasons he had fled the town: one was that Duke Alfonso still withheld from Tasso his manuscripts, and the other was that he wanted protection from those who were "persecuting" him (1: 287). In response to Tasso's requests, the duke said he would take him back if he would renounce his obsessions and listen to the doctors. Once again, we see the familiar fear of persecution and the poet's insistence on some fatherly person to protect him. Tasso's reentry into the court of Ferrara, however, proved disastrous. When he arrived, the whole town was busy with celebrations of the duke's wedding, and because it was the eve of this long-awaited union, the duke was unable to see him that evening. Tasso became so outraged that he publicly insulted the duke as well as the entire Estense court (1: 306–7). In response, the duke had Tasso taken to the adjacent "hospital" of Sant'Anna where the poet was "put in chains as a madman" [e come pazzo, e messo alla catena] (1:309). Tasso's absences and presences, departures and returns, were abruptly put to an end by six years of forced confinement. Needless to say, being put under lock and key did more to seal Tasso's literary reputation than anything since the publication of the *Gerusalemme liberata* four years earlier. One wonders whether this loss was not Tasso's supreme gain.

A better sense of Tasso's recuperation of his melancholic madness can be acquired if we turn now to some of his reclusionary writings, especially his dialogue *Il Messaggiero* and his canzoni, "O figlie di Renata" and "O magnanimo Figlio."[10] To be capitalized upon, loss must be repeated, and it was Tasso's talent to turn one loss into another. Such a self-perpetuating spiral of "loss" that is also understood as defining a unique subjectivity is what Tasso in *Il messaggiero* (written from Sant'Anna) called *soverchia maninconia*, an excess of melancholy. The need to repeat loss also suggests Freud's relation between repetition compulsions and the death drive as Tasso's play between the courts

[10]*Il messaggiero*, in Tasso, *Prose*, pp. 3–37. "O figlie di Renata" and "O magnanimo figlio," in *Poesie*, ed. Francesco Flora (Milan: Riccardo Ricciardi, 1952), pp. 834–37 and 837–39. All translations are my own.

comes to resemble the *fort/da* game described by Freud as a way for the child to master the mother's absence. The same Freud essay, in fact, describes the Tassian character of Tancredi as "the most moving poetic picture" of the compulsion to repeat." But whether or not the Tassian enactment of loss is motivated by *thanatos* and the repetition compulsion, the symbolics of melancholia become apparent when we consider how the display of multiple losses works to establish his identity as martyred genius.

Begun in 1580 and finished in 1583, *Il messaggiero* is noteworthy for the nearly clinical self-awareness with which the poet discusses his melancholia even as the discourse is structured by the unconscious forces that condition that state. The dialogue begins at dawn with an auditory hallucination when a spirit visits the poet, a spirit whose sweet voice, *voce così piana e così soave* (p. 6), is there not to admonish him for his errors but to assure him that his vision is "real." Responding to the poet's request, the spirit appears to him in a form not unlike, the messenger says, the poet's own *anima*. The poet then devotes approximately two pages to the subject of melancholy, especially his own form of melancholic madness, which is here said to resemble a Hydra. The dialogue then proceeds to a lengthy discussion of the phenomenon of spirits and demons, and finally ends with an analysis of the nature and duty of the ambassador, understood as he who goes between the prince or representative of the state and the individual subject or citizen. The first two sections of this text, Tasso's vision and his discussion of melancholia, are of interest here.

Let us begin at the beginning, at the dawn or morning of his mourning.

> Era già l'ora che la vicinanza del sole comincia a rischiarire l'orrizonte, quando a me, che ne le delicate piume giaceva co'sensi non fortemente legati al sonno, ma così leggieramente che il mio stato era mezzo fra la viglia e la quiete, si fece al orecchio quel gentile spirto che suole favellarmi ne le mie imaginazioni, e mi chiamò con quel nome che è comune a tutti quelli i quali son nati nella mia stirpe. (p. 6)

> It was already the hour when the nearness of the sun begins to re-illuminate the horizon, and I was lying on delicate

---

"Freud, *Beyond the Pleasure Principle*, S.E. 18: 22.

feathers with my senses not tightly bound up in sleep but
loosened in a state somewhere between wakefulness and repose
when that gentle spirit who speaks to my imagination made
itself known to my ear and called me by that name which is
common to all those born in my clan.

The disembodied voice of the matinal spirit announces itself to the poet
much as the archangel Gabriel announced to the virgin that she was to
give birth to Christ, whose conception in her womb took place through
the ear that listened to the messenger angel's inseminating words. For
Tasso's spirit generates in the poet a desire to give birth to something
beautiful in "some gentle and beautiful souls" [in alcun animo bello e
gentile] (p. 16), a phrase by which Tasso characterizes himself in this
dialogue and which accordingly signals the exclusivity of this extraordinary group of souls among whom the poet finds himself. The exclusivity of this brotherhood and its indebtedness to a Ficinian eros are
brought forth when the poet asks to see the body of the voice he hears,
a body that the spirit says is an image not unlike that of Tasso's soul,
which the latter would have taken with him from the heavens when the
soul became united to his body. The poet desires to see the body of
this spirit, which putatively mirrors the spirit in his body, and is granted
his wish. In a dramatic moment, with a gust of wind and a profusion
of sun rays, the spirit reveals his form to Tasso while the poet is still
lying in his bed. What appears to Tasso in this literal incorporation is
a young man [un giovane], beardless [non avea le guance d'alcun pelo
ricoperte], of white skin and blond hair [bianco e biondo], and with
only a thin veil [sottilissimo velo] that covered nothing of his beautiful
person [che nulla ricopriva de la sua bella persona] (p. 13).

This erotic figure of a young man, who embodies the spiritual in-
terlocutor whose body reflects Tasso's own soul, inspires in the poet that
Ficinian desire to generate, to *partorire* or give birth, to something
beautiful (p. 16). This birth, he is quick to qualify, is not corporeal but
spiritual. And picking up the Ficinian school of love psychology, he says
that such desire is born in him through the virtue he sees descending
from the spirit's eyes into the poet's heart. The metaphor of birth is
continued as the poet says that he now feels the "itch" [prurito] of "new
wings" [novelle piume] sprouting on himself, wings that his soul, again
following Ficino, had unjustly lost in its violent descent into its body
(p. 16). But since the poet is sure that now his experience is not a dream,

he asks whether he is not in the grips of fantasy, of the imaginative force of the *vis imaginativa*.

In raising the question of a possible "mental alienation" [alienazione di mente], the text then turns around the epistemological problem of the veracity of sensory perception. Always aware of his condition as a *déraciné*, Tasso frames the discussion of the epistemological and onto-logical alienation wreaked by the imagination within the context of his own melancholia and already celebrated madness. The poet says that his mental alienation is related to two types of melancholy. And in an unusually self-conscious move, he proceeds to analyze his melancholy. In so doing, Tasso follows Aristotle and Ficino in distinguishing between two forms of melancholy, melancholy *per infermità* or based on an ac-cidental illness in an otherwise healthy self, and melancholy *per natura* as the essential condition of a certain kind of self. The outburst of melancholia as disease, as a sudden but extreme form of mental alienation [infirmità di pazzia] is exemplified for Tasso by such figures as Pentheus and Orestes. In the best Ficinian tradition, he links the gifted, innate form of melancholia to the Platonic notion of divine furor, and he says (again following both Ficino and Aristotle) that it can be brought to the surface by love or by drink. Tasso says that although he does not recognize his own melancholic madness in the figures of Pentheus or Orestes, he nevertheless does not deny his being mad. He proposes that *his* melancholia, this new form of madness [questa nova pazzia], which is peculiarly his own (at least in his mind), has other sources. Perhaps it is, as he says, a *soverchia maninconia*, a surplus of melancholy: "But since I am in no way conscious of being similar in madness to Orestes or Pentheus, just as I do not deny my being mad, it behooves me at least to believe that this new madness has other reasons. Perhaps it is a surplus of melancholy" [Ma perché di niun fatto simile a quelli d'Oreste o di Penteo sono consapevole a me stesso, come io non nieghi di esser folle, mi giova almeno di credere che questa nova pazzia abbia altra cagione. Forsè è soverchia maninconia] (p. 18).

Having just placed himself in a class by himself, Tasso then none-theless proceeds to cite, with a little help from Ficino, Aristotle's list of outstanding melancholics. The positive Ficinian inflection Tasso gives to the condition of melancholia is further evidenced by his apparent trans-lation of *perittoì* by *di chiaro ingegno*, of clear or bright mind, thus condensing the Ficinian virtues of translucence and cerebralness. And where Aristotle cites Homer on Bellerophon's melancholic wandering in deserted places, Tasso substitutes Petrarch's famous "Solo e pensoso." He thus both adds Petrarch to the list of great melancholics and implicitly places himself in the same rank as his predecessor, while explicitly putting Petrarch in the place of Homer. Concluding that those who are thus melancholic by nature and not by illness are of a singular mind [Comunque sia, coloro che non sono maninconici per infermità ma per natura, sono d'ingegno singolare], Tasso then reaffirms his absolute difference from all other melancholics by claiming that he is melancholic *both* by nature and by illness [e io son per l'una e per l'atra cagione]. The sequence of non sequiturs and illogical jumps by which Tasso both claims and disclaims the unprecedented originality of his madness seems itself to be a proof of his mental illness at the same time that he demonstrates an eloquent mastery of the literature on melancholia. Moreover, the self-proclaimed "originality" of Tasso's condition is underscored by his repeated use of the word *maninconia*, an old form for the modern Italian *malinconia* and an alternative spelling for (Latin) *melancholia*. Interestingly enough, a still common though archaic expression for a mental hospital is *manicomio*.

In addition to betraying a primitive association between melancholia and mania (which, as Freud argues in "Mourning and Melancholia" [*S.E.* 14: 254–58], is merely the flip side of melancholic mourning), the proximity of these words on the level of the signifier also underscores the *institutional* connection between the invention of the asylum and the representation of melancholia as an exemplary and privileged form of madness.[12] Tasso's *maninconia* derives both clinical gravity and symbolic prestige from its situation in a space of incarceration. Perhaps the poet is right to say that his is a new kind of madness, a melancholia that is both illness and nature. This self-conscious if rambling discourse about his melancholy thus discloses the persona of its author as in a state of mental alienation yet within this state still able to reason, to discourse on the epistemological problems associated with a subjectivism whose only source of affirmation comes from a mirrored dialogue with an Ideal, which as we have seen is no more than a fictional representation of the subject itself. Yet this fiction is the motivating force that drives his eros onto the scene of knowledge.

Saying that he suffers from both melancholy as illness and melancholy

[12]Cf. Michel Foucault, *Madness and Civilization: A History of Insanity in the Age of Reason*, trans. Richard Howard (New York: Random House, 1965), esp. chap. 9, "The Birth of the Asylum," pp. 241–78.

as divine inspiration and even more so from this *soverchia maninconia*, the poet is led to describe through a certain analogy the problems associated with this excess: persistent doubt and an implicitly defensive splitting of the ego. The analogy is with a mythological creature, the Hydra. Melancholy resembles a Hydra more than a chimera because, says the poet, as soon as one of the melancholic's thoughts is truncated [tronco un pensiero], two are suddenly born in its place [che due ne sono subito nati in quella vece] (p. 19). As a figure of limitless and unmasterable difference, the Hydra is a fearful symbol of inescapable entrapment at the hands of some other who refuses to go away. At the close of his *De vita*, Ficino calls on the help of a contemporary Hercules in the form of his friend Poliziano to help combat "this hundred-headed Hydra that is now threatening our books" (p. 189). In the long preface to the *Anatomy of Melancholy*, Burton would also evoke the frightening specter of the Hydra as a metaphor of endless dispute: "To have written in controversy had been to cut off an hydra's head, *lis litem generat*, one [dispute] begets another, so many duplications, triplications, and swarms of questions . . . , that having once begun, I should never make an end" (1: 35).[13] Later, in a more pointedly political reference, which also alludes to his own embroilment in the proliferating categories of melancholia itself, Burton says that "every multitude is mad, *bellua multorum capitum* [a many-headed beast], precipitate and rash without judgment, *stultum animal*, a roaring rout" (1: 78).

A daunting figure of social as well as textual turmoil, the Hydra recalls the upsetting effects of Medusa's head, especially as described by Freud and more recently, Neil Hertz.[14] Like Medusa's head, the Hydra is a fearful image of sexual difference associated with the fear of castration and with a general misogyny: not only does Tasso's "truncated" thought obviously recall castration, but as Freud points out, the "multiplication of penis symbols" such as found in the Medusa's serpentine hairs or, for that matter, in the Hydra's many heads, also signifies castration "for they replace the penis the absence of which is the cause of the horror."[15] As such, the Hydra, like the Medusa's head, can be read as a represen-

---

[13]Marsilius Fieinus, *The Book of Life*, ed. and trans. Charles Boer (Irving, Tex.: Spring Publications, 1980; Robert Burton, *Anatomy of Melancholy* (London: Dent and New York: Dutton, Everyman's Library, 1932), 3 vols.
[14]Cf. Neil Hertz, "Medusa's Head: Male Hysteria under Political Pressure," in *The End of the Line* (New York: Columbia University Press, 1985), pp. 161–82.
[15]Freud, "Medusa's Head," *S.E.* 18: 273–74.

tation, to quote Freud once more, "of woman as a being who frightens and repels because she is castrated."[16] As we know from Hesiod's *Theogony*, the Medusa and the Hydra are related. Keto, the mother of the Medusa, also bore the serpent goddess Echidna, the mother of the Hydra, who was, in turn, nurtured by that most threatening of godmothers, Hera.[17] Both the Medusa and the Hydra are misogynist representations of women that ward off the threat of sexual difference through a (male) logic of identity wherein what is not the same is represented as utterly and horrendously different. Not surprisingly, both Medusa and Hydra turn up in Tasso's depiction of hell.[18]

Hence, the messenger who visits Tasso not surprisingly resembles his own projected, idealized self, framed within a Ficinian context of divine love and inspiration, a context whereby eros and desire for another are suppressed by a divine madness that excludes alterity while at the same time appropriating a feminization to the extent that the poet posits himself in bed as the passive recipient of the Logos. It is thus not surprising that within such a framework, the Hydra comes to represent the subject's own fears of castration, namely the recognition of his finitude and inscribed limitations within a preexisting symbolic order. Thus Tasso's metaphor of the Hydra for the melancholic's excess of thought not only signifies a denial or turning away from the recognition of one's communality with women as, for example, in the experience of disempowerment, but it also mobilizes what Freud calls an apotropaic defensive screen such that the fact of sexual difference is denied even as the fear of that difference, castration, is taken in as a symptom so that the ego can subsequently divest itself of the fear. The Hydra thus functions in the same way as melancholia because each time a sad thought has been "truncated," or a loss mourned for, the loss is then doubled or two mournful thoughts are born in the place of one. This ferocious brand of melancholy, *soverchia maninconia*, turns the work of mourning into a perpetual labor, a more-than-Herculean task, one whose excessive—or rather infinite—production of its own loss comes to define the ego precisely in terms of its loss as the condition of its selfhood: a self

[16]Ibid., p. 274.
[17]Hesiod, *Theogony*, ed. and trans. Apostolos N. Athanassakis (Baltimore: Johns Hopkins University Press, 1983), ll. 270–314, pp. 20–21.
[18]Tasso, *Gerusalemme liberata*, ed. Fredi Chiapelli (Milan: Rusconi, 1982), pp. iv, 4–8, English translations with some modifications are from *Jerusalem Delivered*, ed. and trans. Ralph Nash (Detroit: Wayne State University Press, 1987). Tasso's use of the Medusa motif also appears in his love lyric; see, for example, *Poesie* v. ll. 9–14, p. 690.

forever mourning the loss of its own self. Perhaps it is through the uncanny arithmetic of Tasso's Hydra that we can understand the "something more" in melancholia that escapes Freud, namely an endless production of loss that endlessly signals narcissistic gain, and a positing of sexual difference that is both a denial and an appropriation of that difference.

The gap left by the truncated thought can be seen to be filled in, though, by the production of an imaginary system such as Tasso's long ensuing discourse on demonology, which mobilizes late Renaissance notions of "sympathy" and mutual attraction in an attempt to explain away all sorts of phenomena that remain inexplicable within the framework of current "scientific" thought. Chief among these explanatory devices, the *horror vacuus*, imputed to nature by the Aristotelian tradition and appropriated here by Tasso,[19] is merely the replication on the level of theory of the subject's more primordial fear of that void that is the unknown. While at least one critic has argued that Tasso's particular, historicized horror was aroused by a post-Copernican cosmology of infinite space,[20] the fear of the void is also readily decipherable in psychoanalytic terms as the fear of castration and of woman. Like Freud's "open wound," and in the particular context of melancholia, Tasso's *horror vacuus* tries to tame the Hydra of proliferating loss by converting the threatening gap of (sexual) difference into a theoretical principle of

---

[19]In *Il messaggiero*, while discussing the phenomena of sympathies and attractions, the spirit says that nature "herself" fearing to perish because of nature's relationship with the void, calls to "her" aid air, which is a body and thus fills "herself" up so that "she" does not fear to perish [si riempie in modo ch'ella non teme di perire] (p. 26).

[20]Fausto Montanari, *Riflessioni sulla poesia del Tasso* (Savona: Sabatelli Editori, 1974), pp. 17–33. Montanari claims that Tasso's lyric was influenced greatly by the mathematical propositions of Copernicus, particularly the idea of the "infinito-indefinito." The new mathematical concept of infinite space gives Tasso, according to Montanari, a feeling of horror and doubt: "The new Copernican hypothesis unleashed the imagination by infinite linear projections onto the emptiness of space and generated a feeling of an infinite nothing as the dark womb of the universe" [La nuova ipotesi copernicana scatenava la fantasia sulle rette infinite proiezioni verso il vuoto dello spazio, e generava un sentimento di un infinitivo nulla come oscuro grembo dell' universo] (pp. 18–19). Montanari maintains that Tasso's sense of the infinite is born out of these mathematical and cosmological concepts. In order to confront this new world, Tasso assumes a heroic stance, construed to affirm life and thereby create an individual meaning out of life. The poet is able, through heroic posturing, to defy the uncertainties produced through the idea of space as something void (p. 19). What we must continually question is whether one can assume that Tasso's position is heroic and if so, then whether it implies a new understanding of heroism. My contention, however, is that to speak of heroism in Tasso is to confuse a classical ideal, based on Homeric tradition, with the sort of angst (in this case unheroic in classical terms and even in terms of the well-rounded and well-grounded individual of the early Renaissance) that pervades so much of the poet's life and work.

interpretive closure. The gaping hole is covered over, or sutured, by its being raised to the level of "objective" theory. At the same time, the subject's anxiety about lack, which psychoanalysis refers to as the castration complex, becomes available for its narcissistic self-representation as the stigmata of melancholia; the open wound (of castration anxiety) becomes the blessed wound (of unappreciated genius).

The relation between castration anxiety and melancholia is given an especially dramatic rendition in the celebrated twelfth and thirteenth cantos of the *Gerusalemme liberata*, written before the onset of Tasso's madness. There we find another scene where truncation is at issue within a context of loss and lack. Tancredi unknowingly kills the woman he loves in a duel which moves like an erotic and macabre dance and within which Thanatos conquers.

> Tre volte il cavalier la donna stringe
> con le robuste braccia, ed altrettante
> da que' nodi tenaci ella si scinge,
> nodi di fer nemico e non d'amante.
> Tornano al ferro, e l'uno e l'altro il tinge
> con molte piaghe; e stanco ed anelante
> e questi e quegli al fin pur si ritira,
> e dopo lungo faticar respira. (XII, 57)

Three times his strong arms clasp around her, as she, each time, loosens herself from those tenacious knots, bonds of a ferocious enemy and not of a lover. They take up their swords again and fight one, then the other, color it with many wounds, until weak and breathless, they both retire after their long labor to breathe again.

Too late, the Christian Tancredi realizes that his opponent was his beloved, the pagan warrior-maiden Clorinda:

> Ma ecco omai l'ora fatale è giunta
> che 'l viver di Clorinda al suo fin deve.
> Spinge egli il ferro nel bel sen di punta
> che vi s'immerge e 'l sangue avido beve;
> e la veste, che d'or vago trapunta
> le mamelle stringea tenera e leve,
> l'empie d'un caldo fiume. Ella giá sente
> morirsi, e 'l più le manca egro e languente. (XII, 64)

But now, alas! the fatal hour arrives that Clorinda's life must come to its end. Deep into her bosom he drives the point of his sword which sinks and avidly drinks her blood and her embroidered vest that tenderly and lightly clasps her breast hotly swells with gold. She already feels herself dying, and her foot gives way, weak and languid.

The tragedy of this death scene lies, on one level, in the necessity of her death [che 'l viver di Clorinda al suo fin deve]. On another level, the tragedy is excused by the fact that Tancredi was unable to recognize Clorinda, since we already know from a previous canto that Clorinda went out to fight without her usual armor. The guilt Tancredi experiences at her death/murder is fraught with this "error" of misrecognition and also with the inevitability of the event. In the following canto, we see how this event finally cripples Tancredi's ability to act, specifically, to act according to his duty as a soldier and to cut down the cypress tree so as to free the enchanted forest of its incantation.

In these two cantos, we read the necessity of immobilizing the threatening powers of Clorinda's amazonian femininity. Already in Canto III, her first appearance in the epic, the loss of her helmet reveals her gilded head of hair [chiome dorate] which, medusa-like, turns Tancredi to stone [veggendo impètra].[21] A few strophes later, her battlefield manner is compared to a huge bull turning his horn [corno] on a pack of dogs. Such an obviously phallic woman needs to be rendered powerless, and her prowess, represented as pagan, unfeminine and virulent, must yield to an orthodoxy of Christian beatitude. In canto XII, Clorinda's aggressivity (which is understood to be the fruit of her upbringing) is sundered through her death by a beloved from whom she receives baptism. Accordingly she is redeemed through the Christian rite, which renders her benign and "feminine" by locking her up and away into a beatific, Christian heaven. In other words, her murder is somehow absolved by her rebirth, through baptism, into a state of unworldly happiness and peace (XII, 68). She has become gentle and gentrified. What is then supposed to happen but does not, as we shall see, is for Tancredi to become the hero of the Christian mission, the conquest of Jerusalem, by cutting down the cypress tree. The sadism implicit in the murder of Clorinda as well as in the desire to conquer Jerusalem, the city of Christ, from the infidels is never

---

[21]As Marilyn Migiel suggests in "Tancredi and Clorinda: The Battle with Fatal Authorities," *Stanford Italian Review* 11 (Fall 1991), "Clorinda is a figure around whom are concentrated many of the horrifying and reassuring feelings about masculinity and femininity excited by the vision of the Medusa herself."

really an issue in the *Gerusalemme*. If there is any casualty of this overriding presumption, it might be Tancredi himself. For in canto XIII, Tancredi pays dearly for Clorinda's death precisely by his incapacity to *cut* the tree, an act that would free the forest of its evil incantation so that siege machines, made out of the forest's trees, could be manufactured to ensure the Christian conquest of Jerusalem.

This is not to imply, however, that the ability to cut down the tree (as Rinaldo does several cantos later) is any less implicated in the logic of phallocentrism. Whether Tancredi acts "according to his duty" or whether he remains transfixed by his brooding thoughts, what is at stake is a question of cutting, of truncation, hence of castration. Therefore, whether he acts or does not act, he remains situated in terms of a dilemma that reduces the field of possibilities to the simple opposition between "castrate" and "be castrated," an either/or alternative whose reductive formulation *is* the repressive work of phallocentrism itself. For the latter, consequently, any other possibility cannot be understood and is thus cast into the category of the "monstrous," such as the Hydra whose response to the tactic of cut or be cut is to undermine the very sense of the opposition by twice replacing whatever has been lost.

Certainly Tasso, as the epic narrator, is aware of the price extorted by such blatant acts of aggression. For Tasso represents, in the figure of Tancredi, the merciless fixation of a subject caught between word and deed, between representation and experience. Tancredi cannot cut the cypress on which are inscribed the "evil" words of the magician Ismeno:

> O tu che dentro a i chiostri de la morte
> osasti por, guerriero audace, il piede,
> deh! se non sei crudel quanto sei forte,
> deh! non turbar questa secreta sede. (XIII, 39)

O you, audacious warrior, who dared set foot into death's cloister, Woe! if you are not as cruel as you are strong, Woe! do not disturb this secret place.

Briefly, the inscription reads: let the dead rest in peace. How strange it seems that these should be the words of the evil sorcerer. When cut, the tree begins to bleed, and we cannot help but remember the previous canto where the sword drank in the blood that killed Clorinda [I sangue avido beve]. At this moment and in a Dantesque vein,[22] her voice pleads with him not to cut down the tree since she is literally embodied within it:

> Clorinda fui: né sol qui spirito umano
> albergo in questa pianta rozza e dura,
> ma ciascun altro ancor, franco o pagano,
> che lassi i membri a piè de le l'alte mura,
> astretto è qui da novo incanto e strano,
> non so s'io dica in corpo o in sepoltura.
> Son di sensi animati i rami e i tronchi,
> e micidial sei tu, se legno tronchi.   (XII, 43)

I was Clorinda: yet not the only one of human spirit who lives within this crude and hard plant, but others still, Christian or Pagan [who] leave their members at the foot of the tall walls, are confined here by new and strange spells [and] I do not know if embodied or entombed. The branches and trunks are alive with sensation, and a murderer are you, if you cut a limb.

Though Tancredi has been forewarned that the voice that speaks in his lost love's name is not Clorinda's but simply another of Ismeno's tricks, he still cannot help but act as if those sounds really are the sounds of Clorinda's voice. The mimicking of Clorinda's voice thus closes this scene of eerie seduction by the represented forces of evil in a way that leaves Tancredi powerless and transfixed. As in the *Messaggiero*, a disembodied voice exerts a powerful seduction over a listener, who is anxious to misrecognize fiction as fact, illusion as reality—or otherwise put, readily willing to believe in ghosts. It is because of this incapacity to act in the face of such simulacra that Tancredi has been heralded as *the* melancholic character of the *Gerusalemme liberata*.[23] In the following cantos, Tancredi comes to symbolize the melancholic who is transfixed

---

[22]See Dante Alighieri, *Inferno*, ed. and trans. Allen Mandelbaum (Berkeley: University of California Press, 1980), 13, 22ff.; also see Freud, *Beyond the Pleasure Principle*, where Tancredi at the cypress tree is described as "the most moving poetic picture" governed by the compulsion to repeat which overrides the pleasure principle" (*S.E.* 18: 22). On the relation between this passage in Tasso and other "bleeding tree" scenes in Vergil, Dante, Boccaccio, and Ariosto, see Ferguson, *Trials of Desire*, p. 215n.

[23]Cf. Giorgio Petrocchi, *I fantasmi di Tancredi: Saggi sul Tasso e sul Rinascimento* (Caltanisetta: Salvatore Sciascia, 1972): Giovanni Getto, *La malinconia di Torquato Tasso* (Naples: Liguri, 1979); Bruno Basile, "Archeologia di un mito Tassiano: Il poeta malinconico," *Lingua e Stile* 5 (1970), 293–308; Ferguson, *Trials of Desire*, esp. pp. 123–28.

because of his literal incapacity to *cut his losses*, to curtail the incremental momentum of his brooding thoughts [tronco un pensiero che due ne sono subito nati in quella vece], and he thereby reaffirms the motif of the melancholic's Hydra in *Il messaggiero*.

For the false Clorinda, here inextricably bound up within the tree, acts like the Hydra to produce an infinite repetition of loss and mourning as the sign of the suffering lover. It is not the beloved, Clorinda, whose death is mourned but Tancredi's melancholy plight; it is not just his inability to complete the work of mourning but also his inability to live up to the heroic expectations of his fellow Christians that appears as the object of poetic pathos. For Freud to describe Tancredi's dilemma as "the most moving poetic picture" of the compulsion to repeat is to accredit once again the sentimentalization of the crusading hero. More-over, to see repetition in Tancredi's acts, as Freud does, is either to forget that Tancredi *cannot* follow through on chopping down the tree or to fall into the trap that beguiles the hapless knight, namely that of confusing the sorcerer's impersonated ghost of Clorinda with Clorinda herself.

Yet both Clorinda's auditory image and its emanation from within the phallic symbol of the cypress tree point also to woman as other within Tasso's epistemological and moral system.[24] Perhaps the differ-ence between the "true" or beatified Clorinda up in heaven and the "false" one induced by the sorcerer's ventriloquism should be read as a splitting of the representation of woman into good and bad objects. The "good," non-other Clorinda is made into a safe, non-sensual, nec-rophilic love object, relieved of her womanly experience. The "false" Clorinda is woman as other, is like the Hydra herself: an enigmatic source of horror that castrates the male by virtue of "her" assault on his consciousness, by virtue of the ever-insisting character of her difference, which ceaselessly *re*-marks itself even in its denial. Even when slain by the male sword, woman simply returns as two, not unlike the Hydra's

[24]On questions of truncation, body fragmentation, and dismemberment as a sort of love sequence whereby truncation paradoxically signifies unification with a beloved within the context of Pauline theology, see Walter Stephens, "Saint Paul among the Amazons: Gender and Authority in *Gerusalemme liberata*," in *Discourses of Authority in Medieval and Renaissance Literature*, ed. Kevin Brownlee and Walter Stephens (Hanover: University Press of New England, 1989), pp. 169–200. While Stephens goes on to argue that Tasso's desire to recu-perate or "save" woman from herself points to a feminist subtext in Tasso's *poema* that runs counter to its entrenchment in Christian misogyny, it seems to me that such a view of women as creatures to be "redeemed" supports rather than undermines a misogynist ideology.

doubled head. Incapable of being castrated, she thus continues to haunt the male subject as a fearful, phantasmic gap within his defensive interpretive construct, the one that sees her as other and wants to render this strangeness benign.[25] In some way, then, the *horror vacuus* is really a metaphor for a repressed aggressivity toward the feminine, as the male subject—particularly the male poet who attributes to himself the aura of privileged suffering—attempts to make of that repression the driving mechanism of his own eros: an eros maintained by an endless supply of lack. The totalizing empowerment of a discourse based on such aggressivity, fueled by the desire to reduce difference and legitimated by an ethos of aesthetic victimization, persists throughout the reworkings of Tasso's major epic under the guise of a Christian ideology that sets out to hegemonize and homogenize Jerusalem: the topographical equivalent of the female other as that which must not only be *liberata* (in the epic's title of 1575) but also, and more definitively, *conquistata* (in the title of the revised epic of 1593).

In counterpoint to this celebration of male aggressivity is the persistent linkage in the epic between the danger of women and their role as mourners. In canto IV, the "treacherous" Armida leads off a large portion of the Christian army through the power of her tearful lament and mournful recounting of a life begun with the death of her mother. Godfrey himself is virtually helpless before the power of Armida's grieving performance to sway his troops. A narrator's intervention even be-

---

[25]Jane Gallop goes so far as to define feminism as "the defense and validation of such monsters" ("The Monster in the Mirror: The Feminist Critic's Psychoanalysis," in *Feminism and Psychoanalysis*, ed. Michael Feldstein and Judith Roof [Ithaca: Cornell University Press, 1989], p. 23). On the transformations of monsters as misogynist depictions of the feminine into positive representations of woman, Hélène Cixous states that "you only have to look at the Medusa straight on to see her. And she is not deadly. She is beautiful and she's laughing" ("The Laugh of the Medusa," trans. Keith Cohen and Paula Cohen, in *New French Feminisms: An Anthology*, ed. Elaine Marks and Isabelle de Courtivron [Amherst: University of Massachusetts Press, 1980], p. 255); Teresa de Lauretis argues in *Alice doesn't: Feminism, Semiotics, Cinema* (Bloomington: Indiana University Press, 1984), that to see the Medusa "straight on [as Cixous does] is not a simple matter for women or for men" (p. 135). What is at stake for de Lauretis is that "the relation of female subjectivity to ideology" bears upon the real and the historical in such a way that the political issue of femininity, that is the context of women and the representation of women, is greater than "a politics of the unconscious" (p. 136). Barbara Spackman argues, on the other hand, that to side either with the enchantress or the "hag" is to remain within an opposition between essence and appearance that perpetuates the notion that truth is ungendered ("Inter musam et ursam moritur: Folengo and the Gaping 'Other' Mouth," in *Refiguring Woman: Perspectives on Gender and the Italian Renaissance*, ed. Marilyn Migiel and Juliana Schiesari [Ithaca: Cornell University Press, 1991], pp. 19–34).

speaks a certain male envy and resentment of the feminine rhetorical force:

> Or che non può di bella donna il pianto,
> ed in lingua amorosa i dolci detti?
> Esce da vaghe labra aurea catena
> che l'alme a suo voler prende ed affrena. (IV, 83)

Now what cannot be achieved by the tears of a beautiful woman, and sweet speeches on an amorous tongue? From her lovely lips depends a golden chain that captures souls and bridles them as she wills.

The fear of women's tears, and ultimately of the feminization that tears might bring about in men, explains why Raymond later speaks against Godfrey's decision to fight Argantes in the place of Tancredi:

> e disse a lui rivolto: "Ah non sia vero
> ch'in un capo s'arrischi il campo tutto!
> Duce sei tu, non semplice guerriero:
> publico fàra e non privato il lutto." (VII, 62)

and he said, confronting him: "Ah let it not be that in one head the whole army be imperiled! You are a leader, not a mere soldier; the mourning would be public, and not private.

Throughout the epic, the "other" of the crusading army is less its symmetrical opposite, the pagan soldiery, than that wailing multitude of women and *vulgi* by which the population of Jerusalem is consistently represented and which is also the object of the two armies' strife.

One figure does distinguish herself from "the common womanly crowd" [del vil femineo volgo] (VI, 86) and presents an alternative to the risk of contaminating men with the feminization of tears. Erminia, perpetually in tears, seems to figure mourning itself. Her arrival in Jerusalem is followed by the death of her mother, and she is accordingly "swathed in black garments" (VI, 59). It is Erminia who, in the wilds outside the city, comes upon the apparently dead Tancredi and brings him miraculously back to life through the "inexhaustible spring" and "refreshing dew" of her tears.[26] The black-clad and comatose knight is an obvious object of mourning, yet Erminia continues to treat him as such even after her tears and sobs have begun to revive Tancredi: "Open your eyes, Tancred, 'she cries,' for these last obsequies that I make you with my grieving' " [Apri gli occhi, Tancredi, a queste estreme / essequie," grida, "ch'io ti fo co 'l pianto] (XIX, 110). She then binds his wound "with the very hair that she had been wishing to cut" [con le chiome che troncar si volle] (XIX, 112) in accordance with the traditional rites of mourning. The salutary quality of Erminia's cut hair also offers a domesticated or neutralized alternative to Clorinda's threatening, Medusan locks.

The lessons of the *Gerusalemme liberata* seem quite clear. Mourning is women's work and for men to partake in it is to risk their feminization and castration—caught in the clutches of Armida's spell, Rinaldo is so disabled that even his sword is said to be "made effeminate" (XVI, 30). On the other hand, to be mourned for is to be restored from death either literally as Tancredi is with Erminia's help or figuratively in the warrior's continued existence after his death as an object of speech and lamentation.[27] Within the chivalric (and masculinist) ethics of honor, the compensation for a noble death is everlasting fame, and it is the domesticated function of women to ensure the promulgation of this fame through their appropriate mourning of the fallen hero. That the desire to be mourned is the knight's highest aspiration is revealed by Godfrey's reaction to the massacre of Sven's troops:

---

[26]In an unpublished manuscript, Lynn Enterline eloquently argues that not just a proliferation of dead fathers but also phantoms of dead mothers are in need of mourning. Furthermore, she reads Erminia (and Armida) as taking on the task of mourning, one that poignantly recalls Tasso's own loss of his mother as expressed in his "Canzone al Metauro." Enterline sees Tancredi, Erminia, and Armida as generating sympathy as "figures of mourning." I wish to thank Enterline for allowing me to read her excellent analysis. My own discussion of mourning and melancholia differs, however, from Enterline's in that I am arguing that these figures of mourning are given only a devalued access to a symbolics of grief that remains male-dominated and thus institutes the difference between mourning and melancholia as the sign of that gendered difference in value. Also see Marilyn Migiel, "Tasso's Erminia: Telling an Alternate Story," *Italica* 64 (Spring 1987), 62–75, and "Secrets of a Sorceress: Tasso's Armida," *Quaderni d'Italianistica* (Winter 1987–88). Migiel argues that both Armida and Erminia serve as author surrogates for Tasso's anxieties concerning epic narration. See my "The Victim's Discourse: Torquato Tasso's *Canzone al Metauro*," *Stanford Italian Review* 5 (Fall 1985), 25–36.

[27]On the Greek tradition of heroic death as the price for infinite blessings, see Nicole Loraux, *The Invention of Athens: The Funeral Oration in the Classical City*, trans. Alan Sheridan (Cambridge: Harvard University Press, 1986).

"Ma che? felice è cotal morte e scempio
via più ch'acquisto di provincie e d'oro,
né dar l'antico Campidoglio essempio
d'alcun può mai sì glorioso alloro.
Essi del ciel nel luminoso tempio
han corona immortal del vincer loro:
ivi credo io che le sue belle piaghe
ciascun lieto dimostri e se n'appaghe." (VIII, 44)

"Yet what of this? happy is such death and slaughter, far more than gain of gold or provinces; nor ever could ancient Campidoglio give example of any laurel so glorious. They in the shining temple of Heaven possess the immortal crown of their victory: there I warrant that each one happily displays his lovely wounds, and takes pleasure in them."

To mourn is to lapse into a debilitating femininity; to *be* mourned is to receive infinite life and bliss in return for the display of one's finitude. In psychoanalytic terms, two relations to castration are described: a disempowering one that brings the male subject into an identification with women, and an empowering one that recuperates the lack the subject displays by redesignating the implicit "femininity" of that position as super-masculine, as the apotheosis of heroism. By the late Renaissance, of course, this recuperative ethos was already well on the way to becoming anachronistic as the feudal warrior gave way to the courtier and the *honnête homme*, as courage and defiance became decorum and flattery.[28] On the other hand, an aggressive individualism predicated on the narcissistic display of one's wounds crystallizes in the rising figure of the melancholic, who not only desires to be mourned but mourns the fact that he is not being mourned, or not being mourned enough. Typically on the margins of power as a poet or philosopher of bourgeois origin (Petrarch, Ficino, Tasso) or as an exiled or disenfranchised aris-

[28]For some philosophical reflections on the dialectics of noble consciousness whereby "the heroism of dumb service passes into the heroism of flattery," see G. W. F. Hegel, *The Phenomenology of Mind*, trans. J. B. Baillie, 2d ed. rev. (London: Macmillan, 1931), p. 533 and the entire chapter "Culture and Its Realm of Actual Reality," pp. 514–48. Also see, along these same lines, Louis Marin, *Portrait of the King*, trans. Martha M. Houle (Minneapolis: University of Minnesota Press, 1988).

tocrat, the melancholic imagines an elite birth for himself, the noble status of Saturnian descent, for example.[29]

This uncertain social status is doubled by an *apparent* blurring of gender lines. If he mourns his not being mourned, his relationship to the two types of "feminization" mentioned above become vexed and unclear. The display of his wounds may be narcissistic but it is not "happy" if he must shed his own tears. But since these wounds are not physical but psychological (the narcissistic wounds, for instance, of not being sufficiently accredited by the symbolic order of court power), they can only be displayed by the subject's display of his own grief, which following the lessons of the *Gerusalemme liberata* would lead him into a non-recuperable *identification* with the feminine, to his effeminization. The melancholic, in other words, enters into a vertiginous relationship with lack which he must somehow reconvert into an endless narcissistic gain. *Soverchia maninconia* is Tasso's original response to this dilemma, in which he can never be sure whether his castration will be sutured or not, whether his psychical dismemberment (in the form of his "truncated" thoughts) will be forever re-membered or not. The *horror vacuus* evoked by the Hydra's many heads is not, as I have already suggested, just an intrapsychic inability to accept finitude but also an inter- or extrapsychic fear of and aggressivity towards women. Mourning his not being mourned, the melancholic can never be sure whether he is dealing with the docile, male-subservient, and restorative Erminia or the treacherously deceptive and dominating Armida. He does not know whether he will be properly catered to as a lauded object of grief or will lose himself in woeful wailing and shrieks of lamentation. Mourning his not being mourned, the melancholic must both appropriate a "feminine" position as his own *and* deny his resultant sense of castration. To put himself in the place of Erminia is to fall prey to Armida. At the same time, this "risky" appropriation implies a certain rage against their insufficient mourning of the subject, which requires him to take a "feminine" position in order to assure his own mourning, to be impregnated, as in *Il messaggiero*, by a ghost image of himself. The problem is that the male

---

[29]On the relationship between genius, melancholy, and artistic productivity see Rudolf Wittkower and Margot Wittkower, *Born under Saturn: The Character and Conduct of Artists: A Documented History from Antiquity to the French Revolution* (New York: Random House, 1963), esp. pp. 102–8.

hero or melancholic cannot seem to circumvent the necessity of the female mourner, yet that mourner is persistently seen as unreliable.

From such a projected fear and dependency, we can better grasp the intra-psychic motivation of the humanist attempt to regulate the rite of mourning. Erminia, though, as the paragon of that regulation, can still turn out to be Armida. Not only can one never be sure whether the tears are real or faked but the ritual itself necessitates some breakdown of the difference between private and public, which is in itself a prelude to civil turmoil. Remember Petrarch's admonition that compares the tumultuousness of women mourners in the streets to madmen on the loose or the city under siege. And in the case of the siege of Jerusalem, nothing could be more devastating to the Christian cause, as Raymond warns, than the *public* mourning should Godfrey die. Like the two Clorindas, Erminia and Armida, as the phonic similarity of their names suggests, are simply good and bad versions of the same, and following the logic of the Hydra, their split merely reproduces the civil strife and dissension it is supposed to contain. And if the epic is read, as Tasso himself asserts in the "Allegoria del poema," as an allegory of the individual soul, then melancholia would lead to psychical disintegration, that is, precisely that process of infinite splitting that Tasso describes in *Il messaggiero* through the metaphor of the Hydra, and that would testify to the "novelty" of his madness. The city under siege is also a representation of the melancholic ego.

This overtly split subject is one who proceeds to split woman as object in turn—only to have this attempt to master gender difference open onto the Hydra's limitless proliferation of differences. Mourning his not being mourned, the melancholy subject appropriates a femininity he can never possess, all the while characterizing that difference, that lack, as a monstrous threatening femininity. Perhaps it is this resistant insistence of the feminine, his inability to do without women, that is the origin of the melancholic's narcissistic wound, of that open sore of perpetual anti-cathexis.

In the reclusionary poetry written from Sant'Anna, Tasso oscillates between the desire to situate himself as victim in the place of women and the depiction of powerful female figures that victimize him and determine his fate. Already in the prereclusionary "Canzone al Metauro," we saw his appropriation of his mother's death as *his* loss, on the one hand, and his blaming the feminine figure of Fortune [crudel Fortuna] for his woes, on the other hand. In the reclusionary "O figlie di Renata," the poet, in no uncertain terms, calls on the daughters of the exiled former duchess of Ferrara to intercede on his behalf with the duke, their brother.

He begins by telling them he is *not* addressing the funeral pyre of Eteocles and Polynices, those feuding sons of Oedipus whom death itself could not bring together. The poet makes it quite clear that he will not be *mourning* those badly born [malnata] siblings but singing the praises of the well-born daughters of a regal mother whose name, Renata, means to be reborn:

> ma parlo a voi che pio
> produsse e real seme
> in uno istesso seno,
> quasi in fertil terreno
> nate e nodrite pargolette insieme,
> quasi due belle piante
> di cui serva è la terra e il cielo amante.

> but I speak to you whom
> a pious and royal seed produced
> in one same breast,
> as in a fertile terrain
> born and nourished together,
> like two beautiful plants
> who are served by the earth and the loving sky.

Tropes of genetic purity and harmony (royal seed, fertile terrain) oppose the good daughters to the vexed ancestry of the bad brothers. As "sisters of the great, invincible Duke Alfonso" [suore del grand'Alfonso invitto], they are further said to be a match for Juno and Diana and to achieve more through their offerings [vóti] than Berenice, Ptolemy's spouse, who ensured her husband's battlefield success Erminia-like by cutting off her hair [offrí chioma votiva]. Of course, the votive offerings of the daughters of Renata are said to shine more brightly than Berenice's hair, which the gods placed in the heavens as a new constellation. And concluding the panegyric moment of his canzone, the poet states that he is addressing himself to the daughters because they bring about a "harmonious concordance" of "honesty, intelligence, honor, beauty and glory": [A voi parlo in cui fanno / sì concorde armonia / onestà, senno, onor, bellezza e gloria].

Symbols of an overriding unity and genealogical distinction ("off-spring of heroes, of kings" [prole / d'eroi, di regi]), the daughters are then called upon to hear Tasso tearfully narrate his bitter story [narro, e'n parte piangendo, acerba istoria]. They are there to receive the great tears his grief spills out on or to them [lagrime larghe il mio dolor vi spande], to mourn his losses, to reunite him with all that he has been split off from by remembering him—and, of course, by beseeching the duke on his behalf (although this last request does not appear till the poem's end). Split off from the court, or as he says from humanity itself [d'umanità perdute], by his "hospitalization," Tasso appeals to the daughters' lauded synthetic qualities to put his life back together again. If, however, the united daughters of Renata are supposed to be some kind of counter-Hydra, the emblematic creature of melancholia rears another head in the rhetoric of the poet's appeal: listing his losses with egoistic self-obsession and self-display (as Freud might say), Tasso's lyric repeatedly falls into the broken syntax or parataxis of potentially endless enumeration. Significantly, the list begins with the temporal split between what he *is* and what he *was*:

> qual son, qual fui, che chiedo, ove mi trovo,
> chi mi guidò, chi chiuses,
> lasso!, chi m'affidò, chi mi deluse.
>   . . . . . .

> Cetre, trombe, ghirlande,
> misero, piango e piagno
> studi, diporti ed agi,
> mense, logge e palagi
> ov'or fui nobil servo ed or compagno;
> libertade e salute
> e leggi, oimè!, d'umanità perdute.

> what I am, what I was, what I ask, where I find myself,
> who guides me, who shuts me out,
> alas!, who gives me faith, who deceives me.
>   . . . . . .

> Lyres, horns, garlands of flowers,
> unhappy, I cry and I lament
> studies, courtly diversions and activities
> banquets, lodgings and palaces
> where I was sometimes a noble servant and sometimes a companion
> freedom and good health
> and laws, oh my!, of lost human civility.

The rhetorical fragments of enumeration dramatize a dismembered self, one whose only hope appears to be in the daughters' salutary remembering.

Ever the narcissist, Tasso nonetheless tries to mitigate such an obvious—and to him undoutedly fearful—dependency on women. He does not simply ask them to re-member him; he says that he will renew in them the memory of them *and* of himself [ed in voi la memoria / di voi, di me, rinovo]. In other words, it is *through them* that he will remember himself [gli anni *miei tra voi* spesi]. A further implication is that he will return to the daughters the memory of themselves [la memoria di voi], by tearfully talking about himself.

Some explanation for this rather strange claim can be found if we juxtapose the desire for renewal or renovation with the name of the mother in whose name the daughters are implored to preside at Tasso's re-membering. By addressing the *figlie* as daughters *of Renata*, and by claiming a circuit of remembrance that implicates himself in their memory as well as themselves in his memory, Tasso suggests an analogy between himself and the victimized ex-duchess. As Ugo Foscolo once remarked, "Tasso, addressing them as 'Daughters of Renata,' hoped to excite their sympathy by the association of his own misfortunes with those of their mother—an expedient, however, which, like many others, proved unavailing to him."[30] And if the daughters represent the overcoming of difference, their common mother, Renata, *is* the principle of their unity. As the daughter of the French king, Louis XII, Renata is also the source of their royal heritage [real seme, prole di regi].

The marriage between Duke Alfonso's father, Ercole II, and Renata, in 1528 was a marriage based on secular interests. Historically, the Estes had always maintained a close alliance with France. When Ercole II married Renata she, interestingly enough, became a follower of Calvin while at the court of Ferrara. One historian has pointed out that a Protestant chapel was actually constructed within the castle of Ferrara around 1536. And in due time, both Ferrara and Modena were called the new Geneva. Not only had Clèment Marot, the French poet and reformer, been at the court in 1535, but also Calvin himself, in 1536, came to visit Renata.[31] Ercole's attitude toward Renata's conversion to

---

[30]Ugo Foscolo, *Saggi e discorsi critici*, ed. C. Foligno (Florence: Le Monnier, 1953), p. 519.

[31]The following sources describe, in passing, Renata's presence at the court of Ferrara and her Calvinist sympathies: Solerti, *Vita*, vol. I, in particular pp. 136, 179–80, 259–60; Solerti, *Ferrara e la corte Estense nella seconda meta del secolo decimosesto to: i discorsi di Annibale*

Calvinism was one of tolerance. This was so not because of any religious fervor on his part but because, as Mario Roffi has argued, Ercole had to make a political calculation: he was not sure that Protestantism would not win over in Italy. In fact, Ercole tried at the risk of excommunication to prevent the execution of the heretic Camillo Fannio (Fanin) in 1550.[32]

By the time Renata's son, Alfonso II, came into power, the tensions between Ferrara and the papacy had increased, and the *Santa Sede* was both suspicious and hostile toward Ferrara. In order to maintain civic propriety, Ferrara's court had to insist on a certain display of protocol given the climate of religious counter-reform taking place in Italy. Furthermore, Ferrara was not an autonomous unit. It had been ruled uninterruptedly, it is true, since 1317 by the Estes, but they were entitled to do so not as independent lords but only as papal vicars. The Estes, as long as their dynasty continued, were the rulers of Ferrara. When Tasso first arrived at the court, the Este line was almost at an end, having no direct heirs. In fact, as Solerti, the biographer of both Tasso and the Estes, informs us, Alfonso II attempted to pass the dynasty over to his cousin Cesare. What was thus at stake during Tasso's presence at the court was the progressive devolution of Ferrara to the papacy. The papacy refused to recognize Cesare as a legitimate heir, and when Alfonso II died in 1597, Cesare was forced to abandon Ferrara or else be excommunicated. Increasingly threatened by the possibility of not securing an heir for the Estes, the same Duke Alfonso who would later incarcerate Tasso decided, on Rome's request, to send his mother away from Ferrara. She was banished from the court and it was the threat of not ever seeing her children again that forced her publicly to recant her religious affiliation.[33]

Rome: (Città di Castello: S. Lapi, 1900), pp. 32–33. Very little scholarship has been done on what significance Renata's presence might have had for Ferrara and Tasso. One of the most illuminating articles on the issue of Ferrara and Renata is Mario Roffi, "Un concorso di poesia francese a Ferrara alla corte estense di Renata di Francia," in *Il Rinascimento a Ferrara e i suoi Orizzonti Europei*, ed. Walter Moretti (Ravenna: Mario Lapucci–Edizione de Girasole, 1984), pp. 263–71. Also see E. Rodocanachi, *Renée de France* (Paris: Ollendorf, 1896), esp. chap. 4. On the subject of the Reformation in Italy see John Tedeschi, "I contributi culturali dei riformatori prostestanti italiani nel tardo Rinascimento," *Italica* 64, no. 1 (1987), 19–61.
[32]For a provocative description of these events, see Roffi, "Un concorso," in particular pp. 263–66.
[33]Solerti, *Vita* 1: 212–14; J. Salmons, ed., *The Renaissance in Ferrara and Its European Horizons*, pp. 123–26. For a general description of the historical context of the Estes rise to power until they were forced to relinquish control of Ferrara see Solerti, *Ferrara e la corte Estense*; also see Werner L. Gundersheimer, *Ferrara: The Style of a Renaissance Despotism* (Prince-

It is noteworthy that Tasso's father, Bernardo, had been in Renata's service in Ferrara before passing into the service of Sanseverino in Naples.[34] Also, before becoming the official court poet for Duke Alfonso, Tasso served under the patronage of Alfonso's Luigi, a cardinal. In 1570, the cardinal made a trip to France (rumor had it that he was going there to *scardinalarsi*—to undo his being cardinal).[35] He took Tasso with him, and on the way they stopped at Montargis, where Tasso met the cardinal's mother, Renata, who had taken up residence there after being forced out of Ferrara. Renata must have been in some way an idealized figure for the poet. He wrote "O figlie di Renata" in elegiac praise of the lineage of her daughters, honoring the seed from which they came, that is, Renata herself, and Renata was also celebrated later in one of his dialogues, "Discorso della virtù feminile e donnesca."[36] His appeal to the sisters on behalf of their mother seems to have been motivated by something much deeper than a rhetorical nicety. Rather, Tasso identified with their mother, someone who like himself had been excluded for asserting an individual preference. Such an identification with a prominent heretic might also explain Tasso's peculiar insistence on his being himself a heretic, going so far as to accuse himself before the confessor at Ferrara. But when the confessor absolved him because of melancholy and *not* because of heresy, Tasso felt impelled to petition for a confession to the Inquisition in Rome. As I have already remarked, Tasso's need for absolution from the *Santa Sede* must be read against its background. Ferrara had been a refuge for Calvinists during Renata's presence at the court some twenty years before Tasso's arrival there. Solerti informs us, in an almost ironic tone, that he denounced his so-called enemies to the duke—*and* to the inquisitors: "Suddenly he fears that he is a heretic, but at the court, oh, how many heretics!" [A un tratto teme di essere eretico; ma nella corte oh quanti eretici!][37] As long

---

ton: Princeton University Press, 1973); and most recently, David Quint, "Political Allegory in the *Gerusalemme liberata*," *Renaissance Quarterly* 43 (Spring 1990), 1–29. Quint reads Tasso's epic as a "topical allegory" where "Rinaldo's differences and eventual reconciliation with Goffredo maps out a sufficiently ambivalent relationship between the Este and the papacy" (p. 12).

[34]For Bernardo Tasso's relation to the Este court and the events that followed when he passed into the service of Sanseverino in Naples see Solerti, *Vita*, vol. 1, chap. 1; Brand, *Torquato Tasso*, pp. 16–18; and Ferguson, *Trials of Desire*, pp. 70–81.

[35]Solerti, *Vita* 1: 136 and passim.

[36]Torquato Tasso, "Discorso della virtù feminile e donnesca," in *Le Prose Diverse*, ed. C. Guasti (Florence: Successori Le Monnier, 1875), 2: 213; and "O figlie di Renata," in *Poesie*, ed. Francesco Flora, pp. 834–37.

[37]Solerti, *Vita* 1: 258.

as Tasso confessed this sin in Ferrara, all would be well. He would simply be forgiven within the home court as a man suffering from melancholy. But his appealing to the inquisitor in Rome could complicate Ferrara's relation to the *Santa Sede*, especially with Ferrara's dynastic future in question. The city was already looked upon by Rome with great suspicion, because of the possibility that heretics still filled the chambers of the Ferrarese court.[38] (And this may also throw some light on the severity with which Tasso was later treated by Duke Alfonso, being thrown in chains when he spoke out against the court.)

It is from the enclosed space of his cell that Tasso addresses the daughters of Renata in the hopes of inciting their sympathy for his woes. As in the "Canzone al Metauro," the poet's identification with a woman's loss (his mother's, Renata's) serves as an appropriation of their position as victim and as a pretext for the poet's display of himself as the privileged subject of loss. Moreover, this portrait of the artist as feminized victim is accompanied by the evocation of threatening feminine figures responsible for the poet's victimization. In "Metauro," this work is done by the figure of Fortuna. In "O figlie di Renata," it is Circe, who appears at the moment the poet laments his *umanità perdute*: "Who, oh my!, divides me from the descendants of Adam? Or, what Circe pushes me below the herds?" [Da' nipoti d'Adamo, / ohimè!, chi mi divide? / o qual Circe mi spinge infra le gregge?]. The Hydra rears another head as the poet is subject to more dehumanizing splits that separate [divide] him from the human species itself [nipoti d'Adamo] and cast him below the level of beasts [infra le gregge]. As in the *Gerusalemme liberata*, the risk of male identification with women is that of a loss of humanity, understood as a loss of manhood, as the work of castration. And in the following strophe, Tasso himself can no longer seem to believe his own rhetoric in praise of the daughters as the *summum* of harmonious concordance. Now he conjures up the dread possibility of their remaining deaf to his pleas [se voi mi sete sorde?] or, even worse, of their disagreeing with each other:

> Deh!, se voler discorde
> in sì gran'uopo mio vi fa diverse,

<hr>

[38]Ibid., 1: 257–59. On Tasso's imbrication (and writing of the *Gerusalemme liberata*) in the political intrigue and turmoil of the precarious Este court vis-à-vis Rome's desirous eyes, see Quint, "Political Allegory in the *Gerusalemme liberata*."

> in me fra voi l'esempio
> di Mezio sì rinova, e 'l duro scempio.
>
> Alas! if discord wants
> in my great distress to make you go separate ways
> in-between you, I will renew in myself
> the example of Mezio, and his harsh torment.

There seems no assurance that the symbol of unity might not turn out to be that of disunity. The *rinovo* of Tasso's re-membrance would then renew or renovate his dismemberment, which is compared to the execution of one Mezio Fuffezio who was tied to two carts driven in opposite directions. Instead of being reborn (*qua* Re-nata), the poet risks the ultimate castration of death. Mirroring the split between the "good" Renata and the "bad" Circe, the daughters' discord renews in the poetic subject that split they were called upon to suture.

Caught in the middle, as the name as well as the execution of Mezio suggests, the poet can only plead for that beautiful consensus and virtuous harmony by which the daughters might present his case to the duke:

> Quell'armonia sì nova
> di virtù che vi face
> sì belle, or bei per me faccia concenti,
> sì ch'a pietà commova
> quel signor...
>
> So renew that harmony
> of virtue that makes you
> so beautiful, now make beautiful consensus for me,
> so that pity might move
> that lord...

If women are unpredictably unifying or disunifying, then they must be an unreliable source of dependency for the melancholic. What is recalled in the final strophe of the canzone is that the only way to suture the split in the poet represented as the split in women is to posit a superior paternal figure, who is both castrating *and* able to offer the definitive suture of an absolute re-membering. For Ficino, the split between the heavenly and the vulgar Venus is superseded by that castrating but redemptive father, Saturn. For Tasso, the solution is to address the duke directly as that terrifying but also potentially clement prince. While still nominally addressing the daughters of Renata at the close of the canzone, Tasso aims his words quite clearly at the duke, that lord more displeased by the poet's faults than moved by his torments [quel signor per cui spiace / più la mia colpa a me che i miei tormenti]. Not easily moved to tears, like the true epic hero and unlike women and commoners, Alfonso can only be appealed to in terms of the acquisition of greater honor and glory:

> ond'a tanti e sì egregi
> titoli di sue glorie,
> a tante sue vittorie,
> a tanti suoi trofei, tanti suoi fregi,
> questo s'aggiunga ancora:
> perdono a chi l'offese ed or l'adora.

> among so many and so outstanding
> titles of his glory,
> of so many victories,
> of so many trophies, so many spoils,
> this one is added on top of them:
> giving pardon to he who offended him and now adores him.

In his other great autobiographical canzone, "O magnanimo figlio," Tasso addresses the duke directly, calling him not by the name of the mother, Renata, but by that of the father, Ercole d'Este, whose mythological namesake, Hercules, was also the slayer of the Hydra. Not just a "magnanimous son," Alfonso supersedes his father, leaving Ercole's "paternal valor," according to Tasso, far behind [che 'l paterno valor ti lasci a tergo]. Later in the poem, connections are drawn between Alfonso and the god Jupiter (son and castrator of Saturn, the god of melancholics), who is decribed as irritable but able to be placated with the right offerings [voti]. From the duke, the poet fears thunderbolts [i fulmin tuoi] and horrendous arrows [l'orrende saette tue]. Holding the phallus, and wielding penetrating weaponry, Duke Alfonso/Jupiter upholds a patriarchal order wherein all paternal figures of authority seem to stand for each other. In the "Canzone al Metauro," the poet's biological father, Bernardo, is conflated with God the father. In "O magnanimo figlio," Alfonso is not only Jupiter but also Phoebus and Mars. He is also called the son of Alcides, the Greek name for Hercules *qua* descendant of Alcaeus, thus gracing the Este line with a genealogical link with the hero of Greek mythology and ultimately with the gods themselves. Analogous with the gods, and in particular with their ruler, Jupiter, Alfonso is also the last in a long line of superhuman fathers. Jupiter being the father of Hercules, Alfonso seems to be described as the father of his father, the supreme phallic feat. In the person of the duke, Tasso seems to be addressing the Symbolic Father himself, the overdetermined condensation of all patriarchal figures of authority.

Alfonso is, of course, also the good father who first gathered in the poet from exile into his regal palace [a te che da l'essiglio / prima in nobil riposo / mi raccoglesti nel reale albergo]. It is to this father figure, then, that the poet displays himself in the most abject way as victim, detailing his body parts as so many dismembered offerings:

> a te rivolgo ed ergo
> dal mio carcer profondo
> il cor, la mente e gli occhi:
> a te chino i ginocchi,
> a te la lingua scioglio:
> teco ed a te, ma non di te mi doglio.

> and to you then I turn
> from my deep cell
> heart, mind and eyes:
> to you I bend my knees,
> to you my cheeks flooded only with tears,
> to you I loosen my tongue:
> with you and to you, but not about you do I lament.

Continuing his enumeration, Tasso paints himself as a pitiable object of moribund debilitation whose squalid and dried-out body lacking in blood alludes to Ficino's physiological depiction of melancholia:

> il tuo già servo esangue
> gemer pieno di morte orrida il volto,
> fra mille pene avvolto
> con occhi foschi e cavi,
> con membra immonde e brutte
> e cadenti ed asciutte
> de l'umor de la vita e stanche e gravi

> already your bloodless servant
> beholds the full face of horrible death,
> he is cloaked in a thousand pains,

with eyes that are gutted and caved-in,
with limbs that are disgusting and ugly
and falling off and dried out
from a tired and weary humor of life

It is on this destitute body of lack, whose own eyes are gutted, that the poet asks the duke to turn his "clement eyes" [Volgi gli occhi clementi e vedrai].

This request for a privileged and redemptive gaze is doubled by the poet's claim of a privileged suffering. In the Ficinian tradition of melancholic elitism, Tasso wants his grief to be distinct from that of the *vil volgo*, whom he sees as nonetheless receiving the duke's pity. Further proof of the poet's exemplary and uncommon suffering is found in the conspiracy of the stars in the sky against him as well as that of the princes and rulers of the earth (those who wear purple and gold):

Ah! congiurate a prova
in ciel le stelle, e 'n terra
contra me son coloro
che 'ornan d'ostro e d'oro

Oh! it is shown that
the stars in the sky have conspired
against me with those on earth
who are clothed in purple and gold

Referring pointedly to the many criticisms leveled against his major epic production, the *Gerusalemme liberata*, Tasso states that everyone has gone to war against his poetic genius, his Parnassus [e contra il mio Parnaso ognun fa guerra]. And a suggestion of the Hydra motif reappears in the infinitization of his sorrows: "What new column of infinite misfortunes torments me!" [qual me tormenta / nova schiera infinita / di mali!].

Asking for pity in his Christ-like martyrdom, the poet above all fears the duke whom he describes not as a just or unjust persecutor but as someone he has *offended*: "And I have offended you more than any other" [e te via più d'ogn'altro offesi]. And it is at this point that the Jupiterian analogies are introduced, as the poet both fears the lord's wrath from above and seeks to placate him by the offering of words that makes up the poem itself. More important, what is starkly revealed in Tasso's self-accusation, as in his accusing himself of heresy, is the oedipal undercurrent of melancholia. What matters in these self-accusations is not, as Freud would say, whether Tasso is being "more or less unfair" to himself but that they seem to be displayed for the benefit of some man in authority, some version of the Symbolic Father: the inquisitor, the censor, the duke. Recalling that Freud's analysis of melancholia led him to discover the superego, that agency of conscience formed by the introjection of the father, we can surmise that oedipal guilt motivates the melancholic. Yet the guilt of having given offense also, as it does in Tasso, leaves open the possibility of atonement and reconciliation with the Father. Able to be placated, the Father appears much less threatening to the melancholic subject than those persecutory "feminine" figures who bring dissension without warning: Fortuna, Circe, the Hydra, Clorinda, Armida. While these ladies are seen as unpredictably but unambiguously castrating, the subject's split can be repaired when it is, as in Ficino's Saturnian scheme, the father who castrates. Tasso fears the phallic impregnation of the duke's lightning bolts, but a simple nod of assent from the ruler would allow our poet, describing himself as an "unhappy swan," to take flight again:

> temo, cigno infelice, i fulmin tuoi;
> e sol pronte le penne
> colà saran dove il tuo ciglio accenne.

> an unhappy swan, I fear your thunderbolts;
> and the feathers are ready
> whenever your eyebrow gives the sign.

Wrathful though he be in his Jupiterian majesty, the duke is also Tasso's last chance to recover piety and courtliness:

> Per me pietade è spenta
> e cortesia smarrita,
> se 'n te, signor, non nasce e non si trova

> For me, piety is spent
> and courtliness is gone
> unless, lord, it is born and found in you

The key to being welcomed back into the father's protective arms lies in the eloquence of the votive offering, in the words themselves. Language, however, then takes into itself the unpredictable bipolarity between what offends and what placates. There is the "good" *lingua* that is loosened [scioglio] in the duke's honor but also the "bad" *lingua*, the *lingua audace*, that the poet dares not extend [stender]. Back in "O figlie di Renata," the poet both confesses to his offense and blames it all on his tongue, his *lingua*:

> Merto le pene: errai,
> errai, confesso; e pure
> rea fu la lingua, il cor si scusa e nega

> I deserved the punishment: I erred,
> I erred, I confess; and the tongue
> was pure evil; the heart is excused and absolved

True to the paradigm of Freud's split in the melancholic psyche, Tasso, in accusing himself, accuses a part of himself, his tongue (grammatically feminine in gender), as inferior to the unquestionable nobility of his guiltless "heart."

As we remember from Freud, such a self-accusatory arrangement internalizes the ego's aggressivity against an object by which the ego feels abandoned or slighted. In Tasso's case, self-accusation erupts into the full-blown aggressivity of accusing others, on the night of March 11, 1579. Having just returned to Ferrara from his self-imposed exile, Tasso wishes to see the duke, who is too busy—unsurprisingly, since it is the eve of his wedding—to bother with the tortured poet. As Solerti has pieced it together, the story then goes as follows:

> 11 marzo, Torquato esce di casa: tutta Ferrara in festa accresce il suo turbamento, che presto si muta in un impeto d'ira. Va al palazzo di Cornelio Bentivoglio e non trova che le dame: la moglie Isabella Bendidio e, forse, la sorella di lei, Lucrezia; le figlie Laura e Margherita; la loro visita non basta a frenarlo, prorompe in escandescenze e in parole ingiuriose verso il Duca, verso la sposa, verso i principi Estensi, verso tutti. Di là, furioso, s'avvia verso il castello ducale: vuole parlare alla Duchessa, pregarla che gli faccia rendere i suoi manoscritti, il suo poema, il suo onore, che lo salvi dai nemici che lo perseguitano, lo vogliono eretico, lo vogliono morto; le dame, la Peperara, la d'Arco, la Cavriani, la Costabili e le altre, spaventate, lo trattengono, ed egli scaglia nuove invettive, nuove contumelie; accorre gente, il Duca è informato di quanto avviene: Torquato è portato all'ospedale, lì a cento passi dal Castello, e, come pazzo, e messo alla catena. (*Vita* 1: 309)

On March 11, Torquato leaves his house: his mental turmoil is heightened by all of Ferrara being in celebration, and soon it transforms into an impulse of rage. He goes to the palace of Cornelio Bentivoglio and finds there only women: the ladies Isabella Bendidio and, by chance, her sister Lucrezia; the girls Laura and Margherita. Visiting them does not quell his frenzy, he bursts into a hot temper and injurious words hurled at the Duke, at his spouse, at the Este princes, at everybody. From there, in a mad rage, he goes off towards the Ducal castle: he wants to speak to the Duchess, he pleads with her to bring about the return of his manuscripts, of his poem, of his honor, that she save him from the enemies that are persecuting him, that want to see him a heretic, that want to see him dead. The ladies of Peperara, of d'Arco, of Cavriani, of Costabili and others, out of fear detained him, and this led to new invectives, new arguments. People came running, the Duke was informed about what had happened: Torquato is carried off to the hospital, a hundred yards from the Castle, and he is placed in chains as a madman. (translation mine)

Feeling slighted by the duke, Tasso hurls insults on him and on the ducal family, but finds only women to whom to vent his ire. Prefiguring Hamlet's similar outbursts against women, Tasso, as in his appeal to the daughters of Renata, demands help against his persecutors from the court women, including the duchess, *and* accuses them of being among his enemies. Like those of a jilted mistress, his actions demand attention from those (women) who obviously have the duke's attention, which he feels he has been refused. Desirous of the duke, he displays his anger before those whom the duke desires. Taking himself to be excluded from the duke's company, he desires the place of those he takes to be included, yet he is unsure whether they are rivals or potential allies, whether he wants to appropriate their role or appropriate them for himself, whether he wants to be them or have them. Railing, in any case, against his exclusion, he nonetheless finds himself decisively excluded from the court when he is thrown in the inclusive space of the prison-hospital of Sant'Anna, from which he writes the *Messaggiero* and the reclusionary poems I have been analyzing.

For him, to accuse his *lingua* in these works is more than to admit that ill-spoken words put him in his cell. It is to betray again the sexual politics of his melancholia as an oedipalized *display* of loss and victimization, predicated on an exclusion of women that appropriates their presumed "lack" for symbolic gain. Whether or not Alfonso can be said to have overreacted in putting the mad poet under lock and key, Tasso's loss of personal liberty, as I have noted, constituted his symbolic triumph, turning him into one of the great exemplars of misunderstood genius. That genius being a poetic one, the *lingua* is his gift as well as his bane, the source of his successes as well as failures. If words put him in his cell, it is on words that he likewise relies to get him out of there, knowing full well (as the poet who wrote Armida's lament) the seductiveness of sorrow. Portraying his body as victimized lack (deprived of everything from blood to *cortesia*), the poet anticipates that lack being filled by a paternal authority.

All depends on the workings of the *lingua*, whose bipolarity (beneficial/harmful) seems to qualify it in the same ambiguous way as the figure of "woman" in Tasso. Like his women, the *lingua* is called upon to perform a mediating role with authority, to intercede on the poet's behalf, but that mediation is never sure. The poet can never be certain whether he is dealing with an ally or a persecutor. At the same time, his recourse to such a mediating figure points to his own alienation from phallic authority. That figure accordingly signifies his own castration even as it is meant to assuage it. The *lingua*, in particular, can be seen in its function as a fetish, both revealing and denying the poetic subject's castration, for the *lingua* is not only language as a signifying system but also a part of the body, that "unruly member" in Norman O. Brown's phrase, that makes speech possible.[39] In the first strophe of "O magnanimo figlio," it is the last of the body parts displayed to the duke, but it is also the privileged part since it is the one through which the offering is made, insofar as the votive act is a *verbal* one. In offering his *lingua* to the duke, Tasso offers himself in his essence as poet; and as the privileged member of his textual body, the *lingua* is a displaced phallus (a substitute penis, i.e., a fetish in the Freudian sense). In offering it to the duke in so rhetorically eloquent a form as his canzone, he denies his castration while asserting it, displays his verbal mastery as poet while placing it in the service of his lord. In response, the duke can either strike him with the phallic might of his thunderbolts [fulmin] or with a mere movement of his eyebrow, let that "unhappy swan" of a writer take poetic flight with the feather of his pen [penne] and so truly "loosen"

[39] As Norman O. Brown notes in *Love's Body* (New York: Vintage Books, 1966), speech was "resexualized" as a means of "overcoming the consequences of the fall. The tongue was the first unruly member. Displacement is first from above downwards; the penis is a symbolic tongue, and disturbances of ejaculation a kind of genital stuttering" (p. 251).

his tongue. Either way, the poet would seem to get the phallus. Or, is it at the price of sexual difference?

Within the apotropaic workings of such imaginary systems as the demonological section of *Il messaggiero* or the crusading ideology of the church militant as revealed in the *Gerusalemme liberata*, that is, in systems reactively defined by the *horror vacuus* that seeks to deny sexual difference, we read the self-doubts to which the melancholic is subject precisely because of his inability to accept castration, to recognize the limits that define him. Paradoxically, he needs to assuage that doubt, which remains as the telltale sign of a castration that would be denied. The paradox of this logic, as in the case of the Hydra, is that the more the poet attempts to assuage his doubts, the more he is driven into doubt and the more therefore he needs to build certitude according to the logic of identity foregrounded, for instance, by *Il messaggiero*'s epistemological content. Mirroring the analogy of the melancholic's multiplicity of thoughts as similar to the Hydra, however, and refracting the melancholic's constitutive loss of self is his depiction of the fragmented body, whose parts then become available for fetishization. What is therefore at stake in the disembodied voice, ear, or tongue is the double function of displacing the fear of castration into a denial of it while privileging it as that which represents the embodiment of the ego's self-presence, thereby engendering a psychosis of elite difference and thus of exclusionary sameness.[40] In other words, Tasso's "lack" is not that of the *vil volgo*, and its sight is one presented to princely eyes, which are the only ones endowed with the clemency to properly suture that lack. Or, the body is presented to the ghost image of its soul (the "messenger") in an auto-erotic celebration of narcissism.

In psychoanalytic terms, by *soverchia maninconia* the poet is unconsciously representing, in an economic framework, the excess of narcissistic libido dammed up through the repression constituted by a model of purity and sacredness, an excess whose overflow is redirected into a discourse that would exclude alterity. An avenue is thus left open for the *vis imaginativa*, conditioned by a Western metaphysics of immanence, to imagine the self in the likeness of a higher being. Therefore the melancholic proceeds to a double appropriation or incorporation. On the one hand, he appropriates a feminine position by making of himself the exclusive subject of difference through metaphors of birth and re-

[40]See my "Tasso's Tongue: The Lingua as Fetich," *Italian Culture* 7 (1989), 35–53.

ceptivity, which are simultaneously corporeal and noncorporeal. On the other hand, he engenders a fetishized model of the body that both points to the subject's rejection of the female body (since for him it must stand for corruptibility and limitation) and to his desire to replace it with a preferred body, the body of the text, of disembodied words, which inaugurates his mourning fantasy and signifies his privileged relation, as poet, with the divine.

For Tasso, the ear, the gap that receives the voice (i.e., the disembodied voice of the messenger) needs a tongue—the poet's tongue—in order to be transcribed and transmitted as text: the text of *Il messaggiero*. This text, as in his reclusionary lyric, points back to the tongue of the poet, a phallic material that in turn attests to the "reality" and self-sufficiency of his vision. The vision of the messenger, as the closed circuit between the poet's ear and his tongue, thus reveals itself to be a sort of intra-subjective copulation, the only eros available to the subject within such a self-enclosed system, or in Lacanian terms, within an imaginary seeking the foreclosure of all otherness.[41] This system, dependent on its intra-corporeality (the ear and the tongue), attempts to render present the impossible: the union of sexuality and *anima*. It can be represented, therefore, only by the Logos. Tasso can then circumvent the unreliable mediation of women (such as the daughters of Renata) or even of the tongue directed toward the ear of another, or of an other (the duke).

But in this case, Logos as eros belongs only to a privileged few. As the messenger says: "Amongst a few there exists a secret conformity of nature, not known by many, which is Love" (p. 26). [Fra alcuni c'è una segreta conformità di natura non conosciuta da molti, la quale non è altro che amore]. The ear receives this message of love, as in the early amatory sonnets, in which the poet is stricken by love for his lady through the ear.[42] Here, as in his sonnets, the power of love's seduction

---

[41]On the notion of foreclosure, see Jacques Lacan, "On a Question Preliminary to Any Possible Treatment of Psychosis," in *Ecrits: A Selection*, trans. Alan Sheridan (New York: Norton, 1977), pp. 177–225, esp. pp. 217–21.

[42]Tasso, *Rime*, ed. Angelo Solerti (Bologna: Romagnoli-Dall' Acqua, 1898–1902), vol. 3, Parte Prima, sonnets 1 and 2, pp. 7–9. In sonnet 1 we read: "when a woman appeared to me very similar to a pure angel in her voice" [quando m'apparve donna assai simile *ne la sua voce* a candida angeletta] (lines 5–6; my emphasis). In sonnet 2 the aural motif becomes even more pronounced: "but of the minor risk too late I realized / that my heart was wounded through my ears / and the words went where the face did not reach" [ma del rischio minor tardi m'accorsi / che mi fu *per le orecchie il cor ferito* / e i detti andaro ove non giunse il volto] (lines 12–14; my emphasis). Tasso, by defining his poetic inspiration as an effect of his beloved's

through the ear signals its difference from the traditional Petrarchan and Ficinian topos of a love that is communicated through the eyes, since this aural mark of enamoredness has primacy over the visual. In the *Messaggiero*, the poet wants to see the voice that *first* he *hears* and that beckons to him. This auditory insemination reveals a further displacement from any poetic relation that situates the fictional beloved woman as the narcissistic mirror of poetic inspiration, and appropriates, in her place, the *conformità di natura*, like unto like. Furthermore, the aural and oral dialectic marks this poet as the privileged receptor of sound, a medium that in the appropriately poetic form of music could be considered a cure for the troubled ear, even a cure for melancholy. We need only think of the biblical figure Saul whose own brooding spirit was pacified through melody, or Ficino's remark that melancholics find "remedy and solace" in the "pleasures of song."[43] Such an *écoute* points back to the text we are reading as the talking that, in psychoanalytic terms, is to cure what is talked about. Nonetheless, the text seems to stage this cure for melancholia through a dialogue wherein transference can never be any more than its own projected fantasy, which is to say that transference does not occur. What is therefore in the text and what we read is nothing more than an idealized discourse, that is, a discourse that takes its strength from an ideal dialogue between the poetic subject and *his* version of his own projected self-idealization, that spirit of love, the *Messaggiero*. What seems to be other and radically other because of its unworldly character betrays itself as non-other through its epistemological and rhetorical origin in a *conformità di natura*.

In other words, the dialogic possibility of transference, which requires as a corollary to the enactment of a change in affect at least some

---

voice, significantly revises the traditional love lyric, which had found its pretext in the visual, in the inaugural gaze exchanged between lovers. In this way, his poetry becomes other than Petrarchan even if homage is still paid to his literary father. In Tasso's lyric, thus, the focus of sensuality has been shifted from the addressees of his love poems, Peperara and Bendidio, and onto the words themselves. The inseminating power of words replaces that of the gaze as Tasso privileges and eroticizes the Logos. The mystificatory power of the auto-affective circuit between ear and voice has also been extensively analyzed by Jacques Derrida as the logocentrism of "s'entendre parler," from his early *Speech and Phenomenon*, trans. David B. Allison (Evanston, Ill.: Northwestern University Press, 1973), and *Of Grammatology*, trans. Gayatri Spivak (Baltimore: Johns Hopkins University Press, 1974), through his more recent "Otobiographies: The Teaching of Nietzsche and the Politics of the Proper Name," trans. Avital Ronell, in *The Ear of the Other: Otobiography, Transference, Translation*, ed. Christie McDonald et al. (Lincoln: University of Nebraska Press, 1985), pp. 1–38.

[43]Marsilio Ficino, *Commentary on Plato's Symposium On Love*, ed. and trans. Sears Jayne (Dallas, Tex.: Spring Publications, 1985), p. 122.

dimension of conflict or difference between the partners in dialogue, is trammeled by the inflexibility of the poet's ideal self, which is merely mirrored onto the spirit's imaginary, the fictional dialogic other who represents but the *exemplum* of the poet's mythological self-production. The discursive function of the *Messaggiero* thus seems to be to mirror the telos of the subject's desire for absolute certainty and thus for unquestionable self-presence. Consequently, doubt is only a textual strategy that functions as the catalyst of a dialogue whose speakers are already essentially consenting. Doubt in this text functions to produce a textual reconstruction of the self, one self-engendered by an endless display of loss, but doubt also functions as the catalyst for the aggressive appropriation of a space for the melancholic who then paradoxically remains transfixed in his non-transferential incapacity to cut his losses, in the trans-fiction of his loss as the condition of selfhood. The dialogue, through the weapons of reason and epistemological veracity, thus works to build the ego's defense by using verbalism as a talking cure and accordingly attempts to make of this delirium an ideal that necessarily turns back on itself because it requires, in order to survive, a perpetual lack to motivate its fictionality.

Female analogues, Clorinda or the Hydra or Circe, for example, threaten this production of loss by proposing in themselves figures of otherness, the possibility of transference proper since their very representation presents another version of experience, one whose alterity may unpredictably seduce or horrify by virtue of an imbricated play between sameness and difference. In addressing the daughters of Renata, for instance, Tasso does not and cannot know whether he will be remembered by them or dismembered like Mezio. He cannot know whether he will be fetishized or castrated. The Hydra's many heads can be said to represent, on one level, the plenitude of the phallus multiplied, but paradoxically, on another level, otherness, the monstrosity that points to the horror of lack, otherwise codified as that which remains radically unknown, the terrifying sign of radical difference, whose other name in Tasso's imaginary is Jerusalem, the pagan city of women and commoners, the phantom body of the other. The melancholic seems thus to mourn the loss of that whose presence he fears. Tasso's attempt at self-diagnosis can do no more than reproduce what it points to, that is, do no more than foreground itself as the *case* of Tasso the mad poet. Small wonder his appeals for clemency met with no success, even as the "scandal" assured his immortality.

But in portraying himself as the subject of a clinical investigation and cure through the magic of dialogue, could Tasso in his mo(u)rning fantasy not be said to situate himself at the dawn of psychoanalysis, at the inception of an eminently modern form of subjectivity? Perhaps it would be more accurate to say the "horizon" or historical and conceptual limit of psychoanalysis, for with Tasso as the subject of melancholia, in a gendered myth legitimating that neurosis, we read the symptoms of a specifically male subjectivity that characterizes itself through the production of loss. The melancholic model, therefore, can be understood not simply as the incorporation of a lost object of desire, but rather as the incorporation of a loss that needs to be endlessly reproduced *as loss* to sustain its myth. In other words, an interpretation of melancholia ought not to be reduced to simply discovering lost objects of desire but, ought, rather, to show how the lost object, itself mythologized, mirrors the subject's desire. By privileging an ideal through absence and deferral, the self not only reconverts the loss into its own self-display (which Freud well understood) but also legitimates its display as part of a cultural myth. Freud himself, as I have argued in an earlier chapter, can be said to participate, whether consciously or unconsciously, within this myth. It is not the "deserted bride" or the self-deprecating wife who emblematizes the melancholic condition but Hamlet, signaling the fact that a well-known *male* such as the gloomy prince of Denmark is indeed a nameable subject, and a subject of literary and psychoanalytic interest precisely because the canon legitimizes his "neurosis" as something, even when it is "ironized" as the experience of nothing. The clinical opposition between the banality of mourning and the neurotic but culturally more prestigious (if not romanticized) category of melancholia is commanded by a gender opposition, which while certainly not precluding the concrete existences of male mourners or melancholic women, works to maintain the peculiarly privileged artistic and literary status granted the *homo melancholicus*, since at least the time when Torquato Tasso gained his laurels.

Chapter 5

Mourning the Phallus?
(Hamlet, Burton, Lacan and "Others")

In his classic study, Lawrence Babb categorically states that "Eliza-bethan melancholy began as a fashionable affectation, as an imitation of an Italian attitude."[1] Babb's assertion confirms the powerful influence the Ficinian/Tassian paradigm had on the establishment of a melancholy ethos distinct from the disease analyzed in medical discourse. In the Elizabethan tradition, this effect is apparent in the difference between Timothy Bright's still simplistic and physiological *Treatise of Melancholia* of 1586[2] and that complex compendium and supreme monument to the Hydran logic of *soverchia maninconia*, Robert Burton's *Anatomy of Melancholy* published in five increasingly expansive editions from 1621 to 1638.[3]

At the same time, Babb's comment diminishes the rise of melancholia in Elizabethan England to a faddish "imitation" of a questionable foreign "attitude," to an "affectation" of a type typically associated in the British mind with continental and especially Latin culture. Melancholia would be a kind of Italian masquerade, but as Babb adds, "unlike most fads,

---

[1] Lawrence Babb, *The Elizabethan Malady: A Study of Melancholia in English Literature from 1580 to 1642* (East Lansing: Michigan State College Press, 1951), p. 185.
[2] Timothy Bright, *Treatise of Melancholia* (New York: Facsimile Text Society/Columbia University Press, 1940).
[3] Robert Burton, *Anatomy of Melancholy* (London: Dent and New York: Dutton, Everyman's Library, 1932), 3 vols.

[233]

it did not flourish briefly and die" (p. 185). Instead, this imitative conduct, the feigned behavior of melancholia, persisted in England well into the eighteenth century and "even" into the "Age of Wordsworth" (p. 185). That the, in Babb's terms, "medical and pathological implications had faded" by the time of the Romantics (p. 185) does not necessarily imply the historical death of the disease. Rather, it confirms the argument I have been making throughout that melancholia is to be understood as a cultural category rather than as a medical one, even though its cultural dimension may have been legitimated by a clinical discourse.

As a further sign of Italian fashion in Elizabethan England there is the record of a play put on in London in 1594 titled *Tasso's Melancholy*. As C. P. Brand notes, a 1598 inventory listed props for the production of that play; and a revised version of it by Thomas Dekker was performed in 1602, the same year *Hamlet* was first staged.[4] Unfortunately, no version of this play remains today and so we have no way to know its exact content. It is certainly significant, however, that a play not merely about Tasso but specifically about the poet's "melancholy" should have appeared in England only fifteen years after his incarceration and with Tasso still alive (he died in 1595). The play was also popular enough to have been staged a number of times and brought back for a new run around the same time as Shakespeare's dramatization of the melancholy prince from Denmark. But if Hamlet, as Bridget Gellert Lyons has argued, is himself a compendium of the various symptoms associated with melancholia,[5] just as the Tasso of *Il messaggiero* claims to embody both types of melancholia, it is interesting (to follow up on Babb's comment) that one of the key problems posed by Shakespeare's play has to do with the extent to which Hamlet is mad or just "feigning" madness. Strangely enough, early seventeenth-century biographers of Tasso suggested that the Ferrarese poet's madness was also feigned and for the same reason as Hamlet's, so that he might protect himself from courtly intrigue and from Alfonso's wrath.[6] Inasmuch as these biographies were all published well after *Hamlet*, Shakespeare's play could have

<hr>

[4]C. P. Brand, *Torquato Tasso: A Study of the Poet and of His Contribution to English Literature* (Cambridge: Cambridge University Press, 1965), p. 206.

[5]Bridget Gellert Lyons, *Voices of Melancholy: Studies in Literary Treatments of Melancholy in Renaissance England* (London: Routledge & Kegan Paul, 1971), pp. 83–112.

[6]Cf. Brand, *Torquato Tasso*, pp. 207–9; Alessandro Guarini, *Il farnetico savio overo il Tasso* (Ferrara, 1610), p. 49; Gianbattista Manso, *Vita di Torquato Tasso* (Venice, 1621), pp. 48–49; Scipio Errico, *Le rivolte di Parnaso* (Messina, 1625); Angelo Solerti, *Vita di Torquato Tasso* (Turin: Ermanno Loescher, 1895), 2: 499 on Muratori.

influenced the development of the Tasso legend just as the by then well-known case of Tasso's melancholic madness could have inspired or inflected Shakepeare's dramatization of the old Saxo Grammaticus story. The concept of imitation or "feigning" is obviously not simple here, and it certainly is not as simple as the suggestion Babb makes that Elizabethan melancholy imitated "an Italian attitude." In fact, this imitation or "affectation" would then also imply that what the Elizabethan was imitating was already an imitation. According to this view, the otherwise sober English would, as they like to say, have taken leave of their senses by falling under the faddish spell of Latin decadence. What this anglocentric point of view forgets, however, is not only the reciprocity of the movement between cultures but also the persistence of the relation between melancholia as a "moral state" and various kinds of imitating, feigning, deception, and role-playing. Freud's discussion of the ostentatious display of one's woes among the symptoms of melancholia is a key insight in this respect, for it also affirms that the imitation of melancholia is itself a sign of the melancholic condition. Not only is imitation an obvious component of Ficinian Neoplatonism but it is also prominent in both the social and the textual behavior of Tasso with his exiles incognito, appropriative identifications, and aggressive self-positionings as victim. Whether or not Tasso's madness was feigned, Hamlet's taking on of the "antic disposition" would have been taken by the Elizabethan audience as an overt sign of his melancholic madness.[7] In this way, then, the English imitation of the "Italian attitude" could just as easily be viewed as the effect as well as the cause of their melancholia. In fact, it is this kind of appropriation of a cultural or sexual "other" that is fundamental to the discursive practice of melancholia as I have been analyzing it.[8] As Freud's analysis of the melan-

---

[7]Lyons, *Voices of Melancholy*, pp. 94ff. Burton also describes feigned behavior at length as symptomatic of melancholy: "To see a man turn himself into all shapes like a chameleon, or as Proteus, *omnia transformans sese in miracula rerum* [who transformed himself into every possible shape], to act twenty parts and persons at once for his advantage, to temporize and vary like Mercury the planet, good with good, bad with bad; having a several face, garb, and character for every one he meets; of all religions, humours, inclinations; to fawn like a spaniel, *mentitis et mimicis obsequiis* [with feigned and hypocritical observance], rage like a lion, bark like a cur, fight like a dragon, sting like a serpent, as meek as a lamb, and yet again grin like a tiger, weep like a crocodile, insult over some, and yet others domineer over him, here command, there crouch, tyrannize in one place, be baffled in another, a wise man at home, a fool abroad to make others merry" (*Anatomy of Melancholy* 1: 65–66).

[8]While I have been paying attention throughout this study to the gender politics in melancholia, one could also profitably study the roles of class, race, and ethnic differences in its development and such topoi as the "last" Indian, the broken worker, prisoners, etc. Let

cholic split in consciousness showed, the superego's mistreatment of the ego takes place as an internalization of the subject's rage against a lost object of desire who has supposedly slighted or wounded it. Narcissistic revenge is given free rein in the melancholic psyche whether we speak of Tasso, of Hamlet, or of the English gentleman "fashionably affecting" an "Italian attitude."

When we speak of melancholia as a cultural or discursive practice, we can no longer differentiate the affect or sense of loss from its display. Furthermore, as I have noted a number of times, this display of loss is indistinguishable from the *self*-display of the *subject* of loss. Melancholia, as a cultural category (or as a "moral state," as scholars of the condition like to think of it) if not as a medical category, is essentially theatrical. Even the symptomatic desire for solitude is filled with the narcissistic desire to be viewed as lonely, isolated, exiled. We need only recall Tasso's self-imposed exiles and his ostentatious donning of the "unknown pilgrim's" cloak, or the character of Hamlet, that exemplar of melancholic theatricality, whose shifting roles and personality changes provide a source of frustration not only for the other characters in the play but also for centuries of critics.

Recent critics of the play, including Francis Barker and Terry Eagleton,[9] have seized upon the theatrical problem in Hamlet's character to propose a postmodern reading of the melancholy prince as the figure of "an incipient modernity" (Barker, p. 27). According to these critics, the condition of the soon-to-be modern subject is analogous to Hamlet's theatrical display of melancholy behavior. Their "claim" to Hamlet as what they perceive to be a model of the modern subject is that his "interiority" is autonomous. Hamlet's interiority, according to them, is thus independent of the depthless surface that is supposed to characterize feudal society with its absence of any separation between the private

---

me give such an example. In discussing the role French psychiatrists played in constructing a racist ideology, Frantz Fanon discusses how the Algerian's character was described as violent and aggressively homicidal, unable to sustain Cartesian logic and thereby "prey to melancholia." These psychiatrists, however, are quick to distinguish the homicidal melancholia of the Algerian from the (French) melancholia that is the "illness of the moral consciousness." They argue that "since by definition melancholia is an illness of the moral conscience it is clear that the Algerian can only develop pseudo-melancholia, since the precariousness of his conscience and the feebleness of his moral sense is well known" (*The Wretched of the Earth* [New York: Grove, 1968], pp. 298–99). This racist ideology seems to dovetail with Kristeva's view of French melancholia as a superior form.

[9]Francis Barker, *The Tremulous Private Body: Essays on Subjection* (London: Methuen, 1984), pp. 21–41; Terry Eagleton, *William Shakespeare* (Oxford: Blackwell, 1986), pp. 71–75.

and the public. On the other hand, the same character who claims to have "that within which passes show" (I, ii, 85)[10] by virtue of the number of masks he doffs and dons would also deconstruct or reveal the nothingness or "void" behind appearances: "Hamlet has no 'essence' of being whatsoever, no inner sanctum to be safeguarded: he is pure deferral and diffusion, a hollow void which offers nothing determinate to be known" (Eagleton, p. 72); "Hamlet . . . is truly this hollow reed which will 'discourse most eloquent music' but is none the less vacuous for that. At the center of Hamlet, in the interior of his mystery, there is, in short, nothing" (Barker, p. 37). For these critics, Hamlet is an "anachronistic paradox" (Barker, p. 41); that is, as a character he both figures modern subjectivity in its historical onset and radically decenters that same subjectivity in a prefiguration of the postmodern critique of all depth as nothing but a mystifying play of surfaces.

It certainly seems that neither Eagleton nor Barker fears any Greenblattian charge of anachronsim or redundancy, although they (tremulously or not), date modern subjectivity from Shakespeare's *Hamlet*. And it would be pointless, not to mention pedantic, to argue that the same contradictory subjectivity (claim to a privileged interiority and to utter determination by surface exteriority, etc.) could already be found stirring about in the melancholic discourse of Ficino and full-blown in Tasso (as well as in other key continental figures of the Renaissance such as Montaigne, Melanchton, and Loyola). Rather, I suggest that the Tassian logic of the Hydra is instructive in re-situating some of the terms by which Hamlet is cast as a kind of postmodern hero.[11] In the case of Tasso's *soverchia maninconia*, as I argued in the last chapter, melancholia is driven by a *horror vacuus* that seeks to cover over that lack understood as sexual difference (namely castration) but that keeps rediscovering lack in the disintegrative quality of melancholy thought: like the Hydra's unseverable heads, two melancholy thoughts appear in the place of each one. Thus Hamlet's rather enigmatic reference to the slayer of the Hydra and to a stereotypical melancholic animal: "Let Hercules himself do what he may, / The cat will mew, and the dog will have his day" (V, ii, 269–70). The melancholic indulges in the vicissitudes of his brooding behavior in order to deny his castration, that is, the hollowness or

---

[10]All citations of William Shakespeare's *Hamlet* are from the edition of Cyrus Hoy (New York: Norton, 1963) and are indicated by act, scene, and line numbers.

[11]Cf. Eagleton: "Hamlet seems to speak to us more urgently than any other of Shakespeare's tragic protagonists" (*William Shakespeare*, p. 75).

nothing within him, the fundamental lack that, according to Lacan, is the very condition of his being a subject.

Both Eagleton and Barker would be correct then in their intuition of the "void" at Hamlet's center, which does indeed make him *a* figure (among others) of the modern subject in his construction/deconstruction. It is precisely the theatrical aspect of melancholia in its narcissistic and aggressive dimensions that neither critic sufficently recognizes, all too readily betraying an uncritical identification with the melancholy prince as the epitome of the sensitive man (and this in spite of their neo-Marxist, even "feminist" aspirations). For while we all can identify with and appreciate Hamlet as *sensitive* man, it should not be forgotten that his cultural success, so to speak, is also a function of his being a sensitive *man*. If the cultural category of melancholia cannot separate the affect from its display, the question remains as *to whom* the possibility of such display applies. "All the world's a stage," perhaps, but it is well known that only men could appear in the Elizabethan theater, queen or no queen on the throne.[12] In Irigarayan terms, the issue of display is one of access to a signifying economy. The development of the Ficinian/Tassian paradigm in *Hamlet* involves more—"something more"—than the relation between theatricality and the birth—or death—of the (male) subject.

First of all, the act of display, and *a fortiori* narcissistic display, is not psychoanalytically innocent. If there is display it is a display for someone, a desire if you will for the gaze of the other. And in the melancholic tradition, there is no question that the display is for the benefit of a superior, patriarchal gaze, whether we speak of Ficino's Saturnian rays, or of Tasso's demand for absolution from all kinds of father figures, or of Hamlet's being literally haunted by his father's ghost but also peculiarly subservient to Claudius, or of Freud's discovery of the superego

[12]Despite the well-meaning claims of some contemporary critics (see for example the editors' Introduction to *Rewriting the Renaissance: The Discourse of Sexual Difference in Early Modern Europe*, ed. Margaret W. Ferguson, Maureen Quilligan, and Nancy J. Vickers [Chicago: University of Chicago Press, 1986], pp. xix–xxi), there is no reason to believe that the mere presence of a female ruler on the British throne during the Renaissance in and of itself made the distribution of gender roles any more interesting or complex than it was on the continent under the influence of Catherine de Medici and Caterina Sforza. For a critique of this institutional bias, see Marilyn Migiel and Juliana Schiesari's Introduction to their edited volume *Refiguring Woman: Perspectives on Gender and the Italian Renaissance* (Ithaca: Cornell University Press, 1991). Furthermore, if Sandra Gilbert and Susan Gubar's *Shakespeare's Sisters: Feminist Essays on Women Poets* (Bloomington: Indiana University Press, 1979) is any indication, the contribution of English women poets during the Renaissance is virtually nonexistent compared with the wealth of the literary production by women in Italy and France.

in his analysis of the melancholic neurosis. And the patriarchal complicity in this gaze is corroborated by way of Claudius's remark (which is also a tip of the hat to Aristotle) to Hamlet that "madness in great ones must not unwatched go" (III, iii, 185). Not surprisingly, a traditional psychoanalytic critic, K. P. Eissler, considers *Hamlet* to be "as much an oedipal tragedy as it is a tragedy of superego."[13] He also refuses to draw the obvious conclusions and tries to defend and distinguish Hamlet's behavior from "the complaint of a melancholic or of a moral masochist; it may be no more than the expression of the *sensitive awareness of ethical man*, as he strives toward closing the wide gaps left by the narrow span of the superego" (p. 285; emphasis added).[14] While Eissler goes on to assimilate Hamlet to sainthood, his defense of Hamlet as "sensitive" is instigated by his commentary on one of Hamlet's many misogynist lines: "I could accuse me of such things that it were better my mother had not borne me" (III, i, 123). What must be recognized here is that Hamlet does not simply say that it would be better had he not been born, but he implicitly pins the blame for such a horrid creature as himself inhabiting the planet on his mother for conceiving him (notice how the father and considerations of paternal anxiety disappear), which brings me to a second point.

As I have tried to show throughout this work, the melancholic's desire for the father's gaze is concomitant to and inseparable from a profound denigration of women, who are typically accused of all the horrible things the melancholic can also accuse himself of: duplicity, inconstancy, inhumanity, animality, and base materiality. Obviously, the melancholic projects on women the lack he would deny in himself, except of course when he addresses himself in the voice of his own superego. What is sometimes termed moral masochism is also a displaced and misogynistic sadism. For Ficino, the nostalgia and regret the melancholic philosopher experiences is the result of his fall from the higher realm of Saturnian masculinity into what he feels is the debased, feminine world of lack, corporeality, and materiality. For Tasso, women are persecutors

---

[13]K. R. Eissler, *Discourse on Hamlet and "Hamlet": A Psychoanalytic Inquiry* (New York: International Universities Press, 1971), p. 286.

[14]Another psychoanalyst, Heinz Kohut, equates (male) artistic sensitivity and genius with an anticipatory historical function, not unlike what other critics impute to the character of Hamlet. For Kohut, the "great" artist "is ahead of *his* time in focusing on the nuclear psychological problems of *his* era, in responding to the crucial psychological issue *man* is facing at a given time, in addressing *himself* to *man*'s leading psychological task" (*The Restoration of the Self* [New York: International Universities Press, 1977], p. 285; emphasis added).

or rivals who reveal his own limitations at the same time that he identifies with them as objects/victims of patriarchal desire. In Hamlet's case, as Ernest Jones most eloquently notes, the prince's cautious and even gentle behavior toward Claudius contrasts with the vicious abuse and scorn he heaps on both Gertrude and Ophelia.[15] Though Hamlet may be plotting vengeance on Claudius for his father's murder, it is the women who—like the court ladies on whom Tasso spewed his rage—always seem to bear the brunt of his (melancholic) aggressivity.

Gertrude, in particular, is the one most commonly blamed for what is "rotten" in Denmark, for marrying her husband's murderer and for supposedly bringing the time of mourning too quickly to a close. In the first soliloquy, Hamlet begins by railing against his own "sallied" or "solid" flesh, wishing it "would melt, thaw, and resolve itself into dew," but ends by castigating his mother for being weak ("Frailty, thy name is woman," I, ii, 146) and below the level of the beasts ("a beast that wants discourse of reason / Would have mourned longer," I, ii, 150–51). Later, after having decided to spare Claudius's life, he proceeds directly to "speak daggers" to his mother (III, ii, 364). Holding back from using his sword on Claudius, Hamlet has no compunctions about using his tongue as a sharp instrument on his mother's psyche. "O, speak to me no more! / These words like daggers enter my ears" (III, iv, 95–96), she pleads. Finally she succumbs to her son's tongue-lashing or slashing: "O Hamlet, thou hast cleft my heart in twain" (160). No Hydra is she. Gertrude's victimization is coincident with a renewed appearance of the paternal ghost as well as with Hamlet's killing of Ophelia's father, who stands hidden behind the infamous arras. Such phallic violence is echoed by the traditional disdain of critics for Gertrude, some like T. S. Eliot going so far as to deny her very worth as a literary character, a criticism Jacqueline Rose has effectively countered.[16] In similar fashion, in his fanciful "sixth" act to *Hamlet*, Nicolas Abraham resolves any lingering hostility between male characters by presenting a dialogue among the young Fortinbras, the ghost, and a resurrected Hamlet. The Christ-like prince is then revealed to be the child of an illicit affair between the Old Fortinbras killed by Hamlet's father and Gertrude. In Abraham's almost comical resolution to a tragedy that comes across as instigated by a woman's fault—as the men find renewed friendship and

[15]Ernest Jones, *Hamlet and Oedipus* (Garden City, N.Y.: Norton, 1949).
[16]T. S. Eliot, "*Hamlet*," in *Selected Prose of T. S. Eliot*, ed. Frank Kermode (London: Faber, 1975); Jacqueline Rose, *Sexuality in the Field of Vision*, (London: Verso, 1986), pp. 123–40.

even literal brotherhood (between Hamlet and Fortinbras)—it comes without much surprise that he makes no effort to bring the queen herself back to life to explain *her* version of the events.[17]

Given what we have learned about melancholia, we should probably take Hamlet's excessive mourning into consideration, which leads to a third point of disagreement with the postmodernist interpretation. For it is precisely Gertrude's lack of sufficient mourning that makes Hamlet quite irascible, even more than his father's murder by Claudius. Although the prince does admit that his mother wept at the funeral ("Like Niobe, all tears," I, ii, 149), he is shocked by how soon she chooses to remarry. On the other hand, Hamlet's sense of time is not the best: it is Ophelia who informs him that it is not "two hours" or two months but "twice two months" (III, ii, 116) since the old king's death. Has Gertrude completed the work of mourning? And is that the source of the incredible hostility she receives?

Her first words are to ask Hamlet to cease his evidently excessive mourning: "Good Hamlet, cast thy nighted color off" (I, ii, 68). Hamlet's response is caustic as he asserts the "uncommon" quality of his grief. He then goes on to make his famous speech (dear especially to critics such as Barker and Eagleton) that his mournful inner essence exceeds the mere ritual and external signs of bereavement:

> Queen: Why seems it so particular with thee?
> Hamlet: Seems, madam? Nay, it is. I know not 'seems'.
>   'Tis not alone my inky cloak, good mother,
>   Nor customary suits of solemn black,
>   Nor windy suspiration of forced breath,
>   No, nor the fruitful river in the eye,
>   Nor the dejected haviour of the visage,
>   Together with all forms, moods, shapes of grief,
>   That can denote me truly. These indeed seem,
>   For they are actions that a man might play,
>   But I have that within which passes show—
>   These but the trappings and the suits of woe. (I, ii, 75–86)

Claudius intervenes here to acknowledge the correctness of "these mourning duties" but insists in the best humanist fashion that the expres-

---

[17]Nicolas Abraham and Maria Torok, *L'écorce et le noyau* (Paris: Flammarion, 1987), "Le fantôme d'Hamlet ou le VIe acte," pp. 447–74.

sion of loss must be kept within proper limits. Otherwise, he says, " 'Tis unmanly grief" (I, ii, 94), Claudius thus reveals that he misrecognizes the situation, for Hamlet's claim to an uncommon essence over and beyond the appearance of mourning is not simply a reprimand directed to his mother but also an assertion of rivalry. This assertion is also an aggressive appropriation of women's ritual that reclaims his "unmanly grief" as the superiority of the sensitive *man*. He overtly contests Gertrude's legitimate prerogative to set the term and conditions of the mourning ritual at her court, a prerogative that is later confirmed by her organizing and presiding over Ophelia's funeral (and thereby asserting her right to reject the vicious claim that the young woman's death was a suicide—a claim repeated by critics even though the text clearly states the accidental nature of her drowning). In typical melancholic fashion, Hamlet not only projects the lack he would deny in himself onto the nearest available woman but he also arrogates to himself the limits of acceptable expressions of loss, as if only he truly feels the father's death as loss. After one of the players emotionally rehearses the death of Priam as recounted by Aeneas to Dido, Hamlet refuses to be upstaged:

> What's Hecuba to him or he to her,
> That he should weep for her? What would he do
> Had he the motive and the cue for passion
> That I have? He would drown the stage with tears,
> And cleave the general ear with horrid speech,
> Make mad the guilty, and appal the free,
> Confound the ignorant, and amaze indeed
> The very faculties of eyes and ears. (II, ii, 525–32)

And later, when he sees the broken-hearted Laertes leap into his sister's tomb, Hamlet cannot restrain himself from coming forth (thereby revealing his return to an unfriendly court) and throwing himself into the same grave. Here, as Hamlet confronts Laertes, what is revealed is a rivalry in the display of excessive mourning: "Dost come here to whine? / To outface me with leaping in her grave?" (V, i, 255–56). Hamlet refuses to be out-unmanned, and certainly not by another man, as he and Laertes agree to resolve their differences here in the final catastrophic duel that leaves everybody dead. Then, ironically then, they are able to be mourned only by the invading army of Fortinbras.

Jacques Lacan, in his seminar "Desire and the Interpretation of Desire in *Hamlet*," has pointed out the extent to which this play is about mourning and specifically about inadequate forms of mourning.[18] And even though Lacan is usually more than able to sustain a cynical attitude toward the melancholy prince, his main thesis seems also to side with Hamlet's initial reproach to his mother. Before engaging Lacan's complex analysis in depth, it would be helpful to consider in addition to the canonical figure of Hamlet that other seventeenth-century monument to melancholia, Burton's encyclopedic *Anatomy of Melancholy*. Offering a panoramic *theatrum mundi* under the mask of "Democritus Junior," a figure wherein melancholia also appears as rationalist common sense, Burton seems to presage "modern subjectivity" at least as much as Hamlet. He also partakes of the same misogyny, submission to patriarchal authority, and appropriation of the voice of mourning.

Viewing melancholia as a malady that afflicts reason, and especially that part of reason known as the imagination, Burton, like Ficino in his *De vita*, writes his book from the standpoint of a doctor. A preventative medical book, it attempts to teach the reader how to "cure" and especially how to avoid the traps of an overwrought imagination. Whereas Ficino's book is primarily for the scholar, *The Anatomy of Melancholy* extends his warnings through the *exempla* of men and women who have been stricken with the innumerable forms of this illness that Burton perceives. Some scholars, for example, Ruth Fox, have certainly seen in *The Anatomy* Burton's desire for a greater understanding of the human condition,[19] but few, as far as I can tell, have questioned just how the reason that melancholy afflicts is constructed. The very premise of Burton's book—that "all the world is mad, that it is melancholy" (1: 39)—nonetheless gives the writer a "raison d'être," a reason that would equate meaningfulness—and hence narcissistic satisfaction—with a reasoned account of how unreasonable, how spiritless (and thus witless) one could become under the influence of melancholy. What are we then to make of such a world, if not that the only possible cure for such profound

---

[18]Jacques Lacan, "Desire and the Interpretation of Desire in *Hamlet*," in *Literature and Psychoanalysis: The Question of Reading: Otherwise*, ed. Shoshana Felman (Baltimore: Johns Hopkins University Press, 1982), pp. 11–52. For a more ambitiously Lacanian reading of lack in Shakespearian lyric, see of course Joel Fineman's phenomenal *Shakespeare's Perjured Eye* (Berkeley: University of California Press, 1986).

[19]Ruth Fox, *The Tangled Chain: The Structure of Disorder in "The Anatomy of Melancholy"* (Berkeley: University of California Press, 1976).

inertia is for reason itself to alleviate, or at best to reckon with, man's spiritlessness? Burton's consequential reckoning with the symptoms and cures of this both spiritual and physical disease would be justified by his claim to be a doctor of the soul as well as of the body. For Burton, doctors and religious ministers need to work together since this malady of which he treats is "a common infirmity of body and soul, and such a one that hath as much need of a spiritual as a corporal cure.... A divine in this compound mixed malady can do little alone, a physician in some kinds of melancholy much less, both make an absolute cure" (1: 37). Thus Burton's *Anatomy* is a grand synthesis of melancholia as a clinical and as a cultural category, as a disease and as a moral state.[20]

Insofar as he claims to be a healer of *both* mind and body, Burton positions himself within a very special genealogy. Titling his introduction "Democritus to the Reader," Burton writes under the mask of the ancient anatomist, imitating by his subdivisions the dissecting work of antiquity's "laughing philosopher" as described by Hippocrates: "About him lay the carcasses of many several beasts, newly by him cut up and anatomized; not that he did contemn God's creatures, as he told Hippocrates, but to find out the seat of this *atra bilis*, or melancholy, whence it proceeds, and how it was engendered in men's bodies, to the intent he might better cure it in himself, and by his writings and observations teach others how to prevent and avoid it" (1: 20). Melancholic though the "laughing philosopher" might be, were he alive in Burton's era *qua* Democritus Junior, "what would he say?" (1: 54). After detailing the horrors of contemporary warfare, Burton *qua* Democritus Junior asks: "Would this, think you, have enforced our Democritus to laughter, or rather made him turn his tune, alter his tone, and weep with Heraclitus, or rather howl, roar and tear his hair in commiseration, stand amazed; or as the poets feign, that Niobe was for grief quite stupefied, and turned to stone?" (1: 59).

But as he situates himself as he who will continue the investigations of Democritus, he also places himself within that other genealogy, the one Ficino popularized, that links melancholy to intellectual creativity. Burton finds some points of identification with "Marsilius Ficinus [who] was *semel et simul*, a priest and a physician at once" (1: 36); and Burton,

---

[20]On the slippage between melancholia the disease of *atra bilis* and the melancholy disposition, see Stanley W. Jackson, *Melancholia and Depression from Hippocratic Times to Modern Times* (New Haven: Yale University Press, 1986), pp. 95–103, and Babb, *Elizabethan Malady*, pp. 175, 184–85.

like Ficino, was a man of letters: "I have lived a silent, sedentary, solitary, private life, *mihi et musis* [for myself and my studies] in the university, as long almost as Xenocrates in Athens, *ad senectam fere* [practically to old age] to learn wisdom as he did, penned up most part in my study" (1: 17). Like Ficino too, Burton was born under Saturn: "Saturn was lord of my geniture" (1: 18).

And like Ficino's writings, Burton's *Anatomy* would be an artifact which testifies to the *techné* of medicine as a praxis of writing which is performed in order to avoid falling ill of melancholy: "I write of melancholy, by being busy to avoid melancholy. ... I was not a little offended with this malady, shall I say my mistress Melancholy, my Egeria, or my *malus genius* [evil genius]?" Being born under Saturn, and thus a son of the father of melancholy, Burton both internalizes and incorporates melancholia as that which spurs him on but from which he must escape, a paradoxical flight from a condition that is the very condition of his creativity. The "offense" to him would be carried out by "this malady"—my lady or "my mistress Melancholy"—who is explicitly a "she" before being transformed into his *malus genius*. Melancholia as the "feminine" offender would originate a creative antagonism between that evil genius *qua femme mortifère* and the genius of the individual who must dominate it (her). Brilliance and creativity are linked to a heroic conquest of a malady whose initial disempowerment potentially afflicts exceptional men, especially men of letters, who walk a delicate line between something fatal and something transcendent. The remarkable convergence of Ficinian melancholic genius with Burton's own malady is unapologetically drawn.

What does, however, separate Ficino's melancholia from Burton's is that with the former the relation between body and (scholarly) mind is predicated on a desire to retrieve the lost object. The erotic dynamics of Ficino's melancholy is the very precondition for representing the trajectory of the scholar as the quest for a lost truth; the libidinal investment into an other object is marked a priori by a philosophical system whereby mutual affection between men, is but a step toward retrieving part of what one had lost. In Burton's world, however, even as he situates himself under the sign of Saturn, it is precisely the erotic dimension that is repressed and shunned. Just as the appropriation of "femininity" remains opaque to his consciousness even as he tells us that it was "mistress Melancholy" who was his *malus genius*, so the loss that makes "all the world" melancholy is de-eroticized as the theological and historical loss of man's original closeness to God, of the purity that was his in Eden. A nostalgia for God and for the original state of man is thus the motivating force of this opus, while eros (as dialectic of desire) is repressed for the sake of encouraging a relentless *moral* conscience that understands man as fallen, as universally melancholic: "Thou shalt soon see that all the world is mad, that it is melancholy. . . . You shall find that kingdoms and provinces are melancholy, cities and families, all creatures, vegetal, sensible, and rational, that all sorts, sects, ages, conditions, are out of tune" (1: 39).

It is no doubt this generalizing of melancholia as the fundamental trait of the post-lapsarian human condition along with the repression of melancholic eros that explains the chief difference between late Elizabethan and Ficinian melancholy. For in the North, a connection is explicitly drawn between melancholia and evil, an ecclesiastical link that Ficino, Petrarch, and even Tasso had displaced. Yet for Burton as for the character Hamlet, the possibility that melancholic inspiration might emanate either from God or from the devil is disturbing and virtually obsessive. From a libidinal economics of Neoplatonism we have come to the economy of the sensible man who tries to avoid the pitfalls of sin through "reason" (which of course is no reason but only a legitimated form of hysteria, most horribly pursued through the contemporary Northern European witch-burning craze). This diabolism of melancholia is also different from the kind earlier proposed by Hildegard, since it certainly does not question the traditional Western association of women with evil, and in fact perniciously follows up on that association.

Burton affirms the writing of his opus as the busywork that acts as the "antidote" (1: 21) to the evil genius of his mistress melancholy, but this antidote is also the affirmation of the positive insights the disease has brought about: "Concerning myself, I can peradventure affirm with Marius in Sallust, 'That which others hear or read of, I felt and practised myself: they get their knowledge by books, I mine by melancholizing'" (1: 22). Solace is found, here as elsewhere in Burton, by recourse to the patronymic authority of citation, which ensconces the writer safely within a masculine tradition, a veritable brotherhood of melancholia with whom the writer can identify in his struggle with his malady, or ma-lady, melancholia. Turning the noun into a verb, "to melancholize," further reasserts the *activity* of gleaning knowledge from his malady, of phallicizing the loss and disempairment brought on by it. In this way, the passivity of succumbing to the malady, to his *malus genius*, can be overcome through a quest for reason and knowledge that is justifiable even according to the moral rectitude of Burton's reformed religion: "I was fatally driven upon this rock of melancholy, and carried away by this by-stream, which, as a rillet, is deducted from the main channel of my studies, in which I have pleased and busied myself at idle hours, as a subject most necessary and commodius" (1: 35). Burton further justifies his "melancholizing" research and abandonment of the study of divinity by citing the endless "controversy" into which the writing of sermons brings one: "To have written in controversy would have been to cut off an hydra's head, *lis litem generat*, one [dispute] begets another, so many duplications, triplications, and swarms of questions *in sacro bello hoc quod stili mucrone agitur* [in this sacred war that is waged with the pen], that having once begun, I should never make an end" (1: 35).

Yet Burton's book with its endless systematizing and proliferating categories exactly reproduces such a Hydra-like dilemma. The busywork of writing that is the supposed antidote to melancholia also exacerbates and prolongs the condition, as the process of distinguishing between different types of melancholia seems to produce even more differences. This question of differentiation structures his *Anatomy*, as different parts of the body belong to a single unit, the body of the work, which is supposed to incorporate all the differences. This anatomized body, however, also foregrounds its own dismemberment, its differentiation into the parts carved out by the anatomist's dissecting pen. Such differentiation is of utmost importance since the inability to differentiate would be the madness of multiplicity: "Every multitude is mad, *bellua multorum capitum* [a many-headed beast], precipitate and rash without judgement, *stultum animal*, a roaring rout" (1: 78). The analogy then with madness or folly is one of a multitude, that is, one in which distinction is lost in the crowd. The Hydra is a monstrous thing that comes back with more than one head, more than one thought; "she" contradicts reason, which would have all the world systematized and understood. And in fact this systematizing reason is contradicted by Burton's key assertion that "all the world" is mad from melancholy. The book is supposed to be the antidote but it is also the source of melancholy; the disease inspires him to write but the writing aggravates the disease. He writes because he is melancholic, but his melancholia is only worsened by writing. The battle with the Hydra can only perpetuate the difference the anatomist would deny or cut out, drawing him into the limitless difference that is also the undifferentiated mass of that many-headed beast that is the entire world gone melancholically mad.

There is nonetheless an ideological moment in this textual movement of differentiation that multiplies the categories of melancholia into the vast corpus of the *Anatomy*, namely the ideology revealed by the fact that *not all* differences are considered the same: "Such as are solitary by nature, great students, given much to contemplation, lead a life out of action, are most subject to melancholy. Of sexes both, but men more often; yet women misaffected are far more violent, and grievously troubled. . . . 'Generally,' saith Rhasis, 'the finest wits and most generous spirits are before other obnoxious to it' " (1: 172). These distinctions and the apparent accrediting of women's melancholia generate and justify a difference between the rare occurrences of melancholia in women *as a disease* offering no cultural transcendence and characterized by inarticulateness and its more common appearance in men, most especially the "sensitive" men of "fine wit," "generous spirit," or scholarly sedentariness. For the latter, there *is* the possibility of Ficinian inspiration, of the beatific suturing of a lack that is banal in women but exceptional in the man of genius. This is how Burton synthesizes the Galenic with the Ficinian tradition, the disease of the black bile with the heightened consciousness of melancholia. From the many-headed beast, he attempts to separate out at least one form of melancholia that is transcendent.

If reason is the antidote to melancholia, then those melancholics obsessed most with reason, namely "great students," blur the distinction between symptom and cure. Burton himself both cites books as a cause of melancholia and attempts to cure his own melancholia through the busywork of writing a book. Inasmuch as the cure and the cause of melancholia thus implicate each other, Burton interestingly empowers his discourse by the claim of personal experience, a claim that distinguishes his work from traditional medical discourse (a doctor's words are legitimated not because he himself has suffered the disease but because he has successfully treated it in others). The result is also to make Burton's text more literary.

Whether reason or unreason, however, this scholarly melancholia is expressed eloquently in books and other creative works. It is thus poles apart from that other melancholia that affects "maids, nuns, and widows." As Ruth Fox has pointed out, the subsection dealing with this overtly feminine melancholia (included for the first time in the third edition) was "the only actual addition to the matter outlined in the synopses." "The significance of such an addition," Fox argues, "lies in the fact that it could occur without changing the basic structure of the whole work" (p. 7). The ease with which the category of a feminine melancholia can be included in Burton's opus is not just another effect of the anatomist's ability to "embrace diverse matters and diverse times in a single form" (Fox, p. 6), but also an eventuality inscribed in his earlier distinction between the rarer but more "grievous" cases of melancholia in women and its more frequent but less grave appearances in men. And in describing the symptoms of melancholia in "maids, nuns, and widows," Burton the anatomist dissects his subject matter by drawing differences of an obviously hierarchical and ideological sort. At first, these symptoms do not seem any different from those of male melancholia:

> They complain many times, saith Mercatus, of a great pain in their heads, about their hearts and hypocondries, and so likewise in their breasts, which are often sore; sometimes ready to swoon, their faces are inflamed and red, they are dry, thirsty, suddenly hot, much troubled with wind, cannot sleep etc. And from hence proceed *ferina deliramenta*, a brutish kind of dotage, troublesome sleep, terrible dreams in the night, *subrusticus pudor, et verecundia ignava*, a foolish kind of bashfulness to some, perverse conceits and opinions, dejection of mind, much discontent, preposterous judgement. . . . They take delight in nothing for the time, but love to be alone and solitary, so long as this vapour lasteth; but by and by as pleasant and merry as ever they were in their lives, they sing, discourse and laugh in any good company, upon all occasions; and so by fits it takes them now and then, except the malady be inveterate, and then 'tis more frequent, vehement, and continuate. (1: 415–16)

Unlike the inspired eloquence of many male melancholics, however, these women's attempts at expression are irredeemably inarticulate: "Many of them cannot tell how to express themselves in words, or how it holds them, what ails them; you cannot understand them, or well tell what to make of their sayings; for far gone sometimes, so stupefied and distracted, they think themselves bewitched, they are in despair; . . . and yet will not, cannot again tell how, where, or what offends them, though they be in great pain, agony, and frequently complain, grieving, sighing, weeping and discontented, still *sine causa manifesta* [without apparent cause], most part" (1: 416). The source of their discomfort, just as for the women in Freud's essay, is supposedly the lack of a good man: "But the best and surest remedy of all, is to see them well placed, and married to good husbands in due time; *hinc illae lachrymae* [hence those tears], that's the primary cause, and this the ready cure, to give them content to their desires" (1: 417). If, as Sarah Kofman has argued, Freud narcissistically interprets hysteria by projecting a need for men onto women who remain disturbingly indifferent to them,[21] Burton similarly finds the antidote to female melancholia in the phallic subservience of women, whether as servants or whores:

> For seldom should you see an hired servant, a poor handmaid, though ancient, that is kept hard to her work and bodily labor, a coarse country wench, troubled in this kind, but noble virgins, nice gentlewomen, such as are solitary and idle, live at ease, lead a life out of action and employment, that fare well. . . . I do not so much pity them that otherwise be eased, but those alone out of a strong temperament, innate constitution, are violently carried away with this torrent of inward humors, and though very modest of themselves, sober, religious, virtuous, and well given (as many so distressed maids are), yet cannot make resistance; these grievances will appear, this malady will take place, and now manifestly shows itself, and may not otherwise be helped. (1: 417).

In short, female melancholia is the result of a breakdown in the patriarchal order, a breakdown for which Catholicism with its celibate orders bears an important responsibility in the discourse of this Protestant theologian:

> How odious and abominable are those superstitious and rash vows of popish monasteries, so as to bind and enforce men and women to vow virginity, to lead a single life, against the laws of nature, opposite to religion, policy, and humanity, so to starve, to offer violence, to suppress the vigour of youth! . . . stupid politicians! ought these things so to be carried? Better marry than burn, saith the apostle. . . . For let them but consider what fearful maladies, feral diseases, gross inconveniences, come to both sexes by this enforced temperance; it troubles me to think of, much more to relate, those frequent aborts and murdering of infants in their nunneries . . . their notorious fornications, those rapes, incests, adulturies, masturbations, sodomies, buggeries, of monks and friars. (1: 418–19)

[21]Sarah Kofman, *L'énigme de la femme* (Paris: Galilée, 1980).

Perhaps no statement better epitomizes the hierarchy of differences within the *Anatomy* than Burton's remark that "the husband rules her as head . . . : no happiness is like unto it, no love so great as this of man and wife, no such comfort as *placens uxor*, a sweet wife" (3: 53).[22]

And nothing can be more upsetting to and disruptive of this gendered body politic than the "unnatural" desire of a woman:

> Of women's unnatural, unsatiable lust, what country, what village doth not complain? Mother and daughter sometimes dote on the same man; father and son, master and servant on one woman. . . . Yet this is more tolerable in youth, and such as are still in their hot blood; but for an old fool to dote, . . . what can be more absurd? what so common? . . . Worse it is in women than in men; when she is *aetate declivis, diu vidua, mater olim, parum decore matrimonium sequi videtur*, an old widow, a mother so long since (in Pliny's opinion), she doth very unseemly seek to marry, yet while she is so old a crone, a beldam, she can neither see nor hear, go nor stand, a mere carcass, a witch, and scarce feel, she caterwauls, and must have a stallion. (3: 56)

Animalistic images drawn from the "natural" world of feline and equine behavior illustrate the "unnaturalness" of a woman's lust, which also supposedly turns her into mindless flesh ("a mere carcass"). Above all, it is the desire of mature women that horrifies Burton and leads him to assimilate such cases to witches. The seriousness of such a charge should not be underestimated in the seventeenth-century context of witch burning, especially when the charge comes from a prominent Protestant theologian in a supposedly scholarly work. Interestingly enough, those phallus-lacking and supposedly desiring women who suffer from melancholia (nuns, widows, virgins) are thought of as being "bewitched" or as believing themselves to be possessed: "They will complain, grudge, lament, and not be persuaded but that they are troubled with an evil spirit . . . they are in despair, surely forspoken or bewitched, and in extremity of their dotage (weary of their lives), some of them will attempt to make away with themselves. Some think they see visions, confer with spirits and devils, they shall surely be damned, are afraid of some treachery, imminent danger, and the like, they will not speak, make an answer to any question, but are almost distracted, mad, or stupid for the time,

---

[22] Citing Plutarch, Burton adds that a "good" wife "should be as a looking-glass to represent her husband's face and passion: if he be pleasant, she should be merry; if he laugh, she should smile; if he looks sad, she should participate of his sorrow, and bear a part with him" (3: 54).

and by fits" (1: 416). The terror of the melancholic woman (both the
terror the melancholic woman holds for men and the terror she herself
feels) lies in her assimilation to the figure of the witch via that sexually
ravenous and male-devouring Dame Mérencolye of Alain Chartier and
others. It is possible, of course, that a man who speaks with "spirits and
devils" might equally be accused of witchcraft, but he *also* has the further
possibility of being hailed as a man of genius, a poet or a philosopher.
It is precisely the absence of this "also," of this positive possibility, that
describes the condition of women's melancholia. If not contained and
"fulfilled" by the phallic institution of marriage, women are considered
to go mad or to become possessed, to become witches, thus confirming
that old Aristotelian view of the corruptibility of women.

Desire and the possibility of a positive dialectics of lack are legitimated and celebrated in men, denied to and punished in women. This
double standard surfaces as an overt contradiction in Burton's discourse:
"But where am I? Into what subject have I rushed? What have I to do
with nuns, maids, virgins, widows? I am a bachelor myself, and lead a
monastic life in a college, *nae ego sane ineptus qui haec dixerim* [it is
certainly very foolish of me to speak thus], I confess 'tis an indecorum,
and as Pallas, a virgin, blushed when Jupiter by chance spake of love
matters in her presence, and turned away her face, *me reprimam* [I will
check myself]; though my subject necessarily require it, I will say no
more" (1: 417–18). In diagnosing, as Freud too would, the female
melancholic as phallicly needy, Burton blushingly foregrounds his own
sexual deprivation, his own "unmanliness." Much later, in discussing
love melancholia, Burton does not mince words when he says outright
that melancholia "turns a man into a woman" (3: 142). In questioning
what he has "to do with nuns, maids, virgins, widows," that is, in
wanting to extricate himself from the "indecorous" subject of women,
Burton betrays his own fearful identification with them. This identification with women is recuperated, and the potential danger of confronting his own castration is averted, by his ensuing appropriation of/
identification with Pallas, "a virgin," who "turned away her face" from
some Jupiterian vulgarities. But here it is not a woman who turns away
from a man speaking about sex but a man, Burton, who uses this feminine figure to turn away from the topic of feminine sexuality, who
masquerades as a woman to cast women out of his discourse: "*me reprimam* [I will check myself]; though my subject necessarily require it,
I will say no more."

Once again, a male appropriation of femininity serves a misogynist end. An equally duplicitous identification/appropriation takes place in Burton's evocation of Dürer's famous etching of melancholia, an evocation that brings out that icon's force as a double representation:

> [Melancholics are] prone to revenge, soon troubled, and most violent in all their imaginations, not affable in speech, or apt to vulgar compliment, but surly, dull, sad, austere; *cogitabundi* still, very intent, and as Albertus Durer paints Melancholy, like a sad woman leaning on her arm with fixed looks, neglected habit, etc.; held therefore by some proud, soft, sottish, or half-mad, as the Abderites esteemed of Democitus, and yet of a deep reach, excellent apprehension, judicious, wise and witty: for I am of that nobleman's mind, 'Melancholy advanceth men's conceits more than any humor whatsoever,' improves their meditations more than any strong drink or sack. They are of profound judgment in some things, although in others non *recte judicant inquieti* [people in a passion do not judge correctly]. (I: 392)

On the one hand, the commentary on Dürer's depressed woman suggests just that, a depressed woman. On the other hand, Burton turns a negative into a positive by deflecting the meaning away from the case of a depressed woman to an allegorical representation of sorrow and dejection. Such sorrow may be represented as a sad woman, as the feminine, as melancholia, but then—as Burton's quick reversal of syntactical and rhetorical strategy suggests—is suddenly associated with a penetrating intellect such that creativity and femininity are then emblematic of him who suffers knowledge of the world. For, in the very next paragraph, Burton goes on to posit how some men dote too much and too frequently on women, causing melancholy in them, while other men who are already melancholy hate women. On the one hand, love for a woman leads to melancholy; but, on the other hand, an already melancholic man often hates women. If either of these men sees a woman, he is thrown into greater depths of melancholy, suggesting that whether cause or effect, woman exacerbates the problem: "[These men] are prone to love, and easy to be taken: *propensi ad amoren et excandescentiam* (Montaltus, cap. 21), quickly enamoured, and dote upon all, love one dearly, till they see another, and then dote on her, *et hanc, et hanc, et illam, et omnes* [this one, and that one, and all of them]. . . . Yet some again *anterotes* [enemies of love], cannot endure the sight of a woman, abhor the sex, as that same melancholy duke of Muscovy, that was instantly sick if he came but in sight of them; and that anchorite, that fell into a cold palsy when a woman was brought before him" (1: 393). If Burton rejects Ficinian eros from his own melancholic discourse, it is to pursue his own misogynist ends. Melancholia is equally the realm of the *erotes* as it is of the *anterotes*, but like the duke of Moscow, it cannot seem to "endure the sight of a woman." And if the *figure* of woman can allegorically represent the melancholic plight as it does from Chartier through Dürer and Burton, what is thereby represented is not the plight of women (whether melancholic or not) but that of the "feminine" within man.

In the same manner, mourning the loss of a loved one can also lead men into a dangerous femininity like that of "those Irish women and Greeks at their graves [who] commit many undecent actions, and almost go besides themselves" (2: 176). "Democritus Junior," looking over contemporary woes, may turn into Heraclitus, the weeping philosopher, or into Niobe, that feminine figure of mourning (1: 59). By renewing Claudius's humanist admonitions against "unmanly wailing" (2: 180), Burton allows that men mourn albeit within certain prescribed limits. He does not "forbid men to grieve, but to grieve overmuch": "The Romans and most civil commonwealths have set a time to such solemnities, they must not mourn after a set day" (2: 180). Apparently, the "feminine" within man can be given free reign only if women are excluded. Burton cites with approval the dying Socrates who "put all the women out of the room" (2: 180) to keep the men from weeping, and "Ulysses that wept for his dog, but not for his wife" because "he had prepared himself for the blow beforehand" (2: 185). Faced with loss, a man may become tearful *like* a woman, but if he is not to become "unmanly" those tears must take place only in the absence of women, and certainly not *for* women.

But what is meant, in patriarchal terms, by such a representation of the feminine within man if not a displaced image of the lack he refuses to see within himself, namely his own castration, his own lack of the phallus? Representing himself as feminine, however, allows the man to figure this lack as potential plenitude, as something "more" possibly there beneath the robes of transvestism. On the other hand, as Tasso's Hydra and the proliferating "sections" and "sub-sections" of Burton's *Anatomy* show, that something more can always reveal itself to be the something less of an "open wound" that cannot be healed. Burton ends his huge opus by meditating on whether suicide should be excused for the gravely melancholic. It just might be that the phallus is not there, whether or not the figure of woman can serve as an illusory screen, in which case the inescapable acknowledgment of that lack will be confronted as a terrible loss that needs to be mourned.

Perhaps it was this strange situation that led the late Renaissance both to "affect" a melancholy disposition as well as to grasp its historical moment as one of dire loss and fall. The age of heroes has passed, the time of weeping has come—but, of course, the right to weep should be restricted to those who would have been heroes. Burton's long preface, "Democritus to the Reader," recounts contemporary horrors at length, all the while (and throughout the rest of the *Anatomy*) buttressing the author's discourse with the authority of countless citations, a homage to or a hope in the intertextual superego of long dead authors.

It is a banality, of course, to view the rise of Renaissance melancholia in terms of the loss of Christian certitude.[23] As Stanley Jackson has noted, it was not unusual to find among other symptoms of melancholia "fears of being beyond salvation, of being in serious danger of damnation, of having been abandoned by God."[24] For Michel de Certeau, the rise of mysticism in this period is likewise to be understood as a melancholic mourning for the disappearance or withdrawal of God.[25] This shake-up in the symbolic order, and in the centrality of its phallic representor, God the Father himself, is what Renaissance melancholia both recognizes and denies through its sense of history, that is, through a distinctly modern sensibility of a loss in time, of belatedness.[26] On the other hand, this same sense of things being past their prime is what is so aggressively, horrendously denied in the obsessive image of the witch, most notably in the form of the old woman who still has desires. The horror of the witch, or of the female melancholic, is that she would all too openly reveal what is projected onto her, a longing for the phallus though it be long gone, unattainable, or perhaps never there in the first place (we need look no further than the examples of nuns and virgins, who as the famous trials of Loudun showed may also be implicated in

---

[23]Jackson, *Melancholia and Depression*, pp. 330ff; Babb, *Elizabethan Malady*, pp. 184–85; Michel de Certeau, *La fable mystique* (Paris: Gallimard, 1982); Walter Benjamin, *The Origin of German Tragic Drama*, trans. John Osborne (London: New Left Books, 1977).

[24]Jackson, *Melancholia and Depression*, p. 330.

[25]De Certeau, *La fable mystique*, p. 8.

[26]The term is borrowed, of course, from Harold Bloom's classic work *The Anxiety of Influence* (New Haven: Yale University Press, 1976).

affairs of witchcraft and possession[27]). The melancholic's sense of history as loss (of God, of textual authority, of heroic possibility, etc.) undertakes a mourning for the (lost) phallus that reasserts a phallocentric privilege. The sense of loss privileges a male subject as historically sensitive or lyrically sentient. *He* is the one privileged to understand and to speak the loss of God in a philosophical register that reinstates God's omnipotence, the loss of textual authority through a proliferation of citations that seeks to reclaim that authority, the loss of a phallus refound by the very discourse that mourns that loss *insofar as that mourning is marked by a masculine prerogative.* To link the melancholic genius with the historical sensibility of modern subjectivity, or with the dawn of some new epoch of being, may or may not be as progressive as it seems.

The idealization of a consciousness of disempowerment equated to a transcendent poetics and a sense of historical loss is also delineated by Walter Benjamin in *The Origin of German Tragic Drama*. Marking a distinction between tragedy (*Tragödie*) and a "mourning play" (*Trauerspiel*), Benjamin links the characteristics of melancholia to this second form. Let me reiterate the differences for, as we shall see, the differences are also echoed in Lacan's formulation of Hamlet as a modern rather than a classical hero. For Benjamin, tragedy is grounded in myth and in silence. The tragic hero recognizes an ethical contract that is in excess of the gods themselves, one that is grounded in heroic sacrifice of which he is cognizant: "Only antiquity could know tragic hubris, which pays for the right to be silent with the hero's life. The hero, who scorns to justify himself before the gods, reaches agreement with them in a, so to speak, contractual process of atonement which, in its dual significance, is designed not only to bring about the restoration but above all the undermining of an ancient body of laws in the linguistic constitution of the renewed community."[28] Thus, for Benjamin, heroic defiance becomes silence that teaches endurance and unchangeability in the face of life's trials. *Trauerspiel*, on the other hand, demands history; it is rooted in time and in changeability. It demands an acting out of lament and sorrow. The German word *Trauer* signifies sorrow and mourning, and

[27]De Certeau, *La possession de Loudun* (Paris: Julliard, 1970); and more recently, Mitchell Greenberg, *Subjection and Subjugation in Seventeenth-Century French Literature* (forthcoming from Cambridge University Press).
[28]Benjamin, *The Origin of German Tragic Drama*, p. 115. Key elements of my reading of Benjamin have been informed by George Steiner's introductory essay to John Osborne's translation of *The Origin of German Tragic Drama*, pp. 1–24.

Spiel signifies both play and game: play in the sense of both a stage performance and of an acting out, a playing out even in the ludic sense. The *Trauerspiel* is an acting out of sorrow, a play of mourning.

For Benjamin, the *Trauerspiel* rooted in history offers a perspective on the relation of the subject to the body politic. In the wake of the Thirty Years' War and the final breakup of any sense of Christian unity, that relation is the sundered, alienated one most typically expressed, according to Benjamin, by the baroque penchant for allegory. Display of sorrow is analogous to ostentation precisely because the sadness of the modern hero is the sign of his alienation and alienation, implies a subjectivity founded in contradiction and expressed only allegorically. In the event of the *Trauerspiel*, the stage becomes the centerpiece for a display of alienation and intense contemplation. The dialectic comes into play in terms of the play's dependence on the spectator to gaze on an inner world of feeling that bears no relation to the cosmos but instead shows that the subject in question is surrounded by, enmeshed in, and absent from the specificity of the situation. While the values of the classical world are lost to the modern hero, the *Trauerspiel* reflects in fact a mourning for this past, not unlike the preface to Burton's *Anatomy*. Melancholy is thus a characteristic of the *Trauerspiel* and, according to Benjamin, "the prince is the paradigm of the melancholy man" (p. 142). The modern prince thus reflects the *taedium vitae* of higher natures. While the suffering of ancient heroes was mute, in the *Trauerspiel* (as in Freudian melancholia) suffering speaks; it speaks of sadness and of betrayal, thus intensifying feeling and cultivating an eros of longing.

For Benjamin, the German baroque drama—the *Trauerspiel*— accentuates the hero's boredom of spirit understood as a fatigue with worldliness, figured in the space of the court. For it is in the prince that melancholy is most fully realized; that is, by seeing the prince *display* his prerogative for privileged subjectivity the spectator authenticates the prince's unhappy consciousness, which is bound up with his memory : "Every feeling is bound to an a priori object, and the representation of this object is its phenomenology. Accordingly, the theory of mourning, which emerged unmistakably as a *pendant* to the theory of tragedy can only be developed in the description of that world which is revealed under the gaze of the melancholy man" (p. 139). The melancholic presents us therefore with a truth about the tedium of life which paradoxically is then the mark of the contemplative man. That *man* is one whom we—the spectators—see and whose excess of feeling we share, a feeling

that in itself exceeds even the material world of objects and object relations, given that it is in the knowledge of one's fate that one finds
satisfaction. The epistemological issue becomes a moral issue whose
morality lies in an understanding of the fundamental immorality and
intrigue of the surrounding world. Melancholia accordingly becomes an
epistemological problem in which knowledge of one's alienation from
the world is in itself having a perspective on the world. Thus melancholy
is both alienation and perspective.

Following this logic, it would seem that women too would share
this sense of alienation and perspective on the way culture instantiates
itself, given that women are both included and excluded by a patriarchal
symbolic. For women to come into their subjectivity through sexual
difference—through, that is, the legislation of the castration complex—
leaves them not only alienated but doubly so. By way of this double
alienation, they should also be melancholic, doubly melancholic, since
the castration complex inaugurates a double alienation—one from the
mother and one from the father—bequeathing a double perspective.
The difference, however, seems to me to be that women's relation to
father, king, state, authority, to let us say the patriarchal symbolic, does
not provide them with the same cultural discourses that install men's
relation to subjectivity and loss as constitutively raising questions of an
epistemological nature. Benjamin, like so many others, then finds in the
figure of Hamlet the very emblem of the melancholic and princely sensitivity that, for him, typifies the baroque and defines the peculiar modernity that that era and the *Trauerspiel* takes on in his work: "For the
Trauerspiel Hamlet alone is a spectator by the grace of God; but he
cannot find satisfaction in what he sees enacted, only in his own fate.
His life, the exemplary object of his mourning, points, before its extension, to the Christian providence in whose bosom his mournful images
are transformed into a blessed existence. Only in a princely life such as
this is melancholy redeemed, by being confronted with itself. The rest
is silence" (p. 158). In this image of the melancholy prince, we see a
Christ-like figure. If only in a prince is melancholy to be redeemed, then
do melancholic women remain excluded from this privileged form of
erotic Christian suffering? And along with women, laborers and the
general populace, those whom Renaissance humanism contemptuously
relegated to the *vulgus*? For without a doubt Benjamin is here positing
a *class* relation whereby melancholy is equivalent to spiritual grandeur

and characteristic of certain men in whom is displayed a nobility of line and a nobility of spirit.

All of which points back again to the character of Hamlet in his cardinal capacity to represent not only the melancholic sensibility who chides women for not mourning enough but also the epochal moment of a historical transition that is at least as intra- as it is inter-psychic, as psychological as it is sociological. For Jacques Lacan, among others, the question of Hamlet is *both* a historical and a psychoanalytic one. Reading the play in terms of a historicization of the oedipal legacy, Lacan raises the question of modern subjectivity in Hamlet as the exemplar of the alienated individual caught within the web of his "feigned" madness: "Feigning madness is thus one of the dimensions of what we might call the strategy of the modern hero."[29] According to Lacan, it is this feigning of madness that marks Hamlet as a new and different kind of hero from his classic predecessor, Oedipus himself. Oedipus, we remember, becomes mad and a man after he discovers the truth of his origin, after he discovers his implication in his own narrative. In traditional psychoanalytic terms, the play *Hamlet* is usually understood to be oedipally motivated as a recasting of unconscious desire for the mother and the consequent desire to kill off the father. But, as Lacan points out, in *Hamlet* the situation is complicated by the fact that the prince's father has *already* been murdered by his uncle, who then also sleeps with Hamlet's mother. The problem, then, is of a desire having already been performed by another with whom Hamlet is nonetheless implicated as an unspeakable rival. His own desire has been subverted by the actual enactment by another of his repressed oedipal agenda.

The oedipal drama is thereby recast as a drama of deferred action wherein the desired action can never occur since it has already taken place prior to the play, and thanks to someone else. The play's action can then only turn around mourning something that never was, can only occur as an excess of mourning, can only display the theatricality of feigned mourning, which is in turn a melancholic mourning since the excessive display of grief capitalizes on a loss that, from Hamlet's point of view, has not been properly mourned. As Jacqueline Rose has pointed out, Lacan too considers that the rite of mourning has never taken place in the world of the play and that the father has not been

---

[29]Lacan, "Desire and the Interpretation of Desire," p. 20.

properly mourned, for which Lacan implicates the failure of the Symbolic to take precedence over the Imaginary.[30] "Swarms of images" come to fill in the hole left in the Real by the death of the father. Since this real loss has not had an adequate ritualization according to Lacan, this hole comes to be filled in by ghosts such as the one who, in the form of Hamlet's father, haunts Elsinore at the play's beginning. In other words, the question of "insufficient mourning" is inextricably tied to the revision of the oedipal scenario that defines Hamlet's modernity, and by implication to the peculiarity of a madness caught in the web of its own feigning.

Rather than simply accredit this confluence of deritualization and modernity, however, I would like to consider once again how women are cast in the supposedly new historical situation of this revisionist oedipal scenario. For if *Hamlet* is a play about modern subjectivity and about improper mourning, it is also a play about male subjectivity. I have already discussed the consequences of all this in terms of Gertrude. Ophelia too, though, is pivotal for our understanding of the gender politics of melancholia, most notably in its Lacanian version. Hamlet's rejection of Ophelia is both an explicit sign of his putative madness and a representation of traditional Western misogyny. Thus it works in the same way as traditional discourses on melancholia work, to produce a certain kind of eros predicated on a self-production through the fetishistic exploitation of an other, that is, woman.

Not only does Lacan tells us that the play *Hamlet* is a "tragedy of desire" (p. 11), but he also describes Ophelia as "that piece of bait" (p. 113): "Perhaps Shakespeare merely extended her function in the plot, which is to capture Hamlet's secret by surprise. But she thus becomes one of the innermost elements in Hamlet's drama, the drama of Hamlet as the man who has lost the way of his desire. She provides an essential pivot in the hero's progress toward his mortal rendez-vous with his act—an act that he carries out, in some sense, in spite of himself" (p. 12). If we read on, though, we find that Ophelia's "essential" role in Hamlet's trajectory paradoxically depends on her effacement, obliteration, or rejection *as* Ophelia, on the denial of her self as woman:

Hamlet no longer treats Ophelia like a woman at all. She becomes in his eyes the childbearer to every sin, a future "breeder of sinners," destined to succumb to every calumny. She is no longer the reference-point for a life that Hamlet condemns in its essence. In short, what is taking place is the destruction and loss of the object. For the subject the object appears, if I may put it this way, on the outside. The subject is no longer the object: he rejects it with all the force of his being and will not find it again until he sacrifices himself. It is in this sense that the object is here the equivalent of, assumes the place of, indeed is—the phallus. (pp. 22–23)

In other words, Ophelia as woman disappears before her instantiation or hypostatization, following Lacan's witticism, as "*O phallos*" (p. 20). Woman becomes a stand-in for the phallus, as she is "exteriorized," "scotomized," such that eros, specifically male eros, can continue to invest its libido onto lack, a lack that signals the lover's extraordinary alienation from the *vulgus*. (Because he defines himself as unlike the mass, a renunciation must take place, one that is also predicated specifically on the negation of women by their being hypostatized as phallic icons.)

It is also not too surprising that Hamlet is a prince, for in the cult of suffering and of lack, the melancholic becomes the privileged site for a nobility of spirit whose specialness is distinguished by the gift of illness. Lacan in his essay on Hamlet also seeks to ascribe some extraordinary characteristic to Hamlet when he says: "Yet the subject's appointment with the hour of his destruction is the common lot of everyone, meaningful in the destiny of every individual. Without some distinguishing sign, Hamlet's fate would not be of such great importance to us. The next question is what is the specificity of Hamlet's fate? What makes it so extraordinarily problematic?" (p. 25). Lacan's answer is that Hamlet in fact lives in a special state of estrangement, of alienation, of ambiguity, and of procrastination— characteristics of the melancholic syndrome since the time of Aristotle. Lacan then asks: "What does Hamlet lack?" (p. 25). For the French psychoanalyst, Hamlet's problem, oddly enough, is one of object choice: "He has never set a goal for himself, an object" (pp. 25–26), which is also to say finally, not as Eagleton or Barker would have it, that Hamlet is nothing, but rather that he *lacks nothing*. He lacks lack, and to locate an identity, he becomes a pivot around which one can pose endlessly the question of his uncommon essence, of whether or not there is more to him than what seems, of whether or not his madness is feigned. These questions are raised at the expense of Ophelia and of Gertrude, whose real losses (murdered husbands, lovers, and fathers, as well as their own deaths) come to naught. Lacking lack, the melancholic has a *sense* of loss predicated on an *impossible* union with some lost object, that loss to be finally understood as the loss from heaven, the loss not of the object of desire (the Ficinian Venus, Ophelia) but of the phallus, of the erotic link back to the father (Ficino's Saturn, the ghost of Hamlet's father). At the same time, the very evidence of the loss attested by the stance of excessive mourning is the proof of one's uncommonness, of one's link with what has been lost.

But what does it mean for a woman to become a stand-in for the phallus, even to become the phallus? Certainly, nothing good, if "what is taking place is the destruction and loss of the object," as manifested by Hamlet's verbal aggressivity toward Ophelia. Supposedly, the subject is upset to find the object of desire to be outside itself, that is, not a part of itself, yet the defeminization or derealization of Ophelia as described by Lacan also suggests a denial of that otherness the subject finds outside itself and the reduction of the other's objecthood (not to mention sub-jecthood!) to what the subject cannot have, the phallus. Indeed, Lacan's insistence on the relation of this syndrome to fantasy production and on the primacy of the Imaginary in it suggests that the exteriorization or loss of the object is also an interiorization of it. In other words, any possible "intersubjectivity" has dissolved into the literal psychodrama of the ego's *imaginary* relationship to the phallus.

Lacan refers to this entire scenario, Hamlet's oedipal revisionism, as "a decadent form of the Oedipal situation, its decline" (p. 45) and argues that "the Oedipus complex goes into its decline insofar as the subject must mourn the phallus" (p. 46). Lacan describes what he means by this process twice, first in traditional Freudian terms and then in his own vocabulary:

> At the moment of the final outcome of his Oedipal demands, the subject, seeing himself castrated in any case, deprived of the thing, prefers, as it were, to abandon a part of himself, which will henceforth be forever forbidden to him. (p. 48)

> The subject must explore his relationship to the field of the Other, i.e., the field organized in the symbolic register, in which his demand for love has begun to express itself. It is when he emerges from this exploration, having carried it to the end, that the loss of the phallus occurs for him and is felt as such, a radical loss. How does he respond then to the necessity of this mourning? Precisely with the composition of his imaginary register

and with nothing else—a phenomenon whose similarity to a psychotic
mechanism I have already indicated. (p. 48)

His oedipal desires effectively interdicted "in any case" by Claudius's
preemptive moves, Hamlet can only live out his "castration" through
the death of his own desire (the loss/rejection of the loved object, Ophelia) and the *imaginary* relation to paternal authority (to the superego)
signified by the ghost. But what discloses the loss of the phallus? Is it
the love object (Ophelia) who, emptied of desire, becomes the phallus
(*O phallos*), or is it the unattainability of the phallus that reveals the
subject's sense of castration as deprivation? While Ophelia is alive, Hamlet vilifies her, but in her death, he will not let himself be outmourned,
not by anyone, and especially not by that male rival who is her dear
brother, Laertes. But then, is he really mourning Ophelia, or is he
"mourning the phallus"?

And while Lacan is certainly more than clever enough to point out
the narcissistic demand at the core of this syndrome as well as the
response of the subject's imaginary to "the necessity of this mourning,"
he does not especially pursue the aggressivity one would also expect to
find (and which one does find in Hamlet, Tasso, and others) as a result
of what seems to be *the* narcissistic wound. The likeness here to melancholia is also striking. Woman as phallus (not the same as the phallic
woman, which is basically a transvestite male fantasy) is the formerly
loved object, now loathed and abused if alive, or ostentatiously mourned
if dead—indeed one wonders if the aggressivity here is not about a
desire to mourn, a desire whose unspoken supposition is nothing less
than the prior death of the object. The lost (or rejected) object reappears
inside the subject as that part of the ego under the judgmental gaze and
punishing force of the superego. And, contrary to Freud, the hatred
directed to that "inferior" part of the self seems easily transposable to
and from those others whom the subject considers socially or culturally
inferior to itself; women, the *vulgus*, foreigners, and so on. Mourning
the phallus does not mean—far from it—any empathy or complicity
with other, disempowered subjectivities!

Even Lacan, whose astute analyses here and elsewhere have disclosed
the ruses of phallocracy, in the last pages of "Desire and the Interpretation of Desire in *Hamlet*" raises (whether gleefully or mournfully) the
question of where the phallus has gone, of its possible death: "One
cannot strike the phallus, because the phallus, even the real phallus, is

a *ghost*" (p. 50, Lacan's emphasis); "the phallus . . . always slips through
your fingers" (p. 52). Assuming, as others have, that Ophelia's death is
"suicide" and Gertrude's presence is "dominating," Lacan's reading still
remains strongly identified with Hamlet's point of view, that "something
is rotten in Denmark" because there has been "insufficient mourning."
Interestingly enough, this charge of insufficiency, as opposed to the
humanist criticism of women mourning too much, comes about when
what is to be mourned is nothing other than the phallus, and it becomes
especially interesting given that those who ask that we mourn that
"something more" whose mysterious lack haunted Freud's analysis are
men or male characters. Perhaps it is a disregard for this particular object
of mourning that constitutes Gertrude's unforgivable crime. Petrarch's
objection, it should be remembered, was to the uproar caused by a
woman's funeral; he did, after all, invite women—along with himself
and all other natural entities—to mourn the loss of the male poet Cino
da Pistoia. In *Hamlet*, the old king is seen to be "insufficiently" mourned,
but the funeral rites given to Ophelia are considered by the clown-
gravediggers and the critics alike in excess, especially given the "questionable" nature of her death. To have *willingly* or intentionally taken
her own life (the legal definition of suicide), Ophelia could *not* have
been mad—or her madness would have had to be "feigned," but nobody
seems interested in raising that question or in crediting her distraught
state of mind with any creative inspiration or illumination. Instead, like
Ficino's heavenly Venus become old man Saturn, Ophelia becomes "the
equivalent of" the phallus,—something men can feel is worthy of mourning, be it in bonding or in rivalry.

As I have tried to show, then, melancholia is a gendered form of
ethos that is empowered by notions of lack; at the same time, it finds
its source of empowerment in the *devaluing* of the historical reality of
women's disempowerment. That is, it appropriates from women's subjectivities their "real" sense of loss. Melancholia works as a form of
possessive individualism that allows one both to publicize and to pri-
vatize one's specific eros at the expense of other marginalized positions
by a conspicuous display of privileged subjectivity. Furthermore, the
specificity of the myth of melancholia is seen to work for those who
have power or leisure (the prince or courtier, but also the artist, the
writer, the intellectual) and are therefore able to entertain loss and to
capitalize on it. Not only does the melancholic credit himself with a

value based on gender and class, but melancholia also points to a particular way in which eros and sexuality are recuperated within the male subject via a given aesthetics. This erotic aesthetics of the melancholic thus internalizes specifically dichotomized relations in society, between men and women, between dominance and disempowerment—and then reproduces them as ideality and as presence. By such a synthetic maneuver, the polarization between power and submission finds its nodal point, as Freud has shown, from a *sense* of loss.

And if, as Freud argues, "the male sex has taken the lead in the production of culture," then are we not to assume that in melancholia the same division reigns? In acknowledging Hamlet's higher moral nature in "Mourning and Melancholia," an essay where, as we have noticed, Hamlet is the only recognizable persona, Freud is taking a literary representation as an exemplum of (male) humanity at its most poignant. This possible generalization is, of course, quite limited. One suspects how substitutible Hamlet would be in historical, literary, and psychological terms by Petrarch, Ficino, Tasso, and others. Could one, on the other hand, credibly substitute for Hamlet either Gaspara Stampa, Isabella di Morra, or Louise Labé? Mournful women are reduced to the banality and particularity of their existences and times, whereas melancholy men become exemplary of the "human condition."

It also seems that when we have a male representation of a melancholic in a literary figure, then that melancholic subject is considered to speak for a larger community. "He" speaks for "our" collective sense of loss, the claim similarly made on "our" behalf (whose behalf?) by the postmodern thinkers cited at the beginning of this study. And indeed the name of Hamlet is not surprisingly invoked by a number of recent postmodernists. Understanding (their) history as loss, male melancholic voices, whether Renaissance or postmodern, speak of some epochal historical change that supposedly leaves them, and with them all of "us," in some state of lack and loss. More than just a clinical case and more than just depressed, the melancholic thinker has an accredited lack (even if he suffers that most impressive lack of lacking a lack, of lacking nothing), one that supposedly speaks for all of us. The question remains, though, of *who* can continue to appropriate the notion of lack in such a way as to phallicize its implications. To mourn the phallus may be a way to maintain its centrality; and in this way, melancholia may serve to assuage the sense of symbolic castration.

One cannot help but wonder whether a certain current male critique of patriarchy is not the ultimate ruse or feint of phallocracy. Lacan's ghostlike phallus that "always slips through your fingers" is all the more imposing for its transcendent immateriality, and as such it recalls a Ficinian eros, whose rejection of the world of matter, as we remember, was also a rejection of women. One wonders too about the recent rise of "male" feminism, and about the implicit displacement of women's positions by those who in their haste to "speak like a woman" must therefore reduce the sociopolitical positioning of gender to nothing more than a position in rhetoric, to a discursive stance or an assumed "voice." If Hamlet's madness, the madness of melancholia, could be "feigned," today's melancholy postmodernists act as if gender could also be feigned. To argue the social construction of gender roles one does not need to contradict or underestimate the material reality of phallic power and of a symbolic order that continues to organize the world we live in according to a hierarchical masculinism. To reduce gender "roles," on the other hand, to the ease of cross-dressing is to risk a facile, and dangerous, utopianism that all too easily allows all of us (women *and* men) to deny or ignore the consequences of the ways in which we *are* implicated in current relations of empowerment and disempowerment. To understand the phallocentric symbolic order of the West as historically bound and therefore changeable is not to misrecognize the difficulty and real political work implied in bringing about an alternative.

Nor is it enough simply to dance on the tomb of phallocentrism in some Nietzschean deconstructive celebration of the end of man or the death of the subject. Not to mention that such a celebration may be premature, a funeral service for the demise of the phallus is not enough. Rather than mourn the phallus or bemoan our supposedly "melancholy" era, feminism today should seek out the possibility of new symbolic orders, feminine ones. From the standpoint of the gendering of melancholia, one could at least envision a more positive accrediting if not working through of women's losses, a radical affirmation of mourning. Even more so, to rethink mourning from a feminist point of view is to revalue the emotional representation of grief as a process of reasoning very different from classic male rationality or its irrational opposites of mysticism and demagoguery. Mourning could thereby provide a model for revaluation of that traditionally disparaged realm of supposed femininity, the emotions.[31] Psychoanalysis, of course, has shown emotional

---

[31]The possibility and necessity of a feminist rethinking of emotion are the subject of

life to be rooted in the unconscious logic of libidinal investments with
the aim of undoing the ego as the privileged site of consciousness. A
feminist discourse of the emotions would go beyond psychoanalysis,
however, by understanding emotional processes such as mourning to
be not just the undermining of the ego but a positive form of social
and psychical reasoning.

ongoing research by Kathleen Woodward and the topic of an important conference, "Discourses of the Emotions," organized by her and the Center for Twentieth Century Studies at
the University of Wisconsin–Milwaukee in April 1990. With reference to the issue of grief
and mourning in a psychoanalytic context, see especially her "Between Mourning and Melancholia: Roland Barthes's *Camera Lucida*," in *Aging and Its Discontents* (Bloomington: Indiana
University Press, 1991), pp. 87–105. Also see Stephanie A. Shields, "Gender in the Psychology
of Emotion: A Selective Research Review," in *International Review of Studies on Emotion*, ed.
K. T. Strongman (New York: John Wiley & Sons, 1991), and her forthcoming book tentatively
titled *Gender and the Social Meaning of Emotion*. For recent scholarship on melancholy and
mourning in medieval and Renaissance texts, see Louise O. Fradenburg, " 'Voice Memorial':
Loss and Reparation in Chaucer's Poetry," *Exemplaria* 2.1 (March 1990), 171–202; and
Timothy Murray, "Translating Montaigne's Crypts: Melancholie Relations and the Sites of
Altarbiography," forthcoming in *Bucknell Review*.

Index

Abraham, Karl, 34n.3, 36
Abraham, Nicholas, 53n, 240
Absence. *See* Lack; Laura; Loss; Women: absence of, from melancholic cultural tradition
Accrediting: of melancholia and lack. *See* Melancholia: as accredited pathology
Acedia, 6–7, 98, 104, 154
Adam's fall. *See* Sin
Agamben, Giorgio, 3n.6, 4n.9, 53n, 98, 104n, 110–12
Ajax, 6, 105
Aleramo, Sibilla, 30n.56
Alfonso of Ferrara (Duke), 191, 192, 194, 195, 216, 218, 219, 221–22, 224–26, 234
Alienation. *See* Marginalization
Allen, Beverly, 4n.8
Allen, Michael J. B., 120n.29
"Alone and filled with care" (Petrarch), 6, 199
Anatomy of Melancholy (Burton), 2, 5, 21, 200, 243–56, 257; definition of melancholia in, 35
Anger: di Morra's, 179–80; Irigaray's, 110; Kristeva's, at women, 89
Anorexia nervosa, 55
Antoniano, Silvio, 194
Anxiety: and melancholia, 98
"Aphanisis of being," 27, 76
Aphorismata, 98n.4
Aphrodite, 106

Apologia (Tasso), 194
Aquinas, Thomas, 140
Aragona, Tullia d', 168
Archelaus (king of Macedonia), 105
Aristotle, 127, 239; and gender differences, 17, 18, 104–8, 113, 114, 115, 139, 151; and melancholic tradition, x, 6, 7, 94, 101–12, 126, 141, 142, 145, 157, 198, 261
Armida (character), 208, 213, 224
Artists: melancholic. *See* Genius
Augustine, 140
Aurélia (Nerval), 87
Avicenna, 14

Babb, Lawrence, 4n.9, 98n.4, 233, 234, 235, 244n
Bal, Mieke, 22n.36
Barasch, Moshe, 162n.2
Barker, Francis, 236–38, 241, 261
Barolini, Teodolinda, 168n.14
Basile, Bruno, 206n.23
Baudelaire, Charles, 83, 110
Beecher, Donald A., 97n.1
Beilin, Elaine V., 4n.8
Belatedness, 255
Bellamy, Elizabeth, 25
Bellerophon, 6, 105, 110, 198
Bembo, Bernardo, 161
Benjamin, Jessica, 76n.31, 145n, 148n.50, 167n.11

[269]

Benjamin, Walter, 3, 17, 21, 142, 255n.23, 256–59
Bennett, William, 2
Bentivoglio, Cornelio, 226
Bernard of Gordon (Doctor), 100
Bernheimer, Charles, 22n.37
Bestiality: in melancholia, 143–48
Bile. *See* Black bile
Billington, Sandra, 51n
Birth metaphors: in Tasso's work, 197, 228–29
Black bile: and melancholia, 6, 8, 97, 102–3, 106, 127, 129–33, 142, 150–51, 155
Black Sun: Depression and Melancholia (Kristeva), 17, 77, 80n, 81, 92n
Blayney, Margaret S., 98n.6
Blood: and melancholia, 126–32, 155; and women, 107; and women's melancholia, 150, 151, 154
Bloom, Allen, 2
Bloom, Harold, 255n.26
Boccaccio, Giovanni, 6
Boer, Charles, 131, 133, 163n.4
Bowlby, John, 16n
Brand, C. P., 20, 193n.5, 218n.34, 234
Brenkman, John, 24n.43
Brennan, Teresa, 27n.51
Bright, Timothy, 233
Brilli, Attilio, 4n.9
Brown, Norman O., 227
Bruni, Leonardo, 161, 180n, 181n.36
Burton, Robert, x, 2, 5, 14–15, 17, 21, 22, 35, 61, 83, 200, 235n.7, 243–57; on women melancholics, 58n. *See also Anatomy of Melancholy*
Butler, Judith, 158n.58
Byron, George Gordon, 19

Calvin, John, 216–17
Cannibalism, 148. *See also* Bestiality
Canon: and repression of women's loss, 187–90
"Canzone al Metauro" (Tasso), 18, 88, 174, 176, 182, 191, 192, 195, 213, 219, 221
Canzoniere (Petrarch), 167
Carrara, Francesco da, 163
"Case of Successful Treatment by Hypnotism, A" (Freud), 57n
Caserta (author of *Isabella Morra*), 177
Castiglione, Baldessare, 146n, 180n
Castration, 158; and lack, 29, 31, 41, 48, 57, 64–67, 70–71, 80, 93, 99, 119, 200–203, 261–63, 265; male identification with women as, 211, 219–20, 252–55. *See also* Hydra; "Open

wound" metaphor; Phallus; Women: devaluing of, in melancholic cultural tradition
Causae et curae (Hildegard of Bingen), 142
Cavalcanti, Giovanni, 113, 117n, 139
Cervigni, Dino S., 4n.8
Chartier, Alaine, 98, 104, 252
Chase, Cynthia, 79n.33, 80n
Chateaubriand, François René, 3, 83
Chatterton (character in Vigny play), 3
Ciavolella, Massimo, 97n.1
Cino da Pistoia, 264
Circe, 136, 219, 220, 224, 231
Cixous, Hélène, 208n
Claudius (character), 238–42, 254
Clinical depression. *See* Depression
Clorinda (character), 203–7, 213, 224, 231
Cocalis, Susan L., 4n.8
Colby, Alice, 99n
Coleridge, Samuel Taylor, 110
Colonna, Victoria, 169
Communicativeness: of the melancholic. *See* Talk: and the melancholic
Community: and women, 66, 76
Conscience. *See* Superego
"Conscientious woman": Aristotle's prefiguring of, 109, 139; Burton's version of, 251; Freud's conception of, 55, 59–61, 65
Convictionem, 145–47
Convivium, 145–47
Copernicus, 202n.20
Corsi, Giovanni, 160
Couliano, Ioan F., 100, 168n.15
Creativity. *See* Genius
Crébillon, Prosper, 91
Crimp, Douglas, 190n.45
Croce, Bendetto, 175, 187
Cropper, Elizabeth, 14n.28
"Cry, women, and let love weep with you" (Petrarch), 171–72
"Cry, women, and let love weep with you" (Stampa), 171–72

Dame Malencolye. *See* Merencolyie
Dame Mérencolye. *See* Merencolyie
Daniele, Antonio, 174n.28
Dante Alighieri, 6, 206n.22
De amore (Ficino). See *On Love* (Ficino)
Death. *See* Funeral practices; Mourning
Debate between Melancholy and Mirth (Filidor), 101
Decadents: and melancholia, 3
de Certeau, Michel, 3n.6, 22n.36, 111n.19, 255, 256n.27

Dehumanization: of melancholics. *See* Bestiality
Dekker, Thomas, 234
Deleuze, Gilles, 84
Democritus, 110
Depression, ix; causes of, 76–77; contrasted with melancholia, 84–85, 93–95; description of, 64; as devalued condition, 16, 75, 93–95; drugs for, 78; as female form of melancholia, 4, 16, 57, 61, 68–69, 86, 88–89, 93–95; and hysteria, 57; Kristeva's cure for, 77–81; refiguring of women's, 68–69, 77, 79, 93; Silverman's cure for, 77, 79; as symptom of melancholia, 98; as women's essential status, 81, 93. *See also* Melancholia
De Quincey, Thomas, 3, 110
Derrida, Jacques, 1n.1, 28n.53, 36, 40n, 133, 230n.42
"Desdichado, El" (Nerval), 86–88
Desire: and lack, 28–29, 111–12, 116–18, 166, 262–63; to be mourned, 210–12. *See also* Incorporation
"Desire and the Interpretation of Desire in *Hamlet*" (Lacan), 243, 263
Devil. *See* Sin
De Vita (Ficino). See *On Life* (Ficino)
di Collato, Collatino (Count), 171
Didi-Hubermann, Georges, 22n.37
"Did Women Have a Renaissance?" (Kelly), 165–66
di Morra, Isabella, x, 18, 166, 173–90, 265
di Morra of Favale, Giovanni Michele, 174
Dionysius, 106
Diotima, 126
"Discorso della virtù feminile e donnesca" (Tasso), 218
Disempowerment: melancholic men's feelings of, 8, 9–10. *See also* Women: devaluing of, in melancholic cultural tradition
"Divine frenzy," 7, 58, 111, 115
"Divine" madness. *See* Genius; Madness; Tasso, Torquato
Doane, Janice, 31–32
Donadoni, Eugenio, 169
Donne, John, 110
Dora, 57n
Dostoevsky, Feodor, 3, 86, 91
Dronke, Peter, 4n.8, 142n.43
Duras, Marguerite, 86, 89–91
Dürer, Albrecht, 2, 5, 12, 61, 110, 125, 154, 253–54

Eagleton, Terry, 236–38, 241, 261
Ears, 229–30, 240

Echidna, 201
Echo, 168
Eckstein, Emma, 41n
Ego and the Id, The (Freud), 36, 65, 70
Ehrenreich, Barbara, 94, 96
Eissler, K. P., 239
Eliot, T. S., 240
Emma (Frau), 57n
Empedocles, 6, 105
Empowerment: Irigaray's understanding of female, 110; of melancholic males, 11–12, 16, 94–95
English, Dierdre, 94, 96
Enlightenment: and melancholia, 3
Enterline, Lynn, 174n.28, 186n, 210n.26
Ercole II, 216–17
Erminia (character), 209–10, 213
Eros: and melancholia, 245–46, 260, 265, 266. *See also* Love; Venus
Eros and Magic in the Renaissance (Couliano), 100
Erotomania, 10n.23, 96
Errico, Scipio, 234n.6
Essentialism, 30n.56, 69n.28, 93
Ethics: mimetic, in Ficino's work, 138–39
Eve: absence of, from Hildegard of Bingen's analysis, 157
Exile. *See* Loss
Eyes, 230

Falagan, Sabina, 142n.43
Fannio, Camillo, 217
Fascism: and nostalgia, 68n
Father(s): devil as, 158n.57; in Freud, 159; and Renaissance children, 181–85; Tasso's appeals to, 192–93, 221–23. *See also* Alfonso of Ferrara; God; Law of the Father; Patriarchy; Superego; Tasso, Bernardo
Feldstein, Richard, 25n.48
Felman, Shoshana, 22n.36
Female: characteristics of, according to Aristotle, 106–8
"Female Sexuality" (Freud), 70, 71–72
Femininity: Hamlet's appropriation and exclusion of, 21; as a *horror vacuus*, 48; Kelly's definition of, 30; men's appropriation of, x, 10–14, 31–32, 186, 252–54; and mourning, 210–12; as representation of men's loss, 165, 167–68; Tasso's appropriation of, 20. *See also* Feminization; Males: sensitive; Mother(s)
Feminism: its critique of discourse of melancholia, 21, 25–32, 266–67; male participation in, 266

Feminist criticism: di Morra's strategy of, 189–90
Feminization: men's fear of, 31–32. *See also* Castration; Males: sensitive
Ferenczi, Sandor, 34n.4
Ferguson, Margaret W., 174n.28, 183n.40, 193n.4, 194n.9, 206n.22, 218n.34
Ferrand, Jacques, 96n
Ferrara, Duke of. *See* Alfonso of Ferrara
Ferroni, Giulio, 187–88
Fetishism: of the body, 224–30; and melancholia, 47–48, 85–86, 89, 260; of women's absence, 165
Ficinian tradition, 62, 94, 170, 197, 198, 223, 233, 262
Ficino, Dietifeci, 128
Ficino, Marsilio, 22, 84, 145, 146, 148, 154, 200, 220; on death and mourning, 160–61; gender bias of, in discussions of melancholia, 18, 239; as melancholic, ix, x, 3, 7–9, 55, 211, 237; and melancholic tradition, 11, 13, 17, 61, 93, 101, 104, 110–43, 150, 157–59, 166, 222, 243–45, 265. *See also* Ficinian tradition; *titles of works*
Filidor, 101
Fineman, Joel, 243n.18
Finitude vs. infinitude: in melancholia, 19, 29, 140, 170–71, 190, 211, 212
Fliess, Wilhelm, 41n
Flores, Angel, 4n.8
Flores, Kate, 4n.8
Fool: as metaphor for melancholic, 51
Forgiveness. *See* Pardon
Fortinbras (character), 240–41
Fortune: in di Morra's and Tasso's works, 175–77, 179, 213, 219, 224
Foscolo, Ugo, 216
Foucault, Michel, 27, 36, 199n
Fox, Ruth, 243, 248–49
Frandenburg, Louise O., 267n
Freccero, John, 167n.12
Freud, Sigmund, 21, 25, 73, 83, 84, 102, 108, 110, 124, 150, 158n.57, 206n.22, 215, 224, 225, 232, 238, 263; and castration complexes, 63, 179; gender bias of, in discussions of melancholia, 17, 33–63, 65, 76n.31, 105, 144, 145, 164, 187; influence of the Renaissance on, 26; and melancholic tradition, 3, 18, 21, 22, 93, 110–11, 118–19, 148, 195–96, 200–202, 207; and Oedipus complex in girls, 70–71. *See also* "Mourning and Melancholia"; Superego; *titles of other works*
Freud, Sophie, 35n

Fuffezio, Mezio, 220, 231
Funeral practices: Renaissance, 160–66, 213
Fusco, Mario, 186n, 193
Fuss, Diana, 30n.56

Galen, 97, 98, 111, 115, 248
Gallop, Jane, 27n.49, 208n.25
Garner, Shirley Nelson, 67n
Gaze: God's, 156; and love, 120, 122; patriarchal, 238–39; redemptive, 223; women as object of male, 166, 167, 170
Gender. *See* Female; Femininity; Males; Melancholia: discourse of; Women
Generation of Animals, The (Aristotle), 107
Genius: and melancholy, ix–xi, 5–9, 11–12, 16, 19, 49, 84–86, 95, 101–16, 128–33, 141–42, 203, 244–45, 248, 252, 256; Tasso as model for melancholic, 185–86, 191–232
Gertrude (character), x, 10, 83, 96, 240–43, 260, 261, 264
Gerusalemme liberata (Tasso), 20, 193, 194, 195, 203–12, 219, 223, 228
Getto, Giovanni, 206n.23
Giard, Luce, 141n.39
Gilbert, Sandra, 238n
Gilman, Sander, 12n.24
God: melancholy as loss of closeness to, 246, 255–56
Godfrey (character), 208–9
Goethe, Johann Wolfgang von, 19, 185, 191
Greenberg, Mitchell, 256n.27
Greenblatt, Stephen, 23–25, 26, 237
Grief. *See* Mourning; Suffering
Grosz, Elizabeth, 92n
Group Psychology and the Analysis of the Ego (Freud), 36, 40
Guarini, Alessandro, 234n.6
Guattari, Félix, 84
Gubar, Susan, 238n
Guglielminetti, Marziano, 194n.7

H., Mathilde, 57n
Haizmann, Christoph, 57
Hamlet (character): Burton's view of, 246; as melancholic, ix, x, 2, 3, 5, 8–11, 20, 21, 49, 58–62, 65, 96, 226, 232, 258; as sensitive man, 238–39, 242. *See also* *Hamlet* (Shakespeare); Lacan, Jacques; Rose, Jacqueline
Hamlet (Shakespeare), x, 10–11, 55, 88, 110, 233–43, 256, 265. *See also* Claudius; Fortinbras; Gertrude; Hamlet; Laertes; Ophelia

Index

Happiness: Ficino's view of, 140
Hegel, G. W. F., 211n
Hera, 201
Heracles, 6, 102, 104, 110
Heraclites, 110
Hercules, 221–22, 237
Hereos (illness), 100
Heresy: Tasso's self-accusations about, 193–94, 218–19
Hertz, Neil, 200
Hesiod, 201
Hildegard of Bingen, x; analysis of melancholia by, 18, 98, 141–59, 246
Hippocrates: on melancholia, 97, 244
Hirsch, Marianne, 76n.31
Histoires d'amour (Kristeva), 80n
History: as loss, 255–56, 257, 265
History of Animals, The (Aristotle), 107
Hodges, Devon, 31–32
Holbein, Hans, 86, 87, 89
Hölderlin, Friedrich, 3, 19
Hole: women as, 64–65. *See also Horror vacuus*; "Open wound" metaphor
Homer, 198–99
Homoeroticism, 120n.29, 121–24
Homosexuality, 120n.29, 121–24
Horror vacuus, 48, 202, 208, 212, 228, 237
"How a Ruler Ought to Govern His State" (Petrarch), 163
Hughes, Diane Owen, 12n.25, 163n.4, 165
Humanism: and the enforced privatization of women, 161–65
Humoral medicine: and melancholia, 18, 96–112, 115–16, 126–28, 141–59. *See also* Black bile; Blood
Huysmans, Cornelis, 110
Hydra: Burton's use of, 247–48; as misogynistic metaphor, 83; as Renaissance metaphor, 21, 221, 237; Tasso's use of, 196, 200–207, 213, 219, 223, 224, 231, 254
Hyperactivity. *See* Talk
Hysteria, 246, 250; difference from melancholia of, 17, 36, 44–46, 52, 55–57, 61–62; ideological paradigms and, 22, 61; Irigaray's view of, 66, 110; in melancholia, 85–86, 89

Identification: and melancholia, 43–47, 54–56, 60, 72, 76
"I do not envy you at all, holy angels" (Stampa), 170
Inarticulateness. *See* Talk
Incorporation: of lost object of desire, 52, 73, 80, 111–12, 116, 147–49, 185, 228, 232

Infertility: in women, 151–54
Infinitude. *See* Finitude vs. infinitude
Inspiration. *See* Genius
Interiority: in *Hamlet*, 236–37
Intersubjectivity, 76n.31, 166, 262
Introjection: of loss, 52, 80
Invective. *See* Anger
Irigaray, Luce, x, 72, 138n; and essentialism, 30n.56; and hysteria, 110; and question of female melancholia, 17, 63–69, 74–75, 93

Jackson, Stanley W., 4n.9, 15, 16n.33, 244n, 255
Jameson, Fredric, 23n.40
Jayne, Sears, 140
Jewell, Keala Jane, 4n.8
Jonard, N., 186n
Jones, Ann Rosalind, 168
Jones, Ernest, 33–35, 240
Jordan, Constance, 4n.8
Judaism, 91n
Jung, Carl Gustav, 23n.39
Jungian movement, 22, 23n.39
Jupiter, 117, 221–23, 252

Kahane, Claire, 22n.37, 67n
Kaplan, Alice Yaeger, 68
Kelly, Joan, 30, 54n, 165–66, 180
Kennedy, William J., 165n.8, 170n.20
Keto, 201
King, Margaret L., 165n.8, 181n.36
Kittel, Muriel, 4n.8
Klapisch-Zuber, Christiane, 162n.2
Klein, Melanie, 15–16n.32
Klibansky, Raymond, 4, 6, 12n.24, 97, 98, 104, 112, 115, 153, 167
Knowledge: Ficino's view of, 116, 118
Kofman, Sarah, 178n.33, 181n.36, 250
Kohut, Heinz, 239n.14
Kristeller, Paul Oscar, 120n.29, 133
Kristeva, Julia, x, 1n.2, 22, 236n.8; and matricidal therapy, 17, 77–93; and melancholic tradition, 17

Labé, Louise, 173, 265
Lacan, Jacques, 111n.20, 118n, 145n, 168n.15; and *Hamlet*, 10n.23, 21, 238, 243, 256, 259–64, 266; revision of psychoanalysis by, 23–29, 64, 67, 76, 148; terminology of, 8, 13, 24, 76, 93, 108, 158, 229. *See also* Law of the Father
Lack: definition of politics of, ix; gender bias in psychoanalytic views of, 27–31; in Hamlet, 237–38; in melancholic tradition, ix–xi, 8, 11, 111–41, 226, 264;

Lack (*cont.*)
 poetics of, 167; women as, 64–65, 73–
 76, 107, 118, 178. *See also* Castration;
 Desire; Erotomania; Loss; Phallus
Laclau, Ernesto, 32n.60, 183n.39
Lacoue-Labarthe, Philippe, 11n.4
Laertes (character), 242, 263
Laplanche, J., 44
LaRochefoucauld, François, 83
Laura (Petrarch's), 149n.52, 165, 167–68,
 171
Lauretis, Teresa de, 30n.56, 32n.60,
 179n.35, 189n, 208
Law of the Father, 26–27, 53–54, 56, 60,
 65, 68, 73–74
Le Doeuff, Michèle, 56n.18
Leonardo da Vinci, 26
Lévi-Strauss, Claude, 40n
Life of Dante (Boccaccio), 6
Lilium medicinale (Doctor Bernard of
 Gordon), 100
Lingua, 225–28, 240
Loraux, Nicole, 210n.27
Loss: cultural representation of men's and
 women's, ix, 5, 10–13, 165; poetics of,
 1–2, 27–28, 160–90; imaginary vs.
 actual, 5, 10–13, 186–87, 259, 261–62,
 265; sense of, in melancholia, 36–48,
 261–62. *See also* Desire; Lack;
 Melancholia; Mourning; Narcissism;
 Nostalgia; Separation
Love: Ficino's view of, 116–28, 134–35
Loyola, Ignatius of, 237
Lucretius, 127
Lycanthropy, 147n.49
Lyons, Bridget Gellert, 97n.1, 234, 235n.7
Lyotard, Jean-François, 11n.3, 3n.5, 68n,
 177n.31
Lysander the Syracusan, 105

MacCannell, Juliet Flower, 27n.51, 145n,
 148n.51
McGrady, Donald, 192n
MacLean, Ian, 106n
McManamon, John, 165n.8
Madness: and feigning of, 234–36, 259,
 266. *See also Soverchia maninconia*; Tasso,
 Torquato
Males: sensitive, x, 10, 12–14, 21, 31–32,
 120n.29, 248; and superego, 53–54. *See
 also* Hamlet: as sensitive man; Men
Malleus Maleficarum, 100
Manetti, Giannozzo, 161
Mania: and melancholia, 39–40, 49, 57–58,
 145, 199. *See also* "Divine frenzy"

Manso, Gianbattista, 185, 191, 234n.6
Maracus the Syracusan (poet), 103, 105,
 110
Marginalization: and male melancholy, 10,
 20, 50–51, 197–98, 257–58
Marin, Louis, 211n
Marivaux, Pierre de, 91
Marot, Clèment, 216
Mars (god), 135, 221
Mars (planet), 114
Martino, Ernest de, 162n.2
Martyrdom: of melancholics. *See* Suffering
Mater dolorosa, 13n.27
Matricide: as cure for women's depression,
 77–81, 83, 89–93
Medici, Catherine de, 238n
Medici, Cosimo de, 128, 139
Medici, Lorenzo de, 125
Medici family, 140
Medusa: as misogynistic metaphor, 83,
 200–201
Melancholia, ix; as accredited pathology, 9,
 17, 28–29, 38, 62, 68–69, 94–95; as
 affliction women bring on men, 18, 94,
 96, 99–101, 136, 253–54; and
 appropriation of women's losses, 175–90,
 191–232, 264; boundaries of age of, 2–
 3; cultural tradition of, x, 1–32, 74–75,
 94–95; definitions of, 35–40, 43;
 discourse of, 15–17, 61–69, 74–75, 236,
 258–59; Elizabethan, 233–34. French,
 83–84, 91, 236n.8; and imaginary losses,
 5, 10–11, 32, 36–43, 93, 186; as male
 disorder, 56, 61, 75, 105, 112, 143–50;
 185–86; medical tradition of, 14–15,
 96–112, 243–56; origins of word, 6, 94;
 symptoms of, 97–98, 102–4, 143–50,
 249, 261. *See also* Castration; Genius;
 Loss; Mania; Melancholics; Morality;
 Mourning; "Mourning and Melancholia";
 Self-display; Women.
"Melancholia" (Freud), 55
Melancholia and Depression (Jackson), 33
Melancholics: children of, 149–50; named
 and unnamed, 58–61, 88–89, 105, 164
"Melancholy and Melancholia" (Radden),
 93–96
Melanchton, 237
Meltzer, Françoise, 22n.36
Men: feminist, 266; lack of, as cause of
 female melancholia, 14–15, 58, 60–61,
 250–52, 255–56. *See also* Males;
 Patriarchy; Phallus
Menstruation. *See* Blood
Mercatus, 249

Mercury (god), 135
Mercury (planet), 129, 130
Merencolyie (character), 98–99, 104
Messaggiero, Il (Tasso), 195–97, 206–7,
  212, 213, 226, 228–31, 234
Michelangelo Buonarroti, 8, 26, 110
Migiel, Marilyn, 186n, 204n, 210n.26,
  238n
Misogyny: in Aristotle, 106–9; in Burton,
  243–254; in Ficino, 124; in *Hamlet*,
  260; images of, 83, 136, 200–201; in
  Kristeva's work, 77–93; and melancholia,
  144–45, 243, 245, 250–52; in
  melancholia discourses, 18, 96–101, 239,
  250–51; in seduction rituals, 146
Mitchell, Juliet, 25
Modleski, Tania, 32n.59
Moi, Toril, 30n.56, 56n.18
Molière, Jean Baptiste, 8
Montaigne, Michel de, 19, 237
Montanari, Fausto, 202n.20
Montecatini, 193–94
Moon, Michael, 190n.45
Moral conscience: and Burton, 246. See also
  Superego
Morality: in Hamlet, 58–60; heightened
  sense of, among melancholics, 5, 8–11,
  49–54, 265. See also Truth
Mother(s): daughters' relations with, and
  melancholia, 17, 63–95; fixation on, 48;
  Freud's repression of, 41n; in male
  writers' nostalgic fantasies, 32; in Nerval's
  work, 88; as primordial lost object, 54,
  78; in Tasso's work, 182–86. See also
  Matricide; Separation
"Motherhood According to Bellini"
  (Kristeva), 92n
Mouffe, Chantal, 32n.60, 183n.39
Mourning, ix, 17, 160–90; Burton's view
  of men's, 254–55; call for affirmation of,
  266–67; and concrete losses, 5, 16, 36–
  39; in contemporary society, 1–2;
  devaluing of women's, 95, 208–10;
  differentiated from melancholia, 35–38,
  232; as female ritual, xi, 12, 18, 61–62,
  77; Gertrude's, 240–42, 261; Hamlet's,
  259–64; men's appropriation of, 219,
  242–43, 256; poetics of, 166;
  Renaissance assault on women's, 18,
  160–66, 213; women's communal, 168–
  73, 190; women's reasons for, 17; of
  women's relationship to their mothers,
  75–77, 80, 190. See also Desire; History;
  Melancholia; "Mourning and
  Melancholia"; *Trauerspiel*

"Mourning and Melancholia" (Freud), x, 5,
  8–12, 19, 33–63, 66, 73, 81, 83, 112,
  187, 235–36, 250, 264, 265; gender bias
  in, 17, 75
Murray, Timothy J., 67n, 267n
Mysticism, 255

Names. See Melancholics: named and
  unnamed
Nancy, Jean-Luc, 190n.46
Narcissism: in di Morra, 178–79; in girls,
  63–67, 70, 72, 74, 178–79; in
  melancholia, 17, 36, 43–52, 54–57, 119–
  21, 159, 238, 263; in Tasso, 178–79,
  192, 202, 203, 211, 213, 215–16, 228.
  See also Self-display
Neoplatonism, 114–16, 161, 235. See also
  Ficino, Marsilio
Nerval, Gérard de, 3, 19, 83, 86–88, 91,
  92, 110
Newfield, Christopher, 32n.59, 112n,
  120n.29
New Introductory Lectures on Psychoanalysis
  (Freud), 36
Newman, Barbara, 142n.43
Nostalgia: and fascism, 68; and
  melancholia, 11, 31, 32, 167–68, 239,
  246
Nostalgia and Sexual Difference (Doane and
  Hodges), 31
Nothingness. See Lack

Obedience: and women, 109
Objectification: in melancholia, 9–10, 11
Oedipal rivalry. See Father(s)
Oedipal tragedy: *Hamlet* as, 238–39, 259–
  64
Oedipus complex: female versions of, 69–
  77, 80, 83, 87
"O figlie di Renata" (Tasso), 195, 214–22,
  225, 231
"O magnanimo Figlio" (Tasso), 195, 221,
  227
"On Femininity" (Freud), 53, 60, 70, 71
On Life (Ficino), 18, 113, 114, 128–30,
  142, 200, 243
On Love (Ficino), 18, 115, 121–22, 125,
  129, 131, 134, 137–38, 145
"Open wound" metaphor, 40–41, 47–48,
  52, 57, 202–3, 254. See also Castration;
  Hole; *Horror vacuus*
Ophelia (character), x, 10, 55, 96n, 240,
  242, 260–64
Orestes, 198
Orgasms: Kristeva's views on, 89

Origin of German Tragic Drama, The
(Benjamin), 256–59
Orwell, George, 29
Ovid, 168

P., Frau, 57n
Pallas, 252
Panofsky, Erwin, 4, 6, 12n.24, 97, 98, 104,
112, 115, 153, 167
Pardon, 86; Tasso's search for, 192
Parthenope, 183
Pascal, Blaise, 83
Pateman, Carol, 164
Patriarchy: and female melancholia, 17, 60,
67, 250–51; and Hamlet, 59; in Lacan's
scheme, 24, 26–27; and male
melancholia, 13–14, 93; reinforced by
Kristeva's views, 77–93; women's
invective against, 179–85. *See also* God;
Law of the Father; Misogyny; Phallus;
Superego
Penia, 116–18, 120
Pentheus, 198
Persecution: Tasso's, 193, 195
Petrarch, 199, 246; as melancholic, ix, x, 3,
6, 12n.30, 149n.52, 166, 211, 265; and
poetics of loss, 167–68, 170, 188; and
women's mourning, 18, 163–65, 213,
264
Petrocchi, Giorgio, 206n.23
Phaedrus (Plato), 127–28
Phallus: need for, as cause of women's
melancholia, 14–15, 58, 60–61, 250–52,
255–56; and the "open wound," 48;
relation of, to social order, 24, 25, 27,
93; woman as, 262–64. *See also*
Castration; Father(s); *Lingua*
Phoebus, 221
Philomel, 168
Philosopher: Ficino's depiction of, 140
Pico della Mirandola, Giovanni, 125
Pistoia, Cino da, 171
Plato, 133, 138n, 145, 146; Ficino's citing
of, 130–31, 134, 140; as melancholic, 6,
7, 105, 113, 125; works of, 115, 116,
117n, 127–28. *See also* Neoplatonism
Plutarch, 25n
Polan, Mary Lake, 105n
Politics, The (Aristotle), 109
Pontalis, J.-B., 44
Pontormo, Jacopo da, 110
Poovey, Mary, 25n.48
Porus, 116–18, 120
Problems XXX (Aristotle), 18, 101–12, 113,
114, 127
Procne, 168

Proust, Marcel, 83
Psychoanalysis: and feminism, 25–32; and
literature, 22–25, 62; as methodological
approach to Renaissance texts, x–xi, 21–
32
Ptolemy, 138n

Quarquagli, Cherubino, 139, 161
Quint, David, 218n.33, 219n

R., Lucy, 57n
Rabine, Leslie, 30n.56
Radden, Jennifer, 4n.7, 93–96
Rape: male fantasies of, 122
Rashkin, Esther, 53n
Rebel: melancholic as, 50–51
Renaissance: influence on Freud, 26; and
melancholia, 3, 21, 25; and nostalgia, 31,
55
Renata (Duchess of Ferrara). *See* "O figlie
di Renata"
Resistance: women's, in depression, 77
Revolution in Poetic Language (Kristeva), 81
Rhazes (Rhasis), 127, 248
Riley, Denise, 31n.56, 142n.43
Rimbaud, Arthur, 87
Rime sparse (Petrarch), 171
Robinson, Lillian S., 180n
Rocke, Michael J., 120n.29
Rodocanachi, E., 217n.31
Roffi, Mario, 217
Romances (medieval): melancholia in, 98–
99, 136
Romanticism: and melancholia, 3, 20
Roof, Judith, 25n.48
Rose, Jacqueline: and feminism, 25n.48,
32; on Hamlet, 9n.20, 10n.22, 59, 96n,
240, 259; on Lacan, 24n.42; on mothers,
182n
Rousseau, Jean Jacques, 3, 19, 83, 88
Ruggiero, Guido, 120n.29
Russell, Rinaldina, 175n

Salmons, J., 217n.33
Salutati, Coluccio, 161
Salviati, Lionardo, 194
Sanazzaro, Jacopo, 168
Sandoval Castro, Diego (Don), 174
Sappho, 96n, 143
Satan. *See* Sin
Saturn: and melancholy, 7, 97, 113–14,
117, 124–25, 128–30, 134–37, 139,
148, 158, 220, 221, 245
Saxl, Fritz, 4, 6, 12n.24, 97, 98, 104, 112,
115, 154, 167
Scarry, Elaine, 178n.32

Schiesari, Juliana, 4n.8, 109n, 147n.48, 184n, 210n.26, 238n
Schizophrenia, 84
Scholars: and melancholia. *See* Genius
Scholes, Robert, 30n.56
Schor, Naomi, 30n.56, 179n.33
Sedgwick, Eve Kosofsky, 32n.59, 120n.29
Seduction, 146–47
Self. *See* Subjectivity
Self-criticism. *See* Self-display
Self-display: Hamlet's, 257; and melancholia, 5–6, 9, 12, 43, 48–51, 226, 232, 235, 238–39, 264; Tasso's, 20. *See also* Narcissism
Sensitivity: in males. *See* Males: sensitive
Separation: from the father, 124; from the mother, 27–29, 72, 76–81
Sforza, Caterina, 238n
Shakespeare, William, 26, 88. *See also* *Hamlet*
Shields, Stephanie, 267n
Showalter, Elaine, 10n.23, 96n
Sibyls, 103, 105, 108
Silence: and women, 109, 181, 187. *See also* *Talk*
Silverman, Kaja, x, 27, 56n.17, 60n; and question of female melancholia, 17, 69–77, 79
Sin: and melancholia, 154–58, 246
"Since you have clipped the wings of the fine desire" (di Morra), 173
Sirens, 136, 183
Slavney, Philip R., 22n.37
Socrates, 109; as melancholic, 6, 105, 115, 125–27, 146, 254
Solerti, Angelo, 19n, 174n.28, 193, 216n.31, 217, 218, 225, 234n.6
Solitaires, Les (Rousseau), 88
"Solo e pensoso" (Petrarch), 6, 199
Soverchia maninconia, 198, 200, 201, 212, 228, 237; defined, 195
Spackman, Barbara, 99n, 101, 208n
Speculum of the Other Woman (Irigaray), 63, 72
Speech. *See* Talk
Spivak, Gayatri, 30n.56
Sprengnether, Madelon, 28n.53, 35n, 41n, 67n, 76n.31, 79n.34
Stallybrass, Peter, 180n
Stampa, Gaspara, x, 18, 166, 168–74, 189, 265
Stanton, Domna, 4n.8
Steiner, George, 256n.28
Stephens, Walter, 207n
Stepmothers (wicked), 83
Stierle, Karlheinz, 174n.28

Strindberg, August, 110
Strocchia, Sharon, 12n.25, 161–63, 165, 166n.11
Subjectivity, 21, 26–29
Suffering: of melancholics, 7–9, 11–13, 19
Superego: and melancholia, 5, 9, 11, 36, 46–47, 83, 123, 156, 193; and social order, 26, 53, 65, 139, 238–39, 263; in women, 53–54, 60, 73–74. *See also* Morality
Superiority: of the melancholic, 103, 197. *See also* Morality
Sylvie (Nerval), 87
Symposium (Plato), 115

Taciturnity. *See* Talk
Talk: and the melancholic, 48–51, 55, 81–82, 84–86, 103, 108, 249. *See also* Self-display; Silence
Tancredi (character), 203–7, 209–10
Tarabotti, Arcangela (Suor), 149n.53
Tasso, Bernardo, 174, 182, 192, 194, 218, 221
Tasso, Porzia, 174, 182, 186, 213
Tasso, Torquato, 254, 263; contrasted with di Morra, 174–90; as melancholic, ix, x, 2, 3, 5, 18–21, 49, 61, 88, 191–232, 234–37, 246, 265; and women, 239–40. *See also* titles of works
Tasso's Melancholy (lost play), 20, 234
Tatossian, Arthur, 56n.18
Tedeschi, John, 217n.31
Tenenti, Alberto, 162n.2
Theogony (Hesiod), 201
Theriaca (pharmaceutical compound), 133
Timaeus (Plato), 130
Tongue. *See* Lingua
Torok, Maria, 53n, 67n, 241n
Torquato Tasso (play), 20, 234
Tragedy. *See* Trauerspiel
Traité de l'espérance (Chartier), 98
Transference, 230–31
Transvestism: rhetorical, 88
Trauerspiel ("mourning play"), 256–59
Treatise of Melancholia (Bright), 233
Tristesse (character), 98
Tristitia, 98
Truth: melancholics' claim to, 49–53, 55, 58–60. *See also* Genius; Rebel; Universal truths

Ulysses, 254
Universal truths: Freud's categories as, 22, 23
Uranus, 117

Vagina dentata, 83, 99, 101
Van Den Abbeele, Georges, 29n.54
Veith, Ilza, 22n.37
Venus, 115–17, 123–24, 126, 128, 134–37, 148, 220, 262
Vickers, Nancy, 167–68
Vigny, Alfred, 3
Virgilio Adriani, Marcello, 160
Vittorini, Edwina, 192n
Von R., Elisabeth, 57, 61–62
Vulgus: and melancholia, 114–15; and mourning, 161. *See also* Genius

Waller. Marguerite R., 167n.11
Warnke, Frank J., 4n.8
Was woll das Weib? (Freud), 148
Weinberg, Bernard, 194n.7
West, Rebecca, 4n.8
Weyer, John, 14
"When I come before those beautiful eyes" (Stampa), 169–70
Wife. *See* "Conscientious woman"
Willis, Sharon, 22n.37
Wilson, Katharina M., 4n.8
Witches, 21, 246, 251–52, 255–56
Wittkower, Margot, 4n.9, 7n.17, 212n
Wittkower, Rudolf, 4n.9, 7n.17, 212n

"Wolf Man's" sister, 57n
Wolters, Al, 120n.29
Women: absence of, from melancholic cultural tradition, 3–4, 11–12, 18, 53–57, 64–68, 95, 97, 105, 110, 136, 226, 254; as cure for melancholia, 100–101; devaluing of, in melancholic cultural tradition, 10–14, 16, 58–62, 94–95, 143–50, 186–90, 239, 264; disaccrediting of voices and feelings of, 169–90; as melancholics, 14–15, 17, 58–95, 142–43, 150–53, 248–53, 255, 258; as other, 200–209, 231, 260; and Renaissance public funerals, 162–64; as representation of melancholia, 12–14, 98–101, 110, 245, 253–54; repression of, in patriarchy, 25, 63–67, 70–77. *See also* "Conscientious woman"; Depression; Female; Femininity; Gaze; Hole; Lack: women as; Melancholia; Misogyny; Mourning; Phallus; Witches
Woodward, Kathleen, 267n
Worthlessness: melancholics' feelings of, 60–61
Writing: for women, 172–73, 179

Zatti, Sergio, 193

Library of Congress Cataloging-in-Publication Data

Schiesari, Juliana.
    The gendering of melancholia : feminism, psychoanalysis, and the
symbolics of loss in Renaissance literature / Juliana Schiesari.
        p.   cm.
    Includes bibliographical references and index.
    ISBN 0-8014-2686-3 (cloth : alk. paper). — ISBN 0-8014-9971-2
(paper : alk. paper)
    1. Psychoanalysis and literature.   2. Feminism and literature.
3. Loss (Psychology) in literature.   4. Depression, Mental, in
literature.   5. Grief in literature.   6. European literature—
Renaissance, 1450-1600—History and criticism.   I. Title.
PN56.P92S35   1992   91-55529
809'.93353—dc20